What Think You of Christ?

Meditations on the Daily Mass Scriptures

What Think You of Christ?

Meditations on the Daily Mass Scriptures

By

Bishop John A. Marshall

Ambassador Books, Inc.
Worcester • Massachusetts

ISBN: 1-929039-13-1

Library of Congress Control Number: 2003102253

Published in 2003 in the United States by Ambassador Books, Inc.
91 Prescott Street, Worcester, Massachusetts 01605
(800) 577-0909

For current information about all titles from Ambassador Books, Inc. visit our website at: www.ambassadorbooks.com.
Printed in Canada.

— Table of Contents —

Foreword

In all times, all places, and all circumstances, we are called to a closer relationship with Christ. He calls us because he loves us and because he wishes to give us life in abundance. An essential part of an abundant life is knowing and loving and worshipping God.

For Catholics, the central act of worship is the Mass, the great prayer of the Church. It is here that we are nourished by the Eucharist and instructed by the Word of God through the Scripture readings.

In the Scripture readings, we experience anew Christ's birth, life, death, resurrection and ascension, the coming of the Holy Spirit, and the daily journey of the Christian soul. On that journey we come to know Christ's love at a deeper level while he affirms, consoles, chastises, reprimands, instructs and empowers us.

However, for this to happen, we must do more than let the Word pass lightly through our minds. We must hear it, allow it to sink deeply into our consciousness, and receive it into our hearts. We must take the Word into the very center of our being, and let it burrow through the hidden recesses and the dark corners of our souls.

For the Word is spirit and truth, and it has the power to change us, to set us on the journey to become perfect as our Father in heaven is perfect.

The reason this book is being published is to help us hear and receive the Word of God. Bishop John A. Marshall spent his life in service to Christ, to his Church, and to his people. He pondered the daily Scripture readings, seeking to plumb their depths in order to better understand the Lord's message to himself and to his flock.

Bishop Marshall's writings are an effective companion to the daily Scriptures. For those taking tentative steps on a new spiritual path, the daily meditations offer a discipline and a method for understanding Christ's words and applying their meaning to their own lives. For those who are more advanced, the meditations provide a daily retreat, into the hills, away from the crowd, where they can sit at the feet of Christ and not only be nourished, but also be sustained by his words for the journey ahead.

How to use this book

What Think You of Christ? is intended to be used as a companion to the daily Mass Scriptures, although, it is not necessary to read the daily Scriptures in order to use it.

Daily Masses are in a two-year cycle. Year One occurs in odd numbered years and Year Two occurs in even numbered years. For example, 2003 is in the Year One cycle.

Each cycle of the liturgical year is divided into Advent, the Christmas Season, the first part of Ordinary Time, the Lenten Season, Holy Week, the Easter Season, and the second part of Ordinary Time. To find out the week of the liturgical year, consult a church calendar.

Optimally, one would first read the Scriptures for the day in a Missal and then turn to the corresponding meditations in *What Think You of Christ?* However, it is not necessary to have a Missal since the Scripture references for each day are given in *What Think You of Christ?* Indeed, one can read the meditations without having read the Scriptures, since Bishop Marshall gives details about each Scripture.

What Think You of Christ? will draw the reader into a closer relationship with God's word. It will help him or her grasp the depth and breadth of the Scriptures, and in doing so it will promote spiritual growth.

Advent Season

First Week of Advent

Monday

First Reading (B & C cycles): ***Isaiah 2:1-5***
First Reading (A cycle): ***Isaiah 4:2-6***
Gospel: ***Matthew 8:5-11***

The liturgy of Advent gives us the expectations and predictions of the coming Messiah as found in the Old Testament. The major prophet Isaiah wrote magnificently about the future Messiah and the glorious Messianic Age to come and his predictions are realized in Jesus, our Lord. Today's readings teach us that the key to peace and justice in the world is the acceptance of God's teaching. He teaches us his ways and asks us to walk in his path, and, if we do so, salvation will be ours. Priests share in this mission in a special way, and they need to be aware of the need to teach by word and example, in season and out of season. We cannot be certain that people will walk in God's path as a result of our teaching and example but that depends on their acceptance of God's grace and the use of their free will. It takes many people to make a world. One person, under human limitations cannot do everything. But by the grace of God and our own determination, we can do the work that God has given us to do. We need to understand our calling and its limitations and adhere to it faithfully.

Today's gospel shows how in reality, because of Jesus, Israel became the focus of worldwide attention and religion. The centurion was a Gentile and the symbol of innumerable Gentiles who will be guests at the Messianic banquet. The centurion understood well the division of work that must be in place, if a great project is to be accomplished. Each must do his assigned share and not duplicate what others are doing. This is the way an effective army must operate, and it is the way that Christ and we must accomplish the immense task that is before us, the conversion of the world. Christ should not waste time going to the centurion's house, if the boy can be saved by a simple act of the will. The centurion believed that Christ had such power, so that is what he requested. And the Lord, realizing that he could do so and recognizing the opportunity to accept the centurion's act of faith as a means of instructing all the bystanders, healed the boy from afar.

In every assignment, we need to learn to do our part faithfully and to depend upon others to do theirs. Many times we may fail to meet our responsibility since in human affairs this is what happens. However, we need to assist one another especially in the work of evangelization.

TUESDAY

Isaiah 11: 1-10; Luke 10: 21-24

The chapters of Isaiah predicting a future great King of Peace are called the "Book of Emmanuel." Today we read about this Emmanuel. Isaiah pictures the Messiah as one who is filled with the gifts of the Holy Spirit: knowledge, wisdom, understanding, good judgment, reverence, fear of the Lord, and fortitude. These are the signs of a godly person. Isaiah prophesies that the Messiah will overcome the wicked and the ruthless with the word of his mouth. It is truth that reigns in the kingdom of God not physical and material power. If we wish to be members of God's kingdom, we must struggle to uphold truth and love in all that we say and do; otherwise, we are choosing to follow the ways of worldly kingdoms.

In today's gospel, Jesus, in the Spirit, thanks the Father for the style of life which the Spirit prompts us to live, a way similar to the innocence of little children. By nature, children are trusting, loving, affectionate, and gentle. The beauty of the life which the Spirit prompts us to live is hidden to the worldly-wise and powerful; it is totally opposed and not even comprehensible to them. And this way of life, the childlike way of Christ, manifests God to the world. God, who is love, is like the innocent child, unlike the powerful domineering worldly rulers. How many oppressed people have longed to hear about this way of life and have not heard it!

If we take Christ's words seriously, evangelization of the unchurched, the alienated, and those who have never heard of Christ must be a very high priority for us.

WEDNESDAY

Isaiah 25: 6-10; Matthew 15: 29-37

In today's reading, through Isaiah, the Lord reveals that he will make himself known. He will overcome the world and even death, freeing his people from reproach and granting them full happiness. In times of difficulty and heartache, this is the promise that the Lord holds out to us. If we but remain faithful, he will surely fulfill all his promises and grant us eternal peace in union with him. Life is very simple but we make it complex. All we need to do is remain faithful. It seems easy but often it is easier still to succumb to temptation.

Anyone witnessing the multiplication of loaves and fishes and remembering the above prophecy of Isaiah would have no doubt that Jesus is the Messiah. He went up on a mountain; he cured the most afflicted and sorrowful people; he fed them all with next to nothing; he revealed his divinity, both through the miracle and more especially by the fulfillment of prophecy. He showed the people that he did not need the things of this world and neither would they, if they came to believe in him.

Again, all we need is unwavering faith in Christ, which leads us logically to live as he did. We need not worry about the details of our living—what we need to do is believe in Christ, deepen our faith and make it permanent in love, and then place all our hope in his promises.

THURSDAY

Isaiah 26: 1-6; Matthew 7: 21, 24-27

In today's reading, Isaiah gives us a memorable picture of God as the Rock of Israel, a source of protection, strength, and trust for those who keep true faith in him. In order to win God's favor and be one with him, it is necessary to be one with him in mind, will, and action. We cannot simply presume that God will do everything for us. If we had no free will, that would be the case. But since we have free will, we must exercise it and say "Yes" to God if we wish to be saved. In addition, we must persevere in saying "Yes" through frequent repetition; thus, our fidelity to God will become firm and permanent. It is not enough for a person to wish to have a good house, nor even to build a good house; he must build it in such a way that it is strong, permanent, and secure against all and any adverse winds.

As the first reading implies, it is through God's grace and our faith that we build such an "edifice" with our lives. The way to peace is belief in God and acceptance and practice of his way of life, so that we are always strong, honest, and holy as we wait for the happiness to come when God will reveal himself to us.

FRIDAY

Isaiah 29: 17-24; Matthew 9: 27-31

In today's reading, Isaiah predicts the future Messianic age. He says that it will be a time when even snow-covered Mount Lebanon will become green. In addition, the lowly and underprivileged will be treated with justice and charity. The tables will be turned. When the Messiah comes, those who were powerless and oppressed will find themselves strengthened and consoled. Those who were deaf to the Word of God or blind to his way of life will have their eyes and ears opened. The lonely and the poor will find joy. Everyone will be given a new and equal opportunity for conversion. The Lord does not promise salvation to a poor and lowly person simply because he is poor and lowly, nor does he condemn a rich and powerful person simply because he is rich and powerful. The Messiah brings a new opportunity for everyone to hear the Word of God clearly and then to accept or reject it.

Spiritually, the opportunity is like that given to the blind men in today's gospel narrative. The restoration of their sight did not automatically make them successful or happy in the world. Their cure simply gave them a new and better opportunity for worldly success and happiness. The miracle did not automatically make them more holy. We know from personal experience how short-lived spiritual renewal can be. Although we work for him and for his kingdom, we continue to be blind, confused, weak, and fallible. The thrill of a spiritual experience such as a good confession can be extremely intense and yet our tendency to evil can dim that luster and see us returning to a life of sin.

Because God has given us free will, the most he can provide for us is opportunities of grace. It is our decision whether we use them, take advantage of them, or refuse to do so.

SATURDAY

Isaiah 30: 19-21, 23-26; Matthew 9: 35-10: 1, 6-8

Through Isaiah, the Lord promises great prosperity to his people. He uses the terms of everyday life. In the days of Isaiah the people were prosperous and happy if they and their animals had enough to eat and drink and multiply. The bigger the family, the happier they were as long as there was enough to support them. Isaiah also speaks of something else which might be of little interest to them. Through his prophet, God tells them that he will guide them in his way of truth and justice.

In the gospel this prophecy is fulfilled. Christ is the Messiah because he preaches the truth, the way of God. He also cures illnesses and diseases; he restores sight to the blind, hearing to the deaf, and speech to the dumb. The reign of God is at hand. He is moved with compassion for the people. But although this compassion is shown in a visible, material way, it is clear that the Messiah's major interest is the spiritual welfare of the people, who are like sheep without a shepherd, like a vineyard full of grapes without any gatherers. He sees that the people are of good will but they do not know the way of God. True enough, many will not accept that way when they do know it, but they need a chance when their spiritual leaders have failed them. Great numbers of the faithful can fall away from the faith and yet there is hope as long as the spiritual leaders continue to proclaim God's truth. But if they get tired, if they give up hope, if they abandon God's message, all is lost.

Some say, "We live in exciting times." However, the real excitement, the real drama concerns men's souls. Surely, like the Jews of old, many will be saved because of ignorance and lack of understanding of God's message. But what about those who do know and appreciate God's truth, that is, the adult world and especially the religious leaders? Will they stand up to the challenge? When the Lord comes, will he find any faith on the earth?

Second Week of Advent

Monday

Isaiah 35: 1-10; Luke 5: 17-26

In the second week of Advent Masses, Isaiah briefs us on the messianic dreams of the Old Testament. In today's reading, Isaiah speaks of an exodus from misery to glory to be achieved once the Messiah comes. There will be no obstacles on this road, no one lurking on the side to attack or tempt us. The way of the Lord will be clear and straight. Those who walk on it will be joyful and glad having been redeemed from a life of sadness and oppression.

Today's gospel tells of one of the more dramatic miracles of Jesus that reflects the dream of Isaiah. The Lord healed a paralyzed man, forgave his sins, and brought him back to health and happiness. Because the Pharisees questioned the Lord's ability to forgive sins, he, knowing their reasoning, addressed their question head on: "Which is easier to say, 'Your sins are forgiven,' or to say, 'arise and walk'?" A doctor might be able to do the latter, or through some accident or even psychic power, a physical healing might take place. But how does this help one toward salvation? In terms of salvation, it might be just as well or better that the person not be cured. We are called to be much more interested in our own interior spiritual life than in our visible material life; to prize the interior over the exterior gifts. Anyone might be able to cure an external problem or adjust to it and get along. But who can forgive sin except God alone? Our dream must be sanctity: a sinless life spent in the imitation of Christ; a life spent doing God's will.

Tuesday

Isaiah 40: 1-11; Matthew 18: 12-14

Today's reading is from Second Isaiah seemingly written by disciples of the old Isaiah. Written in the sixth century B.C. it revealed an expectant spirit of deliverance because the Babylonian Captivity was ending. The captives will return to Jerusalem. Israel has suffered terribly for its sins but God does not abandon his people. Once again, he is to show them his mercy. Left to himself, man is like the grass or a flower. He may appear bright and beautiful but his life is short. Eventually he withers and fades from the scene, forgotten by all—except God, who rewards with eternal life those who have used their frail human existence to love and serve him.

The Israelites understood human progress the way we do. One thing that can make life a lot easier and more productive is a good road network. They did not have the means to develop one, but they and the Romans did their best. Now we can actually succeed at leveling hills, filling in ravines, making roads wide, smooth, straight, and protected from wandering animals. But even as we have made this material progress, how little we have done in a figurative or spiritual sense to prepare such a way for the Lord by flattening the obstacles in our path, by casting out of the way all temptations, by making a straight, broad path toward the Lord. It has been possible for all men of all time to construct this spiritual road to salvation with the help of God's grace, but how few have done it!

The Messiah is portrayed as the Good Shepherd, just as kind and solicitous for us as a shepherd is for his sheep. We know this; we find comfort in the concept; and yet we wish to escape him, do what we please, and live our own life. We can see ourselves in relation to God by considering little children. They cannot get along without their parents, who gave them their life and continue to provide for them. Yet the childhood years are a continual struggle to "escape," and to be on one's own.

We have experienced the warmth of parents and family. It is comfortable to be protected by them. Yet, we want to be on our own, too. Only when we have broken away, do we realize what we have lost and what great responsibility we have taken upon ourselves—this is normal, natural, and to be expected. What we should learn from the experience is that we should never feel alone or abandoned—even with the death of parents—because we have a heavenly Father, who can truly give us the same and even greater protection and love than parents. Surely both readings make this clear. The Lord is indeed the Good Shepherd, who desires nothing more than "to gather his lambs in his arms."

WEDNESDAY

Isaiah 40: 25-31; Matthew 11: 28-30

Isaiah counsels the people not to give up their faith in God. It may appear from time to time that he has abandoned them but that is not so. He is present to all his people as their strength and hope. If we look for him, we will find him. Our problem, often enough, is that we are not truly looking for him. We demand his presence and are ready to tell him what to do for us, or we seek him in some self-serving way. God is God, so he cannot be used or come to our aid in any way except his way. God must be sought as he is in himself, for his own sake. Thus, if we truly want him, it must be according to his way of doing things, not our own. We must want and be ready to accept him and his way totally and be prepared to give up ourselves and our way completely.

This requires humility, an admission that we are dependent upon God, who is the only independent one. When we surrender ourselves in this fashion, if and when we become meek and humble of heart, then we find how simple, easy, peaceful life can be. Problems may rage around us and embroil us, but we will have an inner core of peace in union with the Lord.

THURSDAY

Isaiah 41: 13-20; Matthew 11: 11-15

Today, the first reading is from Second Isaiah. Using earthy language and examples of material prosperity, the Lord makes clear that everything is possible for him and that he will grant peace and joy to those who trust in him. The key to a happy life, whether here or hereafter, is faith in God's existence, hope in God's promise, love of him manifested in love for those made in his image and likeness. If we live in this spirit, that which looks hopeless will be turned to perfection. Just as the Lord by his power can change a desert wasteland into a fruitful land, so can he change human misery into supernatural joy.

Christ applies the above to himself by a comparison with the prophets. All the prophets were great people; they addressed the people when they were in desperate situations, their message was to trust in God rather than material or human strength. When the people accepted their message, a much more prosperous and joyful period of history was initiated. If the people of Christ's time—or even we, in this day, would do the same, we too would enter upon a period of peace and joy. But we do not, except perhaps for short periods of time, and so we have wars and threats of wars, violence and immorality of all kinds. Fear replaces faith; pessimism replaces hope; enmity, or at least suspicion, replaces love.

Still, even though society does not embrace God with faith, hope and love, it is eminently wise for the individual to do so. A prevailing materialistic culture may frustrate our desires for the reward of peace and joy in this world, but life is short and the life of perfect happiness is everlasting. It is well worth the effort to be a sign of contradiction for a few short years on the face of the earth in light of the reward that is to come.

FRIDAY

Isaiah 48: 17-19; Matthew 11: 16-19

Once again Isaiah returns to what the Messiah can and will do for us. Most of the Advent passages exhort us to root from our lives the obstacles to virtue. Today's reading reminds us of the Christian theology that we do not have the power to save ourselves. It is the Redeemer who does. He does so by his teachings—by word and example. If only we accept his teaching and keep his commandments, we shall have spiritual serenity in this world, and the pleasure and consolation of an extended family consisting of those who follow the same way of life. The deepest sorrows that we experience in life are those which we or our families and friends bring upon us. What a joy it would be to have all of us living the Christ life.

Some think that we should go through life in a solitary penitential spirit; others take a more joyful attitude of celebration among people. Either way can be good. For example, the contemplative life as opposed to the apostolic life; religious life as opposed to married life. Wisdom is found in the realization that we are to follow faithfully the calling that God has given us for a particular vocation. But above all, wisdom urges us, regardless of our special vocation, to follow the universal call to holiness. This implies that we give God a place in our lives, that we accept his grace, that we follow his teaching, and that we try to be as one with him.

SATURDAY

Sirach 48: 1-4, 9-11; Matthew 17: 10-13

Today's first reading from the book of Sirach praises the many great ancestors of the Israelites among whom was Elijah. We read praise of the prophet's life and an expectation of his return. As a preacher, Elijah was a firebrand. Israel would have been better off if the people had accepted his message. Because they did not, they suffered and they were forced to wait for his return, or at least for the return of another who would give the same message and offer Israel another chance to believe.

When Christ came, the apostles asked him about the Second Coming of Elijah. He replied that Elijah had already come and the apostles thought that it might have been in the person of John the Baptist. The latter, a true prophet after centuries of prophetic silence, created intense messianic speculation and anticipation. Who might have figured in the Second Coming of Elijah is unimportant. What matters is that Elijah's message was given to Israel a second time—and it is constantly repeated for us. Shall we reject it as the Israelites did?

Third Week of Advent

Monday

Numbers 24:2-7, 15-17; Matthew 21:23-27

Today the reading from the book of Numbers tells of an ancient prediction of future glory for the people of Israel. The prediction was made when the Israelites reached the Plains of Moab where a famous wise man, Balaam, praised the Jewish nation and predicted future glory and kingship for it. He compares the future Israel to that which is most prized in nature. Fresh water was in short supply, so he compares Israel to a free-flowing well, a well-watered garden. The Lord will send someone who can accomplish this. Ultimately it was Jesus who fulfilled this prediction.

The importance and authority of John the Baptist are stressed in today's gospel. The chief priests and elders came up to Jesus and asked him: "On what authority are you doing these things? Who has given you the power?" If Jesus had answered the question of the priests directly, they would not have accepted his answer. It was necessary to use the priests against themselves. They feared the people, who were the base of their power; they did not wish to offend them. But the people believed that John's baptism was of God; however, the priests, although they feared to attack John, disbelieved in his prophetic power. By raising the question of John the Baptist, Jesus was implying his own divine origin.

In a sense, the first reading today answers the question asked in the gospel. Jesus has the authority of the promised ruler of the entire nation. The readings are also connected by the allusions to water and baptism. The prophet speaks of Israel—its people—as a well-watered garden. John baptized with water. Jesus' disciples would baptize with water and the Holy Spirit and Jesus had greater spiritual power and authority than John.

TUESDAY

Zephaniah 3: 1-2, 9-13; Matthew 21: 28-32

As part of Advent, today's liturgy gives us another noteworthy Messianic passage and prophecy of the Old Testament. The prophet Zephaniah who lived in the decadent times of seventh century B.C. points out the wickedness of a big city, how all are caught up in its ways. The voices of reason and correction are drowned out by greed. The population of the city becomes a tyrant, as it were, with its insatiable demands. In its pursuit of worldly goods, it also loses sight of God.

Through the prophet, the Lord promises to change this situation. It is interesting to note the characteristics that will mark the converted as opposed to those of the "tyrant city." "Proud braggarts" will be removed and replaced by "a people humble and lowly," a people who are morally upright, who have special regard for the truth. Truth is one of the most basic virtues. This is made clear both in Scripture and in the pronouncements of Popes. Jesus, who shows forth the Father, refers to himself as truth. If all that we think, do, and say is patterned after the teaching and the example of Christ, all other virtues follow. If we know the truth, accept it and practice it, we will be Christ-like. It is essential, then, to search for the truth; that is, to humbly accept and practice the truth as God reveals it to us.

Today's gospel should be understood in light of the above. It may take a long time to discover the truth, but that is only human. To remain open to the truth is what is important. Pride, as long as it exists, is an insurmountable obstacle. No matter how sinful a person may be, there is always hope; the wretchedness of the sinful person may provide the fertile soil of conversion for the seed of God's grace. But if a person "knows it all," there is little hope. The two sons exemplify the "smart guy," who came up with good reasons not to go to the vineyard, while the other son was moved to go by his remorse.

WEDNESDAY

Isaiah 45: 6-8, 18, 21-25; Luke 7: 18-23

Again we read an important Old Testament statement about the coming Messianic age. Today's reading is from Second Isaiah. He tells the people in exile to expect deliverance and salvation even if their situation appears hopeless because God is their Savior. The Creator of heaven and earth and all that is on the earth wills that "justice spring up." He has not created the earth to be a waste, but he has designed it to be lived in. And the only way that we can live in the world—in the sense of living peacefully—is to have "justice spring up" among us. "There is no just and saving God but me; let justice descend like dew from above, like gentle rain." God not only creates us but he gives us the grace that we need to live according to his design. And being a God of justice, his design is that we should live justly with one another.

What is justice? "To me every knee shall bend." It is justice that creatures should love their Creator with their whole mind, heart, and soul and with all their strength. "Turn to me and be safe, all you ends of the earth." Moreover, we are to love one another as ourselves because that is what he does. "Only in the Lord are just deeds and power" in their fullest expression. It can also be said that God's activity consists only in just deeds. And since he asks us to imitate him: "let justice spring up" from the earth—it is clear that we are to treat our neighbor justly and with love. Human beings are the only ones with whom we can practice justice and through whom we can demonstrate that we are fulfilling justice toward God; we do so by loving and being just toward those whom God loves and treats justly.

The fulfillment of Old Testament prophecy by Jesus is in itself a sign of his divinity. But even if there had not been such a specific prophecy, his actions would be powerful signs of justice and love, the only kind of activity that can exist in God.

THURSDAY

Isaiah 54: 1-10; Luke 7: 24-30

In today's reading, Isaiah gives a beautiful, consoling message to Israel pictured as a childless widow. God himself will marry her in an irrevocable covenant of peace. Glorious is this glimpse of the coming Messiah. God's action is like that of a husband separated from his wife. The separation is an embarrassment for the wife. But now that the Lord takes Israel back as a spouse, there is no longer need for fear. The Israelites can increase and multiply again because the Lord is with them.

Even when God offers himself to men with the fullness of his love, there are those who reject him. One cannot very well receive God into his heart when there is no room for him, because of pride and the fear of losing material goods. All must be like John the Baptist who thinks for himself, has the courage of his convictions and is not "a reed swayed by the wind," and is not overwhelmed by the luxuries of this life.

John was sent ahead of Christ to prepare the way, to take people out of themselves, away from selfish concerns and the things of this world. "The entire populace" received the baptismal bath John administered, and many of them accepted the way, the truth, and the life of Christ. However, the Pharisees and the lawyers failed to receive John's baptism and defeated God's plan in their regard.

FRIDAY

Isaiah 56: 1-3, 6-8; John 5: 33-36

In today's reading, Isaiah encourages Israel to be truly religious. He prophesies that God is about to reveal the fullness of his justice (in Jesus Christ) so all should make a special effort to do that which is right and just. Although he does not quote from Deuteronomy, Isaiah describes the just man as the one who does not profane the Sabbath because of love of God and keeps his hand from all evil doing through love for neighbor. However, Isaiah prophesies something else that is most unusual. When this time comes, foreigners, non-Israelites, will be welcomed, as long as they too strive in their own way to love God and neighbor. He speaks of God's covenant with these people, confirming St. Paul's teaching in the first chapter of Romans that we can know God from nature; and confirming Paul's teaching that the law of God is written in the heart of every person. "My house will be called a house of prayer for all peoples."

John's gospel speaks of God's justice and truth having come into the world. If the Jews were attracted by John's message, all the more should they be ready to accept Jesus' message and the works that prove the source of his Word. John was like a lamp in darkness which needs another light to start its flame. Jesus, however, shines with his own light!

The Second Part of Advent: December 17 to December 24

DECEMBER 17

Genesis 49: 2, 8-10; Matthew 1: 1-17

From December 17 to 23, the liturgy uses short prayers that summarize the Messianic hope expressed in the Old Testament. These are called antiphons used as the Alleluia verse of the Advent Masses.

The first reading for today describes a dramatic scene where the patriarch Jacob lies on his deathbed surrounded by his twelve sons. Jacob prophesies about the future of each tribe to descend from each of them. For the tribe of Judah, Jacob predicts supremacy—he will rule over his brothers. This is fulfilled in Jesus Christ, the Son of David, of the tribe of Judah.

In the gospel, Matthew gives the genealogy of Jesus and emphasizes Christ's descent from Judah and the royal house of David.

DECEMBER 18

Jeremiah 23: 5-8; Matthew 1: 18-24

In today's reading, Jeremiah speaks of the Messiah as "the Lord our justice." He will be one who reigns wisely, the prophet says, because "he shall do what is just and right in the land." There is real security in such a leader.

In the midst of war and promise of war, we need to look to Jesus with faith, even as the prophets did of old. They looked ahead with hope. Perhaps we need to redefine our terms as to what we mean by peace and security—they have to do with the spiritual life more than with temporal conditions; reliance upon the truth revealed by Jesus is better than reliance on arms. If it comes to making a choice between preserving our earthly lives by mass killing or entering upon eternal life by dying in defense of justice, clearly there is no choice but the latter for one who believes in Jesus.

Today's gospel passage explains how Jesus was adopted into the royal Davidic line. Joseph became his legal father. At first, Joseph was in difficult straits. Before Mary and Joseph lived together, Mary was with child through the power of the Holy Spirit. Joseph did not want to have Mary stoned for adultery, nor did he want to suffer humiliation himself. He wanted to preserve the worldly reputation of each of them. Divine wisdom, however, decreed otherwise. Joseph took Mary into his home as his wife. He risked the worldly problems, had faith in God, did that which was just and right in God's eyes, and "let the chips fall where they may." Certainly we can be grateful that he did.

DECEMBER 19

Judges 13: 2-7, 24-25; Luke 1: 5-25

In today's liturgy preparing us for the Lord's birth we hear of the annunciation of the birth of Samson and, in Luke, of the birth of John the Baptist. The stories of Samson and John the Baptist have several similarities. Their mothers were sterile; an angel announced that they would conceive; both Samson and John were under the nazirite vow as people dedicated to God's service. They were not to take wine or strong drink; they would do wonders for their people, Israel.

Our faith in the present day needs to be strong enough to move mountains. God can touch the minds and hearts of large numbers of people as well as individuals. Nothing is impossible to him. Many of the problems that we face in our world today seem to be insurmountable. But even in such a world, God's grace is always present; it works in strange ways. The ingredients that are always most needed are our acceptance, our faith, our hope and trust in God.

DECEMBER 20

Isaiah 7: 10-14; Luke 1: 26-38

In today's reading from Isaiah, we read of the most famous Old Testament prophecy about the future Messiah. The Jews were always looking for signs from God, but typically human, when God offered them one, they declined the offer! The headstrong young King Ahaz refused to listen to Isaiah's message. Nevertheless, he and his entire house were told that a virgin would bring into the world Emmanuel that means God-with-us.

The gospel speaks of the fulfillment of Isaiah's prophecy. An angel appears to a virgin of Nazareth, who conceives through the power of the

Holy Spirit. The one to be born of her is to be called the Son of God. The Virgin Mary gives total acceptance to God's wishes transmitted by the angel and her "Fiat" brings about the Incarnation.

The contrast between the manner, in which the prophecies are received, is noteworthy. Neither message is easy to believe, but Mary is trusting and Ahaz is not; Mary is humble and devoted to God, Ahaz is not; Mary is willing to let God work in her life, Ahaz is not.

With its attention to Mary, today's liturgy influenced the development of the Hail Mary and the Angelus prayers.

DECEMBER 21

Song of Songs 2: 8-14; Luke 1: 39-45

Today's Advent liturgy centers on the visitation of Mary to Elizabeth. There is a joyful spirit about this Mass directing our thoughts to the birth of Christ. The first reading is from the Song of Songs, a lyric love poem expressing delight and joy. In order to describe joy, the Old Testament very often uses figures of speech from nature. This time the author uses the image of a deer whose innocence, seeming affection, and fear of human beings who stalk and kill its kind to presage the coming of Christ. When one thinks of the suffering of Christ in his lifetime and on the Cross, no figure is appropriate. However, the deer seems to invite us to live a life of freedom, innocence, beauty, peace, and appreciation of God and nature. Likewise, Christ asks us to love life and take part in it fully and trustingly, even though our earthly fate is death, and perhaps death in some "unfair, unjust" manner. That should not inhibit our appreciation for life, because another more beautiful life awaits us as human beings.

The story of the visitation of Mary to Elizabeth echoes the Song of Songs. Mary, filled with the Holy Spirit, goes off to the hill country. She is joyful and happy. Hearing Mary's voice, the baby leaps for joy in Elizabeth's own womb. Yet, there are many hardships to come; not everything is pure bliss; into the lives of John and Jesus much sorrow will find a place. This is true in the case of the deer mentioned above, searching for food and water, hunted by men, and subject to the killing instincts of so many animals. However, our overall impression is that the deer is a thing of beauty and so let us picture Jesus and Mary that way.

DECEMBER 22

1 Samuel 1: 24-28; Luke 1: 46-56

In their better and saner moments, all parents would agree that what they really want for their child is goodness, godliness. If parents could foresee that their child was going to be an embarrassment to them—a criminal or notorious sinner of some kind—there are parents who would surely wish to be childless rather than face that situation. Therefore, parents should be more consciously aware of their true inner aspirations for their child and, like Hannah and Mary, offer the child to the Lord, pray and work that the child, as long as he lives, be dedicated to the Lord. A child is a gift of God in the first place, as both Hannah and Mary make clear. God has done great things for the mother and will continue to do so for her child, as well. Her greatest responsibility is to communicate to her child her own gratitude and love for God so that, in turn, the child will be equally grateful and loving toward God.

In the "Magnificat" we learn that eventually God will show to individuals and to the world the folly of any other approach to life. Ultimately the proud will be crushed and the humble exalted. The poor will become spiritually rich and the materially rich will be devastated. Granted that faith is necessary to accept these assertions, as St. Paul reveals in the first chapter of Romans, it is quite possible and easy to learn this truth just from an examination of nature. However, because natural motivation is weak and quickly overcome by the instinct of self-preservation, we need faith in God and the strength of his grace to retain our belief that the spiritual is more important than the material.

DECEMBER 23

Malachi 3: 1-4, 23-24; Luke 1: 57-66

Today's reading is from the prophet Malachi, who is regarded as the last of the prophets because after him prophecy was silent. Malachi predicted that God's messenger would one day come to purify the Temple and he criticized the priests of his time. In other words, before the coming of the Messiah, the Lord will give ample time to the people to reform their lives, to be converted to his ways. He will send a messenger—one like Elijah—ahead of the Messiah to warn the people. But when the Messiah comes, his holiness will be such that further purification will not be needed. "People will feel the piercing heat of his holy example; they must allow themselves to be melted and then reshaped in his image and likeness. This is not easy for human beings because this takes immense humility. The human detritus encrusting the Old Testament revelation will have to be scaled away, so to speak.

Today's gospel story of the birth of John the Baptist is not only wondrous but totally public. Nothing more dramatic could have taken place than to have Zechariah struck dumb in the holy of holies. Then, his mother was barren and advanced in years. The message that he was to preach later was surely in keeping with the words of Malachi. He called for repentance, conversion, a new direction in keeping with what the people knew from the prophets to be God's will. He was "like the refiner's fire," sent to purify God's people, to make straight the way of the Lord. There is a spirit of joy and wonderment in the story—a realization that the hand of God is active again!

DECEMBER 24

2 Samuel 7: 1-5, 8-11, 16; Luke 1: 67-79

This day is the last of Advent and it gives us a famous Old Testament Messianic prophecy, and in Luke's gospel, the final episode before the Nativity.

Thus the first reading is the prophecy of Nathan to King David. The royal house of David will continue forever—this promise was fulfilled in Christ. David served God faithfully and wished to do him honor. He had a good perspective on his relationship to God—creature to Creator, servant to master. It was good of David to wish to build a Temple, but God made clear that he did not want a Temple so much as he wanted all men to be saved. God gave David the tools with which to carry out his will and David used them well. So the Lord promised "immortality" to David and his descendants.

Filled with the Holy Spirit, Zechariah takes up Nathan's prophecy once again. Through the power of God, a descendant of David is once again to rise up and deliver God's people from their enemies in accordance with his covenant. God's kingdom on earth is realized; however, not only when enemies have been subdued, but also when, rid of fear and delivered from the enemy, the people serve God devoutly and in all their days remain holy in his sight. God is always fulfilling his part of the covenant that is realized when man does his own part. Zechariah sees in John's birth the fulfillment of all the promises made to Israel from that of the covenant with Abraham, the promise of Sinai, the promise of Nathan to David and the assurance of delivery from captivity. John the Baptist is to be the prophet heralding the arrival of the Messiah, who in his mercy will forgive the people's sins. When from the beginning forgiveness of sins was announced as the reason for the Messiah's advent, it is amazing that, in our time, we see ourselves as sinless—so few use the sacrament of penance! Christ preached the need for forgiveness of sin throughout his public life, in his passion and death, and even on the night of his resurrection. If there were no sin, there would be no need of the Incarnation and redemption.

Christmas Season

The Octave of Christmas

December 26

St. Stephen, first martyr

Acts 6: 8-10, 7: 54-59; Matthew 10: 17-22

In today's first reading we hear of the first martyr, Stephen. He was a Greek-speaking Jewish Christian ordained among the first seven deacons chosen by the apostles. Filled with grace and power he worked miracles among the people. Members of the synagogue of Freedmen came to debate with Stephen. But, they were no match for the wisdom and spirit with which Stephen spoke. Raging with anger, the Freedmen accused Stephen of blasphemy and had him stoned to death. In Matthew's gospel, Jesus foretells the future persecution of his followers. Stephen was the first to implement the prediction not only of persecution, but also that when the hour came, the persecuted would be told what to say because the Spirit of God would be speaking in them. Death made Stephen's victory complete. His last words were: "Lord Jesus receive my spirit," and certainly Jesus received him with open arms in his kingdom. However, we must not give up hope on those who persecute us. As Stephen was being stoned, his killers were laying their coats at the feet of Saul. It was this man, Saul, who later was converted and, as Paul, became a great apostle and a major writer of the New Testament.

December 27

St. John, apostle and evangelist

John 1: 1-4; John 20: 2-8

Joy and mystery are the major elements in today's readings. In his first letter, the apostle John says that he actually heard, saw, and touched the one who is the Word of Life. Those are the strong qualifications that support his comments on the life of Jesus. In this first letter written many years after the events of Christ's life, John is still filled with unbelievable awe and tremendous joy. In the second reading, John the evangelist, recounts how on the morning of the first Easter he and Peter raced to the tomb after Mary Magdalene came with the news that it was empty except for a few wrappings and the cloth that covered the head of Jesus. They discovered with their own eyes that Jesus was not there—he had resurrected! Can we imagine the sense of awe and the profound joy these two men experienced? They had just suffered a terrible loss. They had been thinking that Jesus was dead. The one they had followed and loved and believed to be the Messiah had suffered a brutal and ignominious death. He had been mocked, reviled, and, in the eyes of the people of Jerusalem, discredited. They felt abandoned, leaderless, and totally on their own. Then they view the empty tomb and realize that Jesus is alive! Perhaps we become accustomed to the idea of the resurrected Jesus and are not conscious of that extraordinary event and its indelible effect on our lives and on the world itself. On that Easter morning everything changed both in the lives of the apostles and in that of the world. Nothing has ever been the same again. Jesus is Lord. He has opened the door to eternal life!

DECEMBER 28

Holy Innocents, martyrs

1 John 1: 5-2: 2; Matthew 2: 13-18

In the first reading, the apostle John announces that God is light and there is no darkness in him. It is very important for us to recognize the truth of this statement. Only light and goodness come from God. Evil has other sources. It is necessary to remember these words when things go wrong in our lives or in the lives of others close to us. Especially today, on the Feast of the Holy Innocents, the significance of John's words cannot be overestimated. In the gospel narrative, the evangelist recalls how Herod, in his frantic efforts to destroy the Messiah, sent his soldiers to Bethlehem to kill all male children under the age of two. Historians estimate that the number of little boys murdered was between twenty and thirty. The suffering of these very young children and of their parents, indeed of all of Bethlehem, is almost beyond our imagining. Yet, in our time, we have experienced events of such magnitude that thousands and even millions of people have been seriously harmed or killed. We may be tempted to blame God for allowing such happenings. In those instances we need to recall John's words that there is no darkness in God—only light. Evil is not of God's doing. Indeed, he sent his only Son to be the antidote for evil and did not immunize him from suffering at the hands of evildoers. Indeed, it was from the suffering of Jesus that our salvation came. Goodness triumphed over evil, which in many ways carries the seeds of its own destruction. But goodness will never be destroyed! The Holy Innocents did not die nor did their parents suffer in vain. Their suffering is bound up in the mystery of Salvation. In faith we believe that, in the end, God will right everything and will wipe away all tears.

December 29

Fifth Day in the Octave of Christmas

1 John 2: 3-11; Luke 2: 22-35

Knowledge of God's teaching through the revelation of Christ is not sufficient. We must keep God's commandments; we must practice his teaching. Better still, "the way we can be sure that we are in union with Christ is if one . . . conducts himself just as he did." That certainly is a large order but certainly not beyond us with the help of God's grace. One is not asked to perform miracles but simply to do what is in conformity with our God-given nature—to love God with our whole mind, heart, and soul and to love our neighbor as ourselves. As St. John says, this is not a new commandment since it was clear in the Old Testament. It is new only in the sense that we have witnessed it lived perfectly in Christ. We have his grace and abiding presence and every possibility of following in his footsteps. We cannot measure directly the degree of our love for God. It can only be evaluated in terms of our love of neighbor. Love is not just in the mind and heart but it must lead to action. And since we cannot lovingly minister directly to God, we must show our love in the way we treat our neighbor. "As long as you did it for one of these my least brethren, you did it for me." Love of our brothers and sisters is of paramount importance!

In the second chapter of his gospel, Luke describes the events that followed the Nativity. Every first-born male child had to be "bought back" as it were from the service of God. Mary and Joseph gave the example of obedience. They consecrated their first born to the Lord "in accord with the dictate in the law of the Lord," a sign that they "knew" God. They not only knew and accepted God's revelation through the prophets, they put it into practice. Simeon and Anna also acted in obedience. For years, they waited faithfully to see the Messiah. Simeon went to the Temple that particular day in accordance with the inspiration of the Holy Spirit. He gave testimony that God fulfills his covenanted promises if only man remains faithful. He speaks of Christ as "a revealing light to the Gentiles, the glory of your people, Israel." Simeon also reveals that the coming of the Messiah will not change human nature. Some will still insist upon loving themselves instead of loving God. Jesus will be a lightning rod for opposition and those who are loyal to him will suffer deeply. This is an especially important concept for us. We must be ready to accept the unfair, unjust attacks that will certainly be made on us, if we faithfully and perseveringly love and follow Jesus Christ. The more innocent we are, the more we try to love our neighbor, the more vulnerable we are to attack. But if our love is genuine, the more readily will we stand up against this injustice. Indeed, this is another way to discern our faithfulness. If we waver in our loyalty to Christ under the unjust attacks of others, our love is superficial. Genuine love will emerge from this crucible of fire in a shape that is more beautiful, durable, and attractive than ever. Martyrdom is the epitome of such trial and love.

DECEMBER 30

Sixth Day in the Octave of Christmas

1 John 2: 12-17; Luke 2: 36-40

Today, the reading is drawn from the First Letter of John addressed to all age groups. In this letter, John tells young and old about the meaning of Christ—that they are not to live for this world nor all its allurements. However, John's lesson is far more important for us who live today in a much more enticing world than John's. There is no substance to the things of this world. What produces anything of lasting value is faith in God, love of him, and actions according to his will.

We see this illustrated in the case of Mary and Joseph. They had little of the world's goods, yet they made the prescribed offering to God. They did so out of faith, love, and obedience, for there was no material benefit to be gained. Anna, the prophetess, was the same. We claim that we would do anything to see God and to be in his presence. However, we are hardly ready to do as Anna did who was "constantly in the Temple, worshipping day and night in fasting and prayer." The grace of God is upon us, as it was upon Jesus, the invitation and the potential for holiness are given to us. The ingredient that we lack is our commitment to do God's will. This is what Christmas is all about! "He humbled himself to come among us like man. . . He became obedient, even to death on the Cross."

HOLY FAMILY

December 30, if Christmas falls on a Sunday

First Reading (A B C cycles): ***Sirach 3: 2-6, 12-14***
Second Reading (A B C cycles): ***Colossians 3: 12-21***
Gospel (A cycle): ***Matthew 2: 13-15, 19-23***
Gospel (B cycle): ***Luke 2: 22-40***
Gospel (C cycle): ***Luke 2: 41-52***

Today's feast celebrates the family of Jesus, Mary and Joseph, and in doing so the Church honors and celebrates all families. The readings for today acknowledge the fact that family life has difficulties as well as joys, and pain as well as love. Both Sirach and Colossians focus on the mutual respect that is fundamental to sound family life. Paul reminds us that as Christians we should clothe ourselves with mercy, kindness, humility, meekness and patience, and to forgive as the Lord has forgiven us. Sirach exhorts us to honor our parents, indeed, that by honoring our parents we atone for sin. Love is the glue that holds families together. It is what gives them life and energy. It is the affirmation that every family member seeks.

The gospel readings recount incidents from the life of the Holy Family. In Matthew we are told how an angel instructed Joseph to take his family to Egypt to escape the massacre ordered by Herod. And the readings from Luke recount the Presentation and how Simeon and Anna recognized Jesus. But the reading also foretells the pain that Mary will suffer as mother of the Lord. Luke also recounts how as an adolescent Jesus remained behind in the Temple teaching while his parents, not realizing it, were returning home. It is a poignant, bittersweet experience. Families must have unity but they must recognize the individuality of each member. Family life has its tense moments, but love and respect smooth them over.

DECEMBER 31

Seventh Day in the Octave of Christmas

1 John 2: 18-21; John 1: 1-18

Today's Mass brings a profound theological lesson about the meaning of the birth of Christ for our lives. Today's reading is from the First Letter of John and that letter is thought to be the litmus test of genuine Christian living. What does the birth of Jesus mean for our pattern of life, now more than twenty centuries later? John warns against false teachers and tells us that in Christ there is all knowledge and truth. The Antichrist will come from our own ranks. This is why the present period of history is so difficult. It harbors a spirit of indifference, but what hurts the Church most is not its alienated but supposedly "good" members. The latter never really belonged to Christ, for if they did, they would not have abandoned him.

It is a beautiful thing to see how closely we are united to Father, Son, and Holy Spirit. Before anything could be created, God had to conceive of it and, of course, since everything is contained in the one perfect idea that God has, John can rightly say that "through him all things came into being (by the will of the Father) and apart from him, nothing came to be. And whatever came to be in him, found life." Why? Because what God conceives must have a certain perfection and if he wills that perfection be given existence outside of himself, if he wills that perfection to be manifest, it can only be due to his "admiration" and love for that idea. So it can also be said that through love, all things came into being. Moreover, it can also be said that we ourselves are the idea of God; we are the word made flesh meant to dwell among one another. That is our calling to be God—to manifest God—to one another.

The whole notion of being an idea of God, brought to life as a word of God, who is to make God visible to those around us is indeed an exalted concept! But that is who we are. This word, conceived in the image and likeness of God, is intended to echo and reverberate in the lives of others. With such a calling, strengthened by the grace of the sacraments, what a waste it is and what a loss to mankind, if we should surrender to sin and send a different message. May all around us see in us God's glory. It will happen, if we are filled with the goodness of his grace and staunchly loyal to his truth.

Before Epiphany: From January 2 to Epiphany

JANUARY 2

1 John 2: 22-28; John 1: 19-28

The Father and the Son are one. He who denies the Son denies the Father also. In this reading John does not give proof of the fact but proof is contained in the life and in the teaching of Jesus, which life and teaching are communicated in the sacraments and in the anointings that the people have received. In order to be baptized and confirmed one must accept the teachings of Jesus. Above all this is true for those ordained to the priesthood. So St. John urges that these believers remain steadfast in their faith, not drawn away from Jesus by the enticements of worldly teaching but adhering to Jesus with firm faith in what Jesus himself teaches through the apostles and in his promise of eternal life.

Faith, hope and love for Jesus is the key to eternal life. It comes down to an acceptance or a rejection of him (love), his teaching (faith) and his promises (hope). Although this does require faith in what is unseen and inexperienced, we know from what we do see and experience that there is no one who has such goodness and concern for us (love), who has the truth which unlocks the secrets to life (faith), who has a power to promise rewards which far exceed the passing pleasures of this world (hope).

John the Baptist is an illustration of this truth. He was seen by the people of his time as the greatest person living. They placed their faith, hope and love in him. And he, rejecting the honor, directed their attention to the Messiah, Jesus, in whom he (John) placed his faith, hope and love. If the greatest of the ages have done so—prophets of the Old Testament, saints and martyrs of the New Testament—should not we do so as well?

JANUARY 3 (if before Epiphany)

1 John 2: 29-3: 6; John 1: 29-34

Today's reading from the First Letter of John reminds us that we are called to be God's dear children, and therefore, we are to be holy, pure, and sinless. John's primary purpose in writing is to make us understand how privileged and sublime is our status of Christian. We are to be holy as God is holy and if we have this holiness, it is clear that we have been "begotten" by him and that "we are God's children now." That holiness consists in being like God, which requires that we keep ourselves pure as he is pure and that we remain free of sin. To indicate the degree to which we must be holy, notice that we are not to compare ourselves to one another, as so many do and see ourselves as better. Our standard of holiness is God himself. We are to be holy as he is holy; we are to be perfect as our heavenly Father is perfect. Surely the Lord understands that we will not reach that standard of perfection; on the other hand, he is not satisfied unless we are constantly striving for that standard. It follows that if we live this holy life, we shall be rejected by society as was God's Son. People will not recognize our way of life as the course which all should follow.

The foolishness of a sinful life for any Christian is clear in the fact that the reason he revealed himself was to take away (our) sins. If this was the whole purpose of Christ's life, surely we cannot be considered as people who love him and believe in him, if we give ourselves over to sin.

John the Baptist is an example of one who recognized Christ for the person he is. He is the "Lamb of God who takes away the sins of the world." It is not easy to recognize such a person. John the Baptist did not do so of himself, he needed the revelation of the Father to do so. We constantly need to pray for this same grace, for neither can we recognize God in man or in nature without his help. Our prayer must be, "Lord, I believe; please help my unbelief."

JANUARY 4 (if before Epiphany)

1 John 3: 7-10; John 1: 35-42

Jesus came into the world for the purpose of saving us from sin and showing us the way to holiness. Inasmuch as a distinction is made at the end of the reading between holiness and love of neighbor, it would seem that holiness should be understood as union with God, loving him with one's whole mind, heart, soul, and strength. Yet, both love of God and love of neighbor are necessary if a person is to be free from sin.

Again, John the Baptist identifies the Messiah for his disciples; he points out to them the way of the Lord, and the disciples follow Jesus. They accept his invitation to join him, to listen to him, and to find out what he is all about. Apparently, they became convinced from what Jesus said that he was the Messiah. In any event, that was the way that they related their experience to Simon. Jesus immediately calls Simon by name and then changes that name to Peter, which means rock. He does not speak of Peter as being all holy, sinless, but he is to be a person of strong faith, whose faith will support others, enabling all to retain their unity with God and their love for neighbor despite lapses into sinfulness.

JANUARY 5 (if before Epiphany)

1 John 3: 11-21; John 1: 43-51

Today's first reading is again from the First Letter of John. That letter is noteworthy because it joins belief and life, faith and conduct. John maintains that the gospel of love has been revealed from the very beginning. The reason that we don't love one another as we should is envy, as in the case of Cain and Abel. Rather than envy other people, we should work and try to be as good or even better than the other person in virtue. When it comes to material goods there is never a reason for envy. The way that we come to understand love clearly is in the example of Jesus Christ, who "laid down his life for us." We, too must lay down our lives for our brothers and sisters, at least by practicing justice and charity towards them. If we fail in justice and charity, we can hardly say that we love others. There is an obvious contradiction. And we must keep in mind that every sin, fault, imperfection of ours is due to a breakdown in the ideal of justice and charity. Love is not a matter of wishful thinking but a matter of practice. "Let us love in deed and in truth and not merely talk about it."

Nathanael was a person who said what was on his mind, but he was like all other people, filled with prejudice about people and events. "Can anything good come from Nazareth?" He was opposed to Nazarenes as some today are opposed to Blacks, Hispanics, and the poor. Prejudices are unjust and uncharitable. Every person should be given a chance. It is to Nathanael's credit that he did give Jesus a chance and, despite having been so outspoken, he repented and believed that someone good could come from Nazareth. "Rabbi, you are the Son of God; you are the King of Israel." Would it not have been so much better, if he had reserved his judgment in the first place?

Nathanael believed because Jesus knew something about him, but his eyes were really opened when he saw "much greater things than that." Obviously the greater things are Jesus' revelation of the Father—truth, justice, charity in word and deed, culminating in the giving of his life for his friends. This is love; this is what the gospel is all about.

JANUARY 6 (if before Epiphany)

1 John 5: 5-13; Mark 1: 7-11

In today's reading from the First Letter of John, the author says that the birth of Christ means eternal life gained through faith. We are ever so ready to accept human testimony—might makes right, money talks, it is who you know. We see these strategies work for a time and then fail when a person with greater might, more money, better connections appears. Even if the strategy works for a long time it is always overcome by death.

If we see that all the truths of worldly wisdom collapse and fail, why are we so reluctant to place our faith in God's word, God's testimony, God's truth? Yes, we must make an act of faith, but we also make an act of faith in human beings, when we accept their worldly wisdom. And we do so even though we know for certain that their strategy is doomed to failure. As long as we have moral certitude that God is speaking to us—and the life of Christ surely gives us the certitude that he is God—why can't we have absolute faith in what he tells us? For if we do believe that Christ is God and we fail to follow his testimony, we are branding God as a fraud!

The major testimony Christ gives us is that God loves us—enough to give his life for us—and that God wants us to share in his life, his love, for all eternity. What is wrong with the message? Is there anything lacking? What more could a person want than to be united with God in perfect love and happiness for all eternity? If the people stayed with St. John the Baptist in the desert for days on end, how much more should we wish to be united with "one more powerful than he," whose sandal straps John was unworthy to tie! Indeed it was this very John the Baptist, whom the people so admired, who testified that Jesus was the Messiah and who instructed his disciples to follow the Christ.

JANUARY 7 (if before Epiphany)

1 John 5: 14-21; John 2: 1-12

St. John tells us that, "if we pray for anything that is in accord with God's will, it will be granted." But, surely, it is in accord with God's will that every person should turn from sin and lead a holy life. Therefore, if we petition God for the sinner that we are "life will be given to the sinner."

John excludes the "deadly sin," whatever that may be. But still if we believe enough in God that we pray to him, we can hardly be in the grip of "deadly sin." So we should have the greatest hope in praying for ourselves and other sinners that we may be freed from sin. God can do it and will do it, even if we cannot.

God protects those who are begotten of him, who have his grace. Those who accept and use his grace will not sin. On the other hand, we can lose God's grace and protection. John warns us to beware of idols. These are not only inanimate objects but any worldly good that becomes so paramount in our lives that we give it first place. Is this the deadly sin? Who knows? Who cares? The important thing is to avoid "idol worship," cling to God's grace, pray that he preserve us from sin.

The gospel tells us about the first sign that Jesus gave to his apostles of his divine power. "Thus, did he reveal his glory, and his disciples believed in him." Although we were not present for the miracle at Cana, we have far more in the past two thousand years on which to base our faith. Mary believed without previous signs in his public life; the apostles believed after the first sign. How many manifestations have we been given and still we do not believe as firmly as we should? "Jesus, I believe; please help my unbelief!"

After Epiphany to the Baptism of the Lord

MONDAY (or January 7)

1 John 3: 22-4: 6; Matthew 4: 12-17, 23-25

God will support us if we keep his commandments. His commandments are to believe in his Son, Jesus Christ, love God, and love one another. If we do this, we remain as one with God. Everything should be tested against these two commandments. If a person does not love his neighbor, he is not one with God. If a person does not accept what Jesus said and did, he is not one with God.

The key question in Christianity has always been whether or not a person accepts the fact that Jesus established a Church with a visible authority. If he did so, it becomes necessary not only to believe in him but to believe in those to whom he has given charge in the Church. If we do not accept the Church and we maintain that we believe only Jesus, it becomes every person for himself interpreting Scripture as he sees fit. The latter course ends in countless contradictions, confusions, disputes—a situation in which it is next to impossible to carry out the other commandment of loving others as we love ourselves.

The above is not a step beyond what St. John has written. First, it is only common sense to argue that one who believes in Jesus must believe in what he said and did. Secondly, those who have the spirit of the Antichrist, those who are false prophets, use "the language of the world" and "the world listens to them." This clearly infers that we need to listen to the language of Jesus, a language not of this world.

The conclusion to today's reading proves the point that the words and deeds of Jesus must be heard and followed, but it also proves that Jesus established a Church that can speak authoritatively in his name and that the word of Jesus' Church must be accepted. "We belong to God and anyone who had knowledge of God gives us a hearing, while anyone who is not of God refuses to hear us." The "us" refers to no one other than the apostles and his associates, whom Jesus had gathered around him.

Jesus asked the people to listen to him by referring to Isaiah, who had spoken much about the Messiah. He gave witness that he was the great light come to a people living in spiritual darkness. He kept the commandments of loving God and loving neighbor by going out of his way to assist God's little ones. By the same means, he taught that he was one with God. And finally, he urged others to do the same by saying, "Reform your lives." Let us turn from the world's ways to God's ways; let us turn outward also toward our neighbor, putting aside all selfishness.

Tuesday (or January 8)

1 John 4: 7-10; Mark 6: 34-44

God is love! Regardless of whatever good qualities we may think we have, if we have not love, we have not God. For the most part, we have ourselves convinced that we have love in our hearts, whereas the truth is that at best we have justice. Love goes beyond justice to charity, and beyond ordinary charity to sacrifice. Love consists in this: "God has sent his Son as an offering for our sins." "He died for us while we were yet sinners." The test of love is whether or not we love our enemies and do good to those who hate us. And to the extent that we are lacking in love of this kind, we are not in union with God.

In today's gospel, the first thought of the disciples for the vast crowd who followed Jesus was not one of charity. The people would stay as long as Jesus preached, so he should stop and dismiss the crowd so that they could buy themselves something to eat. Almost immediately it became evident that the disciples were thinking as much about themselves as they were about the crowd. They were not about to share with the crowd and certainly they were not going to spend everything they had to buy bread for them. With that, Jesus showed the disciples what it means to say "God is love." He had true compassion for the ordinary poor people. In this anecdote, his compassion extended to the multitudes and he fed them all.

Wednesday (or January 9)

1 John 4: 11-18; Mark 6: 45-52

Today in the First Letter of John, we hear that the birth of Jesus means a magnificent inner spiritual change. It means that God dwells in our souls with love. One cannot be said to love God unless he loves his neighbor also. This is obvious to human reason from the fact of creation; we are all God's creatures with the same nature, rights, and responsibilities. "If God has so loved us, we must have the same love for one another."

In Christ, however, we have gained a special means of understanding our relationship to others. God is love. Christ showed this beyond the shadow of a doubt in his preaching, the conduct of his life, and especially in his death. "When anyone acknowledges that Jesus is the Son of God, God dwells in him." If God's Spirit has been given to a person, God dwells in him. And if we see a person "who abides in love," since God is love, we know that person "abides in God and God in him."

In these conditions, to refuse love to one's neighbor is to refuse love to God, and that would be absurd! We would be the losers, for God continues to dwell in us only if we love one another. Fear is a test of our love. If we hold back from loving our neighbor because of some slight, or even great fear, we do not fully possess God. "Love is not yet perfect in one who is afraid."

Certainly the apostles were faced with a great fear by the storm on the lake, but they had also just witnessed a great sign of Jesus' power in the miracle of the loaves and fishes. The two balance off to a great extent but serve to remind us of how weak we are as human beings, how urgently we need the grace and love of God to sustain us. Our union with God, while on this earth, is never strong enough. We must constantly pray and work at it by our practice of charity, if we are to persevere in God's love through the storms of life.

THURSDAY (or January 10)

1 John 4: 19-5: 4; Luke 4: 14-22

The key to salvation is our belief that Jesus is the Christ. Everyone who believes this is begotten of God, is a child of God. That means that not only am I a child of God, but everyone else who believes in Christ is also a child of God. And since every child loves his father, and does what he asks of him, so we love God and keep his commandments. His commandments, which are not burdensome, are to love him with our whole mind, heart, and soul, and to love our neighbor as ourselves. If a person says that he loves God but not his neighbor or vice versa, there is no truth in him. It is in the keeping of these two great commandments that we overcome the world.

When Jesus began to preach the gospel of love, goodness, kindness to man, his message was received with great joy and praise. It was clear that he was giving the people a great gift. They received his message well and spoke favorably of him. It was not until he made clear that all of his followers must imitate his example that he began to run into trouble. The ordinary person received his message well, but the Pharisees had him put to death and won the people over temporarily to their view that Jesus was a dangerous person. After his death, however, many regretted their abandonment of Jesus, accepted his message, sought baptism, and followed in his footsteps.

FRIDAY (or January 11)

1 John 5: 5-13; Luke 5: 12-16

We are ever so ready to accept human testimony but we tend to hesitate, when it comes to accepting divine revelation even when the evidence is far stronger.

As St. John says, when we fail to accept that Jesus is the Christ, even though he has fulfilled Old Testament prophecy, performed miracles, lived an exemplary life, and many have died for faith in him, we are making a fraud out of God himself. Like the Pharisees, we are always asking for another sign and we never have enough to make a definitive act of faith. But only those who believe in Jesus are able to overcome the world. Only they will have eternal life.

We need the faith of the leper. "If you will to do so, you can cure me." That needs to be our prayer as well. And indeed, if we placed ourselves at the disposition of Jesus in this way, we would do what the leper did—we would spread the word about Jesus far and wide! These signs were enough for the ordinary people. Are we going to be like the Pharisees or like the ordinary people who believed in him? Notice how Jesus "overcame" the world—by retiring to a deserted place to pray, to be in union with his Father. We need to do more of this, too. We should shut the world out of our lives at least from time to time to be at one with the Lord.

SATURDAY (or January 12)

1 John 5: 14-21; John 3: 22-30

If we ask God for anything that is in accordance with his will, we can be sure that we shall receive it. Therefore, if we do not receive something that we pray for, we can be sure that it is not for our good and is contrary to

God's will. Instead of complaining that we do not receive what we seek from God, we should take another look at the situation and probably see what is wrong with our request.

If we are in possession of God's grace, we cannot sin; God protects us. However, we are able willfully to withdraw from God and then sin is well nigh inevitable. Notice that this is always the procedure. We reject God in some fashion or become indifferent to him before we sin. It is only when we set him aside, as it were, that we sin; when we attach ourselves to some "idol."

Both John the Baptist, and later Jesus, told their disciples that they should never be envious but have respect for any person who does wonders for people in the name of God. No one can truly do anything through the power of God without his willing it. And so, if something is done that has no other explanation than the power of God, then for some mysterious reason God is permitting the wonder to take place. In the case of Jesus at the Jordan, John the Baptist had no doubt. All signs were so strong that they indicated that the One, whose herald he was to be, had come. Instead of being angry, he was joyful and sent his disciples to Jesus. "He must increase, while I must decrease."

We are all instruments of God. If God wishes to accomplish something through one rather than another, so be it. We are surrendering to God when we encourage another person's gifts. There are so many lessons to be learned, applications to be made in our own lives of John the Baptist's utterance at the sight of Jesus: "He must increase, while I must decrease."

Ordinary Time

First Week of Ordinary Time

Monday

Hebrews 1: 1-6; Mark 1: 14-20 **YEAR I**

God spoke to men and women in different ways and always in an effort to convince them of who he is. His first message was through the creation of the universe, in all its splendor, and the creation of men and women, in his image and likeness and with his law written upon their hearts. This law, God put into print, on the tablets bearing the Ten Commandments. To persuade the people to follow these Ten Commandments God provided "signs and wonders"; he sent the great prophets and—at the people's request—the kings to guide and rule them in his name. Finally, God, as his full and final word, spoke through his Son, whom he has made heir to all things and through whom he first created the universe. We are destined to celebrate with the Son of God the life of perfect holiness for all eternity.

The Son of God, because he is God, is the revelation of the Father in the world. In Christ, we have the perfect manifestation of God; who he is, what he thinks, how he acts. It was God's plan to have Christ live for only an ordinary life span at a particular moment in history. By his Providence, God provided us with a Church under the leadership of the Vicar of Christ and under the guidance of the Holy Spirit. Within that Church, the Scriptures describe the words, the ideas, the acts of Christ, and they constitute the basis for the living tradition of the Church and proclaim God's message for all time. Finally, as we learn in The book of Revelation, we are in the last epoch before Christ will come again, and in this age we are given "signs and wonders" once again to remind us to heed the Word of God—wars and rumors of war, violence, chemical dependency, sexual permissiveness, breakdown of family life, earthquakes and other natural disasters—all of these intended to rouse us from our religious and moral lethargy.

Christ is the linchpin of all creation, the fulfillment of the prophets, the promise of future glory. Everything depends upon what you think of Christ. If we accept him as God, then everything falls in place and we are obliged—even by common sense—to lead a good life. If we do not accept Christ as God and his message as the way, the truth, and the life for ourselves, we are the most foolhardy and unfortunate of individuals. But we believe that one way or another God calls every person to himself. The response of the apostles, as soon as they recognized the Christ to be God, was immediate and their commitment total. We need to follow their example.

1 Samuel 1: 1-8; Mark 1: 14-20 **YEAR II**

Difficulties and obstacles always seem to attend God's call to his service. In the first reading we are told the story of Hannah who became the mother of the great prophet Samuel. For many years Hannah was barren, and suffered constant upbraiding by another of her husband's wives. Later, Hannah's great faith was rewarded by the birth of Samuel.

In Mark's gospel, we are told that after the arrest of John the Baptist, Jesus appears in Galilee proclaiming the good news and exhorting his listeners to believe in it. He also calls two pairs of brothers, Simon and Andrew and James and John to follow him. All four men stop what they are doing and immediately follow Jesus.

Why did the four men respond so eagerly? They recognized that Jesus was exceptional—unique—and they answered with alacrity because inside of them, they sensed a desire to know, love, and serve God. They did not know the difficulties and the challenges they would encounter. But they must have recognized the authority of Jesus to issue the call, and they must have known, at some level, that his authority came from God. Who would have believed that great events would take place because Hanna was a woman of faith or because four men dropped their fishing nets and followed a teacher who was little known at the time? We, on the other hand, already know who Jesus is. It is a sign of discipleship that, when we bear his call in big or little things, we drop what we are doing and hasten to follow him. To follow Jesus is worth all the challenges and difficulties we may encounter.

TUESDAY

Hebrews 2: 5-12; Mark 1: 21-28 **YEAR I**

It seems unimaginable, but it is true, that heaven exists for men more than for angels. We are less than they are now, but one day, if we merit heaven, all including the angels will be "subject" to us. It is also amazing that the very Son of God should have been made less than the angels for a time so that he could become one with us in our humanity—becoming our brother, suffering as a man, taking our place as it were, in order to redeem us. We accept these truths of our faith, but they are truly mysteries because we have no knowledge, only speculation, as to why God did things this way. That he did so, however, is true and wonderful, leading to unending joy on our part as we reflect upon God's goodness and love toward us.

Curing the man with an unclean spirit is a sign of God's love and compassion even more than it is a sign of his divinity. The manner in which he performed the miracle and spoke to the people with confidence and authority is a sign that Jesus was God. The person of God within Jesus allowed him to overcome all earthly and supernatural powers, even though he was man as well and had the appearance of a man. When we reach heaven we, too, will have overcome all worldly powers even though our person will remain that of a human being. But we will have become glorified human beings. What we are now, children of God, is a wonder. But, as St. John says, we have no idea what we shall be like in glory, when our state will be even above that of angels.

1 Samuel 1: 9-20; Mark 1: 21-28 **YEAR II**

Today, Mark's gospel gives us a powerful reminder of just who Jesus is and the nature of our relationship. To hint, Mark tells us that on the Sabbath, Jesus goes to the temple and begins to teach. The people are spellbound because he teaches with authority. Authority comes from God, and so his listeners are amazed. Jesus casts out a demon from a possessed man. Now, the onlookers are stunned. Here is a man casting out demons and speaking with a spirit of authority. "What does this mean?" they ask one another. Sometimes when we ask a question it leads us to the answer, and sometimes we ask a question to avoid knowing the answer. If we accept that Jesus teaches with authority, then we have to follow his teaching or somehow rationalize our way out of coming to grips with our relationship to him and our obligation, as believers, to follow him. It is easy to cling to what makes us feel comfortable. But we are not called to live superficial lives; we are called to look beyond appearances in order to discover what is real and true.

The first reading continues the story of Hannah. Distraught at being childless, she goes to the temple to implore God to give her a son. Her prayer is so intense that she is mistaken for a drunken show-off. Yet, God sees her deep sincerity, and her prayer is answered. She conceives and bears a son whom she names Samuel.

Hannah was misunderstood by Eli because he misinterpreted the way she prayed. Likewise, some of the people in the synagogue were disturbed because Jesus was different from all others who preached and they were not ready to cast aside their preconceived notions in favor of the truth.

WEDNESDAY

Hebrews 2: 14-18; Mark 1: 29-39 **YEAR I**

By his death on the cross Jesus freed those who, through their fear of death, had been slaves their whole life. If we have any fear of death, therefore, we are not unlike other human beings. At the same time, we must realize that, if we have this fear of death, it is because of our sins, which make us slaves to our own passions and the ways of the world. Too many people seem to think that they are free when they exercise the power to choose pleasure and evil over that which is true, good, and beautiful. In fact, they are freely choosing to bind themselves ever more tightly to the chains of sin. Their evil habits strengthen the bonds that hold them in the grip of evil practices and make it ever more difficult to escape. The virtuous, on the other hand, may not be able to gain worldly power and prosperity, but they experience a sense of freedom that the sinner can never know. This freedom given to the virtuous is described by St. Paul in his letter to the Galatians where he details the fruits of the Holy Spirit which are charity, joy, peace, patience, goodness, kindness, faith, mildness, and self-control.

Since the purpose of the Incarnation and eventual death of Christ was not to redeem angels but men, Jesus had to be fully human, experiencing human life with all of its real problems just as we do. He could not, in the Father's plan, go through life as a purely spiritual being and still have the solidarity with mankind that would convince us that his way of life was far superior to a worldly way of life; indeed, that his way was the only way to salvation.

So Jesus experienced all of human misery, either vicariously through the misery of others or in his own person when he suffered insult, rejection, hunger, thirst, persecution, beatings, crucifixion, and all the rest. He met misery in other people and experienced it intensely and with deep compassion. He overcame his own trials by his resurrection and the trials of others by healing them of sickness, disease, and physical handicap.

We see all this in today's gospel as Jesus heals just about everyone in Capernaum. The lesson we need to learn is not only the way of life of Jesus but also how to practice that life. Jesus' way of life is not something passive as the mere avoidance of sin. The way of life of Jesus is eminently active and positive. Avoiding sin is one thing but to practice his way by helping others is another. This is witnessed throughout the gospel. An example is the cure of Peter's mother-in-law who was healed by Jesus. As soon as she was better, she went about assisting others. Doing for others may well be the way of experiencing heaven right here on earth.

1 Samuel 3: 1-10, 19-20; Mark 1: 29-39 **YEAR II**

"Speak Lord, for your servant is listening." At last, what a wonderful response! Young Samuel had never heard the voice of the Lord, until one night, when he was asleep, the Lord called him. Samuel thought it was Eli, and so he went to the priest and asked him what he wanted. Three times the Lord called Samuel and three times Samuel did not recognize his voice. Finally, the Lord called, "Samuel. Samuel. Samuel." And Samuel did as instructed by Eli and answered, "Speak Lord, for your servant is listening." It was the beginning of a long and powerful relationship.

The Lord calls each one of us and perhaps, like Samuel, when we are young, we may not recognize his voice, or perhaps we do not want to hear it because we know that responding to the Lord will change our lives. Yet, when the call comes, it is for each of us a unique moment when we can say Yes or No to divine love! If we surrender ourselves and respond, "Speak Lord, your servant is listening," we are choosing to join the cast of the heavenly legions and deep joy fills our souls. Our lives take on a new meaning and we are marked forever.

In today's gospel narrative, Jesus makes it clear that he wants the good news to be available to all. The many miracles he performed were to attract the attention of the crowds and prepare them to hear his words. If we want to hear the call of Jesus we must at all times listen intently, not only with our ears but also through the events around us and be ready to say, "Speak Lord, for your servant is listening." Thus, first, we must want to heed the call and then be prepared to live by its demands.

THURSDAY

Hebrews 3: 7-14; Mark 1: 40-45 **YEAR I**

In the first reading, we are warned against hardness of heart and indifference to God's grace—which, in effect, means that we have no need of God and we can take care of ourselves. When everything is going well, such a philosophy seems acceptable and workable, but when reversals come into our lives, we have nowhere to turn. We continue in our worldly ways which lead to actions that can be both immoral and illegal and our last state becomes worse than the first. We need to recognize at all times that we are creatures dependent upon a Creator both for our present existence and for the after-life. This amounts to having a "soft heart," humble and aware of the true facts of life. We need to encourage one another because, in the eyes of the world, humility is weakness and others will take advantage of our innocence. Indeed, it is next to impossible to keep the faith and to live on a spiritual level without the moral support of like-minded people.

The leper is an example of a person who recognizes Christ as the Son of God, who created him, and who therefore has the power to cure him. It is true that the leper, being an outcast, could not appeal to a worldly power for a cure. He had only one hope. Unlike the many lepers who, in those days, cursed their fate, he turned to the Creator for the spiritual support and the cure which he needed.

Scripture authorities do not seem to hold the leper guilty of any "crime" for publicizing his cure even though it caused Jesus some difficulties. In disobeying instructions, the leper was able to encourage others, especially his fellow lepers, to recognize Christ who had the power to cure. He was trying to show them to look at life as he did and come to the realization that trust in the Creator is the only effective way of dealing with the world and human problems.

1 Samuel 4: 1-11; Mark 1: 40-45 **YEAR II**

There is a very powerful lesson to be learned from today's first reading. The Philistines living in the seacoast region were the archenemies of Israel. The Ark of the Lord was a portable tent of worship that the Israelites used in the desert after their exodus from Egypt, and its loss was an indescribable catastrophe.

The Philistines were about to go into battle against Israel when they heard a joyous shout from the Hebrew camp. They learned that the Ark of the Covenant had been brought into the camp accompanied by the two sons of Eli. The Philistines became fearful because they knew God had brought the Israelites out of Egypt by striking down the Egyptians. Yet, with great courage they engaged in battle, defeated the Israelites, took possession of the Ark of the Covenant, and killed the sons of Eli.The Lord had foretold the death of Eli's sons because, although they were priests, they were wicked men who abused those who came to the temple to sacrifice. With public manifestation of importance, they had marched with the Ark into the Hebrew camp, but God rejected the Israelites and allowed the Philistines to be victorious, It was a disastrous defeat! However, the Lord did not allow the Ark to remain with the Philistines. The Israelites repented of their sins and when the Philistines again attacked them, the Lord gave the Israelites victory and the Ark was returned to the Hebrew camp.

God allows us to pay a penalty for our sins. It is often the pain we experience because of our sins, which causes us to return to God.

FRIDAY

Hebrews 4: 1-5, 11; Mark 2: 1-12 **YEAR I**

Crucial to the practice of a religious and moral life is the acceptance of God's word and obedience to it. One without the other is useless. One cannot obey God's word unless he first accepts it. Without total acceptance, obedience is impossible.

Generally speaking, life-long Catholics obey God's word out of habit. They settle into a comfortable style of life and see themselves as more or less perfectly in accord with God's word. However, when a preacher jogs them from complacency or when a new situation develops, they find it very difficult to obey what they know to be God's word. They have never truly accepted the whole message, or they have taken it so much for granted that their conviction is not sufficiently intense to command obedience.

The paralytic and his friends had certainly accepted that Christ was God, so they let nothing stop them from getting to him. The paralytic had no hesitation in getting to his feet, when Christ commanded him. Both acceptance and obedience were complete. The Pharisees, on the other hand, could not bring themselves to accept what they had seen demonstrated with their own eyes. And, therefore, they were incapable of obeying the message that Christ was revealing to them.

In all of this, we can see that obedience to God's word comes easily if we are firmly convinced of its truth. This conviction comes only from reflection, meditation, and prayer. Faith is a gift. We can dispose ourselves as best we can to make an act of faith, but we cannot bring it about by our own power. This is why it is so important, once we have faith, to retain it by a devout life. "To him who has, more will be given," from others who have little, even that little will be taken away unless they cultivate the gift of faith.

1 Samuel 8: 4-7, 10-22; Mark 2: 1-12 **YEAR II**

St. Teresa is reported to have said that there are more tears shed over prayers that have been answered than over unanswered ones. God instructs us to petition him, and there is nothing wrong with asking God for favors. However, God knows what is best for us, and often we are far better off seeking his will than asking for specific things.

The Lord had set up judges to rule over Israel, but in today's first reading, the Israelites decided, in light of Samuel's advancing age, that they wanted to have a king just like other nations. When Samuel, who was serving as judge at that time, complained to the Lord, the Lord replied that the Israelites were not rejecting Samuel, rather they were rejecting God himself as their king. And the Lord told Samuel to give them whatever they wanted.

There followed a long line of kings, beginning with Saul and then succeeded by David and Solomon. Many of the kings turned away from God and the nation followed their example. The results were disastrous and the Israelites were finally led into captivity. When people do not understand that God's ways are not our ways and his thoughts are not our thoughts, the results are confusion or disaster.

In today's gospel, some of the scribes are scandalized when Jesus heals a paralyzed man by forgiving his sins. Instead of realizing that the power of Jesus comes from God, they immediately jump to the conclusion that Jesus is blaspheming. Yet, the goodness and power of Jesus should have been clear to them.

The Israelites did not see how graced they were to have God as their ruler instead of a human king, and the scribes refused to recognize the Messiah they had in their midst.

Saturday

Hebrews 4: 12-16; Mark 2: 13-17 **YEAR I**

"God's word is like a two-edged sword." It separates good and evil in our souls; makes clear the difference between principle and mere carnal desire; and between good and evil thoughts within the same person. As we read elsewhere in the gospel, the Word of God separates people one from the other, even among family members, depending on whether they accept or reject the Word of God. God's word is not hard or cruel or intended to cause pain—just the opposite, it has all the qualities of truth insofar as it is in accordance with principle and serves as a fundamental doctrine and motivating force.

Many people do not realize how important it is to accept and abide by God's word. That is the reason why we often compromise with the truth, thereby abandoning Christ, who is the Word of God. Christ understands our human dilemmas; he knows our weakness; he sympathizes with our difficulties. Still, he calls us to live by his truth. And that very truth, further strengthened by grace, provides us with the means to remain faithful.

So often in his public life Jesus confounded the Pharisees. They would question his association with tax collectors and others who violate the Law. Christ does not justify sin, but he recognizes that we are all sinners and we need his mercy. The Pharisees from earliest times were very clear in their Scripture and liturgy but they did not put the truth into practice. Christ's statement makes a true distinction between Pharisees and sinners. The latter know their sin and seek mercy; the former are blind to their sin, and do not look for mercy. They recognize the truth, but they cannot accept and live by it. Pride, position, power, and possessions blind and hold them back.

1 Samuel 9: 1-4, 17-19; 10: 1; Mark 2: 13-17 **YEAR II**

So often we read in the Scriptures that God calls into his service people who seem to lack the necessary qualifications, probably people we would not choose if we had the opportunity. In the first reading, a lad named Saul is sent by his father in search of the family asses, which had wandered off. As he carries out the search, Saul encounters the prophet Samuel who, upon the Lord's request, anoints him to govern Israel. According to the Scripture, the most significant thing about Saul was that be was handsome, hardly a necessary qualification to become the first king of Israel.

Mark's gospel recounts how Jesus saw Matthew at his tax collector's post and selected him to be one of his followers. In the eyes of the Pharisees, Jesus could not have made a poorer choice. Tax collectors were looked upon as crooks and seedy types; good people did not associate with them. This prompts Jesus to tell the Pharisees that he has come to call sinners and not the self-righteous.

There is a further lesson to be gained here. When God calls us and we follow him, we are expected to do his will and not to be self-willed. After his initial success as king of Israel, Saul began to do things his own way. Because of this, the Lord rejected Saul as king, and he commanded Samuel to anoint David. As king, David was not perfect and be also made mistakes. However, the great difference between Saul and David was that David, unlike Saul, delighted in the Lord and wished, from the depths of his being to serve him. For that reason, David is remembered as the greatest king of Israel.

Second Week of Ordinary Time

Monday

Hebrews 5: 1-10; Mark 2: 18-22 **YEAR I**

God's providence is surprising and revealing. It exposes God as soft-hearted and full of mercy. How else can we explain the fact that, for his priesthood, God chooses sinners from among sinners to offer sacrifice to him? If priests are to be human, there is no other choice—all of us are sinners—and yet it is marvelous that God should condescend to do this. Probably, we would choose to have no priesthood at all, if it were necessary to have sinners as the mediators between God and man. This is why man cannot in any way take the priesthood upon himself but must receive a special calling from God.

Although all priests are sinners, sinfulness is hardly a characteristic that we want to identify with the priesthood. Therefore, it is totally fitting that Christ should be our High Priest. What he needed to do in order to become an efficacious priest was to take upon himself everything human except sin. And if Christ was to be a perfect man, it was necessary that he live as a man in obedience to the Father's will, subject to suffering and even to death. And that is what Christ did, that is how he saved us, that is how he exercised his priesthood and became for us not only High Priest but victim as well.

While Christ lived, there was no need of other priests to offer sacrifice for sins. It was not necessary that the apostles offer their lives in sacrifice, while Christ—true God and true man—was doing so in their midst. After his resurrection, however, they were called upon as members, leaders, priests in the Church of Christ, not only to offer the Eucharistic sacrifice, but to offer themselves in sacrifice too.

1 Samuel 15: 16-23; Mark 2: 18-22 **YEAR II**

One of my first recollections of sports has to do with the St. Paul's baseball team, on which my brother played. In the late innings of a close game, the priest told the best hitter on the team to bunt. He went to the plate, hit a home run, and St. Paul's won the game. The priest would not let the hitter play on the team for the next several games.

In today's reading, Saul does much the same thing. He is told by God to destroy the enemy and all his possessions, but Saul's men capture some of the booty and use it to offer sacrifice to God. Saul had far exceeded God's expectations, so he thought. But God rebuked Saul: Samuel tells him that sincere obedience is more important than all external rituals. "Does the Lord delight more in holocausts and sacrifices than in obedience to the command of the Lord?" Obedience is better than sacrifice, as it is taught in both Testaments, but ever so clearly in the writings of St. John. If we love God, we are to prove it by keeping his commandment which is to love one another.

The gospel expresses a similar thought. John the Baptist and the Pharisees were given to fasting, but Jesus' disciples were not. The people saw fasting as a sign of holiness, associated in their minds with doing God's will. They were to realize that "God's ways are not necessarily man's ways, nor God's thoughts man's thoughts." God's word and not man's idea is the standard according to which one's obedience is to be weighed. Fasting is more fitting for those who only hope for the Savior, but celebration is a more appropriate action and a sign to indicate the presence of the Savior. The Pharisees were rejecting the instructions of "the coach," the one who had proven his authority in so many ways. They preferred to follow their own insights which, even though they were objectively good, were contrary to what the Lord God was asking of them at that time.

TUESDAY

Hebrews 6: 10-20; Mark 2: 23-28 **YEAR I**

St. Paul urges his readers to show their love for God in their love for others, in their good works and service to all around them. Not by wishful thinking, but through concrete actions are we to show our love for God and for our neighbor.

To many people a holy life is nonsense. Why should we sacrifice ourselves because of love for other people? St. Paul gives a whole host of reasons, but all of them have their basis in faith and hope—faith that God exists and hope that God fulfills his promises. But who cannot believe and hope in God?

If God exists, surely he is just, surely he keeps his promise of eternal life to those who serve him. He has sworn an oath that this is true. His own Son lived a self-sacrificing life, rose from the dead, and ascended into heaven. Countless other people have followed in his footsteps.

What we need in addition to faith and hope is patient endurance in these virtues and in the practice of the corporal and spiritual works of mercy.

All men and women, although imperfect and weak, are the focal point of all creation. Everything was created for their benefit, not vice versa. This is a sign of how much God loves them and wants them for himself. When turned to God, a person's free will makes that person God's prize; but, when turned away from God, free will makes that person the most despicable of creatures. Do we believe, hope, and trust in God? Or do we believe, hope, and trust only in ourselves? It may be difficult to believe, hope, and trust in what we have not seen, but it is foolish to believe, hope, and trust in what we have seen, namely ourselves. What we hope for is a happy life for all eternity. It is obvious that neither we nor any other human being can provide that for us. Human experience shows us clearly that "it is appointed unto all men once to die." And conscience makes us very much aware that "after death there will be a judgment." And who is there to judge us but the One whom we call God? So faith, hope, and trust in God are not idle and vain. Belief in God's existence removes the absurd from life and makes sense of human existence.

1 Samuel 16: 1-13; Mark 2: 23-28 **YEAR II**

"Not as man sees does God see, because man sees the appearance but the Lord looks into the heart."

The Lord had looked into the heart of Saul and saw that he no longer wanted him to rule his people. He had grown powerful, however, so Samuel could not see how Saul could be overthrown. Samuel also misjudged in trying to figure out which of Jesse's sons was to be anointed king. In Samuel's eyes Eliab seemed to be the perfect choice for king, but that was not God's will. If Samuel had lived to see David's reign, he would have realized that the judgment of the Lord was far superior to his own.

In the gospel, the same lesson is taught. The Pharisees simply do not understand the ways of God. Surely the Lord wants the Sabbath observed, but God created the Sabbath for man's good and not man for the Sabbath. Man's life and welfare must be preserved even on the Sabbath. There is a hierarchy of values, and the Pharisees in making up their rules and regulations had not understood that hierarchy. In effect, they were not so concerned about the violation of the Sabbath as they were about the violation of their laws. The Sabbath was to be observed; that was a commandment of God. But how was it to be observed? Was it necessary to observe it the way that the Pharisees had commanded—even at the price of the God-given gifts of life and physical health—or did these God-given gifts have priority over the pharisaical law? The answer is obvious.

WEDNESDAY

Hebrews 7: 1-3, 15-17; Mark 3: 1-6 **YEAR I**

Melchizedek means "King of Justice"; he was king of Salem, which means "King of Peace." Nothing is known of Melchizedek's ancestry or what happened to him after his encounter with Abraham; but he offered gifts of bread and wine to God on behalf of Abraham, and Abraham gave him a tithe (10%) of the booty he had taken in the victory over his enemies.

Melchizedek prefigures Christ in that he had no human ancestry; Christ came into the world as the Prince of Peace and to establish justice; Christ offered gifts of bread and wine to God; and after his death and resurrection, he disappeared from earth.

Our lives should be characterized in the same way, but are they? How important it is that we have good breeding! Indeed, it may make a great difference in our lives from a material standpoint. And how concerned we are to leave behind us a good name and numerous descendants? On the other hand, we can be so indifferent to peace, justice, and worship—all of which were central concerns to Christ. Obviously, we are not as Christ-like as we should be.

The cure on the Sabbath makes clear that there can be no contradiction between worship and peace/justice. Yes, we should set aside a day each week for the Lord, but that does not preclude doing what we can to help our neighbor. That we are to love God with our whole heart and soul does not forbid that we love our neighbor as ourselves. Rather, love of God demands that we love our neighbor, whom God loves. Indeed, our love of neighbor is a proof that our love of God is real and fraternal love leads to still greater love of God.

"You can't take it with you." On Judgment Day our ancestry and posterity will be of no account. What will count is what we have done with our lives on earth. And what we must do is love God with our whole heart and soul (worship) and love our neighbor as we love ourselves (justice). Then, we have the tranquility of good order which is peace.

1 Samuel 17: 32-33, 37, 40-51; Mark 3: 1-6 **YEAR II**

This reading is the story of young David's victory over Goliath, the Philistine giant.

The latter had been a warrior from his youth, but David, from his youth, had been a person of faith. Tending sheep, the Lord had never allowed him to succumb to bears or lions, so he would surely not allow him to fall into the hands of the Philistine. David spoke with such assurance that Saul, the old warrior, believed him and his faith was justified as he overcame Goliath, the Philistine.

In the gospel, Christ faced a different kind of enemy, the Pharisees. He performed a miracle in order to convert them but they would not believe. David was soon to find out that he was in the same position. Undoubtedly his victory over the Philistine and Christ's triumph over the withered hand had convinced many people not only of God's power, but also that God's favor rested upon Christ as it had upon David. But God's favor toward them was a challenge to the power and authority of those who claimed to be godly but who trusted in the world. Soon they would be seeking to remove them as obstacles to their plans for continued control of the temporal situation. We too have our choice between worldly ambition and faith in God. Which shall it be?

Another consideration is the unexpected nature of the appearance of the man with the withered hand. So often we have our whole day planned; we desire to accomplish many good things. Something unexpected happens and rather than giving it any consideration, we brush it aside. We don't allow it a chance to compete with our program even though it may be a higher good than our self-designed projects. Indeed, it is very likely a higher good coming into our lives providentially—contrary to our own designs. In the gospel, Jesus does the opposite; he chooses the unexpected, providential, and higher good over that which he had planned and which others considered inviolable such as the observance of the Sabbath.

THURSDAY

Hebrews 7: 25-8: 6; Mark 3: 7-12 **YEAR I**

That which singles out Jesus as the High Priest, is his perfect holiness, innocence, and freedom from sin. This is what he had to offer to the Father—a perfectly holy life—and that is why his sacrifice is acceptable for all times. However, without his divine Sonship, he would not have been perfect. His holy life, offered to the Father as man, allowed the Father to forgive our sins once again and to offer us the life of grace.

It behooves all priests, therefore, to be holy. This surely rules out mediocrity from our lives and satisfaction at being better than others. This attitude of itself condemns us as it did the Pharisees. We must strive for humility so that Christ may live in us and act through us. We must strive to live a life of holiness, free of attachment to the things of this world, living only for the world to come in a spirit of faith, hope, and love. Our holiness must be such that people look forward to our Mass, our preaching, or simply our very presence in their midst. This is the phenomenon which marks the Holy Fathers, Mother Theresa, and the Cure of Ars. And if we are not this holy—as most priests are not—we may still be adequate priests but we need to devote ourselves more zealously to the task if we sincerely love the priesthood and if we wish to be priests after the mind and heart of Christ.

1 Samuel 18: 6-9, 19: 1-7; Mark 3: 7-12 **YEAR II**

Today's reading tells of Saul's jealousy of David's growing popularity. Jonathan intercedes for David and placates Saul. Jealousy is a terrible thing, especially among those who are supposedly serving the Lord. If we are indeed serving the Lord, he is the one gaining all the credit and we should rejoice over that; all of our human effort is pooled together. When we start fighting among ourselves, everyone loses—the Lord, ourselves, and the people. A reconciler is a great person to have in the Church and the willingness and the humility to be reconciled is a precious gift. Jonathan was a reconciler and was able to do his work effectively because he loved much, he loved his father, Saul, and his friend, David. It would have been the easiest thing in the world for Saul and David to remain obstinate from a human perspective, but their humility overcame their pride. It is an art to be able to praise people without fostering pride in them and jealousy in others. Disharmony can be fostered by one single person but harmony requires the cooperation of many.

Today's gospel text shows the great popularity of Jesus. People came from the south, the east, and the west to hear him. Granted that all happens according to God's providence, it can be said that, if the crowds had not given Christ such adulation, if they had listened to his pleas for discretion about his miracles, he might have been able to win over the Pharisees gradually. But the praise of the crowd, although it did not make Christ proud, made the Pharisees jealous. They were in power and they were not about to have that power taken away.

Pride and jealousy are difficult vices to overcome. Humility is a strong antidote against pride and prudence, in the one dispensing praise, can help a great deal in abating both pride and jealousy.

FRIDAY

Hebrews 8: 6-13; Mark 3: 13-19 **YEAR I**

St. Paul attempts to make clear to people that they cannot live forever in the past. God is faithful; he fulfills his promises. However, because God has been so long in coming, the people have developed for themselves a comfortable religion. They now prefer human traditions to God's revelation. Although it is difficult to believe that the promise has been fulfilled in my time, I must change my ways based on that very belief. I must do likewise with respect to the Vatican Council. God has spoken through the bishops in union with the Pope under the guidance of the Holy Spirit. We must alter our ways, not in accordance with the worldly wisdom of some bright men, but according to the understanding of the Pope and bishops. They exercise the authority of the apostles, who received it from Jesus himself.

We note again, as we do every Christmas and Easter, that the greatest gift of the New Covenant is forgiveness of sins. The last words which St. Paul quotes are these: "I will forgive their evil-doing and their sins. I will remember no more." If anything could make a Jewish person of the time of Christ believe that the Messiah had come, it was forgiveness of sins. Reflection on the gospel story makes clear how much stress Christ placed on this belief as he preached and performed his miracles.

If only we understood that even though we are sinners, God is ready to forgive our sins. What more than forgiveness of sins can we expect of God? What greater blessing and sign of love can we anticipate? What more can we ask of religion, of our Church? This is what Christ and the Church are all about. "Your sins are forgiven! Go and sin no more! Love God with your whole heart and soul and your neighbor as yourself!"

1 Samuel 24: 3-21; Mark 3: 13-19 **YEAR II**

In today's reading from The First Book of Samuel, we learn of the nobility of David who respects King Saul as the "Lord's anointed." Saul likewise acts nobly on this occasion.

All God asks of human beings is justice motivated by love toward one another. Only he acts constantly with mercy and compassion. In today's reading, however, we have an example of "divine" mercy exercised by a human being, David. Love is the motivation but it is obedience to God, rather than any special love for Saul, that prompts David to preserve Saul's life. It is such a striking example that Saul sees it as a sign that David is truly called to be king. Although God does not demand anything more than justice from us, surely he is pleased when we are merciful as he is merciful. It is also a sign to ourselves that we are truly acting in the image and likeness of God. As David does, so should we leave judgment to God. We should accept to be considered fools here on earth and thereby store up rewards in heaven. This is a passing world.

In today's gospel narrative, Jesus, on the mountain, calls those he wants and they come. The Twelve Apostles are the foundation of the new Israel of twelve tribes. From what we know of the lives of the apostles, most of them were like David; yet at least one was like Saul. It was Peter who was chosen to be the head of the Church. Being chosen by God for some special responsibility is certainly no guarantee of salvation. Earthly honors and responsibilities mean nothing. Everyone will be judged by the same standard, obedience to the will of God and his commandments, the practice of justice, and the exercise of mercy toward others. This is what St. Augustine may have been referring to at least in part, when he said how joyful he was to be a Christian with the rest of the community, and how fearful he was about what he was expected to do for them because pride can so easily afflict the leader and have terrible repercussions for so many. As many have said, if we are to err, let us err on the side of justice and mercy rather than on that of severity.

SATURDAY

Hebrews 9: 2-3, 11-14; Mark 3: 20-21 **YEAR I**

The old order is compared with the new, but there can be no real comparison. How can one compare the sacrifice of animals to the sacrifice of the very Son of God? Although God attributed validity and responded to the sacrifice of animals, of how much greater value is the sacrifice of the Son of God?

In the desert wanderings, the Jews looked upon the tabernacle, which enclosed the Ark of the Covenant, as the holy of holies. There can be no comparison between the tabernacle of the Jews, and God made man! How much more powerful in the sight of the Father, and how much more capable of producing holiness in others is the Son of God? We believe with absolute certitude that, at his personal request, the Father forgives our sins.

And yet, because he taught a truth which was opposed to that of the Pharisees, because the crowds were stirred into a frenzy over his miracles, because to outward appearances he seemed like any other man, Christ's relatives thought him to be unbalanced and the Pharisees declared that he was possessed by Satan.

As Christ went along preaching and performing miracles, these allegations were utterly disproved. Then, why did the people not accept him as God? For all time, the question remains: "What think you of Christ?"

2 Samuel 1: 1-4, 11-12, 19, 23-27; Mark 3: 20-21 **YEAR II**

Today, the reading is from The Second Book of Samuel where the major figure is David. When David learns of the death of Saul and Jonathan, he expresses his sorrow in a beautiful poetic lament. To David, the fact that Saul was God's anointed meant everything. He loved Jonathan deeply because they were personal friends, who had much in common, and who enjoyed each other's company. Saul, however, was of a different generation; they disagreed; they were enemies. But still, David loved Saul and grieved over his death because God loved Saul, had chosen him, and had him anointed as king. This is a good lesson for us. We should love and respect superiors as David did Saul, especially when we disagree with them.

In today's gospel narrative, we learn that the relatives of Jesus did not understand what he was doing, resented him, and considered him unbalanced. Likewise, in the eyes of the world David was, in a sense, out of his mind. However, both Jesus and David loved people who were believed unworthy of love. But God loves all those people because he made them and longs for their conversion. Our work in the world is God's work, so we should take our cue from him and do as he does. "If we love God, we should love one another also."

Third Week of Ordinary Time

Monday

Hebrews 9: 15, 24-28; Mark 3: 22-30 **YEAR I**

The sacrifice of Christ on the cross is contrasted with the Temple sacrifice on two levels. Christ does not merely enter into the holy of holies and plead as a stranger for God's favor; rather he marches right into heaven, and pleads on our behalf as a son would to his father. Secondly, Christ's sacrifice is offered once and for all because it is infinite in value. Christ does not need to offer himself time and again the way animals were offered over and over again in Old Testament sacrifices. The two sacrifices are similar in that they are both offered to atone for our sins, but they are very dissimilar in that the sacrifice of Christ is totally efficacious because he is the Son of God.

During the sacrifice of the Mass, that is the re-enactment of the death of God's Son for our sins, we should be filled with faith, contrition, love, and hope. Beforehand, we should take time to recollect ourselves and reflect upon the meaning to us of the mystery of the Mass. It is truly overwhelming and far in excess of one's imagination and understanding that such a sacrifice should have been offered for us. But since it is so, how devout we should be in offering each Mass!

The Jews could not accept that Christ was God; instead some of the Pharisees saw him as the devil incarnate. Jesus tells us that either we are for him or against him. We cannot be lukewarm, indifferent, or on both sides of the fence, so to speak. We should pray constantly that the Lord increase our faith, hope, and love for him. We want to be consistent, unwavering signs of his presence in the world for the sake of those whose faith is weak and lukewarm, and for those who, until now, do not have faith in Christ.

2 Samuel 5: 1-7, 10; Mark 3: 22-30 **YEAR II**

In today's reading from the Second Book of Samuel, we continue to hear of the history of Israel's kings. Initially, David reigned over Judah for seven years and six months. When the elders from the Jerusalem area anointed him as their king as well, he ruled for thirty-three years over all of Israel and Judah. After becoming king of the entire nation, David conquered Jerusalem and made it the national capital. David was the forerunner of Christ in many ways. Christ descended from David. We see in David's story parallels and contrasts with that of Christ. It was the mission of Christ to save and thereby unify all men, but his word was a two-edged sword that caused people to take sides for or against him. Christ was anointed, so to speak, by the people who welcomed him to Jerusalem on Palm Sunday. He took the city, not by storm, but by peaceful means, by curing the blind and the lame, the very ones who were supposed to deter David from entering Jerusalem. David reigned for 33 years but Christ may have reigned only 33 hours until the city began to turn against him. But then he reigned for all eternity.

The background of today's gospel was the confusion of some over the identity of Jesus. When Christ went up to Jerusalem, the scribes accused him of being possessed by an unclean spirit. Christ demonstrated that such was impossible. He could not be both for and against his principles at the same time and under the same circumstances. That would be a destructive contradiction. The truth of the matter was that the unclean spirit was within his accusers, as Christ pointed out on several occasions. He was very much at one with himself but his words and actions were like a two-edged sword and were received differently by different people. The problem was not in Christ, but in his hearers. His word was a grace to some and a condemnation for others who could not accept it. So today, although the Church has an all too human appearance, one cannot maintain that Christ is good and the Church is evil. The Church is Christ's Body and is divinely protected. We must accept both Christ and his Church or neither.

TUESDAY

Hebrews 10: 1-10; Mark 3: 31-35 **YEAR I**

It was always possible for God to forgive sin but to remind people of their sinfulness was all that the sacrifice of animals could do. The blood of animals could not bring about the forgiveness of sins. Only the sacrifice of a very special human being could accomplish atonement. Indeed, if the sacrifice were to be truly worthy and of infinite value, it had to be the sacrifice of the Son of God, Jesus Christ, God-made-man.

Faith compels us to believe that Jesus can be both God and man. Since it is clear that the most appropriate and the way for the Father to forgive sins was through a sacrifice of infinite value, it was necessary that the Son of God take on our human nature and be offered to God for the remission of sin. There was no other way.

Gratitude and awesome wonder at the goodness of God should fill our hearts when we think of the way our sins have been forgiven. Unfortunately, we take this wondrous event so much for granted. We need to meditate on the death of Christ on the cross and on its significance in our lives. The central mystery is that Christ, who is true God and true man, died a horrible death on the cross in atonement for our sins. It was the mystery of the Incarnation that made possible the death of Jesus on the cross bringing about our redemption—an occurrence made totally credible by the Resurrection. Meditating on these awesome events every day of our lives would not be enough time to plumb the depths of God's kindness. However, a most devout prayer of adoration, thanksgiving, reparation, and petition can be the daily fruit of such a meditation.

The gospel makes us realize that each one of us, through our appreciation of this mystery and our consequent love of God and total dedication to his will, can become one with the Redeemer. Since Christ had to become man to accomplish our salvation, he had to have a mother, relatives, and friends. If Christ was to be human, he had to have a family. It was fitting, of course, that his mother—the instrument, through whom Christ became man—should be one with him in holiness. But we have an equal opportunity, with his family and associates, to be among his most beloved brothers and sisters. It is not human relationship but a spiritual relationship that brings about closeness to Christ. How close, how committed to getting closer to Christ are we? It should be our ardent desire to be as close as possible to Christ because of his role in our salvation and in the forgiveness of our sins.

2 Samuel 6: 12-15, 17-19; Mark 3: 31-35 **YEAR II**

In today's reading from The Second Book of Samuel, we learn that King David transported the ark of God to Jerusalem and located it in a tabernacle or tent. This made Jerusalem the religious center of the kingdom—the holy city of God's people. The ark contained the tablets of the Law—the Ten Commandments. The devotion that the Israelites had for the Ten Commandments is something for us to emulate. Instead of celebrating the commandments, we often look upon them as a burden, an obstacle, an unfair restriction. They are just the opposite. To abide by the commandments is to find a clear pathway to heaven. It is of the utmost importance to follow them strictly. Although there may be difficulties in life, we shall nevertheless be at peace because the commandments lead us to love God with our whole heart and soul and our neighbor as ourselves.

The commandments are in complete accord with human nature. In fact, they are the written, visible expression of "the law written on our hearts" from the moment of our creation. It was because human beings did not follow the unwritten law that it was given in writing. It was because human beings did not follow the written law that we were given the life of Christ. "O Felix Culpa!" Christ did not come to set aside this law but to fulfill it. In a very real sense, although incomplete, the commandments are one with Christ.

Today's gospel reading teaches us that the real relatives of Jesus were those who accept him fully. The keeping of the commandments was so important in the mind of Christ that he considered the person who obeyed them to be far better and far closer to him than his own parents and family. Sinlessness—obedience to the commandments—is the most important measure of God's regard for a human person. We should remember this when we think of the various offices in the Church. As St. Augustine put it, high rank in the Church is not a sign of holiness. High rank simply adds responsibility and, if anything, makes it more difficult to keep the commandments because the higher the position, the greater the temptation of pride and the greater the demands from larger numbers of people.

WEDNESDAY

Hebrews 10: 11-18; Mark 4: 1-20 **YEAR I**

The death of Christ on the cross is the only means of obtaining forgiveness of sins. If we wish to have our sins forgiven, we must go through Christ. Those who do not know of Christ will nevertheless be saved by him if they make every effort to follow the Law which is written in their hearts. However, those of us who know of Christ must have a tremendous devotion to him; we must keep his commandments and follow in his ways. There are people who think they will be saved by simply being "better than others" as long as they know Christ, realize his love for them, and his forgiveness of their sins. But what does it mean to be "better than others?" It cannot be good enough for one who has received the gospel message and has the knowledge and the grace to be truly Christ-like. If we do not use our free will to become true followers of Christ by imitating his virtues and following in his ways, our salvation will be in jeopardy, not from want of opportunity but from indifference and lack of motivation.

The parable of the sower develops this thought. Everyone in the parables hears God's word. Some are ill-disposed; others have a satanic tendency—they are superstitious and they believe that the devil and occult arts can save them. Still, others receive the Word joyfully at first but with the first difficulty, they yield to temptation; for example, someone makes fun of their Christian belief; a reward (a lucrative job) is offered based on their willingness to betray Christian principles; or they simply crave acceptance at the cost of virtue. Still others abandon the Word of God because of the pleasures of this world such as living for the moment instead of eternity, existing for physical gratification rather than spiritual joy, leading a totally selfish existence—all of which stifle growth in the Christian life.

Good intentions are necessary pre-requisites to attain salvation. In addition, however, there is need of will power to overcome human weakness. Without a doubt, every person will fall short of perfection. But every effort must be made to overcome indifference, self-pity, negative attitudes, repetition of past failures, and worry about perseverance. At all times, our "best" is required if we hope to be saved. Indeed, the spiritual battle is waged within ourselves—we are the enemy. The choice is always between present gratification and future happiness. Only faith in God makes the latter choice possible. Our constant prayer should be that the Lord strengthen our faith.

2 Samuel 7: 4-17; Mark 4: 1-20 **YEAR II**

Today's reading is most important. David wishes to build a house for God, and God promises to build a house for David—to create a dynasty that will rule forever! God's promise is fulfilled in Jesus Christ, who is of the royal line of David. David considers building a Temple but, through the prophet Nathan, God makes it clear to David that a dwelling place for him is secondary. God wants to dwell in the hearts of men as he has done with David, but not done with Saul, and will do with Solomon. Faithfulness to God's will and moral righteousness are what God seeks.

Also, more important to the Church are its members rather than the physical structure of the church. There are no parables about farmers building barns except for the greedy and foolish one. The farmer is always sowing his seed as the follower of Christ should always be preaching and teaching the Word of God, catechizing and evangelizing. We cannot expect that all the seed will fall on good soil; much is left to the hearer of God's word; the preacher is only the initiator. The response to God's word depends on the depth and quality of one's soul. Receiving God's grace, as everyone does, is one thing; accepting and using God's grace is quite another. What good is it to have beautiful churches for people who themselves have fallen away from the faith, who do not evangelize others, and, as Catholics in name only, give scandal and bad example to others, thereby becoming a negative influence?

THURSDAY

Hebrews 10: 19-25; Mark 4: 21-25 **YEAR I**

It all depends on faith. If we believe that Christ is the Son of God, that by his death on the cross he has freed us from our sins, and that all this has been made efficacious through baptism, then we should live accordingly! Otherwise, what good is our faith? We cannot have it both ways as lukewarm souls, the kind that Christ would vomit from his mouth. The lukewarm believe that Christ is God, and that if he has been foolish enough to die on the cross for our sins, he can be presumed foolish enough to save us from eternal death.

St. Paul sees the death of Christ on the cross and baptism as a call to us to undertake our personal part in the work of salvation. It is a glorious opportunity, and we must take advantage of it by using our free will, in cooperation with God's grace, and thereby raising one another to love and good deeds. To do this is to believe in Christ, hope in what he has promised, and appreciate what he has done. Yet, faith and hope are not enough. Love is also needed, love for God's word and for God's children. To act in any other way is a denial that God cares about what we do with our lives.

The illustration of the lamp confirms the point. To cover up a light is to deny its purpose. It is the same with Christ's death and baptism. If we fail to use them to advantage in our lives, our faith in Christ is in vain. Christ's death and our baptism are the motives and the means to conform our free will to his and to live our lives in imitation of his. By so doing, God's grace is increased within us, and our spirit further strengthened in faith, hope, and love. "To those who have, more will be given."

2 Samuel 7: 18-19, 24-29; Mark 4: 21-25 **YEAR II**

God had promised that he would make an everlasting kingdom of David's line. In today's reading, David asks the Lord to fulfill that promise.

The whole passage demonstrates that David is not so much praying for a favor as he is telling the Lord that he thinks he understands the responsibility involved and is willing to accept it. David humbly asks God to bless forever the promised Davidic dynasty. God looks for this kind of prayer whether from Mary and Joseph, Abraham and David, or any of the great saints. "Thy will be done," is the best prayer of all, especially when it is said in a deep spirit of acceptance and with the determination to do God's will with the help of his grace.

Today's gospel reading shows the Lord's simple pattern of teaching. He teaches sublime truths in every day language. Those who hear the Word of God should keep it. Inevitably, this means that the person who hears this word is going to be called upon to be a witness. We cannot believe one way and act in another. Just as the candle gives light to all in the room and is not to be put under a bushel basket, so faith must be professed. God's will must be openly avowed in word and action and for all to see. Thus those who witness God's will in action have the opportunity and the grace to accept God's word and to believe. Faith comes through hearing and seeing.

Friday

Hebrews 10: 32-39; Mark 4: 26-34 **YEAR I**

St. Paul calls upon the Hebrews who have kept faith for centuries not to falter now. They have undergone persecution in the past and lost everything. Why make that sacrifice useless by abandoning faith in the Messiah at this point? The Lord will come. When the difficulties of this world are compared to the eternal glory of the next, even a lifetime is short.

We too should look upon our lives in the same way. What is temporal suffering compared to eternal glory? And why suffer even a little (and everyone in the world does) unless there is to be some reward? Why believe and practice the faith at all, if you don't believe fully in the redemptive power of Christ? There is only one answer to all these questions for a believer—love God with your whole mind, heart, and soul; love your neighbor as yourself.

The gospel parable proves that only God can give the increase. In this case, the spiritual life is likened to a farmer, who does everything necessary to obtain a good crop. He prepares the soil; he plants the seed; he favors growth as much as possible. All the while his life rhythm goes unchanged—he retires to bed and gets up day after day. Through it all the seed sprouts and grows without his knowing how it happens until it is full grown and ready for harvest. The growth is imperceptible but inevitable—so it is with our spiritual life. If we do our part, mindful of God's word in all our daily duties, the Lord will nurture our humble beginnings and bring them to great development. All that God asks for is our faithful adherence to his commands through the exercise of our free will. The hand of God is our guide as we proceed along the path of life. His light shows us the way we are to go, one step at a time. He walks with us!

2 Samuel 11: 1-4, 5-10, 13-17; Mark 4: 26-34 **YEAR II**

In today's reading from the Second Book of Samuel, we learn that David commits a most serious sin of lust and murder. To take Bathsheba, the wife of Uriah, one of his warriors, he arranges to cause the latter's death. David's passions are the cause of his sin, and likewise, our passions are the motives for our failings. We can reason that others tempt us, however, the real problem is that we relax our moral standards. Temptations stay at arm's length and our conscience remains clear if we maintain our moral standards and shy away from immoral decisions. This is surely the case with David and Uriah. David has relations with Bathsheba. To save himself from scandal, he relies on deceit. He tries to cover his guilt by facilitating intercourse between Uriah and his wife, Bathsheba. However, neither royal present nor banquet induces Uriah to come to his wife. When all fails, David engineers the death of Uriah and thus implicates himself in murder. Actually, the undoing of David was the uprightness of Uriah, which stands in contrast to David's immorality and duplicity. There is no doubt that Uriah was the winner before God. And surely it was the innocence of Uriah which infuriated David and led him to make such poor judgments. Evil is no match for goodness and truth. The latter will win out one way or the other, often in this world and certainly in the next.

In the gospel, Christ makes clear that the growth of the kingdom is beyond man's power, is imperceptible and inevitable, and leads from humble beginnings to great development. As we sow, so shall we reap. If our lives are upright, true and good, we shall be rewarded. If our actions are evil, evil will be our compensation. In the world to come, these recompenses will be magnified to the maximum degree because then they will be definitive and eternal. We will be totally happy or totally miserable. For the good person God's grace is crucial—his reward is far beyond anything that a mere human being could earn or expect.

Saturday

Hebrews 11: 1-2, 8-19; Mark 4:35-41 **YEAR I**

"Faith is confident assurance concerning what we hope for and conviction about things we do not see." St. Paul is assuring us that God has given us his word or revelation. If we accept that he has really spoken to us, offering us a reason to live as well as to die, if we accept him and his message of life, we are believers. Furthermore, St. Paul urges us to live by our faith. Again, faith is the sure conviction that God exists, that he has spoken to us, and that he will surely keep his promises. Faith is founded in God's existence; it means holding to God and to our beliefs.

Like Abraham and so many others, we are not likely to see God's promise fulfilled on earth, at least not in a way that is clear and unambiguous. But that should not matter because it seemed even harder to believe on the part of those who did see God's promise fulfilled in Christ. Like most others we shall probably "die in faith"—without witnessing God's power in some marvelous way. However, that is what religion is all about: the confident assurance in what we hope for, belief in things that we have never seen.

The gospel narrative describes the apostles being given an opportunity to witness the fulfillment of the promise of God's power manifested in the calming of a turbulent sea. They were filled with awe and wondered, "Who can this be?" but their faith did not appear to be immediately strengthened, even though they were concerned as to the source of his power. The subtle signs of God's power in our daily lives are more helpful to our faith than the awe brought on by the calming of the sea. What are those signs of God's power so finely woven in the texture of our days? They are all around us in the cycle of each new day, between sunrise and sunset, in the blistering rage of storms, growth and death in nature, the goodness and decency of people, or an unexpected change of heart in ourselves and in others. Major signs of God's power often instill fear and cause us to wonder about a sinister power; the smaller signs are more powerful. So we should not be constantly asking the Lord for great and glorious signs that we may believe. We should simply pray, "Lord, increase my faith. Lord, I believe; please help my unbelief."

There are only two basic ways to live—in faith or without faith. Many are in between, but belief or unbelief will prevail. The only fully happy, peaceful state is belief. Unbelief leads to a life of pleasure masquerading under the disguise of happiness. Those who live between belief and unbelief have the most miserable life of all on earth. They are perennially filled with doubt, worry, and uncertainty. So the only truly happy life is one where total faith prevails, even in the face of misfortunes of all kind. Once we utter the "yes" of faith to God and accept his blueprint for living the fullness of life, the whole world no longer revolves around us, our needs, and gratifications. We are called to go out of ourselves as though we were going out of an old home, and we can never be the same again.

2 Samuel 12: 1-7, 10-17; Mark 4: 35-41 YEAR II

In today's reading, the prophet Nathan, by means of a parable, makes David see the greatness of his sin. David expresses sorrow and obtains God's pardon, but he is punished for his sin. It is clear that we are our own worst judges. We can see faults in others—even small faults—but it is so hard to see even great faults in ourselves. David was quick to see serious sin in Nathan's story and only then did he perceive his own guilt. He could have protested that there was a difference and that the story was not exactly what he did, that there were extenuating circumstances, but he did not. At least when he was trapped by the truth, David surrendered to it, admitted his guilt, and did penance for his sin.

There is little or no connection between the readings today. In fact, they only illustrate by different means how much we need God in our lives. David decides that he will go it alone, ignore God's will, and do what he pleases in taking Uriah's wife. The apostles already have the Son of God in their presence but their faith is so weak that it does no good. David neglects faith altogether; the apostles are filled with doubt.

How hard it seems to advance from lack of faith or from weak faith to full faith. Somehow we always think faith will be there when we need it, and it is not important nor even necessary to grow our faith through frequent acts of faith, hope and love, in prayer. Raising our minds and hearts to God in a total giving of self, adoring him, and being attentive to whisperings of grace is the prayer of choice. Both David and the apostles were embarrassed about their lack of faith and made amends. Have we reached that great turning point of embarrassment?

Fourth Week of Ordinary Time

MONDAY

Hebrews 11: 32-40; Mark 5: 1-20 **YEAR I**

In his letter to the Hebrews, St. Paul gives additional examples of people who lived by faith. He mentions men and women who faced incredible challenges because of their faith in God.

All of these leaders were weak human beings, but they became strong and powerful by virtue of God's grace and their faith in God's promises. Thus, they were able to endure every kind of persecution and hardship, suffer torture, and die peacefully with assurance of the reward that was to come. Indeed, "the world was not worthy of them."

We need to keep in mind how much those who have gone before us have done so that we might have the faith. For example, parents, grandparents, our parish communities, and all those who by word or example have led us to God. We have that same obligation toward our own and the coming generation. What is important is that we keep the faith, in season and out of season, and that we strive to be free of sin, filled with virtue, and committed to love—all motivated by our abiding hope in God's promises.

In the story of the demoniac at least two important teachings are made clear, namely the power of God's grace and the tenaciousness of sin. The demons could see that the power of God was far stronger then their own, but they desperately wished to remain in the man. They would use any strategy and go to any length to control him. By all outward indications, no power could repel the demons. But eventually the perseverance of Christ, his firm determination, his unwillingness to compromise with evil, all contributed to the expulsion of the demons.

In our own lives we need to be as principled and persevering as Christ. Surely we should learn from this story that, although sin does not usually seem that strong in us, it is only because we temporize with it. The strength of evil becomes fully evident only when we determine to eradicate it totally from our lives. At that point there is a real battle and a very uneven one at that, one that we shall surely lose unless we step aside and let the Lord fight the battle for us. That's the only way to win! Prayer and flight from the demon are our only chances of success. Let us not after prayer tell the Lord, "I'll handle it myself now." If we do we will again begin to compromise with evil and fall flat on our face once again.

Thank God our attitude is not as bad as that of the Gerasenes. When they saw what Christ had done, they deliberately chose the demons over him. The people were terrified by the demoniac and they stayed away from him. They wished to be delivered from these evil spirits, over whom they had no control. But when Christ delivered them they asked him to leave their land because the loss of the demons meant the loss of their wealth.

The Gerasenes chose evil over good, their material over their spiritual welfare. But is that much worse than our choices? We choose both. We tell the Lord that we will be loyal to him even though we are unwilling to leave the occasions of sin. We say, "Lord, leave it to us. We know how to deal with these things. We'll work out a compromise. We'll have our cake (holiness) and eat it too (commit sin)." Is our eternal salvation worth the gamble?

2 Samuel 15: 13-14, 30, 16: 5-13; Mark 5: 1-20 **YEAR II**

Today, we continue reading the story of King David. A new tragedy afflicts the royal family when the king's beloved son, Absalom, plots a revolution. David is forced to flee for his life; he does not retaliate insults and shows his greatness. In this instance of Absalom's rebellion, David thought he was in the right. However, he had the humility to realize that he might be wrong even when his own son was against him. Especially, he had the faith to believe that, if he was innocent, the Lord would somehow vindicate him. If, for instance, we are unfairly treated by the media or some other groups, it is usually best to accept the punishment and have faith that the truth will eventually vindicate us. For at the basis of the ill treatment, there is usually enough truth on the side of others that they can make a case for themselves or misunderstand our position. If we cannot have the humility to be charitable, or at least non-vindictive in the circumstances, how can we expect the same virtues in those who attack us? It is not at all certain that the Lord will come to our rescue. David says: "Perhaps the Lord will look upon my affliction," without expecting more than the Lord will give. David knew that much is gained from suffering in silence.

Today's gospel is the puzzling story of the man possessed by a legion of demons. He lived in pagan territory in an area inhabited by non-Jews, the Gerasenes, and it was known as the Ten Cities. The gospel indicates that most of the time we do not know what is best for us. It is better to leave all in God's hands and patiently rely on his Providence. The people wanted the possessed man to be brought under control but when Jesus acceded to their demand they were upset that the pigs plunged over the precipice and drowned! Difficult as this miracle story is to explain, it lends itself to various interpretations one of which is that, on earth, things will never be thoroughly to our liking. There is always something that bothers us. Rather than trying to dictate the way things should be, we should adjust to and accept our situation, always mindful that God will always care for us in the way that is best.

Tuesday

Hebrews 12: 1-4; Mark 5: 21-43 **YEAR I**

St. Paul has the answer for the one who is tempted, but yet wishes to be a holy person. "Lay aside every encumbrance of sin," he says and "keep your eyes fixed on Jesus, who inspires and perfects our faith."

Our problems are nothing compared to those of Christ. We haven't come close to shedding blood for our faith. Look at the hardships Christ endured and realize that if he could overcome them, he can certainly deal with the sufferings in our lives. Our role is to use our free will to get away from the "encumbrances" of sin. Then let us leave him to deal with the evil spirit. We should flee temptation and not attempt to battle with it. Fighting the spiritual battle is the Lord's work; on our own, we cannot overcome these preternatural forces.

The miracles of the gospel illustrate St. Paul's contention in a more concrete way. The woman afflicted with the hemorrhage kept her eyes on Jesus, as it were. All her hope was in him. Just touching his clothing would cure her. She wasn't looking for special attention from Jesus but simply to be in his presence. That's all we need spiritually. If we are close to Jesus, and trying sincerely to get closer, no evil can harm us, for no evil can get close to the Lord and survive.

Likewise, Jairus desired to approach the Lord on behalf of his daughter. He had done all that he could on behalf of the girl's health; he had used all the human resources available to him. Seeing that the illness was more than he could overcome, he fled to Jesus. He admitted that he could not deal with the problem himself and went to the only one who could.

The lesson is clear. Our only hope in physical illness is to realize our incapacity to deal with it; to stop temporizing with it, and to reach someone who can deal with the problem. In the spiritual realm, that one person is Jesus.

2 Samuel 18: 9-10, 14, 24-25, 30-19: 3; Mark 5: 21-43 **YEAR II**

Today, we read that the rebellion against King David is crushed. Absalom dies an ignominious death and the king weeps over his disloyal son. David was certainly a man of great patience and compassion. Although convinced that he himself was God's chosen one, he exercised the greatest restraint in his conduct, vis-a-vis Saul, and now he mourns Absalom, both of whom unjustly attacked him. He had not aspired to be king, so that did not mean so much to him. However, he had the greatest respect for Saul's position and the greatest love for Absalom. Chosen as he was by God, he saw both Saul and Absalom as chosen also. Respect for God's chosen ones and his own love for his son inspire David's actions in response to the quelling of the rebellion.

Today's gospel tells of a miracle within a miracle and of the Lord's concern for secrecy. The confident demeanor of Jairus contrasts with the hostility of the scribes. Jairus asks that Jesus lay his hands on his little daughter so that she may live. In the fray and crush of people around him, Jesus wants to know who touched his garment. A woman suffering from an issue of blood has touched his cloak hoping to be cured. Her behavior as well as that of Jairus reveals an access to Christ in faith. Both sense his holiness and power. He, in turn, senses the power of their faith. Neither the apostles nor the crowd had a faith so transparent that others could detect it. What about ourselves? Can others sense our holiness? Is our own faith such that we can identify it in others, when we are in their presence or talking with them? Sometimes it does happen and we recognize some people who have far more faith than we do. But, if we were truly impressed, we would try more earnestly to follow their example. But our reaction often is only, "I wish that I could be as holy as that person." If we are short on holiness, where is the faith that should impel us to seek out Jesus and beg his favor? Our lives should be characterized by a humble faith, prompting us to be on our knees begging the Lord to increase our faith and holiness so that we might serve him well.

WEDNESDAY

Hebrews 12: 4-7, 11-15; Mark 6: 1-6 **YEAR I**

Toward the end of the letter to the Hebrews, the author gives practical advice. He tells us that life's trials are the means used by God to discipline us and bring peace into our lives. He likens God's use of trials and adversity to the discipline a father imposes upon a son he loves. "What son is there, whom his father does not discipline? At the time it is administered, all discipline seems a cause for grief and not for joy, but later it brings forth the fruit of peace and justice to those who are trained in its school." Those words illustrate that perseverance comes as a result of our training. Whatever the circumstances, the lesson of discipline is worth its weight in gold. As I go around the diocese for confirmations, the happiest children, those who seem closest to their parents, who appreciate one another as a family are the disciplined children. Yet, their parents train them for a short time and according to their own lights—so we should readily submit to our Father in heaven who disciplines us that we may share his own holiness.

As St. Paul asks, if discipline and demands are signs of a good parent in the world, should we not expect the same from God our Father? Should we not expect that there should be commandments? Should we not expect hard times rather than have things given to us on a silver spoon? And through it all, should we not expect—and do we not find—understanding, compassion, love, and grace from God our Father as exhibited in the life of Christ, his divine Son? Should we not expect a life like that of Christ, if we are indeed God's "chosen ones?"

In our prayer and meditation we should reflect gratefully on God's gift of discipline and commandments instead of begging constantly to be delivered from them. We should pray to be delivered from evil and attachment to the things of this world.

In today's gospel narrative, we learn that the neighbors and friends of Jesus' family could not understand how he could be so wise. Yet he was saying nothing completely new to them. He was simply repeating the Law and the prophets. What was new was the way he lived his life. He was practicing what he preached—love of God and love of neighbor. He was accepting God's discipline and demands in his own life while preaching to the people that they should do the same instead of living a life of self-gratification and religiosity.

Today, is not our religion often manifested as mere religiosity? We fulfill the externals of the law. When it comes to the real substance of religion, which means loving God with our whole mind, heart, and soul, loving our neighbor as we love ourselves, we often fail miserably. Many of us struggle to be just. Yet how many are internally very unhappy because they maintain only an outward front of religiosity? Self-discipline that could move us to the practice of full justice by treating others as ourselves and then to open-hearted charity would bring happiness into our lives and remove the veil of phoniness which envelops our worldly existence. Let us pray to be delivered from envy and jealousy which consumed the neighbors of Christ and to be filled with admiration for Christ and attempt to imitate him as closely as a sinner can.

2 Samuel 24: 2, 9-17; Mark 6: 1-6 **YEAR II**

In today's reading we hear that David sinned against God by taking a census of the people—all for selfish reasons—to know how many thousands of warriors he had at his disposal. He later realized that he had sinned against God. Christ, during his passion, said that he could have legions of angels to assist him, if that were opportune. But God is not interested in overcoming man which he can do at any moment by any means. He does not need legions of angels or armies of men, as David was tempted to think, in order to exercise his Providence in the world. David realized that he had succumbed to temptation and had failed in faith. He recognized his sin, and therefore, when he had his choice of punishments, he atoned for his mistake by asking to be chastised by God using a pestilence, rather than by war with men. His choice of punishment was further admission of his guilt.

In the gospel, the people listening to Jesus recognized the power of his word, but they, for the most part, were unwilling to place their faith in the ultimate victory of truth. Amazed as they were by the spiritual strength of Christ's message, thcy still refused to rely solely upon the spiritual. What they felt they needed was physical and material strength. After a while Jesus "gave up" on them, healed those who did have faith, and went his way, repeating the same message. In comparing these readings we wonder how a people of Israel's culture could fail to believe and accept the message of Jesus. We have a similar situation today. The Word coming to us from the Church falls upon deaf ears as much now as it did in the time when Jesus walked the earth.

THURSDAY

Hebrews 12: 18-19, 21-24; Mark 6: 7-13 **YEAR I**

In today's first reading, a contrast is made between the God of the Old Testament and the God of the New Testament. The people who received the Old Law from Moses were not attuned to kindness and love. Primitive man was a hunter and as such was confronted daily with the decision to kill or be killed. Only harsh means could gain his attention. Thus, it was in fearful darkness, fire, lightning, and noise that the Old Law was given by God to Moses on Mount Sinai. Moses himself was terrified and trembling. Today, such an event would be called an "act of God," and it would remind us powerfully of our dependence upon the Almighty. However, in the New Testament, so that we would not be afraid of God, Jesus, God himself, and the mediator of a new covenant came to us as a baby. Later, he died suffering on the cross. No one is afraid of babies nor of people who are suffering. Truly, Jesus has made it easy to feel comfortable and "at home" with him. From the time he walked into our human history, he has led us with love, compassion, and gentle persuasion. He does not want us to be afraid and he wants to convince us of his love.

In the gospel narrative, Christ sends forth his disciples to bring the people to repentance. Note that he instructs them to take nothing on the journey but a walking stick—no food, no traveling bag, no money. They are to persuade with the truth, and show goodness, through healing and other spiritual and corporal works of mercy. They have no means to frighten people, and many of their listeners come to Christ through their persuasive efforts. We must first listen to Christ and his disciples. Then we, in turn, must attempt to persuade others of God's love by living a life based on truth and loving our neighbor in all ways—spiritual and corporal. Let us remember that total love is found only in God.

Even if we think that we are leading just lives, we are still sinners striving for perfection defined as total love. By their deeds, the just demonstrate all the love they can muster. But that love will be total only in heaven when sinners who are living a just life on earth will be made perfect by union with God for all eternity.

1 Kings 2: 1-4, 10-12; Mark 6:7-13 **YEAR II**

Today's reading is from The First Book of Kings and continues the history of the Chosen People from Solomon to the Captivity. When the time of his death is near, David gives advice to his son and successor, Solomon. His instruction to Solomon is "take courage and be a man." This can be interpreted at least in two ways. It can mean David's exhortation to Solomon is to be a warrior, to seek worldly dominion by bravely overcoming his foes in battle; to ignore God, to show everyone how tough he is, and sweep everyone out of his way by whatever ruthless means he has. In other words, he should act as a bully. However, this is not David's understanding of his counsel. To "take courage and be a man," in David's view implies a truly good man, one who is going to reach his full potential, and recognizes that he has been created by God. For him it is necessary to observe God's commandments and to follow in his ways. A man is going to show forth the image and likeness of God, which is spiritual strength, based on his knowledge of the truth and his firm commitment to put that truth into practice to achieve goodness.

The gospel is a good illustration of the first reading. In this reading, we learn of the working orders given by Jesus to the Twelve. At that time in Palestine, the natives had five articles of clothing: a long inner tunic, an outer cloak, a cincture or belt, sandals and the Oriental headdress. Travelers carried a bag for food. Jesus sends out the apostles as poor, simple, generous men. They are not to rely upon material goods in fulfilling their mission. They are simply to preach God's truth and practice goodness in their lives. If they do this, even though they will be rejected by some, many will appreciate what they offer and will take care of their material needs. The greatest need of human beings in this world is not material but spiritual. That is, we need to recognize God as creator, ourselves as creatures, our obligation to keep God's commands, and our need for repentance when we violate those commands. This is the person who is fully human.

FRIDAY

Hebrews 13: 1-8; Mark 6: 14-29 **YEAR I**

In his description of the Christian way of life, St. Paul stresses hospitality to others and sympathy for those in trouble, such as prisoners and those who are ill-treated, purity, and freedom from greed or love of money. He urges adherence to the Christian way of life for two reasons. Firstly, tomorrow, we may be in the same difficulties as those who need our help today. We shall be able to bear our own burdens with greater equanimity, if we are not weighed down by the guilt and shame of having refused aid to others.

Hospitality is not only sharing one's roof, but also one's attention and concern. An old American Indian saying reminds us that "to truly understand another human being, we must first walk a mile in his moccasins." To walk in another one's shoes we must first take off our own. Hospitality is not only sharing food but especially making an honest effort to get out of ourselves and to donate our presence and availability to others in need. All of us know what it is like to knock on a door and get no response—we know what it is like to dial a number with a sense of urgency and receive a busy signal. When others need our help do we open the door and display complete availability?

Secondly, as Oliver Wendell Holmes said, "Catholicism is not an easy religion to live, but it is a beautiful religion, in which to die." We should always look to our goal, which is eternal life and judge everything by that standard: "What is present suffering or deprivation compared to perfect and everlasting glory?"

Let us recall the words of St. Matthew as he portrays the saved coming into the blessedness of heaven: "Come and receive the kingdom which has been prepared for you since the creation of the world. I was hungry and you fed me, thirsty and you gave me to drink; I was a stranger and you received me into your homes, naked and you clothed me; I was sick and you took care of me, in prison and you visited me . . . I tell you, indeed, whenever you did this for one of the least important of these brothers and sisters of mine, you did it for me!"

The example of John the Baptist is given as witness to the truth that present suffering and deprivation cannot be compared to perfect and everlasting glory. Regardless of the way in which he was treated, John remained a man of principle and thereby kept his freedom even in prison. For John the Lord was light and salvation. He did not fear Herod because his hope was in the Lord. Even as death waited at his door, John's trust in God was immutable. Herod seemed to understand that John was a man of principle and he was in awe of him. This attitude in Herod was a cause of sorrow for him when he was asked to deliver John's head on a platter. Because his resistance to sin was low, he succumbed to his sexual appetite for Herodias, as well as the appeal of power and delivered John's head. Holiness is practicing all virtue to the best of one's ability. That was John's salvation and its absence was Herod's downfall.

Sirach 47: 2-11; Mark 6: 14-29 **YEAR II**

Today's reading is from the book of Sirach which contains a lengthy section praising the great figures of Israel's history. Here we read Sirach's praises of David whose story we have already read. Sirach describes the glorious exploits of David and tells of the praise which was heaped upon him. However, the praise did not turn David's head; his whole mind and heart were already turned to God. The more praise he received, the more David directed praise to God, from whom all good gifts come. David is an excellent example for us because he was a sinner too. The past few weeks we have read more about his sinfulness than of his goodness, which in fact dominated his life. David was not only a sinner, he was a repentant sinner. And that is the example we must follow. All too often we either blind ourselves to our sinfulness or come close to despair. David did neither. He recognized his sin, asked God for pardon, and resolved to live a life of virtue. Sin is only a sign that we are human; repentance is a sign of our faith in God and love for him.

Today's gospel tells us that Herod, who has gone down in history as a symbol of evil, had an opportunity to be a David, to lead his people as David did. Herod, too, was a sinner; he had married the wife of his brother, Philip. God's grace touched his soul, calling him to repentance, but he could not bring himself to conversion. Herod who knew John the Baptist to be an upright and holy man feared him and was troubled when he reproached him his sin. Herod had his chance to be converted, but he allowed his chance to pass him by. When temptation came in the person of his wife's daughter, "he went deeper into sin and ordered the Baptist to be beheaded." He chose his own pride "because of his oath and the presence of the guests" to God's grace as made known to him—offered to him—by the Baptist. So often we do the same for the same reasons: pride, vanity, and human respect. Consequently, we do not taste of the joy that David experienced in this world, and our eternal happiness is placed in jeopardy.

SATURDAY

Hebrews 13: 15-17, 20-21; Mark 6: 30-34 **YEAR I**

In this life, we are urged to praise God and obey Church leaders. We should perform good deeds, be generous, and be just. Those are the kinds of sacrifices that please God. Above all, we must be obedient to our Church leaders who as human beings are subject to temptation just as we are. In civil society, we trust our leaders and follow the law of the land. It is the only way for order and peace to subsist. In the Church, we must act on the presumption that our leaders, strengthened by God's grace, are people of integrity, concerned for our welfare, and therefore, deserving of our trust. In addition to heeding their words, we should attempt to assist them in every way possible by giving good example to add strength to their exhortations, by sharing with the poor, assisting the sick, and all those in need of assistance whether spiritual or temporal.

This is especially important in our day when anyone with a message can communicate it to the world, literally. It may be tempting to go off on our own without acknowledging Church leaders, who are for us exemplars of the good shepherd who guides us in right paths. In his day, Christ gathered the people and taught them the truth. He united them in the truth. Then, as now, not all could accept that truth because it required faith in his word and sacrifice to live by his dictates. Apart from listening to our Church leaders, we must, as they must, pray for them and for ourselves. "Apart from me, you can do nothing," Jesus said.

In the gospel narrative, we read that when the apostles came back from their teaching journey, Jesus invited them to come apart and rest. It is important to realize that Church leaders have serious responsibilities, and they need to be supported. We are the ones to offer appreciation and assistance. Again, as the gospel tells us, this is not always possible. The first to be considered are the people. They did not allow Jesus and the apostles to come apart, rest, and eat, but they followed them in the wilderness. Jesus had pity on them because they were like sheep without a shepherd, and he began to teach them at great length.

1 Kings 3: 4-13; Mark 6: 30-34 — YEAR II

"He who humbles himself shall be exalted." Would not most of us be overwhelmed if we were called upon at an early age to lead a whole nation? And yet history tells us that so many leaders are blinded by the panoply of office and begin to think that they are important. Not Solomon; he simply asked for the ability to do his work properly, to be given an understanding heart so that he would be able to judge right from wrong. And as a reward, the Lord gave him not only wisdom, but worldly wealth as well. "To him who has much, more will be given," as Christ says in the parable of the talents.

The gospel reveals the understanding heart of Jesus. The people were attracted to him, not only because of the miracles, but because of his teaching. He taught with authority. He knew the truth and expressed it clearly, distinguishing between right from wrong.

Moreover, Jesus tried to give his apostles an understanding heart. When they returned from their journeys, Jesus took them away from the crowds, "lest their heads be turned," and brought them to a quiet place to settle them down. His plans were frustrated by the crowds, but apparently the time alone in the boat was sufficient in this instance.

We very much need to learn the same lessons, and spend time alone with God. In his sight, we realize who we are, how much we lack, and how much we need him. We especially need his understanding heart if we are to lead our people in the way, the truth, and the life which Jesus has taught us.

Fifth Week of Ordinary Time

All it really takes to be in the presence of God is a simple act of the will. All we need to do is to raise our minds and hearts to him, for he is ever ready to be present. Thus, God provides for the poorest, the most handicapped everywhere in the world, at every moment. If we will to be in his presence, instantly we are with him while he gives us his full attention! This is not to say that the building of the Temple or our offering the Mass and visiting the Blessed Sacrament are superfluous. No, they are meant to increase our devotion and constitute special signs of our love for God.

Monday

Genesis 1: 1-19; Mark 6: 53-56 **YEAR I**

The first story of Genesis is the start of salvation history. It tells us that, before creation, the heavens and the earth were a "formless wasteland." The story is not a scientific presentation, but an artificial arrangement to teach religious lessons such as the goodness of all God's creation and our need to rest on the seventh day. God set his hand to fashion the universe the way he wanted it to be, suitable and adequate for the playing out of the history of salvation.

Early on, God's Chosen People were very much united as a community and, although they sinned, they also repented, reformed their ways, and persevered as God's People. Generations later, when Christ came into the world, mankind had slowly become a "formless wasteland." Men were going astray. The gospel narrative tells us that as Christ walked the roads of Palestine, everything that he put his hand to was re-ordered. Humanity's "formless wasteland" took shape. Sickness was cured, deformations of body were healed, evil spirits were driven out. Hearts were warmed and once again, people's souls were touched by the Word of God. Just as in the beginning, a word or a touch from God made everything good. Those who allowed themselves to be touched by God's Son, the Christ, were made whole and got well, both physically and spiritually.

1 Kings 8: 1-7, 9-13; Mark 6: 53-56 **YEAR II**

In today's narration from the First Book of Kings, we learn that during the solemn dedication of the Temple, Solomon brought the Ark, which contained the Ten Commandments engraved on tablets of stone and placed it in the innermost room of the Temple, the holy of holies. For this partial word in stone, the Israelites showed the greatest reverence. How much more should we revere the Eucharist, which is not stone but the flesh and blood of the God Man, which is not partial but complete, which is not lifeless but living, active, and dynamic in the world!

The reception that Jesus received from the crowds and his growing popularity remind us of the same truth. As Thomas a Kempis has stated, if the Mass were offered only at one time and one place each generation, how we would exert every effort to be present! But because in his goodness, God makes the Eucharist so readily available to us, we take it for granted. Recognizing how little the Israelites received of God and how much they appreciated it, should we not be far more grateful for what we have received in the Eucharist—the very presence of God become Man?

TUESDAY

Genesis 1: 20-2: 4; Mark 7: 1-13 **YEAR I**

When God created the heavens and the earth, the fish of the sea and birds of the air, the animals and seed-bearing plants, he saw that they were good. Then, God gave man power over all these creatures. So it was that the Pharisees had the right to make laws for the people. However, in the application of those man-made laws, they should have been more honest especially when a law was merely a reinforcement of the law of God. One example of similarity between the law of the Pharisees and God's law was the commandment to honor father and mother. But, the pharisaical law allowed children to abstain from parent support by declaring their revenues to be "korban," that is, dedicated to God, while continuing to be used personally, nevertheless. This was a farce. It certainly did not absolve children from parental support as required by God in the Ten Commandments. It is a clear example of the discrepancy between pharisaical law and God's law. Intellectual dishonesty on the part of the Pharisees favored a subterfuge that permitted disobedience to God and obedience to a man-made law. The Pharisees chose to pay more attention to their laws and traditions than to God's law.

In the gospel narrative, the Pharisees reproach Jesus for allowing his disciples to go against the ancestral traditions requiring washing one's hands before eating. The Pharisees seemed to hold their man-made laws and traditions superior to God's law. Jesus tells them that, through the centuries, they have made a practice of setting aside God's commandment in the interests of keeping their own traditions. He reiterates that they have nullified God's commandment to honor father and mother so as to favor traditions which their ancestors have handed down to them. Jesus accuses them of disregarding God's commandment and of clinging to what is human tradition. He repeats to them Isaiah's words: "This people pays me lip service but their heart is far from me. Empty is the reverence they do me because they teach as dogmas mere human precepts."

It is proper for human organizations, including the Church, to make other laws, namely, fast and abstinence, to strengthen us in the observation of God's laws but we must keep in mind that exceptions to man-made laws are allowable, whereas exceptions to God's laws are not permitted. Thus, it was acceptable for the Pharisees to legislate but not to do so while using intellectual dishonesty to favor subterfuge and self-service in the execution of their laws. God desires truth in our innermost being.

1 Kings 8: 22-23, 27-30; Mark 7: 1-13 **YEAR II**

From the First Book of Kings, we hear in today's reading of a dramatic scene—the formal dedication prayer of the newly-built Temple in Jerusalem. Solomon prays that God may always remain in their midst as symbolized by the structure of the Temple. It is amazing to think that God, whom the heavens cannot contain, allows himself to be "confined" to the Temple and in our day of the Eucharist! Two things are essential in the prayer of Solomon—man's utter dependence upon God and his constant need for pardon. Without God, man is nothing and yet, often enough, man rejects God, sets out on his own path, and sins. Man must constantly pray to God to preserve the proper relationship, and failing that, he needs to pray for forgiveness.

Mark's gospel was written for Romans. Thus, in this passage, Mark explains some Jewish customs. "Korban" was a practice whereby a person dedicated something to God while continuing to use it personally. The practice was easily abused. The elaborate regulations of the Pharisees stand out in stark contrast to the simple prayer of Solomon. Jesus says of the Jews: "They teach as dogmas mere human precepts . . . They disregard God's commandments and cling to human tradition." The observance of Jewish unwritten traditions sometimes contradicted God's commandments. "Korban" refers to a practice whereby one would evade the obligation of the written law, the fourth commandment, to support his parents by dedicating his money to God, declaring it sacral by pronouncing over it "korban," a legal fiction that allowed one to retain possession of the money. Although dogma is necessary as we try to draw more and more from Scripture and make application of it to the modern day, it must never displace interior devotion, personal prayer, and the spirit which we inject into our public prayer. Religious leaders should be judged not by their wisdom, regardless of their importance, but by their holiness. Do they draw us only to themselves or do they lead us to God? Are they instrumental in uniting us to him?

WEDNESDAY

Genesis 2: 5-9, 15-17; Mark 7: 14-23 **YEAR I**

Today the first reading in Genesis gives us an account of the second and older creation story. In it, God created man out of the clay on the ground and blew into his nostrils the breath of life making him a living being. In addition, God planted a garden in Eden. Out of the ground he made various trees grow, delightful to look at, and good for food with the tree of life in the middle of the garden. Thus life comes from God and so do the means of sustaining life. Man's role was to cultivate and care for creation around him, including caring for his own health of body and soul. Perhaps the most awesome words in this description of the creation of the first man are these: "You are free . . ." Man is given clear instructions as to what he is to do with his life, however, he is free to follow those directions or not.

The gospel narrative makes clear that we need God to teach us his paths and lead us in his truth—to teach us how to use our freedom. Otherwise, we could have lasting sorrow because of the poor use of it. The Pharisees taught that unwashed food eaten with unwashed hands constituted impurity. They should have explained that this impurity food could not affect the soul; it could only effect one's physical health. Jesus makes bold to say that impure food could not bring evil to the soul. He adds that nothing that enters a man from without can make him impure; only what comes out of him can make him such. In other words, only what comes from man's heart or soul can make him impure, such as evil thoughts, desires, acts of fornication, theft, murder, adulterous conduct, greed, maliciousness, deceit, sensuality, envy, blasphemy, arrogance, an obtuse spirit, and all other personal vices. We are the only ones in control of our hearts and souls; we are free to bring them harm or cause them to contribute to God's glory. The Pharisees were concerned about the laws of hygiene. Jesus makes the point that violating one of these laws (except out of contempt for God) could never cause harm to a person's soul but violating the law of God, which is within, "written on our hearts," can alienate us entirely from the love of God. Accordingly, we should cultivate good thoughts and desires and monitor the actions that proceed from them. Such activity will greatly diminish the effects of outside influences. At all times, let us keep the love of God and his law in our hearts and our steps will not falter. Let us recall the words of the psalmist who tells us, "The salvation of the just is from the Lord; he is their refuge in time of distress. And the Lord helps them and delivers them; he delivers them from the wicked and saves them, because they take refuge in him."

1 Kings 10: 1-10; Mark 7: 14-23 **YEAR II**

The Queen of Sheba visited Solomon because she did not believe in his wisdom and justice. Upon her visit, she realized these qualities are far more important to the happiness, prosperity and security of a country than wealth and weapons. Would that we could learn this in our own day! And so to him who had everything, she gave more and praised God.

The gospel echoes the same sentiment. Material things in themselves are indifferent; how we use them makes the difference. If we have an understanding heart and we follow its wisdom, practicing justice toward those around us, then we are pure indeed. Nothing outside us can truly affect our holiness. Only we, by virtue of our intellect and free will, can make ourselves impure or sinful. Just as the Lord has the whole world in his hands, so we have "our whole world" in our hands. We determine our own fate; there is no one else to blame.

THURSDAY

Genesis 2: 18-25; Mark 7: 24-30 **YEAR I**

Before discussing today's reading, let us remember that in 1948, the Pontifical Biblical Commission noted that the early chapters of Genesis are not objective history. They are written primarily to teach a religious lesson relative to marriage. At the time of creation, God recognized that man was a social being, and thus it was not good for him to be alone. He determined to give him a suitable partner and proceeded to form out of the ground various animals and birds. The man gave each a name. They were all excellent in their own way. But none imaged God as did the man, none had a body and mind like his, none could reproduce with him to fill and rule the earth. For all these reasons, none proved to be an appropriate partner for him. To make up for this lack, God, while the man was asleep, created from his flesh a woman and presented her to the man. When he saw her, the man knew that she wasn't just another animal to identify with a name. She shared his humanity and he immediately declared her flesh of his flesh, bone of his bones, and called her 'woman.' Man and woman are human, equal, and similarly related to God. They are fully good for each other just as they are, are made for each other, and are eminently suited to share each other's life. This original relationship was the way God wanted it. They were to be a mutual help to each other rather than a stumbling block, and a source of temptation to sin. Theirs was not a disposable relationship, but all that changed once they sinned.

In the gospel narrative, the evangelist Mark describes Jesus working a miracle in favor of a foreign woman, one not of Jewish origin. Deliberately, Jesus extends his mercy beyond national boundaries. Thus, through this miracle, he makes a strong statement that his love is universal and knows no boundaries. To our own day, this statement remains of the greatest importance. The reality is that, inasmuch as God has created every person, Jew or Gentile, he loves all of them without distinction. Granted that, at that time, his personal mission was to the Jews, Jesus still recognized the universality of God's love and accepted the plea of the Canaanite woman to treat her as a human being, a person made by God.

1 Kings 11:4-13; Mark 7:24-30 **YEAR II**

Unlike his father David, Solomon did not repent after committing a heinous sin—worshipping false gods because it was pleasing to his foreign wives—even though he had been warned twice by God. Because of David, however, God did not take the kingdom immediately away from Solomon, but he saw to it that Solomon's sons would lose it.

Contrary to the example of Solomon with his pagan wives, Jesus does not succumb to the blandishments of the pagan woman who approaches him. Worshippers of the true God should not dally with those who worship false gods. This woman believed in false gods, perhaps superstition. It would not be proper, it would be misleading to have the One who claimed to be the true God appear to be subservient to false gods, doing the bidding of one of their false worshippers. So Jesus refused. But when she addressed him as Lord, and admitted her unworthiness—that the pagans were as dogs compared to the true believers—when she proclaimed her faith in him, Jesus cured her daughter.

Surely we should continue with our ecumenical efforts; these Christians are not worshipping false gods. But we should be very much on our guard against the pagans of our time, who worship money, sex, power, and everything material. We are being swamped in a moral morass, and to this point, we seem to be doing comparatively little to resist it.

FRIDAY

Genesis 3: 1-8; Mark 7: 31-37 **YEAR I**

Today, the reading from the book of Genesis tells of the temptation and fall of our first parents. The author presents the story in a dramatic fashion using much symbolism. The religious lesson to be drawn is that, as children of Adam and Eve, sin has become a factor in each of our lives. Even before Eve existed, God told Adam he was free to eat fruit from any tree except "from the tree of the knowledge of good and evil, for when you eat of it you will surely die."

Adam instructed Eve about God's command. Satan, the cleverest angel who was punished because of his pride, did not come to Eve while declaring his true credentials. He did not say that he hated God or anyone loved by God. He hid his real identity and his genuine intentions that were to drag Adam and Eve to become part of his cohorts of rebellious angels, the devils. He came in a form that would impress our first parents and with words that would attract them. Satan chose the serpent as his mouthpiece because it was the smartest thing on earth besides humanity, the most splendid speaker Satan could find to deceive Eve. The serpent was more intelligent, meaning crafty, and possibly more splendid than any created being besides humans. Only after the fall did God take away the serpent's attractiveness and made him repulsive. Satan's first order of business was to make Eve second-guess what God had said. He wanted Eve to disbelieve God's word and distrust his character. Tempting someone to be dissatisfied in the beautiful garden of Eden was quite a smart trick. He wanted Eve to feel deprived. Because God had said: "You must not eat fruit from the tree that is in the middle of the garden, and you must not touch it, or you will die," Satan shrewdly told Eve, "You will not surely die . . . you will be like God, knowing good and evil."

Eve thought if it would give her wisdom to match God's wisdom, why not try it? She would rise to God's level! Was it pride that finally convinced Eve? The moment Adam and Eve ate the fruit, something in them died. They did not become like God but they became more like Satan. Since Adam and Eve were afflicted with pride—they wanted to be as gods—one is inclined to understand the phrase "gods who know what is good and bad" as indicating that they wanted to determine what was good and bad. Eve knew good from bad, in the sense of right from wrong, because she understood clearly that it was wrong (morally bad) to do what God had forbidden her to do. It would seem, therefore, that what she was lacking was the power to determine what was right and what was wrong. That is the divine prerogative, God's mind is the standard for judging, and that is what Eve wanted. She wanted freedom from moral responsibility. But as a matter of fact, by going against God's will, by exercising her freedom to do as she pleased, she succumbed to the slavery of sin. To be without sin is the real freedom; we have no reason to fear anyone or anything when our consciences are perfectly clear. After succumbing to the temptation of Satan, Adam and Eve hid in the garden but God found them. After announcing to Eve a judgment mingled with mercy, the Lord turned to Adam. As the woman's punishment affected her in her role as mother and wife, so the man's punishment affected him in his role as worker and provider. We should be thankful that although God has placed us outside of paradise, he has not closed the door forever.

The gospel narrative depicts the deaf and dumb man attracted to Christ who heals him. Contrary to Adam and Eve who while being in God's company in the garden of Eden fled from him, so to speak, by giving their ear to Satan, this man sought the Lord and was taken into his care. The man was drawn, converted to Christ and that union made his healing possible. He was healed physically as a sign of what happens to us internally, when we become of one mind and heart with the Lord.

Physical infirmities are by no means necessarily caused by sin, although they could be, as Christ said elsewhere. As an example, Adam and Eve did not become physically impaired after their sin.

The purpose of joining the two stories in today's Scripture readings is to stress that true freedom comes from union with God; harm comes to us by withdrawing from him.

1 Kings 11: 29-32, 12: 19; Mark 7: 31-37 **YEAR II**

Truth and justice are important virtues in God, even though in our day we place much more emphasis on love and mercy. God carries through on his promise to take the kingdom away from Solomon's heirs, indicating that he does keep his promises and he does punish. That is, if people challenge him by the evil of their lives, God's justice forbids him to exercise mercy because he would then be denying his truth and justice.

In the gospel, on the other hand, Jesus shows his goodness, mercy and love to the deaf man. All the Lord requires for his miracles is faith. He cannot resist that virtue, even though the miracles would eventually be his downfall. The people publicized the miracles so that everyone's expectations for temporal power were raised, cutting short his time for preaching because the Pharisees became alarmed at his hold on the people. They did not understand that the purpose of the miracles was to increase faith still further. Their purpose was not to be a sign of temporal power, but one of supernatural power. They were intended to captivate the mind and heart and lead them to God—not to inflame the sense appetites. But exactly the opposite happened.

SATURDAY

Genesis 3: 9-24; Mark 8: 1-10 **YEAR I**

Today, the reading in Genesis continues to tell the story of Adam and Eve after their encounter with Satan. When God found our first parents hiding in the garden, he had a question for Adam. "Why are you hiding?" he asked. Adam responded that he was naked and that he was afraid. So God said, "Who told you that you were naked? You have eaten then of the tree of which I had forbidden you to eat!" There followed a series of blames and shirking of responsibility on the part of both Adam and Eve. They exemplified the age-old habit of blaming others for one's mistakes. Adam blamed Eve who then blamed the serpent giving us the secret of shedding responsibility on others. God sentenced them to a life of work, pain, and death and he exiled them from the garden of Eden. The serpent lost its attractiveness among animals and was destined to eat dirt for the rest of his life. These punishments were inflicted not only on our first parents but on the entire human race.

If man had remained faithful to God, he would have had everything at his disposal. As it was, through history, man has often found himself in need. One of the great proofs of Christ's divinity is that he could restore that plenty at will. The gospel narrative makes that statement very clear. Christ provided thousands with a miraculous feeding. He told the despondent apostles to give the people something to eat. It was evident that they did not have the resources to feed such a large crowd of people, and their powerlessness was evident. They were totally dependent upon Christ's generosity, compassion, and power which he demonstrated dramatically by feeding some four thousand people. It seems that Christ used for himself the goods of this world sparingly, but there is no sign in Scripture that he experienced need unless it was voluntary. This is in contrast to the apostles and the general population who often experienced anxiety in that regard. If man had kept from sin, need for food or any other necessity would never have been experienced.

1 Kings 12: 26-32, 13: 33-34; Mark 8: 1-10 **YEAR II**

Jeroboam understood that worship of God was a potent force among his people. So strong was it that, if he allowed the people to go up to Jerusalem to worship, he would eventually lose them to the king of Judah. So he persuaded his people to worship false gods and he "consecrated" most anyone a priest.

Perhaps it is more subtle in our day, but we now worship the false gods of money, technology, sex, and the like. From the time of the Protestant Reform, when so many were convinced that there was no power on earth entrusted with God's authority, man has been gaining in ascendancy. If the most intelligent took over, it might make some sense because there would be an effort to base society on truth and goodness. As it is, however, "might (money or some other kind of strength) makes right," so everyone strives for "might" of some kind, or at the very least survival. We end up with the society described by St. Paul in the first chapter of his letter to the Romans, a society not much above that of the animal kingdom.

The Lord has concern for our material welfare, as evidenced when Christ feeds the huge crowd with a few loaves and fishes. But it was much more important that the people had stayed with him for three days, listening to the Word of God, the Bread from Heaven. Actually, if the Lord wished to exercise "less" miraculous power, he could have seen to it that the people reached their homes safely without food. But apparently, he wished to impress the people and the apostles with the fact that all material goods come from God. We need very little, if we follow the lifestyle of the gospel. We should share what we have with others, because faith is worth more than food.

Sixth Week of Ordinary Time

Monday

Genesis 4: 1-15, 25; Mark 8: 11-13 **YEAR I**

It was very clear to Eve that God was the giver of life; "God has granted me more offspring." It was probably more obvious at that time, when Adam and Eve were the only people on earth, that they of themselves could not generate children. In fact, they might have had no idea what would result from their expression of love and dependency upon one another until Cain was born. With time, they recognized that as all creation was God's gift to humanity, so people were also God's gifts to their fellow human beings.

It is mysterious as to why God would accept Abel's gift and disdain that of Cain. Was it that Cain gave the leftovers to God? Although the lamb was to have great symbolism later, grain and grapes would also be important. We cannot answer the question, but we should be able to see that acceptance of Abel's gift was not only a blow to Cain's pride, it was a possible temptation to be prideful for Abel. Given time, Abel may very well have dominated—even killed Cain—for reasons of pride. It is not for us to judge the justice of God, nor to penetrate divine mysteries, but the story teaches us the value of humility and the danger of pride. "Pride goeth before a fall." Temptation is from the evil one. The Lord encouraged Cain to do well and to resist the demon lurking at his door saying to Cain that he could overcome the demon and be its master.

We are our brother's keeper because our brother is God's creation, God's child. We have a very clear responsibility not to harm him and we have the added obligation to do all we can to help him.

Everyone has basic rights by virtue of creation and human dignity and we respect those rights and that dignity when we come to the aid of the needy, the down-trodden, the battered, and the powerless.

In the works of creation the Pharisees had all the signs they needed to believe in God and to lead a moral life. But, somehow they expected "humanly convincing" evidence to prove divinity. They were demanding that God meet their standards, adopt their ways and their thoughts, instead of vice versa. In a way they were questioning God as Cain had done and surely they should have known better. They were prejudiced by their own ways and laws. If they had tried to understand the Old Testament with greater openness and accepted the signs of Christ's countless miracles, they would have been well prepared to accept him as the Messiah.

James 1: 1-11; Mark 8: 11-13 **YEAR II**

James, John, Peter, and Jude contributed to the seven "Catholic" Epistles of the New Testament. Those Epistles are addressed to the universal or Catholic Church and not to a single church. For two weeks we read from the Epistle of James. In today's selection, he greets all Christians and discusses endurance, wisdom, and humility. After listening to James, perhaps we can conclude that the greatest or most necessary gift of all is endurance or perseverance. We can see in the gospel how Jesus was tested in this way. He was constantly besieged by the scribes and Pharisees. Under constant opposition, one begins to doubt one's convictions; one seems to stand alone, and there seems to be no great need to resist because no one truly cares. To hold out in such a situation requires a firm faith that God cares. One also must believe that human beings are worth saving despite their opposition or indifference. In time, when they see the evil of error and the importance of faith, people will come around and seek the truth.

The one who lives by the gospel can be sustained by a certain justified "pride" that he is doing God's work. Other signs are not likely. Not only will the Lord withhold signs from his opponents, but also from his supporters. Both opponents and supporters have the same unmistakable signs of God's truth—Christ's life, the teaching Magisterium, and the example of the saints. For those who live in virtue, there are the joys and consolations of their own just lives. This contrasts with the pangs of the sinner's sinful conscience. Clearly, faith in the signs that we already have, acceptance of God's grace, and perseverance of will are essential to salvation.

Tuesday

Genesis 6: 5-8, 7: 1-5, 10; Mark 8: 14-21 **YEAR I**

The part of Genesis which is today's reading from the Old Testament is a "protohistory"—unrecorded but oral history—stories of the remote ancestors, memorized and handed down from one generation to another. The story tells of general corruption in society in the days of Noah when things were actually worse than they are now. Human beings were so evil that God regretted having created man as well as all other living things and sent the flood to annihilate them so that he could start all over again. In quantity, because of the world's population, evil is much greater today than it was then and there are more organizations and more structures infiltrated with evil. And yet, due to the coming of Christ, mankind is apparently not in the desperate condition in which it was in Noah's time. The wonder of it all is that any time that we make up our minds to bring Christ back into society, as Pope John Paul II urges us to do, we have the power to turn the world around.

In the gospel narrative, the apostles are a symbol of all mankind. Even though they were in the presence of the very Son of God, their minds were on more mundane matters. Yet, in their defense, their obduracy in failing to understand Christ's efforts to teach them and open their eyes to the truth that he was the Messiah springs not from any lack of goodwill as with the Pharisees, but from lack of insight. The apostles were, in many ways, imbued with the nationalist and political views of the Pharisees, and, in the present scene, those views predominate and prevent them from recognizing the true nature of Jesus, the Messiah. Try as he might, it was not until after his death and resurrection that Christ gained the full attention and acquiescence of the apostles to give themselves totally, without reservation, to the things of God. They simply did not understand the need and the urgency to give themselves fully to him. Neither do we. We may do a lot of good things to please God and neighbor but all of us reserve for ourselves pockets of time or possessions from which we exclude even God. Sometimes it's a matter of sin (total selfishness) from which we exclude him and from which he excludes himself. More often it is simply the exercise, on our part, of a "right" to unnecessary pleasure of some kind in food, entertainment, relaxation, or whatever. Too often, like the apostles, we lack insight into the deep meaning of the spiritual life and allow contemporary ideas, beliefs, and understanding to cloud our perception of what could be conducive to our spiritual welfare.

James 1: 12-18; Mark 8: 14-21 YEAR II

It is doubtful that the James who wrote the words we are reading today was an apostle but rather he was the relative of the Lord who later presided over the Jerusalem community as we learn in the Acts of the Apostles. James tells us to persevere in trials and to respond to the magnificent God in heaven. Sin and virtue, life and death, heaven and hell are our free will choices. God does not lead us astray, nor has he predestined us. We are in charge of our own destiny in that we have free will. God does not tempt us. He permits certain circumstances which appeal to our passion, because this life is a test for us to see whether we want to do God's will or our own. The basic choices are ours. We have no one to blame but ourselves; therefore, we must accept responsibility.

In the gospel, Christ warns the apostles to beware of the insidious spirit of the Pharisees and of Herod. The Pharisees claim that man's judgment supersedes God's and Herod views man's power as superior to God's. Once we fall victim to a vice or passion, such as the pride of the Pharisees or the greed of Herod, the tendency is to justify most evil means in order to satisfy our passion. These repeated sins lead to death for the soul.

Wednesday

Genesis 8: 6-13, 20-22; Mark 8: 22-26 **YEAR I**

Today's reading describes the end of the flood, Noah's sacrifice, and a fresh start for humanity. Man had not changed, but God's will to save mankind dictated mercy and the continuation of salvation history. Noah offered a sacrifice to God in thanksgiving for the end of the flood. On the altar he placed clean animals of every species and offered them as holocausts. It was a generous act and an example to us. How unselfish are we in giving up some of what we own for the benefit of others—especially seeing that all we have is from God? In accord with our doctrine on original sin, God knew, that once man had lost his first innocence, once he was affected by concupiscence, the desires of his heart would be evil from the start. God said to himself: "Never again will I doom the earth because of man . . . nor will I ever again strike down all living beings, as I have done."

We Catholics, judging from the whole context of Scripture and from the evidence of free will, interpret the statement to mean that, as a result of original sin, man is always going to have evil desires and will commit sin. It is useless to flood the earth again. If man is going to continue to possess free will, the best that can be done is not to send another flood but to send Christ.

In the gospel narrative, there is a detailed description of another miracle where a blind man's sight was restored progressively—in other words, his eyes improved in two steps, instead of immediately upon the laying of hands.

Possibly that was intended as a hint for us to grasp why the apostles understood only very gradually that Jesus was a suffering Messiah. Christ's major objective in the world was spiritual healing of the soul. Physical miracles were by no means his primary purpose. However, it was good that the people should witness miracles in order that they might believe in Christ, although there was the possibility that they would fail to hear and heed his spiritual message. That could be a reasonable explanation why Christ wanted to keep secret some of his miracles. We, in our day, should repeatedly seek encounters with Christ, not only to be cured from physical illness, but to be helped to see clearly what choices we are to make within God's plans for us as we trudge our way to eternal life.

James 1: 19-27; Mark 8: 22-26 **YEAR II**

What we read today is an outstanding passage of the New Testament. James exhorts us to respond to God's gifts by rooting out vices and developing a religion that makes us self-disciplined and dedicated to the good of others. We are counseled to be "quick to hear, slow to speak, slow to anger, and prompt in putting God's word into action." As we reflect on this advice, we realize that our tendency is to do just the opposite. Certainly it does no harm to listen to others; there is no obligation to accept what we hear, and yet we may very well learn something worthwhile, if we pay attention. At least we may learn something about the other person's feelings and perceptions, if nothing else; and no matter how erroneous they may be, our compassion for the person can grow. If we have listened, our anger will be much less likely to get out of control, and we are at least gaining respect and understanding for the other person. Thus we can make a distinction between the person and the content of his remarks and keep ourselves under control.

Another principle that we need to follow is to judge the other person's remarks always in relation to God's word. This will prevent many errors on our part, and will stop us from placing our thought in opposition to another's judgment. Our reactions will not be so personal and we may dislike what we hear but will continue to love the person. The all-knowing God, and those he has appointed on earth to explain his word, become the final arbiter of truth.

We must speak the truth and put it into practice. In that way we shall always have a perfectly clear conscience and be at peace both with God and our fellow man. Surely we should remember to be kind, polite, even diplomatic in our words and actions—there is no need to hurt—but we should be staunch in speaking and acting in truth. Truth is a two-edged sword, which separates even family and close friends into those who accept it and those who reject it. That cannot be helped as long as we have free will. Like the gradual improvement of the eyes of the blind man whom Jesus cures, the eyes of the person in error may gradually be opened by the consistent hearing of God's truth.

Thursday

Genesis 9: 1-13; Mark 8: 27-33 **YEAR I**

After the flood Noah is given instructions similar to those given to Adam. "Be fertile and multiply and fill the earth . . . Every creature that is alive shall be yours to eat; I give them all to you as I did the green plants. Only flesh with its life blood still in it you shall not eat." In God's precepts it is important to note the special reverence for blood. The ancients regarded blood as the expression of life, and therefore as sacred. Then God adds another very strong and explicit command in light of the murder of Abel. "From man in regard to his fellow man I will demand an accounting for human life . . . For in the image of God has man been made." In other words, the murderer will have to give an account of his evil deed. The Lord then says ". . . I will establish my covenant with you that never again shall all bodily creatures be destroyed by the waters of a flood; there shall not be another flood to devastate the earth." As a sign of this covenant God uses a natural phenomenon, the rainbow! "I set my bow in the clouds to serve as a sign of the covenant between me and the earth." Although after the flood, God promised never to send one again, we see in our own lives and in all of creation, the life/death/life cycle. It happens over and over in nature and in our daily lives many times each day. We are asked in diverse ways to die to self so that we can live for God. As imperceptibly as the symbol of our covenant, the rainbow, builds color by color so must the years of our lives build to the glory of God.

In the gospel narrative, this is the lesson that Christ tries to teach his apostles. If he was to follow the designs of the Father, he, the Messiah, had to experience the life/death/life cycle. It is in this gospel passage that the apostles first recognize Jesus as the Messiah. The story also introduces the theme that Christ is a suffering Messiah. Peter declares Jesus to be the Messiah but, imbued with the popular expectations of his day that the Messiah would be the liberator of Israel, he does not accept a "suffering"

Messiah. He remonstrates with Jesus in those terms. Christ rebukes Peter severely and tells him that his views are strictly human. God's thoughts and God's ways are foreign to man's thoughts and man's ways. The salvific plan of God is to do things in such a way that Christ's death and resurrection will not only be a sign of his divinity but also a sign that he knows, understands, and sympathizes with the human condition. In faith he gives us every reason to accept that his thoughts and his ways are above ours. Paul VI tells us that "Faith in God is the most powerful safeguard of the human conscience and is the solid foundation of those relationships of justice and brotherhood the world yearns for."

James 2: 1-9; Mark 8: 27-33 **YEAR II**

We are tempted to ask, "Who is James, or any of the apostles for that matter, to speak about concern for the poor?" since they were all so anxious, as was Peter in today's gospel, to receive an earthly reward. But James is correct. The good news proclaimed by Christ makes clear that all men are equal in God's sight, and therefore, those who love God should love one another as God loves, without distinction. There must be no partiality or favoritism in the Church. We are all followers of the poor Jesus; we are all rich in Christ Jesus.

We are not to judge, lest we be judged. We are not to judge by the clothes a person wears or by appearance. Looks often mean a great deal to us, at least by way of first impressions. And are we not often deceived? Indeed, our most difficult conversations are with such people who have little or no understanding of compassion or concern for others. A ruthless businessman and a strong politician are very difficult to deal with and yet people bow and scrape before them! Certainly this was not the way of Christ. He went out to the poor, the sick, the homeless, and the afflicted. The message of Christ is that we should love and treat all as we want to be loved and treated by them.

In the gospel, the apostles, previously amazed and mystified, see Jesus at last as the Messiah. The Lord tries to explain to them that he is a suffering Messiah—that is God's plan. Previously, the apostles realized that Jesus was a great personage. They hoped to take advantage of his prestige, and also to gain in a material sense. Now their eyes were opened! What they received, of course, was abuse, suffering, and death for the love of Christ but they were happy to suffer when they came to know and love him. Our attitude too must be that of Christ, who gave up everything for love of us. That should be our life, too.

Friday

Genesis 11: 1-9; Mark 8: 34-9: 1 **YEAR I**

Today's reading is the last one from Genesis—that collection of stories about the distant origins of humanity. It comes to us through the mists of antiquity and traditions of the Orient. It gives us the reason for the division of mankind into peoples speaking different languages and climaxes the whole prehistory of mankind. The sin of the first man resulted in the alienation of man from God and from his fellow man. From sin now results the alienation of all human society from God and men from one another.

The people were not satisfied that they were God's Chosen People. Instead they wished to receive recognition from their fellow men. The evil was in their desire to "make a name" for themselves rather than in the attempt to build a tower "with its top in the heavens." So they built a whole city and a tall tower in order that others would think well of them. In ancient Babylonia, the ziggurat was common. It was a temple tower in the form of a terraced pyramid with each story smaller than the one below it. God punished the wickedness of his Chosen People by confusing their language, so that one did not understand what the other said. They stopped building the city and the Lord scattered them from there all over the earth. God's plan is that we should not be concerned about the esteem of other human beings but that our sole desire should be to follow him in his designs over our lives. The Psalmist says that "The Lord brings to nought the plans of nations; he foils the designs of peoples. But the plan of the Lord stands forever; the design of his heart, through all generations." Praise from humans will profit us nothing; but acceptance of God's will gains the recognition of his Father. The fact that all peoples began to speak different languages is a sign to us that words are of little value, whereas the deeds of the virtuous person, even those that are hidden, are of inestimable worth.

In today's gospel narrative, we hear the doctrine of the cross. Just as the Lord must suffer, so must the Lord's followers. The disciples are instructed to give up even life itself to follow Jesus and reach eternal life. If we wish to be followers of Christ we must be ready to put aside our own will and "deny our very selves." Like the people of Babel, we could attempt to overcome the whole world and still that effort would have no value toward the attainment of eternal life.

James 2: 14-24, 26; Mark 8: 34-9: 1 **YEAR II**

In today's reading James teaches that faith must express itself in good works otherwise it is dead faith. Without inner conviction, whatever actions we perform are without meaning; we are just going through the motions. We are doing what everyone else is doing, following a herd mentality so that we cannot be singled out from the crowd. The person who has faith, however, follows a certain course regardless of the crowd. He is one who takes up his cross daily to follow Christ. He is one whose actions are determined by principle rather than by idle notions and a desire for popularity. Good works not only demonstrate and nourish our own faith, but also inspire others to believe. The good work done for love of God leads others to love God, too. It is the fulfillment of the Law, and the practice of the two Great Commandments in one great work.

In today's gospel, Jesus explains the doctrine of the cross. Just as the Lord must suffer, so must the Lord's followers. Jesus instructs his disciples to give up even life itself to follow him and reach eternal life. They must have faith in him and produce good works to show their allegiance to his teachings. Otherwise they demonstrate that they are ashamed of Christ and his teachings. On the last day, when he comes as judge, he will be ashamed of them and their lack of good works.

SATURDAY

Hebrews 11: 1-7; Mark 9: 2-13 **YEAR I**

In today's reading, the unknown scholarly author of Hebrews shows how faith in God joined together Adam, Abel, Enoch, and Noah, those "men of old." He states that "Faith is confident assurance concerning what we hope for and conviction about things we do not see." This verse accurately describes Christian existence marked by assurance that the goods promised by God will be fully possessed in the future and by conviction that the past and present facts on which the assurance is based are indeed facts and not illusion. The author goes on to say that the Christian's fundamental beliefs are: a) God exists; b) God is creator of all things; c) Man owes God worship; d) God rewards the just and punishes the unjust. With faith all of these truths follow one another logically; without faith it is difficult to accept any of them. Although many may resist an act of faith in God, as St. Paul says in Romans, they cannot fail to see signs of him in nature. With conscious faith in God the world would be a better and safer place in which to live. For, when it is a choice between one's own welfare and sacrifice for another, the non-believer has great difficulty choosing self-sacrifice for the neighbor, an option totally basic to the Christian and God-fearing message.

The gospel narrative, in anticipation of the coming death and resurrection of Jesus, describes the Transfiguration and adds a basic element of faith, which embraces all the other detailed beliefs. Jesus is the Son of God and we are, therefore, called upon to believe all that he tells us. "This is my beloved Son. Listen to him." In the Son, we see the Father. In the words and deeds of the Son we have the fullness of revelation. It is no longer necessary to rely upon the deductions of reason, which argue from the visible to the invisible and could very well be erroneous. In Christ the visible and the invisible are joined. "He who sees the Son, sees the Father."

The ultimate proof that Jesus is the Son of God will be his suffering, death, and resurrection. Suffering and death show that the sacrifice of self, of one's own will, is the best way to worship God. "Not my will but Thine be done."

James 3: 1-10; Mark 9: 2-13 **YEAR II**

The reputation and practical wisdom of James, the author of today's reading, strengthen his authority in human affairs. James teaches a practical lesson on the use and abuse of the tongue. If we allow the senses of sight, hearing, tasting, and touch to function properly, all will affect our thinking. They are stimuli, bringing to the mind phenomena from outside the person. When we use our bodies to act and more often than not, use our mouths to speak, we are not receiving signals but sending signals which indicate to others what we are thinking. The faculty of speech is thoroughly good and helpful to man but it can get us into trouble because we often use it without careful thought. It is worse when we say what is not true even after thoughtful reflection. The mouth should be used to give glory to God by praising him, by revealing his truth, or expressing something that is good and helpful to others. So often we use the tongue for opposite purposes.

In today's gospel, Mark describes the Transfiguration. It was a revelation given to the key apostles, Peter, James, and John in anticipation of the coming death and resurrection of Jesus. Comforted by a wondrous event, of which Peter had no understanding, he was still constrained to say something, when he should have remained silent. He reprimands Jesus for speaking about his coming death. Peter himself is severely reprimanded by the Father and then by the Son for speaking when he did not know what he was talking about. Do we not do the same? It is bad enough when we make some human error. It is unforgivable in us, when we make a mistake with regard to God's truth. "This is my beloved Son, listen to him" should be our watchword. The teaching of the Church is God's truth on earth. The tongue is a small member, yet it makes great pretension and can cause difficulty for ourselves and others when we attempt to teach what we know little about. Let us listen to God through his Church.

Seventh Week of Ordinary Time

MONDAY

Sirach 1: 1-10; Mark 9: 14-29 **YEAR I**

The reading today is from Sirach, whose beautiful Old Testament book is considered an encyclopedia on good religion and wise living. The book of Sirach is also known as Ecclesiasticus, the "Church book," because of the extensive use the Church has made of it.

In this passage, Sirach invites us to contemplate God, the source of wisdom which, in fact, is the power of God. It is not restricted to "brains," to intelligence, but it is the capacity of God to do all things. Wisdom is that which is responsible for everything in existence, large or small. Wisdom has its origin from God but is not identifiable with God. Neither is wisdom accessible because only God fully knows her; yet, she is poured out "upon all his works." Everything depends upon the spiritual power of God. In the face of God's great power, our attitude should be one of awesome respect. If we have this reverential "fear" of God and act accordingly, we shall be blessed with peace and happiness. We share in God's wisdom, if we recognize his power, depend upon him, and seek to accept and follow his holy will.

In the gospel narrative, the father of the boy, who was possessed by the demon did not, at first, fully recognize and accept the divine power of Christ. "If you can do anything," he says to Christ. But when Christ challenges his lack of faith, the boy's father exclaims, "I do believe. Help my lack of trust." And the miracle is performed.

In this case, the apostles as well as the father, the Pharisees, and the crowd lacked faith. The apostles had been trying to cure the boy with no success. They did not pray to God as they should have done. Clearly, we must pray and call upon God not only at the last moment or when we are in desperate need, but we must lift our minds and hearts to him always. If we don't pray as we should, it may be a sign that we don't believe as we should. The two go hand in hand. "If we have faith, we can move mountains." God will act in and through us. This kind of faith and prayer is possible to us but too often we pray and trust only conditionally.

James 3: 13-18; Mark 9: 14-29 **YEAR II**

Today's reading is again from the practical letter of James. In biblical times, people were greatly concerned with wisdom in their way of living. In this reading James exhorts the faithful to follow wisdom as it comes from God. He identifies defects that favor inconstancy and vile behavior. The defects pointed out by St. James marked the apostles themselves. They were always expecting a reward from Jesus, they argued among themselves as to who was the greatest. Indeed, they were afflicted with jealousy, selfish ambition, arrogant and false claims, cunning and strife. St. James was speaking from lived experience and his message had meaning for himself as well as for his hearers.

Today's gospel exemplifies this fact. Instead of resorting to prayer and the power of God, the apostles thought, in their pride, that they had become remarkable people and could cure the afflicted boy in their own name. Jesus criticizes their lack of trust in God and their neglect of prayer. He is disgusted with the unbelieving crowd but even more so with the apostles for their lack of understanding that cures were accomplished solely by the power of God and not by human agency. Everything is possible to one who places his faith in God; however, faith in oneself produces only self-destructive pride.

After the Resurrection, when the apostles learned the error of their ways and gained some humility, they were filled with good sense. They put aside human wisdom and human standards in favor of Christ's teaching. Filled with the grace of his wisdom, they became innocent, peaceable, and lenient.

TUESDAY

Sirach 2:1-11; Mark 9: 30-37 **YEAR I**

The only way to summarize today's reading is to say that in all life's trials one must be faithful to God. The theme can be expressed briefly: "Trust God and he will help you." Every verse is a brief explanation of a different facet of the theme and worthy of a separate meditation. The overriding message is that, regardless of what one's trials are as a follower of Christ, nothing will disturb our equanimity, if we are one with the Lord. The psalmist says: "Commit your life to the Lord, and he will help you."

We need to be sincere of heart, steadfast, accepting of misfortune and humiliation, patient and trusting, faithful to his commandments. If we fulfill our role, do our duty unflinchingly, we can expect the Lord to be merciful, compassionate, forgiving of our sins and faults, and he will give us final vindication. He will show to the world that the way we chose to live, in union with him, was the wise course to follow, the one which will ultimately and everlastingly lead to our happiness.

In the gospel narrative, Jesus attempts to tell the apostles that he is their Messiah who is destined to suffer, die, and rise. Throughout his mortal life, Jesus trusted in God's word and he maintained his equanimity. Life is full of trials, misfortunes, and humiliations that are not necessarily of our own making. There is no point in trying to avoid them once they afflict us, rather, we must accept them as part of God's providence, unite ourselves to him, and rely upon him to be our vindication. In addition, when Jesus discovers his apostles discussing their individual order of importance, he embraces a little child to teach them childlike humility. In our own personal history we realize sooner or later that we cannot overcome all obstacles. We do not have full control of our destiny on earth and the search for power leads to a blind end. That is why Jesus chose to save the world through love rather than through power. The psalmist confirms the words of Jesus in this verse: "The salvation of the just is from the Lord; he is their refuge in time of distress . . ."

James 4: 1-10; Mark 9: 30-37 **YEAR II**

The Letter of James for today's reading is concerned with our day-to-day life. James explains his diagnosis of the conflicts within the Christian community. "Where do the conflicts and disputes among you originate?" is his theme. They originate from inner cravings, envy, desire for pleasure, and love of the world. Again, St. James knows this well because he is aware that the apostles argued about who of them was the greatest right up to the Last Supper. Christ caught them at it several times. The answer to the problem, given by Christ and repeated by St. James, is humility. We must be as innocent and guileless as a little child. St. James tells us that if anyone wishes to rank first, he must remain the last of all and the servant of all. He also maintains that God resists the proud but bestows his favor on the lowly.

In today's gospel, Jesus attempts to tell the apostles that he is the Messiah who will suffer, die, and rise. To teach them humility, he embraces a little child. As was the case with Christ, so it is with us—death is always just around the corner. What does it profit to have been a great person at the moment of death? This is what St. Augustine was talking about when he said that he rejoiced with everyone else that he had the gift of baptism; but as a bishop, he was in fear and trembling because of the extra accountability to which God would hold him. Humility, prayer, and closeness to God are the only answers for all those who wish to be saved.

WEDNESDAY

Sirach 4: 11-19; Mark 9: 38-40 **YEAR I**

Today's reading describes the rewards in life for a person who accepts God's wisdom. When we understand wisdom, not as the virtue of intelligence alone, but as describing the infinite power of God, the readings from Sirach become very meaningful.

God, in his creation, instructs us and tests us sometimes with calamities in the order of nature. In those times especially, we need to trust in him; he is the only one who can save us, even if the calamity overcomes us. Those who truly look forward to eternal life will love God and place their trust in him, and God will shower blessings upon them and also upon their descendants. The most precious gifts we can pass on to generations to come are faith, hope, and love of God.

Accordingly, we should not look upon hardships as anything more than invitations from God to trust in him, to adopt an attitude that, in this world, all things arc passing; thc onc pcarl of grcat pricc is union with God. If wc have him, we have everything. Of course, this is not easy, especially if we are put to the test as the martyrs were. However, this is hardly in the offing for us because our trials are less severe than martyrdom. One thing we can be sure of is that God will never test us beyond our strength so there is still nothing to fear. The one thing necessary for us is the willingness to accept God's will and the determination to hold fast to him.

The gospel narrative supports the point that good works done in God's name by those whose faith is imperfect are still pleasing to him. Despite our ignorance of much about God, if we have faith in him, if we use what grace we have to stay close to him, the Lord will remain with us. "Anyone who is not against us is with us." That statement leads to reflection on daily life and relationships. How often when people offend us are they really against us? Or are they just hurting or insecure?

James 4: 13-17; Mark 9: 38-40 **YEAR II**

In today's reading, St. James says that our whole life depends on God's will. In all our plans, we should seek his will. Imperfect believers can be compared among themselves. One is the person who is new to the faith, who hasn't fully accepted it yet, but who may be on his way to embracing it. We are not to discourage that person but try to support whatever efforts he is making to become a believer. And if his weak faith is rewarded by God with special favors, we are not to complain but try to help the person solidify that faith. The other imperfect believer is the one who has the faith but doesn't use it appropriately. Instead of acknowledging that "without him we can do nothing," this person tries to barge ahead in life on the strength of his human talents. He trusts in himself more than in God. The latter imperfect believer is the sinful person rather than the former. He who knows what he should do and fails to do it is the guilty party, rather than the person who is still struggling to find out what he should be doing.

Today's gospel is a warning by Jesus against jealousy and intolerance directed toward those who do good works but whose faith is still imperfect. Instead of criticizing the struggling person for not having faith, we should do everything to help him. On the other hand, since we have faith, failing to trust in God is a serious danger for us. We must keep faith alive, have a humble attitude, and rely on God lest human reason lead us to make bad choices.

THURSDAY

Sirach 5:1-8; Mark 9:41-50 **YEAR I**

In today's reading, Sirach tells us that no matter how powerful we may think we are, we are as nothing in God's sight unless he can recognize his image and likeness in us. Sirach warns against the sense of power that wealth begets and against false security. He does not condemn riches as such but he points out the dangers of self-reliance which wealth enhances. There are two kinds of presumption. Either we presume on our own capacities thinking that we can save ourselves without help from the Lord, or we presume on God's almighty power or his mercy in the hope that we will obtain his forgiveness without being converted and glory without obtaining merit. Pride and presumption engender sin and deface the image of God within us and lead to our eternal perdition. "Delay not your conversion to the Lord, put it not off from day to day" is Sirach's admonition.

The same point is driven home forcefully in the gospel. Jesus tells his hearers not to cause scandal to anyone in life or not to allow anyone or anything to lead them to hell. He makes this hard statement: "And if your eye causes you to stumble, tear it out . . . better for you to enter the kingdom of God with one eye than to have two eyes and to be thrown into hell." What is our highest value: saving our life, our body, our property, or our soul? We are to strive for conversion, for holiness, for purity of life, even at the expense of the body.

James 5: 1-6; Mark 9: 41-50 **YEAR II**

In today's reading, St. James is exceedingly strong in his condemnation of the unjust rich who have exploited others to acquire luxuries. They have gathered their riches at the expense of the poor and their mere holding of wealth indicates a failure to help those in need. His is a salutary warning to the faithful of the terrible fate of those who abuse riches and perhaps also a consolation to those oppressed by the rich. The wages withheld from the laborers who harvested the fields of the unjust rich cry out against them. In the Old Testament we hear that to take a neighbor's living is to murder him; to deprive an employee of his wages is to shed blood. There is a future judgment of wrath that the unjust rich man has stored up for himself in the form of punishment from God, the Father of all. The concluding phrase of James is a terrifying truth to contemplate: "You fattened yourselves for the day of slaughter." When wc compare ourselves to people of third world countries it is easy to see ourselves as fattened for the slaughter. The picture could hardly be more accurate.

In the gospel, Christ tells us that even the person who gives another a cup of cold water will receive a reward. How much more than a cup of cold water are we obliged to give, and how much do we part with? In this context, Christ seems to be saying that we can lead people astray by acts of omission, that is, by not helping others when we should. How many people have been kept out of the Church by our failings toward the poor not only in our midst but around the world. We present the picture of affluent people who are neglectful and even oblivious of the suffering around the globe. As Christ says, "If our eye gets us into moral difficulties, it would be better for us to be deprived of the eye than to suffer the eternal consequences of sin." The same surely applies to possessions. It would be better to die poor and enter the kingdom of Heaven than to die wealthy and suffer eternal condemnation.

Friday

Sirach 6: 5-17; Mark 10: 1-12 **YEAR I**

In today's reading Sirach instructs us on the subject of relationships to God and to our fellow men. His teaching includes thoughts on the value of true friendship. We should be friendly with everyone; love our neighbor as ourselves, and treat everyone with justice and charity. However, in friendship, caution is the keynote. The basic criterion for discerning a true friend is the ability of that individual to harbor unconditional love for another despite the other's inherent faults and weaknesses. Wisdom counsels us to be very careful about what we say to others and about our choice of friends. We should take very few into our confidence if we want to avoid betrayal which is the source of great pain.

Some are friends as long as it is to their advantage to be close to us. Others can be very good friends for a time but eventually tire of us or break away for some reason and become our worst enemy. Still others are "fair weather" friends, who desert us when we suffer misfortune of some kind; they are nowhere to be found, when the time comes to share our sorrow and pain as well as our joy. "Standing by one's friend in time of adversity brings its reward," and "Be on your guard with your friends."

The passage does not tell us to be suspicious of everyone but counsels us to be wary of confiding indiscriminately in any one who claims our friendship but turns away when misfortune is at our door. Who is a true friend? The true friend is one who fears God and behaves accordingly. A true friend is one who loves God with his whole heart and soul; if one cannot love God, who is perfect and who has given us everything, how will that person be able to love an imperfect human being, who from time to time is going to fail him. Sirach is simply telling us that, if we choose friends on the basis of appearance, power, money, and like interests, we make a serious mistake. All these may be inducements, attractions, but the one thing that is absolutely necessary in a person to whom we are going to give friendship, is love of God and service of him. "A faithful friend is a treasure beyond price; no sum can balance his worth." And friendship works out perfectly, when both people "fear God" in the sense that they love him and serve him with all their heart. One is secure when one has a faithful friend. True piety is the guarantee of true friendship; true friends will be alike in that both fear God.

The gospel narrative speaks of marriage and divorce. Marriage is something more than friendship because of the commitment that one makes to children as well as to spouse, but everything that Sirach says about friendship applies to marriage. How can one person marry another and expect the marriage to last unless both love God and serve him? Granted that no one's love and service of God are perfect, so no marriage will be perfect or faultless, and both spouses must be ready to forgive and to improve. However, if a person is indifferent to God and scornful of him, that person is a poor choice for a marriage partner. The question should be: Does the person love and serve God? If not, that person can hardly be expected to love and serve a marriage partner. Surely there are some non-baptized or non-Catholic people who love and serve God, but alliances with such people require sincere reflection, deep thought, and foresight before a final commitment is made.

James 5: 9-12; Mark 10: 1-12 **YEAR II**

The reading today is again from the letter of James that has been compared to the book of Proverbs in the Old Testament. Both give practical religious teachings, but in no orderly presentation. Today James gives instructions about patience and about false oaths. He urges the people to be steadfast and patient in sufferings. He tells us that the Lord is kind, compassionate, and understanding of our trials which are not evil; but an opportunity for God's grace. Trials are an opportunity of showing our love for God, and, on many occasions, they build up a strong spirit of camaraderie among those who share in the same difficulty.

We are to remain steadfast in our faith and our commitment to God and the Church. Once we have given our allegiance we are to stand by it without wavering. The gospel applies this principle to marriage and gives the directives of Jesus concerning marriage and divorce. When a follower of Christ marries, it should be until death. Jesus proclaims permanence to be the divine intent from the beginning concerning marriage. He reaffirms it with the declaration that what God has joined together, no human being must separate. Unfaithfulness or abandonment violate the bond of marriage.

SATURDAY

Sirach 17: 1-15; Mark 10: 13-16 **YEAR I**

In today's reading, Sirach reviews the history of salvation from Adam to Moses and introduces a treatise on divine wisdom in creation. He interprets creation under the aspect of the economy of salvation by joining to the works of creation the saving acts of God toward Israel. In his outline Sirach shows how wonderful God has been to man, what little God asks of him, and he makes clear that a good and just God cannot but require a response of loving cooperation from man. The history of salvation for each person is as follows:

- God has created us in his own image and likeness and he has set a limit to our life on earth. God has given us some independence, or power, and the means to know, to understand, and to distinguish good from evil.
- The wonder of the created world calls our attention to the goodness and love of God so that we will sing God's praises.
- By inscribing it on our hearts, God gives us a law of life as his inheritance. He reveals his commandments; and he urges us to "avoid all evil."
- Then, God waits and watches to see what we will freely choose to do. Will we keep God's commandments or go our own way? Nothing escapes God's notice; everything that we do, even in secret, is clearly known to him.

The gospel narrative supports the message of Sirach that, indeed, each one of us is a child in God's sight. It behooves us to be as innocent as children. Even though we should be mature in our relations with one another, we should have the attitude of a child vis-a-vis his parents, when good and evil are at issue. Just as parents give their children so much and all they ask is that they obey their instructions for their own good, so God who has given us our very life and everything in creation for our use asks us only to do what is good for us. He sees our every action and, as a loving parent who must treat justly all children in the family, so God by his justice must punish evil and reward good. ". . . the kindness of the Lord is from eternity to eternity toward those who fear him, and his justice toward children's children among those who keep his covenant."

James 5: 13-20; Mark 10: 13-16 **YEAR II**

Today's reading is the last from the letter of James. In it, he gives instruction about prayer and what to do in times of sickness. The power of prayer is tremendous, especially coming from a person closely united to God. We are urged to pray both for spiritual and material needs. The recovery of a sick person will bring glory to God and perhaps conversion to those who witness the healing. Spiritual conversion is even more important, even though it is not visible. The person who is instrumental in bringing a sinner back to the fold, not only helps to save that soul but wins eternal life for himself. Of all the consolations that we can have in this life or the next, the greatest is to be freed from the burden of sin!

Bringing the little children to Jesus was "preventive medicine" in the days when Our Lord was on earth, and it should be the same today. The parents wished to ward off physical and moral evil from their children and Jesus obviously was the person who could do so. On their part, the apostles thought that it was a waste of the Lord's time. Why bother with little children? What power do they have? Better to help those obviously in need who, when cured, can help us. The apostles were not seeing things as God sees them. Theirs was a human, worldly, and materialistic perspective. They were correct and logical in their thinking but their starting premise was wrong—they should have realized that God's kingdom is primarily spiritual and otherworldly. We must never lose our childlike innocence, or if we do, we should earnestly try to regain it.

Eighth Week of Ordinary Time

Monday

Sirach 17: 19-27; Mark 10: 17-27 **YEAR I**

In today's reading, Sirach appeals to sinners to return to God. He also reminds us of the nothingness of this material world and declares that even an evil man has the opportunity to change his status. What he has to do is ask for forgiveness and hate what God hates, namely, sin. On the one hand, we recall that "God loves sinners" but, on the other hand, we easily forget that he loathes sin. And sin is in us. To express our contrition let us pray to God and let us turn to him for forgiveness. This will maintain or restore hope in our hearts.

We have been created to glorify God. But if we are dead in sin and die in sin, we can no more give praise to God than a person who was never born. Only those who are alive and spiritually well can give praise to God. The time for compunction is during this life and we should make haste to repent. Great are the mercy and forgiveness of God! The way to be filled with hope, joy, and love, is to turn to God in fervent prayer, to repent, and to seek forgiveness.

To establish a permanent state of joy in our lives we must "forgive" others as God has forgiven us. Concretely, we must take of what we have, give to all those in need and follow in the way, the truth, and the life of Christ. This kind of detachment not only withdraws us from attachment to the world, which can entangle us in sin, but it makes us more like unto God, and allows us to share in his compassion, mercy, and forgiveness. We are all "in need," if not of material possessions, then of spiritual, moral, psychological, and physical necessities. Whatever we have, we should share with others and thereby "forgive" them their lack in those areas.

The gospel narrative emphasizes the highest ideals of Christianity. This world's riches are a trap for the Christian who must be simple and free to love God without encumbrance. Jesus tells the young man who had great possessions to give up everything and to follow him closely. This was a contradiction of Jewish thought. Indeed, Jesus, in an authoritative way, reverses the common Jewish thought that wealth is a sign of God's favor! The young man chose not to follow him and to remain among the allurements of the world and of his riches. We have no idea what later happened to him but we know that "with God all things are possible."

1 Peter 1: 3-9; Mark 10: 17-27 **YEAR II**

Today's reading is taken from the beginning of the First Letter of Peter. He tells us that we have been given a second birth in baptism, and that certitude gives us the strongest hope. Our lives and trials have new meaning and new hope based on the death and resurrection of Christ. "There is cause for rejoicing here"—this, despite the fact that the spiritual journey is hardly a path of easy certitude and satisfaction. Rather it seems to be a way of unfathomable mystery and contradictions. In this present life there is comparatively little respite and consolation for the person who wants to love and serve God and his neighbor. Ours is a silent God who pursues us quietly in a noisy world and he will forever remain beyond our understanding. The follower of Christ must live in hope and with a relentless desire to hear and respond to God's call.

It was not quite that way with the rich young man. He wanted to do what was right and just toward God and man. But what he didn't want to do was to live only on the basis of faith and hope—literally he wanted the best of both worlds. He wanted to love God to the fullest but he also wanted to retain his possessions. The point is that we cannot love God to the fullest, if we are attached to the goods of this world as a way to sustain our hope. God demands total dependence upon him in faith and hope.

The apostles were puzzled. This was something new. The Jews of the time believed that since God did not reward evil, those who had great possessions were the good and holy people. Those without wealth, especially the handicapped, must have committed some serious sin. This, of course, is far from the truth, but without Jesus's instruction, we may never have known it.

Tuesday

Sirach 35: 1-12; Mark 10: 28-31 **YEAR I**

Today's passage from Sirach teaches us that obedience to God's law and a just life are sacrifices pleasing to God. Sirach also teaches us that we should make offerings to God but always with a cheerful and generous heart.

Merely to keep the commandments is already a great sacrifice to God, which enriches greatly any ritual offering that we make. Justice and charity, especially almsgiving, are further ways of making all of our offerings pleasing to God. We should be motivated to do all this in thanksgiving for God's goodness to us. We should be cheerful and generous in giving according to our means.

The Lord knew human nature very well. How many of us really give until it hurts? Many of us can give more than we actually do and still be giving according to our means without disadvantage to ourselves and our families.

Sirach concludes by reminding us of two things. The Lord is never outdone in generosity; he will reward us sevenfold for our goodness. On the other hand, our gifts should never be given as a form of bribery, to get some favor from the priest, or to try to bribe even God himself to give us what we want. "He is a God of justice, who has no favorites."

In today's gospel narrative, although Jesus gives a polite answer to Peter's question, "What's in this for us?" Sirach and all of Scripture reveal that the question is totally uncalled for. As was mentioned above, God is never outdone in generosity. And so it seems that the question must have been asked with greater innocence than the text implies. In any event, Jesus himself gives the scriptural response. "Truly I tell you, there is no one who has left house . . . or children or fields, for my sake . . . who will not receive a hundredfold . . ." The reward is not necessarily promised for this life, although even on earth spiritual consolation may be great. But certainly in heaven the reward will be greater than we can now imagine. St. Paul tells us that "eye has not seen, nor ear heard . . . what God has prepared for those who love him."

1 Peter 1: 10-16; Mark 10: 28-31 **YEAR II**

Today Peter states that the entire Old Testament pointed toward the coming of Jesus Christ and so those who have received Christ are to be holy as he was holy. Both the sufferings and the glory of Jesus were foretold by the prophets. We must live with total dedication the life that Christ exemplified for us. If we are living a life of sinful pleasure we must renounce it and live in the hope of the marvelous things that God has promised us. This life is one filled with challenges for the Christian in quest of transformation and holiness. Sometimes we will be eager and impatient, sometimes we will be still and peaceful. Always we must harbor a relentless desire to hear and respond to God's call as at every turn in our lives God challenges us to hear him.

In today's gospel, Mark stresses that the one who gives up everything in this world will be overwhelmingly rewarded in the world to come. How do we surrender everything to God? In all our actions we must endeavor to experience life's center: the love of God who holds onto us regardless of the turns our lives take. He comforts and challenges, encourages and questions, directs and compels us to seek always something more. In all that we do and every day that we live, we must try to make more palpable in our lives the love of God for us. God's love implants life within us, so that we can imitate Jesus and respond in ways beyond our normal strength and endurance. Being open to God's action in all we do, expecting it, and trying to acquiesce to his urgings, expectations, and demands will bring us closer and closer to conforming to his plan for us. He knows what is best!

WEDNESDAY

Sirach 36: 1, 5-6, 10-17; Mark 10: 32-45 **YEAR I**

Today, Sirach's message is a prayer to the supreme Lord of the universe acknowledging his sovereignty over his Chosen People and begging for his mercy. In this beautiful prayer Sirach recalls God's past acts of power and asks for new ones, so that Israel's destiny might be achieved and all nations might recognize him as the true God. The prayer is filled with true humility.

In the gospel narrative, we note that the apostles had not learned the lesson of humility which is so difficult for human beings to learn, even though calm, rational analysis makes it so obvious.

Jesus announces once again to the apostles that he is about to suffer a cruel passion and death but that he will rise again from the dead. They hardly hear him. They don't know what he is talking about, but they do believe that he has supernatural powers as evidenced by his miracles. And they wish to stay on Christ's bandwagon, bound for glory. Not only that, they also want the most honored places—not only James and John—but all those who "became indignant" at them.

Patiently, rather than angrily, Jesus goes over the same ground again. He has come as one who serves and the apostles must do likewise. They and we must be like a seed which falls into the ground; we must be humble, self-effacing, God-loving, God-dependent. We must rid ourselves of worldly ambition and desire for power; we must give ourselves to God's will, which is to love and serve those around us in the name of God. The important lesson is to serve rather than be served. How important are recognition and status to us?

1 Peter 1: 18-25; Mark 10: 32-45 **YEAR II**

We have not been redeemed by someone paying in silver or gold for our lives. We have been redeemed by the Son of God giving his life for us on Calvary. It is this sacrifice of Christ which gives us hope. If he has overcome sin and death on our behalf, what is there to fear? If we approach life from a materialistic standpoint, there are many things to be feared, but there is nothing to fear, when we have faith that Jesus is the Son of God.

Peace and joy reign in our souls, not because we are materially prosperous, but because we have received the truth of God, which is a gift beyond price. The truth makes us free and that type of freedom makes us fully human and ready to become filled with the presence of God. However, if our lives are cluttered with worldly wisdom and desires, we are limited in our capacity to receive God and restricted in our power for true love, joy, peace, and happiness.

The apostles are a good example of this materialistic clutter. James and John give evidence that they and the rest of the apostles had not by any means given full acceptance to the truth of God. In the story of Zebedee's sons, James and John, we note their ambition, the resentment of the other apostles, and the important lesson that they must serve rather than be served. They were not ready to suffer; they were not ready to be the servants of all. Why should they be? Did they not have a wonder worker in their midst? They simply did not seem to be able to change from an Old Testament mentality to that of Christ. Neither his word nor example could get through to them until finally he died on the Cross, rose again, and they received the gifts of the Holy Spirit.

THURSDAY

Sirach 42: 15-25; Mark 10: 46-52 **YEAR I**

Sirach rejoices in God's creation, goodness, and beauty as reflected in the world of nature. All created things mirror God's omnipotence and omniscience. Creation is a reflection of God, and an expression of his thought, even as we human beings are living proof of his infinite power and love.

Above all, in creation, it is the harmony amidst so much diversity that manifests divine wisdom. It is in contemplating God's creation that we perceive his perfection revealed through his ability to guide all its parts harmoniously. With all of creation we should revere God.

The gospel narrative tells of a dramatic public healing of a persistent blind man, Bartimaeus. He was loud enough to claim everyone's attention and because of his faith he was cured. In the gospel the blind man begs for sight. We don't know whether or not he understood that sight is good only insofar as it leads us to faith in God. Nevertheless, Jesus gave the man the grace not only to know him through sight and nature but to know him through faith as well. Having had the same blessings ourselves—sight and faith—we pray that we may do as the blind man did, "He started to follow him up the road" to Jerusalem, the road of life to Paradise. The one who follows the Lord will have the light of life.

1 Peter 2: 2-5, 9-12; Mark 10: 46-52 — **YEAR II**

Today, in his first letter, Peter tells those born anew through baptism to develop spiritually by eliminating vices and taking suitable nourishment. The baptized constitute a royal priesthood. They are to be mediators between God and man as Jesus was. This requires that they be ready to offer their lives in sacrifice as he did, not necessarily in martyrdom but in giving themselves tirelessly in the service of others. Their way of life will be rejected as that of Jesus was. There is no excuse for abandoning Christ's way of life, to adopt the habits of the unbelievers. Rather, we, the baptized, should strive to give good example so that, if and when those with no religious beliefs are touched by God's grace they will have before them the inspiration and the example of those who profess the faith. We have found mercy from God; we should be equally merciful to others. The best way to do this is to be channels of love to one another. We can refuse our love to no one.

Each one of us has been chosen by God as the blind beggar was chosen to come forward and be converted. This is the way God's grace continues to work in the world. Regardless of a person's way of life, God's promptings to live as he does are always there to inspire. We are to be intermediaries as the apostles were, people who by their example give converts the encouragement to accept God's grace, to go to him, and to ask with faith for spiritual healing. Since we freely have received the gift of faith, we should provide it freely to others.

Friday

Sirach 44: 1, 9-13; Mark 11: 11-26 **YEAR I**

In today's reading, we hear Sirach's introduction to a lengthy treatise of praise of Israel's great ancestors. The evidence advanced in the treatise points to the conclusion that the wealth of godly men remains in their families, their heritage belongs to their descendants; their families endure. Sirach provides excellent advice to parents of all generations. "Nemo dat quod non habet." One does not give what one does not have. If parents possess good qualities, they are passed on to their descendants; bad qualities of parents are also the inheritance of their children. The latter are free to opt for good or evil but their starting point comes from their parents. Many parents fail to realize the grave responsibility they have not only to themselves but to their offspring and to future generations as well. We are, indeed, our brothers' keepers.

The gospel narrative is a reminder that the Old Testament prophets repeatedly compared the people of Israel to a barren fig tree with leaves but no fruit. Cursing the fig tree is a parable in action expressing God's judgment on Israel for not accepting the teaching of Jesus who called the Pharisees "whitened sepulchers." Was it any wonder that the people were the same? They, who had witnessed the miracles of Christ, nevertheless called for his crucifixion. They exemplified the conclusions of Sirach who stated that "one does not give what one does not have." The Jews living in the time of Jesus were a faithless people, the descendants of faithless ancestors.

Individual people could have and should have known how to worship God in spirit and in truth. However, it was much easier to follow the leaders—those whom Christ called "whitened sepulchers." They made the Temple "a den of thieves," when it was supposed to be "a house of prayer." Leaders in the Church, for this reason, have a great responsibility before God. It is easy for a Church leader to see sin and error in others. It is quite another matter for him to realize that he is either the cause of the error in the first place or the reason why people have failed to convert to God. How often do we adopt the attitude of the Pharisees by doing away with the one who notices the error rather than eliminating the error itself.

The attitude that we should have toward evil in the world is compassion, mercy, and forgiveness toward those who promote it. This will develop within us the attitude which was in Christ Jesus—hatred for sin, love for the sinner; uncompromising on principle, totally receptive to those who are struggling. And if Church leaders treat others this way, they themselves will be treated by God in a similar manner.

1 Peter 4: 7-13; Mark 11: 11-26 **YEAR II**

Today's reading is the last from the First Letter of Peter. The end of life is always in sight and for that reason we should remain calm, and grow close to God if we wish to have the presence of mind to do what we ought. And what ought we to do? We should love one another, and "be generous distributors of God's manifold grace" like the steward in God's spiritual household who dispenses to others what has been entrusted to his care. We should do what God does, treat others as he treats us. We should not be surprised to be considered fools and to be the butt of anger. It was the same with Christ. Eventually, people who hate us will come to their senses, when they realize that trust in God is their only salvation and that trust must be manifested and strengthened by continuous good works.

All of this is illustrated when Christ drives the money changers out of the Temple. His action is an exercise of his Messianic authority and a symbol of God's judgment against the abuses of the Temple. It is interesting to note that the scribes and the Pharisees do not deny that the Temple had been turned into "a den of thieves"; however, they center their wrath on Christ because he is trying to establish, in proper proportions, the spiritual and the materialistic aspects of religion.

The lesson derived from the story of the withered fig tree is related to today's first reading and to the rest of the gospel narrative. It shows that we must truly be one with God and not simply put on an appearance. When the end of life comes, we must be hot or cold, good or bad, fruitful in our lives or unproductive. We cannot be a little of both. Our charity and our generous distribution of God's manifold grace must be total. We must forgive every grievance, regardless of the person involved, and do good to all people regardless of the circumstances, if we hope to be saved.

SATURDAY

Sirach 51: 12-20; Mark 11: 27-33 **YEAR I**

Today's reading is from the final chapter of Sirach. He tells us how, through prayer, persistent study, and holy living, each person should approach wisdom. To Sirach wisdom is a teacher, beloved and respected.

Wisdom is knowledge of God, so it is not at all remarkable that, if Sirach possessed wisdom, he was aware that he had a precious treasure. Because he had this knowledge as a youth, he avoided the foolish mistakes that most of us make. He was grateful for God's gift, showed his gratitude by practicing the virtues that God revealed to him, and he kept growing in holiness. Each of us is offered the same gift; indeed, we are given God himself in baptism. So many of us do not appreciate what we have nor give thanks nor grow in virtue. Would that we knew the value of wisdom. It is as valuable as silver and gold and makes one truly rich in peace and happiness.

In today's gospel narrative, the scribes and Pharisees portray us well. If they had known, loved, and followed God's revelation as they should have done, they would have known who John the Baptist and Christ were. But they were playing politics instead of searching for truth. In their human understanding, they thought that they had cornered Christ; they thought that he would never claim divinity because that would be blasphemy. But they were fooled, when he refused to answer and placed them in a similar predicament by asking them whether John's baptism was from heaven or from men. They lost whatever credibility they had by responding that they didn't know the answer to Christ's question. They feared the crowd and their fear prevented them from voicing a negative opinion against John. The point of the story lies in the pronouncement of Jesus when he said, "Neither will I tell you by what authority I do the things I do." It was Christ's way of claiming tacitly that he possessed Messianic authority from God. In this world, we are expected to use our human intelligence, but wisdom requires that we also use God's revelation and God's grace to address our human condition.

Jude 17, 20-25; Mark 11:27-33 **YEAR II**

Today's reading is from the letter of Jude who warns against false teachers. The apostle urges us to "welcome the mercy of Our Lord, Jesus Christ." The spiritual life, stripped of all the complications which we add to it, can be simple. Before Christ, mankind was in a desperate state. In his mercy he has saved us. All we need to do is to accept that mercy—that is, accept his teaching and put it into practice—and we shall have a happy and peaceful life on earth with eternal, perfect happiness in the next. The only thing to remember is to try to take some one along with us, as Bishop Joyce so often says. As we have received God's mercy, so we should extend it to others.

We need only make the decision regarding Christ that the Pharisees refused to make. How foolish they seem to us now, when we read about their refusal to recognize John the Baptist either as God's prophet or a false prophet, fearing in either case to lose their position and power among the people. All the more so were they afraid to accept the obvious with regard to Christ.

We can be critical of the Pharisees but we are compromisers too. Intellectually we are convinced of the "credentials" of Christ but in practice we often refuse to make a clear-cut choice. If we fully recognized Christ as God and we fully accepted his mercy, our lives would be totally dedicated to his way, his truth, and his life. But as it is, we often waiver between accepting his goodness, mercy and love in favor of our own preferences for some worldly good. And that's exactly what the Pharisees did. Why cannot we see ourselves as clearly as we do the Pharisees and recognize our own compromising nature?

Ninth Week of Ordinary Time

Monday

Tobit 1: 1-2, 2: 1-9; Mark 12: 1-12 **YEAR I**

Today's reading is from the book of Tobit—a most interesting religious story—written around the year 200 B.C. Tobit was one of those who, during the Babylonian captivity, remained faithful to God. He had come close to being executed once for burying the dead according to Jewish custom. Despite this close call, he again performed burial rites when Tobiah, his son, reported that a Jewish person had been murdered and his corpse was lying in the market place. His friends and neighbors mocked Tobit and could not understand his conduct nor his fearlessness; on the other hand, he could not believe that his neighbors were willing to go against the Word of God and accept the misery of living in exile for merely a few more years. Tobit was more concerned about God's will than about life on earth. He probably believed in the immortality of the soul as well.

Tobit showed other signs of faithfulness to God's word. He wanted a poor man to share his meal; he went immediately to get the corpse and left his dinner untouched; he wept for the deceased; and he dug his grave. Those several corporal and spiritual works of mercy gave Tobit peace of mind despite the severe criticism of his fellow Israelites.

The gospel narrative presents the parable of the tenants which is a thinly-disguised accusation by Jesus that his enemies are planning to kill him, the Son of God. It is a unique passage among the parables of Jesus because it shows how Israel's rejection of the prophets reached a climax in the murder of Jesus and how, as a consequence, Israel was dispossessed of its birthright. People who gave clear signs that they were from God, the prophets, were not only criticized but many were also beaten and killed. On the contrary, many others gave into their own weakness, apostatized, or took "the easy way out." The scribes and the Pharisees were the spiritual descendants of these traitors and Christ was the Son of God.

In our modern culture we must be on guard against taking the "easy way out"—the sinful way out—as so many Catholic people do who fail to stand up and be counted. They fail to be a sign of contradiction as Christ was; they fail to follow the example of Tobit, which was basically one of fidelity to God and compassion for one's fellow man.

2 Peter 1: 2-7; Mark 12: 1-12 **YEAR II**

We have been given by God—through knowledge of him—everything we need in order to reject the sinfulness of the world, share in the divine nature and thereby live a good and holy life.

There is an interesting progression of virtues presented to us by the author. Faith strengthens us in virtue; virtue enables us to discern; good discernment gives us self-control; self-control leads to perseverance; perseverance to piety; piety to care for others; and care for others to an all-encompassing love.

In the gospel, we have the parable of the vineyard, in which the tenants refuse to pay their rent. Possibly we can make a direct connection with the first reading—the owner loved the tenants and was not simply demanding justice because he was very patient with them and eventually sent his son, even though other messengers had been put to death. In any event, the sending of the son whom he loved should have been a sign to the tenants that he loved them greatly too. But they even put the son to death.

Of course, the parable is a clear reference to salvation history. God placed man on the earth to use the fruits of the earth not only for their own sustenance but ultimately to enable them to love and serve him, as it had been written in their hearts. Time and again God sent his messengers to Israel not to collect anything material but to gain their souls, to obtain a commitment of love. Each time they killed the messenger and now they were about to put to death God's own Son. Like Adam and Eve, they wanted to be as gods; they thought that, if they killed the Son, they could then take over the world and do as they pleased. They failed to recognize the basic facts about the relationship between God and man. He is Creator, provider, rewarder of good, punisher of evil. We cannot escape his all-encompassing power and authority. To try to do so is a totally foolish delusion.

TUESDAY

Tobit 2: 9-14; Mark 12: 13-17 **YEAR I**

In today's reading, we witness the trials of Tobit. He becomes blind, his caretaker leaves, and his wife Anna ridicules him for being so serious about religion. Despite his goodness to others, Tobit is not so patient in accepting charity as he is generous in providing it to others. This is a problem for many when they fall upon evil times in a country of plenty such as ours. Instead of graciously accepting God's goodness through others, they become resentful and do not wish to receive assistance. While they have good health and a means of livelihood, they deceive themselves into thinking how great they are. When God shows them that "without me, you can do nothing" they become impatient and their pride shows up. When illness strikes they are upset with themselves for not being able to do as much as they would like and disturbed with others for asking them to countenance what they cannot endure in time of illness.

In the gospel narrative Christ displayed humility when caught in a lose-lose situation. The question put to Jesus of paying taxes to Rome was a trap. An affirmative or a negative answer would have been hostile to either Jewish nationalism or to the occupying Roman authorities. Jesus avoided the trap by choosing to admit his dependence upon creatures, his obligation to government in its responsibility to care for the common good. Actually, the people in government depended upon God but Jesus, the man-God, allowed others to provide for his needs unlike Tobit, myself, and others like us.

If we are going to do good for others, we must not deny them the opportunity to do good for us. Indeed, such a refusal is a sign of pride in our own self-sufficiency, and a denial of our dependence upon God who often meets our needs through others.

2 Peter 3: 12-15, 17-18; Mark 12: 13-17 **YEAR II**

What we should really be interested in is "a new heaven and a new earth," that is God's kingdom of perfect peace and justice. Our time on this earth is transitory. We are to accept it as God's will, live at peace with one another but be looking forward with anxious expectation to the coming of the Lord.

This comes clear in the little episode between Christ and the Pharisees concerning the payment of taxes. The Pharisees deliberately set out to entrap him, and even though it's hard to imagine that people can use their lives in that way, some people still deliberately try to embarrass others and/or entrap them in sin, dragging the virtuous from their "pedestal." But our answer to them should be that of Christ. We are not especially interested in this world; we don't care whether we have a little money or a lot; those interested in this world may play their little games, place their images on coins and pieces of paper. We will abide these practices, cooperate with them for the sake of order in the world, but we're really not that interested. Our interest is in "rendering to God the things that are God's."

In giving glory to God, we have "security." We must "be on (our) guard lest (we) be led astray by the error of the wicked and forfeit the security (we) enjoy."

WEDNESDAY

Tobit 3: 1-11, 16; Mark 12: 18-27 **YEAR I**

Two scenes are given to us in today's reading. The blinded Tobit prays for death. Some 300 miles east, a young woman Sarah also despairs and prays for death. Raphael helps them both. Judging from this passage alone it is difficult to know whether Tobit believes in immortality; he speaks of "the everlasting abode" but also about going back "into dust." In any event, it is quite clear that he believes in sin and the consequences of sin when he mentions the sins of his father. He believes that it is not worth living the sinful life. Again, it is hard to know what he might expect after death but he is ready to surrender to God's will—admit that God has the last say—and suffer death for his sins. He thinks that it is better to be removed from the earth by death than to have God calumniated because of his sins.

Sarah has much the same problem. She loves and worships God. She is puzzled about her marital misfortunes but is not about to blame God for them. Still, because others are belittling him because of her situation, she believes it is better to die than to continue being a cause of blasphemy and ruining the reputation of her father as well.

In the gospel narrative, the Sadducees, who do not believe in the immortality of the soul, bring the case of Sarah to Christ's attention. To which of her seven husbands will she be married in the afterlife? Christ makes clear that there will be an after-life but the focus of that life will be God himself and not our fellow human beings. To us, it seems logical that we should have some relationship in heaven with those we love on earth but that will be a secondary consideration. In the after-life our primary activity will be praise and adoration of God.

2 Timothy 1: 1-3, 6-12; Mark 12: 18-27 **YEAR II**

By the laying on of hands, Paul gave Timothy a Spirit which is not cowardly but which is strong, loving and wise. Still, we can suppress that Spirit ever so easily and we often do so by letting shame overcome us. That is, we realize that the truth of the gospel is not in keeping with the worldly values and culture, amid which we live. And so we "hide" the gospel. We don't proclaim it by word or by deed. We are ashamed, we are lacking the courage to do so. And so, St. Paul encourages not only St. Timothy but ourselves as well not to be cowardly but to use the gifts of the Spirit, which provides the wisdom and the fortitude to proclaim and to live the life of Christ.

St. Paul is in prison as he writes but he is not ashamed of that. "I know him in whom I have believed." He has called us to live a holy life in accordance with the commandments and the Beatitudes. If we do that, there is nothing to fear; God will support us in this world and reward us in the next.

As is clear in the gospel, our basic problem is that we don't see the world and our life in it as God does. God looks into the heart; God looks at the spirit; God sees life in terms of creation, redemption and eternity. All too often, like the Sadducees, we interpret life by worldly values rather than the gospel. We are blind to the power of God, the goodness of God, the love of God, which has been revealed to us in nature, through the prophets and especially in Jesus Christ. The most important question in life is whether we are going to trust in God have faith and hope in him—or live for this life only according to the values of the world. Are we going to be ashamed of Christ and his gospel, turn our backs upon him in order to be like the rest of men, or are we going to be loyal to Christ and his gospel and in many instances be out of step with the world, scorned and even ridiculed by the world? We have our choice—selfish pleasure here, which gives a superficial happiness now but eventually eternal sorrow, or a life of self-sacrificing love, which provides an inner peace and happiness in this world but which will be expanded and intensified beyond compare for all eternity in the next life.

THURSDAY

Tobit 6: 11, 7: 1, 9-14, 8: 4-7; Mark 12: 28-34 **YEAR I**

In today's reading, young Tobiah, Tobit's son, is led to Media by the angel Raphael who is using the name Azariah. Tobiah marries the unfortunate Sarah according to the Mosaic Law after her father, Raguel, who does not want the transaction to be carried out under false pretenses, tells Tobiah that this is the eighth time that he has given his daughter in marriage. Truly, the customs in the time of Tobit are hardly appropriate to our culture; it seems that the bride had absolutely nothing to say about the marriage. What is important is that the marriage was entered into according to the "decree of the book of Moses" and it was lived out in the same fashion, that is, according to the law of God.

The gospel narrative portrays a friendly rather than a controversial discussion between Jesus and a scribe. Jesus tells the latter that the fundamental and all-inclusive stipulation of God's covenant with his Chosen People is to love the Lord our God and the second commandment is to love our neighbor as ourselves. The only objective yardstick which we have for measuring our love for God is the way we treat our neighbor. Since God loves us and our neighbor equally well, we should love one another as we love ourselves. Both commandments were central in the religion of Israel, but their combination into a single moral principle appears to be original with Jesus. On this issue Jesus and the scribe agree.

There is no denying the instinct of self-preservation that often prevails, but the test of life is to overcome self, placing God first. It is so easy for us to pray, to go to Church, and convince ourselves that we love God, when perhaps that love is everything but strong. The more "objective" test is our treatment of our neighbor. We must see God in the neighbor and act accordingly.

2 Timothy 2: 8-15; Mark 12: 28-34 **YEAR II**

St. Paul makes clear that the externals of life have little to do with eternal salvation. It is all a matter of the will. There is no possibility of chaining God's word and no possibility of our being prevented from living that word, even though we be in chains, as long as we will to do it.

If we have already died to Christ why should we be concerned with the threats of man? For we shall live with Christ! But God's essence—his very being—is such that, if we deny him, he must deny us; he cannot do otherwise; his mercy cannot extend to those who will not to be with him. This is the great mystery of life—free will. Why did God give man the power to oppose him by granting free will?

How can he do it? We don't have the answers, but we know for a fact that he did. So man has the capability of choosing to be with God for all eternity by loving him with his whole mind, heart and soul and his neighbor as himself. Or, man may choose to be by himself for all eternity, loving whatever he finds in himself and that turns out to be Hell because he discovers that there is no life worthy of the name without the presence of God and that leads him to hate even himself for his own foolishness.

In our present day, we need to keep reminding people of these things. We cannot fulfill our baptismal—and especially our ordination—mission otherwise. The two Great Commandments are known by everyone; they're written on our hearts. When Christ spoke of them the people had no further questions; they perceived that he spoke the truth. So it is in our own day. And that is why the Holy Father is so admired. People are still sinners, self-centered, seeking personal pleasure, but they know and recognize the truth when they hear it. We too must continue to reiterate the truth. It is the only possibility that the people have of converting themselves and thereby saving their souls.

Friday

Tobit 11: 5-15; Mark 12: 35-37 **YEAR I**

With an anointing of fish oil Tobiah, through the power of God, restores his father's sight. Blindness was connected in the minds of the Jews with God's punishment for sin, a curse. It was necessary for salvation to follow the Torah, but without sight, the sacred book could not be read. This is why Tobit speaks of God's mercy—not just his goodness—because God not only restored his sight but also forgave his sins.

Light and the relationship between father and son are also powerful symbols of God's favor. Certainly children were looked upon as a gift of God in those times. When so many children are lost today, either before, during, or right after birth, we can well imagine that the numbers were much greater in Tobit's time. Also, the male child had the potential to rebuild the family which had few children, so God showed his goodness not only in bringing Tobiah back home, but also providing a good wife, according to the Law of Moses.

Darkness was truly black in Old Testament times. There were no bright lights inside or outside the homes—only flickering oil lamps and the embers of a cooking fire. The daylight hours were precious because only then could work be done. Tobit had been deprived of daylight, deprived of the possibility of work, deprived of the Torah, deprived of seeing his wife and children. As of old, we should live as children of light, that is, take advantage of our opportunities to work for God's glory by loving one another and living in the way shown to us by the Light of the World.

Today's gospel narrative needs explanation. The scribes taught that the Messiah would be David's descendant. Jesus quotes from the Psalms of David to show that the Messiah would also be David's Lord. The verse reads: "The Lord said to my Lord: Sit at my right hand until I make your enemies your footstool." If David addresses God as Lord in what sense can God be his son? Here, Jesus insinuates that the Messiah is something more than a mere son of David, having a more exalted, transcendent origin than David himself. In other words, the Messiah had a character transcending mere blood ties with David; so the latter could rightly refer to him by the name otherwise reserved for Yahweh. The words of Jesus are a step in his self-revelation.

2 Timothy 3: 10-17; Mark 12: 35-37 **YEAR II**

St. Paul reminds St. Timothy that he must be mentally, psychologically, spiritually "tough" if he is to fulfill his mission of evangelization. "You must remain faithful to what you have learned and believed."

This is the great problem of our times. Remaining faithful for a lifetime is seen as impossible and reactionary, stifling to one's personality. What we learn and believe, the world thinks, must be constantly changing with the times. Besides, what we learn is derived from authority and that is psychologically unhealthy; we must think for ourselves. The modern world really denies that there is any order in the world, that there are any fixed principles, upon which we can rely. The modern world believes that the knowledge and wisdom of past ages has been supplanted by new discoveries. The modern world rejects the wisdom of the ages in favor of yet undiscovered knowledge and technology which will lead to a utopia of some kind. Meanwhile, man must live in the truly perilous world of total uncertainty. As a result of the acceptance of such theories, countless people try to escape the world through drink and drugs and sex; others try to resolve their problems by human means of psychology or technology. But all are agreed that there is no God, no higher all-directing intelligence; man is the acme of existence.

In the face of this, we must be people of "resolution, fidelity, patience, love and endurance" and expect to suffer persecution. The Lord never promised us an easy life; just the opposite. He has promised that, if we trust in him, he will make the yoke of his commandments and the burden of misunderstanding bearable and he will reward our faithfulness with everlasting happiness. God is the revealer of the truth that we have; through the centuries those that have preserved it for us have given their lives for the faith; and if these be the sources of our principles and convictions, we have every reason for confidence. Eventually, the majority of the crowd will hear what we have to say with delight.

SATURDAY

Tobit 12: 1, 5-15, 20; Mark 12: 38-44 **YEAR I**

In today's reading, the angel Raphael reveals his identity and gives some religious instructions to both father and son. When Tobiah is about to pay Azariah for his assistance, the latter confesses to him and to Tobit that he is Raphael, one of the seven angels who enter and serve before the Glory of God. He admonishes both of them to bless and extol God's name in song. Honor and proclaim God's deeds before all people. Giving praise to God is far superior than any other means of thanking God for his goodness. Lead a holy, righteous life. All this comes first in God's sight—acknowledgement from the mind and heart.

The second great way of giving thanks to God—superior to other kinds of prayer and fasting—is almsgiving. "As long as you did it for one of these my least brethren, you did it for me." Holiness of life and almsgiving in proportion to one's ability, expiate every sin, give joy to life, and offer promise of eternal life.

Sinfulness and greed are opposed to Raphael's instruction and in the gospel we have a perfect illustration of the meaning of the angel's counsel. The poor widow who gives little is giving proportionately more than the wealthy, who are not sacrificing in proportion to their wealth. Worse still are the scribes and Pharisees, who pray for the sake of appearance, who devour the savings of widows, who live a hypocritical life, put on a good show, but in fact are living sinfully. Jesus warns us against their self-serving religion and praises the generosity of the poor widow.

2 Timothy 4: 1-8; Mark 12: 38-44 **YEAR II**

There is no doubt about it that, as long as we are human and living on this earth, we are always going to be tempted and influenced by the attractions/pleasures of this world and our human appetites/concupiscence. There is no fault in that because that is the human condition. But we must recognize and identify these attractions for what they are, distinguish them from the will of God—as made known to us by Scripture and the Church—reject the worldly and remain faithful to that which is of divine origins.

In our better moments, this is easy to do but over the long haul, it becomes more difficult. Why not make a few exceptions? What a fool I am, if there is no God! God would never send everyone to Hell, so all I need to do is be just a bit more holy than others. If others are following a certain line of conduct, there must be something to it; I seem to be all by myself following an "inflexible" rule of life. The temptations go on and on. It should not be difficult to live a holy life but it is even easier and more agreeable to do the human thing, which if we think of it, is animalistic instead of rational—do what comes naturally instead of doing what has been revealed by God.

Christ points out some practical examples. The Pharisees, for instance, performing their own style of pietism allow greed to dictate many of their decisions. He observes the "foolishness" of the widow giving her mite at the treasury—all she had—whereas people much better off than she "prudently" give a measured amount. The Lord points out that hypocrisy is one of the worst of sins, not only in itself, but because it is false teaching/poor example misleading other people. But God sees into the heart. He sees in secret and he will judge all of us justly.

In the face of these temptations, St. Paul points out that it is the person of faith who will be saved. Objectively it's easy to remain faithful. But all of us know the subtle attraction to think/do what everyone else is thinking/doing and then rationalizing our behavior, telling ourselves that we're not so bad because we are "just like the rest of man" and all this time we have lost sight of God's teaching. Then when we must face what he has to say, the decision to convert ourselves is difficult; we've been drawn further away from him than we imagined.

So St. Paul makes clear that it's not just great saints like himself, who will be saved, but anyone—like the poor widow—who retains faith in God, accepts his teachings, and puts it into practice in his/her life.

Lenten Season

The Week of Ash Wednesday

Ash Wednesday

First Reading: ***Joel 2: 12-18***
Second Reading: ***2 Corinthians: 5: 20-6:2***
Gospel Reading: ***Matthew: 6: 1-6, 16-18***

Today we begin a time of introspection and renewal, a time of humbly coming into the presence of the Lord and admitting our sinfulness and our absolute need for his grace. We are called to repentance and self-denial. Think of the athlete whose body is out of shape. The athlete diets and trains, doing calisthenics and sprinting to the point of pain in order to become sound and ready for competition. In our spiritual lives we are called to train to become more spiritually sound so that our lives can be more focused on the Lord, more filled with love, and more effectively witness to Christ in us.

Joel tells the people, "Even now, says the Lord, return to me with your whole heart, with fasting, and weeping, and mourning. Rend your hearts, not your garments, and return to the Lord, your God."

St. Paul implores us "In Christ's name: be reconciled to God." And in Matthew's gospel, Jesus gives practical instructions on how to pray and fast.

He tells us not to perform religious acts for people to see. When we give alms, he says we should not let our left hand know what our right hand is doing. When we pray, we should pray in private, and when we fast, we should not let on to anyone what we are doing.

It is in this way that we turn to the Lord. We do not do it for show we do it to allow God's grace to renew us and strengthen our relationship with him.

After all, our relationship with God is the most important relationship in our lives. Without him, we have nothing, with him we have everything. And yet we are sinners, we turn from God in so many ways, through neglect, through anxiety, through seeking pleasure, through lack of charity, and most of all through self-concern.

As we begin this holy season, let us put aside self. Let us turn to the Father who loves us and who is eager for us to have abundant lives, and let us pray, "A clean heart create for me, O God, and a steadfast spirit renew within me."

THURSDAY

Deuteronomy 30: 15-20; Luke 9: 22-25

At the beginning of Lent we must concentrate on the life of the soul—not on this world.

In the first reading from the book of Deuteronomy, Moses tells the people of God that their choice is between life and death. And just as the Israelites are ready to cross the Jordan River into the Promised Land, Moses reminds them about the facts of life. If they keep God's commandments, they will live and prosper; if they reject his commandments to follow other gods, they will face unhappiness and death. The choice is up to the individual person and to the group. God strongly urges, though, that they choose life and follow in his ways.

We can see from Old Testament history that the people constantly struggled with the choice of life or death. They knew what was right and good for them but more often than not they set aside the ways of God to obtain temporary pleasure and success. Likewise, we lack the faith to believe that with God all things are possible; without him, even with money, weapons, unlimited power we will fall victim to worldly forces. In our own day, the debate on war and peace highlights this fact. "What profits one who gains the whole world and destroys himself in the process?"

In Luke's gospel for today, Jesus mentions his coming sufferings and tells us clearly to put our eternal life above all else. Of course, life is not free of pain and suffering, sacrifice and humiliation. Life and joy in God are not synonymous with a carefree life of ease on this earth. Most often, as in the case of Christ, it is quite the opposite. What God promises is peace of mind, the joy found in the conviction that one is doing what is right and good, and that one is living and acting in union with God. We must "lose" our own life, if we are to share in the life of God. And "losing" our life means that we adopt the thoughts and ways of God, which so often are contrary to worldly thoughts and ways. This demands humility, sacrifice and may bring on poverty and low esteem in the eyes of the world, but it is the pathway to eternal life.

Friday

Isaiah 58:1-9; Matthew 9: 14-15

Today the question is, "What kind of fasting applies to our religious lives?" Isaiah tells us that fasting is not just going without food. Internal fasting is also required and must be accompanied by good living and the practice of the corporal works of mercy.

The Lord instructs Isaiah to try to convince the people that they are sinners so that, when they appeal to God for his favor, they will do so with contrite hearts. The people claim that they are devoted to God, that they want to do his will but actually they have abandoned the law of God. They continue to go through the motions of sacrifice and fasting, as if ritual alone will save them. They keep the letter of the Law but not its spirit. On the very days that they do their fasting, they also persist in acts of injustice towards their employees and fighting among themselves in search of every advantage. The reading from Isaiah applies well to the present generation!

"Rend your hearts and not your garments" we read on Ash Wednesday. External signs are a great form of worship but only when they truly signify the interior state of one's soul. The type of "fasting" which the Lord looks for is fasting from injustice and a mean spirit. He looks for the practice of justice and charity that will always require sacrifice on our part. This cannot be overemphasized. It will insure that our prayer will be heard and that we will be at peace. While on earth, Jesus took time to teach the apostles about justice and charity. He wanted them to absorb these qualities of the spirit, be convinced of them, internalize them, act upon them in their lives, and, in addition, do penance in this spirit. Jesus further insists that fasting is to be an integral part of the life of his followers.

Saturday

Isaiah 58: 9-14; Luke 5: 27-32

The Lord, through the prophet Isaiah, asks the people, if they wish to please him, to be concerned about three things, namely, guarding against lying and malicious speech; exercising charity, especially towards those who are hungry; making holy the Sabbath. It is remarkable that the Lord, in the Scriptures, places so much emphasis on "what comes out of the mouth" and yet we are so careless about what we say! But we know the truth. It is with awe that we say about a person, whom we recognize as being especially holy, "I never heard him say a bad word about anyone."

Because several necessities such as clothing or shelter are not easily placed in common, failure to share food with others has special significance. Food is divisible and it is almost always possible to get along on a little less especially in our country where we eat far more than we should. We ought to feel especially guilty for not sharing food.

Keeping holy the Sabbath is important because it consists in "holding back from your own pursuits . . . not following your ways, seeking your own interests, or speaking with malice." Malicious speech is mentioned again, as if it is such a common fault that we can be expected to give it up at least for one day a week in order to give praise to God on the Sabbath. The Sabbath is made holy by doing God's "thing" rather than our own. It would seem, therefore, that even the type of relaxation that we do on Sunday should not be merely for our own pleasure. Fulfilling one's Mass obligation on Saturday, except in case of need, further exacerbates the situation. We should take Sunday away from ourselves and give it to God. Prayer is an obvious way to fulfill the obligation.

The one who lives this way by worshipping God and performing the spiritual and corporal works of mercy is the true reconciler in society, bringing people closer to one another and to God. The Lenten invitation is surely for changing our pattern of thought and being fully converted to God.

First Week of Lent

Monday

Leviticus 19: 1-2, 11-18; Matthew 25: 31-46

Today, from the book of Leviticus, we learn that it is God's will that we show justice and love toward others. In commanding the people to be holy, the Lord places emphasis on the need to control one's tongue above all else. You shall not speak falsely nor take the name of the Lord in vain. You shall not go about spreading slander. You may reprove a person, when justified, but do not overdo and incur sin.

The people are warned against several other negative practices: stealing; taking advantage of the helpless, by cursing the deaf or placing an obstacle in the path of the blind; and judging falsely by favoring the powerful or excusing the weak. You must not bear hatred for another, cherish a grudge or take revenge; rather, you have a duty to protect your neighbor against harm, come to his aid, love him as yourself.

The gospel strengthens all the prohibitions of the Old Testament by stating the same truths in a positive fashion. It teaches us that the follower of Christ must go beyond justice and charity in dealings with the neighbor. We must see Christ in others—especially the poor and underprivileged of society. We are to feed, clothe, and shelter our less fortunate neighbors. We are to visit and comfort those who experience sorrow. And here we are given the reason why we are to love others and treat them kindly. We are not only one family by the act of creation, but we are also one family now through the Incarnation. We are brothers and sisters of Christ. "As often as you did it for one of my least brothers, you did it for me."

Tuesday

Isaiah 55: 10-11; Matthew 6: 7-15

Today's Lenten Mass is one favoring Scripture and Prayer. The first reading from Isaiah is one of the most compelling of the Old Testament. Isaiah tells us that God's message comes as rain and dew and returns after having nourished holiness in our lives. Regardless of how the world may appear to us at any point in life, the Word of God is constantly making it fertile for conversion in accordance with God's will. Why? He says so through his prophet. We can easily see the truth of this in Jesus Christ. By his life—even though it appeared that everything had ended in disaster—the groundwork was prepared for the salvation of all mankind. Although our efforts to spread the Word of God seem weak, futile, and fruitless we must accept his word that they are like the rain and snow. They seem to be absorbed without effect. But just as moisture provides what is needed for plants to grow, and water accumulates in ponds and rivers for humans and animals to drink and then flows into the sea for the benefit of marine life, so is the Word of God working in hidden but effective ways.

So we should not pray to see what we want to see nor that God should do this or that. Rather, we should pray that we may be receptive to God's will whatever it may be. God's decisions will always be reached. The only thing in question is whether or not we will be "on his side." When the apostles asked Christ how to pray, he answered that we should pray solely to be as one with the Father. May your name be praised, your kingdom come, your will be done by us. These things will happen anyway. The conclusion of the prayer is that he will help us to have the strength of body, mind, and heart to cooperate with him to the fullest. Again the first reading reminds us that God's wishes will inevitably be accomplished. In the Lord's prayer we are told to pray that we may be accepting of God's will whatever it may be, whether we see, understand, and agree with its effect or not.

WEDNESDAY

Jonah 3: 1-10; Luke 11: 29-32

The key to contentment on this earth and to happiness for all eternity is the recognition of our sinfulness. That is the first and necessary step. Of course, we must take steps to rise above our sinfulness. Conversion will surely follow, if the conviction of our unworthiness is sufficiently clear and strong in our minds. However, it seems that we need to be shocked into the recognition of our sin and into the resolve to reform. In a certain way, conscience makes us aware of sin, even if it is half buried in a life of pleasure and material prosperity. Our thinking and protection are that many others are worse than we are. That may "protect" us in this world, but it is hardly a protection against the wrath of God, who "sees in secret."

Even as Jonah and Solomon were signs to the people in their day, so Jesus is a sign not only to his contemporaries, but by his life and his teaching, he remains a sign for so many martyrs and saints, who have dedicated their lives to the love and service of Christ the Lord. We have the signs. What we need is the strength of will not only to recognize our sinfulness through these signs but to act upon them and reform our lives.

THURSDAY

Esther C, 12, 14-16, 23-25; Matthew 7: 7-12

The first reading, today, is from the book of Esther and represents one of the most moving prayers in the Bible. Because a pogrom or persecution had been plotted against the Jewish people in Persia, Queen Esther, herself a Jewess, prays to God before asking the king to protect her people. She prays that God will protect her and her people from the enemy. Perhaps it is better that they be overcome, but surely it is good to pray for God's protection. In any event, she does not tell God how to run his business. She asks in general for the protection that God has already promised. So she is praying that God's will be done and she leaves the means to him.

Whenever we kneel to pray, it seems that we always have a petition of some kind on our lips, and most of them concern insignificant or physical favors. When there is some concern with which we truly need God's help because he is the only one who can help, usually, he is the last one to whom we turn. All of this reveals the kind of relationship we have with God. We use him as someone who is supposed to work for us, bend to our wills, rather than we to his. If our relationship with God were intimate, our prayer would always be the same, "Thy will be done; help me to accept it."

This is the way that we should understand God's promise to answer our every prayer. We will always get an answer and, at that, the very best answer because God treats us as he would have us treat others. He will not grant our every whim nor gratify what are simply short-range desires. He will give us that which he, in his wisdom, sees to be best for us. If we do the same with our children, if we, in response to their pleadings, give them, not what they ask for exactly, but what we know to be best for them how can we expect that God will do any less for us, who are his children?

FRIDAY

Ezekiel 18: 21-28; Matthew 5: 20-26

Today's first reading from the book of the prophet Ezekiel teaches us that God does not punish one person for the sin of another. Each person stands alone before God, who demands the perseverance of the just and the repentance of the sinner. The prophet explains that perseverance is all-important. The so-called virtuous man can abandon his virtue and become subject to eternal death; the so-called wicked man can be converted and be rewarded with eternal life. God's role is always the same. He wills the salvation of all men; otherwise, he is working against himself in the very act of creation. He not only wills our salvation but gives to everyone the means whereby he may be saved.

How can we say that "the Lord is not fair?" Everything depends upon man's free will. Do we want to argue that it was not fair that God gave us free will? Very few would be willing to dispute this point, since human beings consider their freedom to be so precious. Once given this gift, our final destiny is in our own hands, determined by whether or not we accept or reject God's will and God's grace.

The Lord is not only offended by heinous crimes but by what we consider to be lesser offenses, for example, anger and abusive language. It is clear that attitude is at the heart of the matter. Granted that actual sins are the indicators of the sinful person, it is the interior attitude that is responsible. If we truly love another person, we are not likely to offend that person. If we despise a person, it would not he at all surprising if we should treat that person uncharitably. Reconciliation takes place not only in regard to our neighbor but also in vast and very real areas: within the ecclesial community itself, in society, in the relations among nations, in ecumenism, and wherever human beings singly or in groups, large or small, are in need of forgiveness and peace.

SATURDAY

Deuteronomy 26: 16-19; Matthew 5: 43-48

Today's reading holds an inspiring lesson. In the ancient book of Deuteronomy, Moses reminds the people that they are called to fidelity and with them we should renew our covenant with God. God's covenant with his people is that he will reward them with everlasting glory, if they keep his commandments. And since we know that God loves us and wants only what is best for us, we can be sure not only that it is possible to keep the commandments but that as a result of our fidelity our lives will also be happier. God knows better than we do what is good for us. Human experience bears this out. Sin and disobedience to God's commandments lead to embarrassment, remorse, unhappiness, and probably to more sin and a repetition of the cycle.

Sin is due to our insatiable appetite to have more than we need. God gives us everything that is necessary for life and other things as well to make life more enjoyable. But we want more. We are given parents to guide us; we want more freedom. We live in a society to provide assistance to one another; we compete against others. We are given an opportunity to marry one spouse; some prefer more than one, or change from one to another or even reject God's institution of marriage. We have goods, clothing, shelter; but we take that of others either by stealing or buying much more than we need while others go without. Our minds are made for truth; we use them for falsehood, when we think that it is to our advantage. If we would only be content with what we have, we would have happiness in this world and eternal and perfect bliss in the next.

As Jesus told the Pharisees, it is strange that we seem to have such great difficulty in obeying God's law, while we so easily seem to be able to accept and obey man-made laws, for example, hate your enemy, gain revenge on him; love only those who love you. God's law is that we love all people, even our enemies and those who hate us. Today, God invites us, following our ancestors in the faith, to set perfection as our goal.

Second Week of Lent

Monday

Daniel 9:4-10; Luke 6:36-38

Today we learn of the obligation to forgive others if we seek God's forgiveness. The reading from the book of the prophet Daniel is an excellent penance prayer—a national act of contrition. Daniel makes a confession on behalf of the people, admitting that they have clearly broken the covenant with God. "Justice, O Lord, is on your side." The people have not loved and served the Lord as the covenant prescribes; moreover, they have ignored the warnings of the prophets. Daniel throws himself upon the mercy of God.

There is hope for Daniel and the people of his time. At least, they recognize their faults. On the other hand, we seem to be oblivious of our sin. The Beatitudes tell us that the kingdom of God is promised to those who suffer in this world and to those who come to the aid of the suffering (Mt 25). A large part of our problem today is that we do not heed the advice found in the gospel. We are constantly judging others instead of ourselves, or if we judge ourselves, we do so in comparison to others. No wonder we are blind to our sins! In a decadent society to see one's self as better than the neighbor is no great accomplishment because we are called to be perfect as our Heavenly Father is perfect.

In comparison to the other nations of the world, we are wealthy and powerful. Therefore, should we not adopt the virtues most characteristic of God—compassionate, non-violent, forgiving, and generous? It stands to reason that we should develop those traits. There is also much wisdom in being generous because paradoxically those who are generous always seem to be replenished. "To him who has, more will be given. The measure you measure with will be measured back to you."

TUESDAY

Isaiah 1: 10, 16-20; Matthew 23: 1-12

Today's reading from the book of the prophet Isaiah warns us against hypocrisy in our spiritual life. We must avoid the trap of needing to appear religious to impress others.

No matter how seriously we sin against the law of the Lord, we can always be forgiven. God's mercy is continually available to us and we always have it within our power to change from our evil ways.

Most of us, however, are like the Pharisees. We are full of wishful thinking, but when it comes to correcting our ways, we are slow, spineless, and compromising. For anyone in a position of authority to be less than virtuous in private life is especially heinous. By their very position they "bind up heavy loads, hard to carry, to lay on other men's shoulders," or so it appears to those who must obey them. They and we are hypocrites if we do not, at least, give them the benefit of our good example.

Because we are all sinners, it behooves us to be humble. We should not be anxious to display the trappings of power in public, we should be gentle in our use of authority, and we should be conscious of the fact that God will judge us as we judge others. "The greatest among you is the one who serves the rest. Whoever exalts himself shall be humbled, but whoever humbles himself shall be exalted."

WEDNESDAY

Jeremiah 18: 18-20; Matthew 20: 17-28

In today's reading from the book of the prophet Jeremiah, the tenderhearted prophet, victim of a plot, begs for God's understanding and help. The Israelites plotted against Jeremiah because they did not wish to hear what he had to say although his words made sense to their consciences. To still their consciences they plotted his death. They knew that there were plenty of priests, wise men, and prophets available, who were only too willing to tell them what they wanted to hear, so the easiest way to convict Jeremiah was to have his words contradicted by unfaithful priests, sages, and prophets. It is obvious that the Jews of Christ's time used the very same tactic and it is used profitably in our own time. All we can do is to pray, as

Jeremiah did, that somehow the Lord will see to it that the truth will be heard. It may not be heard in our day, but we leave that to God's providence. The book of Jeremiah is a part of the Bible, and the teachings of his foes are not. History will favor the truth!

In the gospel Jesus tries to explain the above lesson to his apostles. They do not understand. No sooner is the lesson explained than the mother of James and John asks for honor, power, prestige for her sons when, as Jesus explains, rejection, persecution, death are more likely to be their lot as his followers. The other ten apostles are of the same mind because they berate James and John for trying "to get a leg up on them." Jesus patiently reprimands them all. "Whoever wants to rank first among you, must serve the needs of all. Can you not see that I, Jesus, am setting such an example?" And do you think that the servant can be greater than the master? "The Son of Man has come . . . to give his own life as a ransom for many."

THURSDAY

Jeremiah 17: 5-10; Luke 16: 19-31

In today's reading, Jeremiah tells us that the people who trust in human beings are cursed. Those who place their trust in God are blessed. He contrasts good and evil by comparing the first to a tree planted near running water and the second to a barren bush in the desert. This simile is very telling. Regardless of one's wealth, the sinful person "enjoys no change of season," for that person, life is barren, fruitless, salty-bitter, without deep and abiding consolations, and in isolation from others. The good person, on the other hand, is full of life and joy, with many friends of a similar outlook, productive and with a sense of fulfillment, always looking forward to the next day, the next person, and the next opportunity to do a good act.

The parallel between the Old Testament reading and the gospel is deliberate. Both draw a line between good and evil people. The story of Dives and Lazarus in the passage from Luke illustrates all of the above. Dives had Moses and the prophets to guide him. He knew what God expected of him and yet he exercised no charity. From a human standpoint, his life seemed most happy but it is clear, when he asks help for his brothers, that his happiness was a thin veneer. Stagnant as his life on earth had been, it was worse in hell. Selfishness dries up a person during the course of life. Wide as the gap was between Lazarus and Dives upon earth, it could always be bridged by a simple act of will on the part of Dives. In the after-life the distance between the two becomes a chasm which cannot be bridged—whether by Lazarus in mercy or Dives in desperation.

FRIDAY

Genesis 37: 3-4, 12-13, 17-28; Matthew 21: 33-43, 45-46

Envy and jealousy are formidable enemies to the soul and two of the most difficult temptations to resist. Goodness done to another is seen as deprivation inflicted on one's self. Good people will always be a temptation to envy on the part of others. We feel justice has been done when receiving something from another because it is, in some fashion, deserved. However, when others receive something it is so often seen as undeserved or even unjust. The best attitude is one of humility, which tells us that even life itself is a gift and we should be satisfied with what we have and be able to accept with equanimity that others have more than we enjoy.

Joseph was sold into slavery and almost killed because his father loved him. Jesus was put to death because he told the truth. Not only did the Pharisees understand that the parable of the vineyard was about themselves—having killed the prophets and now plotting against one who claimed to be the Son of God—they could also see in the parable parallels with Old Testament history similar to the story of Joseph and his brothers. Somehow the tenants perceived justice toward the master as an injustice to themselves, and they killed those who were in the good graces of the master. They were even more envious and avaricious with regard to the heir. Instead of being willing to live peaceably and justly—and even humbly in this world, if need be—they wanted everything. In the process they lost happiness both in this world and the next. We need to give thought to the same possibility. "What does it profit a man, if he gains the whole world and suffers the loss of his soul?" This is the answer to very many of the problems and disappointments in life. "Quid ad aeternitatem?"

SATURDAY

Micah 7: 14-15, 18-20; Luke 15: 1-3, 11-32

Micah appeals to God on behalf of his people. True enough, the people have sinned. But their God is a God of pardon, clemency, compassion, who does not remain angry but forgives guilt. Describing the serenity of nature, the prophet asks that the people be returned to a state of peace and prosperity. When in the gospel the Pharisees object to Jesus dining with sinners, it is evident that there is something wrong with their approach. Micah was neither the first nor the last to plead for mercy on behalf of sinners. Surely, when the Messiah came, therefore, compassion for sinners would be a sign of his presence.

Everyone sympathizes with the Prodigal Son. It is not because he sinned that we sympathize but because he acknowledged his sin and asked only for forgiveness rather than re-instatement to his former honored position as son of the master. His honesty and humility win our hearts. It is not even necessary to win over the heart of the father; the love is ever present. But the son's humility enables him to knock at his father's door, seek his forgiveness, and ask his pardon. Immediately the father's love is freed to express itself; the son had the key. Indeed, the father was more pleased now with his son than he had ever been.

Meanwhile the other son had the reaction of the Pharisees. The Prodigal Son is not worthy of forgiveness. The truth is that the other son is not worthy of anything that he has received from the father either and yet he too shares in everything that the father has. Envy again is at the heart of the matter. Because the father is good to one son, the other interprets the gesture as an act of injustice towards himself, unmindful of the fact that the father has been exceedingly good to him as well. Envy, self-pity, pride are fatal to the life of charity which is the basic characteristic of God's activity and which must be the hallmark of our own lives.

Third Week of Lent

Monday

2 Kings 5: 1-15; Luke 4: 24-30

Today's reading from the Second Book of Kings is the story of the pagan Naaman who came to a physician in Israel, the prophet Elisha, to be healed of his leprosy. Naaman's story provides us with several insights. God works through very human instruments. We must have faith in them regardless of their appearance. It is truly remarkable that Naaman had such faith in a little slave girl that he would make the extraordinary trip to Israel and then have so little faith in her prophet, when he arrived, that he would not perform the very ordinary ritual requested of him. Notice how much support Naaman needed from others in order to carry out his task. All those in his retinue worked to convince him to perform as required by Elisha. We ourselves cannot get along without the help and cooperation of others. Also when great things are to be effected, we look for much pomp but Elisha did not even go out to greet Naaman. The Jordan is a muddy river, bathing required no great effort on Naaman's part. All these details demonstrate that at the heart of every good work there must be faith in God.

Little faith as Naaman may have had, the people of Israel had less. There where plenty of lepers in Israel but they never went to Elisha—but Naaman did! Indeed, the heroine of the story is the little Israelite slave girl with great faith, willing to help anyone—even her masters. She was as instrumental as Elisha in the cure of Naaman but remained completely in the shadows. There are many people like the little slave girl in the life of each one of us: teachers of years ago, religious in contemplative life, friends, guardian angels and saints in heaven. How grateful we should be and so often how thoughtless we are.

Tuesday

Daniel 3: 25, 34-43, Matthew 18: 21-35

So often people pray while posturing a lack of responsibility for their miserable state and they beseech God in words such as "I don't deserve to be in this miserable state. It's not my fault, Lord. Help me." Azariah harbors no such sentiments nor does he pray just for himself but for the whole nation. He does not try to analyze the situation; he simply prays to God in a spirit of absolute faith, begging for his mercy and not for justice. The people are destitute; so poor that they have no offerings to make. Azariah appeals to God that he accept their contrite hearts and humbled spirits. He promises, on behalf of the people, to follow the Lord "unreservedly, with whole heart." "We fear you; we pray to you," he says. And we are not ashamed in the sight of others to trust in you regardless of what others may think. The way to pray is summarized as follows: a) fear the Lord; b) have faith in him; c) ask only for his mercy; d) promise sincerely to follow his ways unreservedly.

The debtors of the gospel illustrate the proper way to pray. Their relationship to the master is like ours to God. We owe him everything and have nothing with which to repay the debt of our sins. They dropped to their knees and begged for mercy. Even in human relations, it is expected in some circumstances that the master will forgive. After all, he has everything; he can afford to be merciful. The fact that the first debtor did not forgive his fellow servant is indication to us that we need to be thoroughly converted to our love for, and faith in God. Are we truly and sincerely repentant? Are we only looking for "freedom" to repeat the same sins? Are we truly sorry or only sorry that we were caught? How deep is our conviction to amend our lives? It is clear that when we do not accept God's mercy by treating others as he treats us—we have no one to blame but ourselves, when punishment is inflicted on us. It is self-inflicted punishment.

WEDNESDAY

Deuteronomy 4: 1, 5-9; Matthew 5: 17-19

The ancient catechumens used to come to the first part of the Mass for instruction and then departed. This Mass, in the third week of Lent, was their first scrutiny or test and it was on the commandments. Both readings, consequently, are about the commandments that were given to the Israelites in order that they might live. The commandments will help them to live happy and fruitful lives on earth. Also, since the commandments come from God, they are the very essence of intelligence and wisdom. If these form the basis of a society and are practiced by the people, there will be perfect order because there will be religion, lawful obedience, respect for life, purity, honesty, and truth. The proper observance of the commandments is also a sign of divine protection.

It is especially important that the commandments not be neglected. Otherwise, the effects will add to the burden of original sin. Granted that the commandments are written on our hearts, they need to be reinforced by our teaching of them in word and example. If this is not done, disorder and mistrust will be the result followed by unhappiness and a further clouding of the intellect and knowledge and wisdom will be reduced. Christ himself confirms the value and usefulness of the commandments. He teaches that the commands of God have lasting validity. We must first observe these rules even in their finest points and then teach them to others. God honors those who keep the commandments, giving good example to others.

THURSDAY

Jeremiah 7: 23-28; Luke 11: 14-23

Again, as we read repeatedly in Lent, the Lord chastises his people for one thing—their disobedience, their lack of willingness to choose his ways over the ways of their own human wisdom. And today he equates that to a lack of fidelity. Surely Israel had been unfaithful to the Covenant, as we have been unfaithful to our baptismal and confirmation promises. But it goes deeper than that. One who is unfaithful to the commandments is unappreciative of the very gift of life, which came to us with the commandments written on our hearts. One is unfaithful to nature and to his own best interests. One is unfaithful also to his neighbor, whose rights are to be respected.

If we do not see disobedience to God's commands as unfaithfulness and most of us do not, we do not understand that the relationship to God is one of love. If we see our disobedience as solely a matter of pride—choosing our ways over God's ways—we are seeing our relationship to God as only a struggle between master and servant. We are defying the master, taking our chances on being punished, even though we can foresee that we are not likely to escape. But God loves us; he created us because he loves us; he gave us the commandments for our guidance because he loves us. He humbles himself by making clear that he loves us and very much wants us to love him. That's why sin is not just a matter of pride and rebellion but it is unfaithfulness and a rejection of God's love.

We are either with God or against him; there is no middle ground. If the actions of our lives are good, we are with God, if they are evil, we are against him, no matter how much we protest to the contrary. And the source of our strength is either God or Satan. So we are giving allegiance to one or the other; again, there is no in-between. We are either with God or against him. We are either faithful or unfaithful. And if we believe that we are in-between, one thing is absolutely sure, we are not faithful. We might just as well deliberately line up with Satan because the lukewarm the Lord vomits out of his mouth.

FRIDAY

Hosea 14: 2-10; Mark 12: 28-34

Today's reading from the prophet Hosea tells about God's love for his people. We should not put our trust in humans, human products or politics, but should trust in God. God loves us, is ready to forgive, and is near at hand to save us. The first step in conversion is to recognize one's unhappiness and the error of one's ways. The second is to have faith that, regardless of what one has done or how late one comes to conversion, God will have compassion and forgive. Recognition of sin must lead to faith, hope, and love, not to despair. God does not promise material rewards. The convert will be humbled, but he will experience an ethereal joy, a joy which comes from being as one with God. It is the height of wisdom and prudence to recognize and to choose God's thoughts and God's ways over man's ways and thoughts and yet how difficult this can be due to pride, from the time of Adam and Eve to the present.

But there is another virtue which makes it all so easy, and that is love. The person who truly loves another constantly humbles himself to that person. One loves because he sees in the other desirable qualities, a certain goodness and perfection, in which be wishes to share. When he recognizes this and wants to have it, he must convince the other person of his sincere appreciation, his need of the other, and his fidelity. We can see all of this illustrated in an authentic human love affair. Therefore, when it comes to God, who is all goodness and we recognize that fact, pride should cede easily, totally and permanently to the humility needed for true love. And once we have given our whole mind, heart, and soul to God, there should be no turning back because we have experienced, even while yet on earth, "the reign of God."

SATURDAY

Hosea 6: 1-6; Luke 18: 9-14

Hosea stresses the importance of sincere religious service to God. He speaks in terms of the Lord wounding his people, but the context makes clear that the blame is entirely upon the people not God. Their piety has been like the dew which so quickly passes away at the beginning of the day. They have not been sufficiently steadfast. They have gone through the motions of sacrifice, but they have not given their minds and hearts to God.

But even more certain than the guilt of the people is the love and mercy of God. All they need do is turn to him; immediately he will heal the wounds and raise them up. They must come to know him in such a way that they will appreciate him, love him in return, be steadfast and faithful to him. It is not difficult to know what our relationship to God should be. What is difficult for human beings is to persevere in faithfulness.

The parable of the Pharisee and the tax collector illustrates the point. The proud Pharisee, despite his external practices, is not truly religious. The humble tax collector is closer to true religion. He realizes how much he needs the help of God. It does not matter how much we accomplish in this world—even working for the Church—if in the process we lose sight of our relationship to God. The tax collector thought that his relationship to God was poor because he saw himself as a sinner. Regardless, be kept up the relationship day in and day out.

Perhaps the Pharisee did too for good periods of time, but basically his relationship was not to the true God but to one of his own making. We need to see ourselves as we truly are, look to God for mercy, and persevere in that attitude for a lifetime.

Fourth Week of Lent

Monday

Isaiah 65: 17-21; John 4: 43-54

Today's reading from the prophet Isaiah is an ideal expression of the joyful spirit expressed the day before, Laetare Sunday. Isaiah uses the figures of peace and prosperity to describe the "new creation" in Christ, which is about to come. There have been times and places in history, where the peace of Christ has abided but, unfortunately, those have been too few. Certainly the simple joys described by Isaiah are the ideal of religious life, and there have been many such communities, but even there we have no guarantee of their enduring presence. The life of Christ seems to be very elusive for human beings who, once they have peace and prosperity, become insatiable for more personal prosperity thereby creating an unjust society and introducing chaos rather than peace.

Today's gospel tells of a welcoming Galilee where people expect more and more wonders from Jesus. It was not his mission to cure everyone in sight and to overcome all human trials. His was a spiritual mission. All else was merely a means to conversion. So it was that, although many pleaded for cures, Jesus chose to heal the son of the pagan official because he was the one who showed great faith in Jesus' divine power and he was seeking only his son's health, and not extraordinary gifts of material value. Christ had come that we might have life and have it abundantly. That is what the official asked for and received—the life of his son and the gift of faith for himself and his household.

Tuesday

Exodus 47: 1-9, 12; John 5: 1-16

The figure of water flowing from a temple or the mount of Jerusalem is a testimony to the grace that will flow from Calvary and from the Church to every nation. It will be plentiful; indeed, more than enough for every person. It will bring life and fruitfulness to all it touches. Unlike nature, however, human beings have the free will to resist life and fruitfulness. It seems incredible that anyone knowing the power of grace could refuse it but some do.

Jesus brings to life the reading from the prophet Ezekiel. By the waters of Bethesda, he performs a dramatic miracle. The cripple is waiting for the water to cure him, but Jesus takes the place of the water. At his very word the man is cured. Jesus insists with the man that his physical cure will gain him not if spiritual healing does not follow. He should sin no more. The Pharisees and bystanders are taken up with the fact that the miracle takes place on the Sabbath, when carrying a mat was prohibited. Although Jesus had shown clearly that his power was greater than any man's, they wished to bind him to their man-made prescriptions for the Sabbath. Over the years, the latter had been accepted as if they came from God. As a result, the gospel ends with an ominous note of persecution.

WEDNESDAY

Isaiah 49: 8-15; John 5: 17-30

Today's encouraging reading from the prophet Isaiah can be understood as addressed to the catechumens of old as well as to ourselves. This day was the one when the catechumens had salt placed in their mouths—a symbol of wisdom. They were given the Creed, the Our Father, and the Four Gospels.

We are also reminded of the Advent readings as we hear from Isaiah that the Lord "will cut a road through all my mountains, and make my highways level." Only now he is not asking us to make smooth his paths, he is promising that the Messiah will do this for us and make our lives eminently joyful. Some still complain that God is far from them, has forgotten them, but the Lord is ever less likely to forget us than a mother to forget her child.

Although everything is painted in terms of sweetness and light, we need to remember that the Lord speaks of spiritual joy. This earth is still a place of trial, not a place of perfection; earth is not heaven; there is a difference. And yet, if we accept the Lord's blessings, we can have complete peace and joy within ourselves.

We shall have the type of relationship with God, while yet on earth, that Jesus had with the Father. We shall be called truly sons and daughters of God.

One very important truth we need to realize is that "without him, we can do nothing." Jesus even says that of himself repeatedly. "The Son cannot do anything by himself." But he—and we too—can do whatever the Father does, if we are one with him. The key is to allow the Father to reign in our lives, through mutual love. From the Father, through the Son, we can share in God's own life. Again, as the life of Jesus shows, life on this earth is a trial—even for him—but that life can still be a happy one, knowing that we are doing the Father's will and trusting in his promise of perfect and everlasting happiness in the life to come.

Jesus and the Father are so much one that "He who sees me, sees the Father." Therefore, we should love the Son with our whole mind, heart and soul; we should receive him and his teaching as we would receive the Father. In this sense, judgment has been given over to the Son. In fact, we judge ourselves. He who accepts and initiates the life that Jesus has shown to us, will be saved; those who do not will be condemned. Jesus is the standard of judgment; we, by our actions, judge ourselves.

THURSDAY

Exodus 32: 7-14; John 5: 31-47

Today, both readings speak of Moses, the great prophet and deliverer of the Israelites. Moses is a type of Christ, interceding for God's people. They are no sooner delivered from the hands of the Egyptians that they forget about the God who has saved them. Because the Lord does not "obey" their every whim as quickly as they would like, they abandon their worship of him for a golden calf. Moses, speaking of God in human terms, foresees that this will anger the Lord, so in his prayer he points out how contradictory it is for God to deliver his people from the hands of the Egyptians and then have them die in the desert. The Lord hears the prayer of Moses and holds back his wrath at least for a time. How often in our lives we turn an indifferent shoulder to God or worship some material thing in our lives by paying more attention to it than to God and he still patiently and lovingly withholds punishment. And how quickly we are to complain when something goes wrong in our lives as a result of our foolish ways and we blame God for our misfortune.

The Jewish people, especially the Pharisees, had turned from the ways of the Lord in Christ's time. In trying to win them back, Jesus admits that even if his own testimony that he has been sent by the Father is worthless, they should accept the testimony of John the Baptist. Greater still, however, is the testimony of his words, his miracles, and his fulfillment of prophecy. How can the Pharisees not believe him! They accept one another's word but they cannot accept his divine word. They claim to believe in Moses, and Moses himself wrote of him. Therefore, if they do not believe in the Christ, they do not really believe in Moses either.

We ourselves fail to recognize that God's thoughts and God's ways are not necessarily our thoughts, our ways. If what God has revealed is contrary to our own thinking, we maintain that God really could not intend to be so cruel as to "cross" us, or even demand that we do something that inconveniences us. As Abraham told Dives, we have Moses and the prophets, and 2,000 years of Christian tradition. We need to hear it, pay attention to it, accept it and practice it in our lives as a source of wisdom higher than our own.

FRIDAY

Wisdom 2: 1, 12-22; John 7: 1-2, 10, 25-30

The reading from the book of Wisdom shows how wicked people act unjustly and reject spiritual values. The passage is often applied to the evil plot against Jesus when dark clouds gathered over him. It makes clear what has been true in every age that those in power, if they are wicked, do not necessarily rule by an objectively true standard. Rather, they judge as to whether or not one agrees with them and accepts their standards. If a person is opposed to their way of life, he becomes obnoxious to them. Therefore, he must be treated harshly and, if somehow he can escape "revilement and torture," he may still be condemned to a "shameful death." If his declarations are the epitome of goodness, truth, and justice, as he claims, he will sway public opinion and thereby save himself. We realize that, as a result of original sin and the persuasiveness of power in human society, the just one does not have a chance.

Obviously every line of this reading pertains to the treatment of the just Christ by the wicked Pharisees. "If you are the Son of God, come down from the Cross, and we will believe you . . . He saved others; himself, he cannot save." Everyone in Jerusalem knew, the gospel tells us, that the Pharisees were out to kill Jesus. It was just a matter of time; it did not matter whether he was just or not; they would have their way when the time came.

SATURDAY

Jeremiah 11: 18-20; John 7: 40-53

In today's reading we hear of Jeremiah who describes himself as an innocent lamb being led to the slaughter. He leaves us a record of the persecution that he endured at the hands of his own townspeople.

If not individuals, at least the world, the flesh, and the devil are always plotting against us, in the sense that their very presence in the form of people, places, things can and do lead us into sin. Like the prophet we should look much more to the Lord than to ourselves for protection. Surely this is what Christ did. He prayed to the Father and asked only that his will be done.

In today's gospel, John acting as a reporter, gives the reactions of the people concerning Jesus. They judge Christ, as he asked them to do in Thursday's gospel. They examine his words and his work; they reflect on Scripture. Their conclusion is that Jesus must be the prophet, the Messiah. The Pharisees, blinded by prejudice judge to the contrary. True, the Messiah was to come from Bethlehem, not Galilee, but if the Pharisees had considered the case with open minds, as Nicodemus had urged them to do, they would have questioned Jesus directly and learned that he was born in Bethlehem. But they still would not have believed; they would have found some reason to discredit the testimony. If they could not accept what they saw with their eyes and heard from him with their ears—as the people did—they were not in any position to question their firmly held prejudices.

Fifth Week of Lent

Monday

Daniel 13: 1-9, 15-17, 19-30, 33-62; John 8: 1-11

The fifth week is the final full week of Lent. The first reading illustrates the superior wisdom of Daniel and tells, in Susanna's story, how innocent blood was spared. Again, there is a contrast, as there was last week, between those who are God-fearing and trained in the Law of Moses, pious, respected, and praying with hope with those who "suppressed their consciences and did not keep in mind just judgments." The judges had "grown evil with age; their past come to term." Susanna preferred to suffer martyrdom at the hands of the wicked rather than to sin. Susanna's virtue was extraordinary but even ordinary virtue is a contrast to the manner in which we would try to arrange a compromise with evil. If we were in Susanna's situation, we might not sin openly but perhaps we would try to "strike a deal" of some kind. Few of us would stand forthrightly for unadulterated virtue like a St. Thomas More. What we might promise to the wicked is a matter of conjecture but probably we would try to do something dictated by our own foolish wisdom rather than rely utterly upon the goodness and mercy of God. God does live; he knows what is going on; he wills our happiness and salvation. It might very well be, due to our sins, that salvation will be gained only through martyrdom. But whatever happens, why not trust God? Why not place our hope in the one who loves and cares for us more than we do ourselves?

In the gospel, the woman did not trust in Christ as Susanna had trusted in God; maybe she did not know of him. In any event, Jesus calls the bluff of the Pharisees. If they had been in the same difficulty as the adulterous woman, they would have used all their ingenuity to "strike a deal." Indeed, as Jesus made them realize, they had been in similar situations and had been able, in a sense, to get away with their sin. They had no right to cast stones at someone else who was different only in that she had been caught. Again, the mercy of God is immense! He not only forgives the woman but he even lets the Pharisees "get away" with their sins. It probably would have helped the Pharisees, or at least it would have been an extra invitation to salvation, if they had been further embarrassed. In any event, we should trust in God's goodness and readily accept whatever, in his providence, we receive from him.

TUESDAY

Numbers 21: 4-9; John 8: 21-30

Today, in both readings, we sense the division between Jesus and his enemies becoming more critical and sharper. In the book of Numbers, source of the first reading, we hear of a curious incident that took place during the desert wanderings of the Israelites. The curative bronze serpent on a pole is a reminder of the crucified Lord, a prophecy of Christ. As the Israelites were saved by looking at the serpent, so can we be saved by looking upon Christ who suffered and died on the Cross. Of course, it is not a matter of looking upon him only but of accepting him as the Son of God and following in his footsteps. If we do not believe in him, surely we shall die in our sins, as he told the people of his time. He does not condemn us; he simply looks into our hearts and asks us to believe in him, to love him, to serve him—not for himself but for our salvation. How could we be so foolish as to ignore his invitation? And yet that is what we do, when we fail to accept him fully into our lives and live only for him.

How many people still blame God for all the evil that there is in the world! Granted that he could prevent the evil, divine providence orders that life in this world should be a trial of our will, a proof of our holiness, and of our readiness to love God above all things. Indeed, he allows us to be tried but he gives us all that is necessary for a good life. Simply because he does not give us everything, does not remove every trial, and does not take away free will is no reason to turn against him. When we contribute so little because all is from God how can we complain about anything?

WEDNESDAY

Daniel 3: 14-20, 91-92, 95; John 8: 31-42

So often in life one who tempts us to forego our principles has already forgone his own and does not understand that this could be a difficulty for others. The pagan king deeply appreciated Daniel and the three young men; it was contrary to principle that he should want them to suffer harm. But he forfeited that principle for his selfish interest, namely, to appear as a god to every one else. We see the same thing in the case of St. Thomas More. He loved the king and the king loved him greatly too. But he sacrificed St. Thomas for his own selfish reasons. These are difficult cases from a human standpoint. We must choose God over all other people, even members of our family. God's word is the two-edged sword that separates us, one from the other. We must be prepared to respond as the three young men did: "If our God, whom we serve, can save us from the white-hot furnace and from your hands, O King, may he save us. But even if he will not, know, O King, that we will not serve your god."

The proof of our convictions is found in our actions. It is easy to say that we love God, it is much more difficult to live by his teaching. The people of Christ's time are an example. They claimed to be "holier than Thou," but if they were, how could they even think of putting to death one whom they could not convict of sin? Like the pagan king and others, they simply wished to do what they found agreeable to themselves and, if anyone stood in their way, he was either to be compelled to join them or eliminated. There could be no tolerance for disagreement. Others in the community might be influenced and their power be eliminated. Truth has a way of undermining tyrants.

THURSDAY

Genesis 17: 3-9; John 8: 51-59

God in making his covenant with Abraham—"I shall be your God and you shall be my people"—promises untold material benefits, such as, great fertility, powerful kings, a multitude of nations. He vows fidelity and expects fidelity in return. Fidelity is the most difficult thing that God asks of weak human beings—always remain faithful, never betray me to satisfy your own pleasure by sin. If we violate the pact we must quickly return to God and the highest motivation to do so is that he always remains faithful. "If a man is true to my word, he shall never see death."

Is it any wonder, when Christ claimed to be greater than Abraham, that the Jews were upset? No man could be greater than Abraham. What they failed to take into account was that to make such a claim was asking for death, so it should have given them pause and they should have considered the claim, unusual though it was. The claimant would need to be either insane or sent from God and Jesus gave no sign of insanity. Again, the real problem was the prejudice of the Pharisees. Their hearts were so hardened, they could in no way hear of an opposing opinion.

FRIDAY

Jeremiah 20: 10-13; John 10: 31-42

So often, is it not through "the whisperings of many" that people lose their reputation? People who we thought were our friends are the "whisperers." And once they start, they begin to look critically at everything. Qualities that had been considered virtues are now thought to be vices. They find fault with everything. And even if forced to recognize that there is some virtue present, the motivation is questioned; there must be some evil intention. This is indeed a severe trial for the person who is unjustly accused. His only recourse is trust in God. It takes perseverance in faith but there is nowhere else to go. And we are safe. The cause of the whisperings, as in the case of Christ, is envy; the goodness of Jesus is detracting from the attention given to the Pharisees. Instead of improving themselves, or leading the acclaim for Jesus, they decide to hold their position in society by pulling down his reputation. They had a tough job on their hands but they succeeded by playing to the lower instincts of others, such as Pilate and the crowd.

Jesus points out that all his deeds have been good. The opponents do not deny it. "Who can convict him of evil?" Instead, they attack his person. He simply cannot be the person he says he is, the person his deeds reveal. He acts through the power of Beelzebub. Repeating these charges over and over again, even though the people were beginning to believe in him, the scribes and Pharisees undermine Jesus, and on Good Friday wreak their vengeance on him.

Notice how the same thing happens today in public life. No politician can compare to Jesus but it is quite clear that, although they make mistakes, many are decent, honorable men who have sacrificed much to serve others. However, their reputation is always in danger. Granted their case cannot be compared to that of Jesus but the undermining process is the same and so is the motivation—insatiable greed for power.

SATURDAY

Ezekiel 37: 21-28; John 11: 45-57

Ezekiel speaks of the day, when the Lord will convert Israel from idolatry to the Covenant. He will unify them, restore them to Jerusalem and grant them peace. And the Israelites shall obey his commandments under David, their one shepherd.

The prophecy of Ezekiel, of course, was fulfilled far more effectively by Christ, and not in the glorious way anticipated in Ezekiel but by his death on the cross. This was the New Testament in Christ's blood. The implementation of the New Covenant is still proceeding, but in Christ we have all the elements for unity, worship of the true God, and peace. What we need to do, as the Jews needed to do, is accept God's commandments and put them into practice in our lives. There will always be some like the Pharisees who will be opposed. But we must have the strength of our convictions, and despite the fact that we may even be put to death—figuratively or literally—we must remain united to Christ, steadfast in principle, committed to doing God's will.

Holy Week

Monday

Isaiah 42: 1-7; John 12: 1-11

Today, from the book of the prophet Isaiah, we read the first description of the Suffering Servant of the Lord. He is chosen by God to preach justice to the nations. The Messiah will be one who is meek and humble of heart, known for his great patience and charity. He will be persistent in his efforts to establish justice among the people. He will be able to do all this because he is of God; he has the spirit of God, who created heaven and earth and governs them by his all-powerful providence. Actually, God has appointed the whole Israelite community to this task of justice but unfortunately they fail to implement it. Ultimately, the Prince of Peace will fulfill this assignment.

Today's gospel tells the story of a meal at the house of Lazarus. The overtones are of death. On this occasion Jesus is trying to convince his apostles that, although he is the Son of God, he is about to be put to death. He wants the apostles to begin to consider more seriously the mission that is to be theirs and the fact that they too will be called upon to suffer death because of their faith in him. During the repast, Mary, the sinner, anoints the feet of Jesus with costly perfume. Judas Iscariot protests that the three hundred silver pieces paid for the perfume could have been used to benefit the poor. He, who stole from the common purse, is actually concerned about Jesus' lack of justice and compassion for the needy and impoverished! How blind we can be to our own faults.

The reading also makes clear that all of us need personal friends and this allows for greater signs of affection than might be given to others. Washing Christ's feet with a perfume was a special sign of love. The criterion for justice or charity is not necessarily one of quantity, but one of attitude. That one gives more to a friend and less to a beggar is not an injustice as long as the needs of both are met. The quantity and quality in the case of a friend is not only a sign of justice but also one of special affection, and possibly of gratitude as well.

Tuesday

Isaiah 49: 1-6; John 13: 21-33, 36-38

For most of us, baptized as infants, Isaiah's prophecy has a personal application. "From my mother's womb, he gave me my name. The Lord called me from my birth." It is a mystery as to why God calls so many of us in this way and at such an early age, but it is a fact. We have a mission in the world. We are to be that "sharp-edged sword" of Truth in God's hand, standing firmly in our convictions concerning the revelation that we have received from Christ. So many are separated from relatives and friends by the sword of God's Truth. At times it seems that we have toiled in vain and spent the strength of our lives uselessly. But this is a temptation. Our faith is in God; he is our strength. And even though we may be rejected as Christ was rejected in his time, we shall be vindicated as Christ was vindicated. The Lord will make us a light to the nations and his salvation will reach to the ends of the earth.

We must be single-minded about our mission, not in the sense that it has a narrow focus but that it is all-consuming. Judas thought that he could eat, make money, and enjoy the love of Christ and be in his service too. But we must serve God or mammon; we cannot have both. Even the apparently strong person such as Peter may succumb to temptation. We need to learn that we simply cannot carry out the mission of Christ merely with our own human abilities or holding to our own agenda. Constantly we need to be united to him in prayer, through the sacraments and by sacrifice. If we have our choice between the brilliant-proud person and the dull-humble person, the option should always be given to the latter. The combination of intelligence and humility, of course, is the optimum. But the humble example of the Christ life accomplishes far more for him than all the arguments of the proud. If Peter had not learned this lesson by the time he came in contact with Paul, who could come on so strongly, there could have been fireworks and a setback for the Church instead of the remarkable spread of the faith which was led by both of them.

Wednesday

Isaiah 50: 4-9; Matthew 26: 14-25

We depend on God for absolutely everything. And he is forever revealing himself to us in nature and in prayer. We must be resolved never to turn our back on him, always to do his bidding. For what are we without our God? Persecution and opposition are as nothing, if not an honor, when accepted for his sake. Judas took the opposite view. He seemed to think that God owed him something. Let Jesus take care of himself. If he is not God, he is an imposter and deserves what he is getting. If he is God, he can take care of himself. Because of his betrayal of Jesus, Judas is richer by 30 pieces of silver and no great harm is done. What Judas fails to understand is that, although God can take care of himself it is his design that in this world we are to protect his interests. This is a great honor; it is also a great obligation. Although God can do what he wills, what he has willed to do is to entrust his "fate" to the free will of human beings. This is a strange and wonderful truth. By his will, we are our brother's keeper; it is our role in life to exercise "divine" goodness, love, and mercy towards our neighbor, and thus to exercise our concern for God and his will for man on earth. How could we do otherwise, when he has been, and is, so good to us? The answer is easy. The Judases of this world, who maintain that God can take care of himself or that God is in his heaven and has no interest in us on earth, proclaim a philosophy of "everyone for himself." And if we wish to get along in the world, it behooves us to accept and practice that philosophy. This is what life is about. Isaiah and Judas present contrasting viewpoints to us. Because of God's gift to us of free will, we must make the choice.

HOLY THURSDAY

First Reading: ***Isaiah 61: 1-3, 6, 8-9***
Second Reading: ***Revelation 1: 5-8***
Gospel Reading: ***Luke 4:16-21***

When Judas betrayed Jesus for 30 pieces of silver, his motivation could hardly have been the money. Maybe he had hoped for much more, but his reason to go through with his crime was undoubtedly the same as that of the "unjust steward." He wanted to make friends with the mammon of iniquity while there was still time. He read the signs of the times and he concluded that Jesus' popularity was waning. The confrontations in the Temple area were Christ's death knell. Judas reasoned that it was best to abandon a sinking ship and salvage what was possible.

On the preceding Monday, Judas valued Mary's jar of perfume at 300 pieces of silver. It would seem that a human being, especially Jesus recognized by some as a "trouble maker," would be worth far more if only "to get him off the streets." And if the apostles were arguing among themselves, even at the Last Supper, as to which of them was the greatest, it is clear that Judas' temptation was not unusual. Anyone of the apostles could have fallen. The lesson for our times is clear. How many theologians and priests have betrayed the Lord for a few pieces of silver! To be popular, they have told people within the Church what they have wanted to hear, and they have been paid well for it. Judas left the Upper Room after the washing of feet and probably before receiving the Eucharist. Surely he was less hypocritical than those who today stay in the Church, call themselves Catholics, receive the Sacraments, but deny the teachings of Christ and of his Church.

Easter Season

Octave of Easter

Monday

Acts 2: 14, 22-33; Matthew 28: 8-15

During the octave of Easter it is time to contemplate the meaning of the Resurrection of Jesus and of the sacrament of baptism. Throughout the week the readings are from the Acts of the Apostles as written by Luke.

Peter tells the people about certain facts. He claims that there is no need to enumerate them, nor to prove them because they were witnessed by many. He refers to the "miracles, wonders, and signs," which Jesus performed. His hearers also know how Jesus died: "You even made use of pagans to crucify and kill him." They know, too, that David died and is buried in their midst, but David made clear that one of his descendants would be the Messiah, who would not undergo corruption. What they do not know, or at least have not accepted as yet, is that God has raised up this Jesus—he is resurrected—and it is to be the work of the Twelve to bear witness to him.

The holy women are half-fearful and half-overjoyed, half-believing and half-disbelieving. However, when they see Jesus clearly, they believe and accept his instruction: "Peace! Do not be afraid!" What we lack is this vision of Jesus. It is not something that he holds back from us. We have it in the New Testament; we have it in the lives of great saints, in spiritual writings, in the preaching and example of those around us. What we lack is a total acceptance of the person of Jesus and all that he stands for to remove from us fear of this world and the next, to free us from our defensiveness and make of us loving and trusting people. Like the soldiers, often we allow ourselves to be bribed by the powers around us. For pleasure and transient peace we forfeit spiritual consolation in this world and possibly eternal happiness in the next. With the help of our resurrected Savior, let us overturn the stone that closes us up in the tomb of sin and spiritual laziness.

TUESDAY

Acts 2: 36-41; John 20: 11-18

Today's Mass reminds us that we are "risen with Christ." Peter had told the Jews the historical facts about Jesus, and they accept those facts without question. Now he challenges them on something that is not totally observable—but which Peter holds with equal certitude—that Jesus is the Messiah! In support of his testimony he uses many arguments but ultimately faith is required to accept something claimed by another person.

Not everyone who hears Peter is now contrite and accepts baptism. Only "those who accepted his message were baptized" while others heard and were not baptized. Why? It is not only necessary to hear the message but also to accept it. "You must reform, have your sins forgiven, and receive the grace of the Holy Spirit." The key is the act of will to turn from the things of the world to the things of God. Everything falls into place after conversion.

In the gospel reading we see through the eyes of Mary Magdalene the wonder and glory of the Resurrection. The scene as narrated by John is filled with tenderness, sympathy, and devotion. We must seek Jesus with the same perseverance and love with which Mary Magdalene searched for him. Even she did not recognize the glorified Jesus. He had to reveal himself to her. We need that grace, too. Faith is not a matter of logic. It is a matter of asking God for the most precious gift we can receive, belief in him. And he, loving us and wanting what is best for us, cannot refuse. We must seek this gift as Mary Magdalene did. The Lord has a mission for those who love and believe in him and that mission is always the same. We are to make every effort to communicate our love for and faith in God to others. "Go to my brothers and tell them."

WEDNESDAY

Acts 3: 1-10; Luke 24: 13-35

Today, we read again from Luke's Acts of the Apostles composed under the spell of the great event of the Resurrection. At the Beautiful Gate of the Temple, Peter works a dramatic miracle in the name of Jesus. He offers the poor beggar seeking alms not a few coins but the ability to walk again.

Like the poor beggar, we need to sort things out for ourselves. In the final analysis, which is more important: a few coins which will be spent and soon gone; or the ability to walk, to work, and to earn a salary for himself? There is no comparison, of course. But it was necessary for Peter to get the man's full attention ("Look at us!" he said.) or he never would have been able to rouse in the beggar the required act of faith. The beggar was completely committed to his way of life. Begging was all he knew, to think that there might be something better for him was next to impossible. However, he finally believed and was cured.

In today's gospel, Luke tells of the Lord's appearance to two disciples on the way to Emmaus. They were talking about Jesus when he drew near and accompanied them without being recognized. Their conversation revealed that they must have given little attention to the words and deeds of Jesus when he walked the roads of Palestine. They had not reached the clear conclusion that he was the Messiah. The apostles were much the same. Jesus had conducted a school, as it were, for three years or so with two main lessons to teach: 1) He was the Messiah; 2) We are to love God and one another as he loved us. The two disciples even chastise Jesus for not knowing the events that took place a few days before. In return, Jesus chastises them for not being able to add two and two. "What little sense you have! How slow you are to believe all that the prophets announced! Did not the Messiah have to undergo all this so as to enter into his glory?" This time the disciples listen intently. Their hearts burn inside as they realize what the events signified. How stupid could they have been? They recognize Jesus. He disappears but they are thoroughly convinced. Nothing can stop them now. They race back seven miles to Jerusalem without lights, amid ruts covering the road, and robbers lurking in the dark in order to announce the Good News to the apostles.

May God give us the grace and the will to believe that Jesus is the Son of God, the Messiah, our Savior, and may we act accordingly.

THURSDAY

Acts 3: 11-26; Luke 24: 35-48

Peter makes clear to the people that faith has given the beggar perfect health. Faith in God—a miracle—was the only reason for his cure. Peter and the apostles are familiar with the perplexity of the crowd. Peter says "I know that you acted out of ignorance" in the past. He does not excuse them—what they did was sinful—but now they have another opportunity, just as he and St. Thomas, and the disciples at Emmaus, and later St. Paul, St.

Augustine, and all of us were given another chance. But it is urgent that we "Turn to God, reform our lives, and have our sins wiped away." Who knows whether there will be another favorable circumstance tomorrow?

"All the prophets have announced the events of these days . . . God sent the Messiah to you first to bless you by turning you from your evil ways because you are the children of the prophets; you are the heirs of the covenant God made with your fathers . . . Anyone who does not listen to the Messiah shall be ruthlessly cut off from the people." This same message is given to us each year as we commemorate the death and resurrection of Jesus and our own baptism. We are God's newly Chosen People. Shall we repeat the incomprehensible mistake of the Israelites?

The gospel reading continues yesterday's narrative to the disciples of Emmaus and later that same night to all the apostles. " 'Everything written about me in the law of Moses and the prophets and psalms had to be fulfilled.' Then he opened their minds to the understanding of the Scriptures." But he did all this to convey the essential truth that their sins were forgiven. "Penance for the remission of sins is to be preached by you to all the nations."

The reason God wants us to recognize our sin is that we cannot appreciate his love and goodness, nor can we receive his pardon unless we realize our sinfulness. The reason for preaching penance is to free us from fear and to give us hope. It is obvious that death comes to everyone, and therefore, we should fear death and be despondent when we think of it, unless we have hope of an after-life. But an after-life is beyond our power; we cannot even retain the life on earth that we already possess. So anything that is to take place in an afterlife is controlled by another Power. How we can please this Power is contained in the message of Christianity.

FRIDAY

Acts 4: 1-12; John 21: 1-14

The newly found courage of the apostles is amazing! They preach in public; jail does not frighten them; they even speak forthrightly before the high priests. When arrested for announcing the Resurrection of Jesus, Peter proclaims Jesus Christ to the influential Sadducee party. He states that Jesus is the stone rejected by the builders and it has become the cornerstone. Peter adds: "There is no salvation in anyone else, for there is no other name in the whole world given to men by which we are to be saved." Although all of this can get the apostles into serious trouble with both civil and religious authorities, they are fearless. In our modern day, how many of us have the courage of our convictions to evangelize and catechize as we should?

In the gospel story it is evident that the apostles are not as yet filled with the Holy Spirit. They look to Peter for leadership but he, apart from Christ, is nothing; under his leadership they cannot even catch fish, not to mention men. However, under the direction of Jesus they not only catch fish, but their faith is on fire as well and they will, in the future, catch men!

SATURDAY

Acts 4: 13-21; Mark 16: 9-15

The courage of the apostles is obviously not of this world. Not only were they normally fearful of authority, but they were "uneducated men of no standing." They were not able to speak in high-sounding theological terms; they simply spoke of "what we have heard and seen." Thus, there is a striking difference between their present fortitude and the timidity they showed when Jesus was arrested and put to death. The lack of courage on the part of the Sanhedrin stands out in contrast to the strength of the apostles. Perhaps they were becoming aware of a grace that had been offered to them all along during the public life of Jesus but that they still had not the humility to accept.

Although the grace was given, the Sanhedrin could not bring itself to look at Jesus as coming from God. In addition, immediately after the Resurrection, the apostles not unlike the Sanhedrin put no faith in those who had seen him after he had been raised. They had a preconceived notion as to whom and how Jesus should reveal himself. They were not about to take the word of outsiders. Jesus took them to task for their disbelief and their stubbornness.

All of us act in a similar way. We are slow to accept God's word from the Church until we have a crisis or we think that we have received some kind of special revelation from God in prayer. What is worse is that we do not give full commitment to the gospel, even after we have accepted it. At least the apostles committed themselves fully to spreading the gospel. When Jesus commanded them to "go into the whole world and proclaim the good news to all creation," they did so as we read in Luke's Acts of the Apostles.

Second Week of Easter

Monday

Acts 4: 23-31; John 3: 1-8

This week, the reading is again from the Acts of the Apostles, a book filled with the marvelous effects of the Resurrection of Jesus. The apostles recognized that what God had prophesied had come to pass. The Jews and the Gentiles had conspired against Jesus, God's anointed, and put him to death. But the apostles believed so strongly in the divinity of Christ that they could not allow that his life be given up in vain. They prayed with so much power that the very building shook. They vowed to be faithful to their mission to preach the gospel, and asked God for perseverance in their proclamation by showing to all around signs and wonders "worked in the name of Jesus." The fervor of the apostles was tremendous, and therefore, they "continued to speak God's word with confidence." Faith in the divinity of Christ gave them confidence in the truth of his teaching and the assurance that nothing could prevent them from overcoming the world.

Some time previously Nicodemus had proclaimed exactly the same kind of faith. "We know you are a teacher come from God, for no man can perform signs and wonders such as you perform unless God is with him." What Nicodemus lacked was the power of the Holy Spirit, which would enable him to do the same in the name of Christ. "Flesh begets flesh; the Spirit begets spirit." In a spiritual sense, the rich get richer. Faith, good works, love of God feed one another, allowing the Spirit a free reign to live in us and work through us in all of our thoughts, words, and deeds.

Tuesday

Acts 4: 32-37; John 3: 7-15

The early Church was characterized by the ardor of its faith and witness to the Resurrection, by its unity among the members derived from respect for the apostles, and charity toward one another. We strive to live by the same virtues and practices in our own day—faith, unity, charity, evangelization emanating from respect for a God-given authority—but with very uneven degrees of success.

These virtues can only be had by those who have been begotten of God's Holy Spirit. Salvation is not from man but from God. Man cannot earn holiness, as it were, by the practice of natural virtue; he must have these gifts given to him from above.

Everything depends on faith. Christ is the only one who has actually seen God and we must have faith in him. The sign by which we believe is the Resurrection of Jesus. "The Son of Man must be lifted up, that all who believe may have eternal life in him." The key is our belief that God so loves us that his only Son gave his life on the cross for us; and the Resurrection shows that Jesus truly is God's Son.

Wednesday

Acts 5: 17-26; John 3: 16-21

In today's reading from the Acts of the Apostles we hear that the Jewish religious authorities arrested the apostles whose popularity aroused jealousy. The apostles preached the gospel, regardless of the foreseeable consequences, in obedience to the command of Christ. They went in the Temple precincts to the very people least likely to receive them and in a place where everyone in Jerusalem would know about their activity. Human wisdom would have counseled that they go underground. Truth counseled that they had nothing to fear—not even death, for death would only aid the cause as turned out to be the case with the martyrs. Therefore, they preached and did not resist, when the Temple guard arrested them. Indeed, the bravery of the apostles had won over the crowds who might possibly have stoned the guards, if they had exerted much force in arresting the apostles.

"He who acts in truth comes into the light to make clear that his deeds are done in God," Jesus told Nicodemus. And the apostles followed that very advice. It is true that, if we are guilty of sin or a crime of some kind, we see no other course of action than to hide it. Jesus came into the world, not to condemn people, but to enlighten them. And when the light shines upon error or sin, the person stands self-condemned. Jesus enlightened the world by manifesting how much God loved the world. He did this by his preaching and by his death on the Cross. But many of those whose guilt was exposed—for the most part, exposed only to themselves—could not bear the

Truth. Instead of being attracted to him, they put him to death and ran from the Truth. It was to such people that the apostles appealed, and to such people that we must preach all through the centuries.

THURSDAY

Acts 5: 27-33; John 3: 31-36

Everyday in every temptation we face the same situation as the apostles. Which is it better to do: to obey God or man? The answer is obvious. But in practice the fact that we choose to obey or please man is equally obvious. And by "man" we mean both ourselves and other human beings. As the Italians put it, even when sin is not directly involved, pride is at work; we want to make a "bella figura" in our own eyes and those of others. Sometimes this can be done without great harm, but often it demands compromise of principle, rationalization on our part, and ultimately sin. Even when sin is not involved, the exercise in pride is unhealthy!

If others can be stung to fury by our actions and be ready to kill us, how can we be so indignant about a loving God, who allows us to break from him eventually, if we so wish? We fear the anger of those who can harm us in this world more than we fear the loss of love for all eternity. This illustrates another difficulty from which we suffer—we tend to prefer immediate gratification to daily, long-lasting, quiet peace, joy, and holiness.

Jesus explains all these points to Nicodemus. We accept earthly authority much more readily than the authority of God. It makes no sense to fear the anger of man more than "the wrath of God"; to choose a temporal satisfaction over the happiness of everlasting life. But sadly, we do.

FRIDAY

Acts 5: 34-42; John 6: 1-15

That which is of human origin comes and goes. It may last for a long time and attain great success and popularity but eventually the originators pass on or the admirers become disenchanted, attracted by something else.

Something of divine origin may have its ups and downs. The difference between what is of human origin and what is of divine origin is that what is divine endures forever. In worldly terms, for example, the Church may be popular, successful, have many members at one time and far less at another.

The sign of divine origin is that the Church does not fail—even through the sinfulness of its members.

Who would ever imagine that a Church founded on the apostles could be successful! They probably had far less talent than Judas. The gospel reveals their many shortcomings. But the principle of judgment given to the Sanhedrin is true. If the Church is founded by God, it will endure and it is foolish to try to fight God. The apostles went right on preaching convinced that Jesus is God. Despite threats, court summons, beatings, and even martyrs' deaths for one after the other, the Church prevailed in their time and still prevails—a certain sign of divine origin.

The power of the apostles—rather, the lack thereof—is clearly seen in the miracle of the loaves and fishes. They admitted that they could do nothing on their own. It seems that Jesus wanted them to admit their personal inability which they could not later deny. Then, he performed the miracle and it was evident beyond the shadow of a doubt to the apostles and all those present, "This is undoubtedly the Prophet who is to come into the world." After the Resurrection and Ascension, the apostles never doubted this. "They never stopped teaching and proclaiming the good news of Jesus the Messiah."

Saturday

Acts 6: 1-7; John 6: 16-21

In the young Church in Jerusalem, the Jews were divided into two groups: the Palestinians who spoke Aramaic and the Hebrews of the Greek-speaking Diaspora. Discrimination has existed through all the ages and apparently apostolic times were no exception. The apostles addressed the problem directly, however, and responded to it as later they would in the matter of circumcision. Seven Greek-speaking men were made ministers to help the apostles. One of the important things to note is that they chose "men acknowledged to be deeply spiritual and prudent" to assist them. Vatican II still insists very strongly on these virtues: holiness and prudence. They do not always go together and they far surpass other qualities such as scholarship and popularity, which we might be inclined to use for making a choice of assistants.

The institution of the diaconate resulted in greater unity, too. "The proposal was unanimously accepted by the community." This was the task of the deacons: to unify the Church through direct, personal service to the people. Meanwhile the apostles went about their work of preaching the Word of God, increasing their numbers enormously and even converting many priests. Regardless of whatever criticism may be leveled against the priest in our own day, our people still recognize them as religious leaders and are ready to follow them, if we give our people a leadership that is truly based on God's word. The sign of this would be humility, quiet authority, courage, and perseverance. As for our deacons, it would certainly seem that evangelization is a fertile field for their ministry.

As were the apostles, we, in our day, are on troubled waters. But all we need do is remember the miracle of the loaves and fishes. The lessons are that we do not need much to work with; of ourselves, we are nothing; with God all things are possible; God wants us to pray to him, to seek his help; we are to be solicitous for others, even when we think that we have little to offer; even though it seems that Jesus has sent us out alone, he is not far from us; and he will never ask us to do anything beyond the means of a person who looks to him for help.

Third Week of Easter

Monday

Acts 6: 8-15; John 6: 22-29

Stephen, one of the seven chosen to assist the apostles, came into conflict with Diaspora Jews because of his beliefs. They were no match for his wisdom and spirit. Like the apostles, Stephen had a phenomenal spirit because of his faith in Jesus. He was filled with the Holy Spirit. He worked great wonders among the people and it was obvious that God was with him. However, God's truth was too much for those who were unwilling to accept Jesus, so they fought Stephen as one who was not obeying the law and the prophets. They used falsehood to attack truth and stoned him to death.

The sole purpose of signs and wonders is to promote our acceptance of Jesus as Lord and Master. There is no other reason. However, the Jews had another motive; miracles were a means to power and the good life and that certainly was what they were seeking. They were not concerned, as they should have been for the kingdom of God; rather they, like all of us, wished to have their heaven on earth. Our principal purpose seems to be one of survival and survival on the best material level. We look upon Jesus as someone to be used, not someone to believe and follow. Why not give priority to the primary purpose for our being on earth, which is to know, love, and serve God?

Tuesday

Acts 7: 51-8: 1; John 6: 30-35

In his defense before the Sanhedrin, Stephen attacked directly the unbelieving Jewish leaders. He accused the Jews of being people who did not wish to hear the truth and were only nominally followers of God. We are much the same. When we are "stung to the heart," the proper response would be to ask why, to search our consciences for the reason. If we did so, we would probably discover that we are living a contradiction, that we constantly rationalize God's law and that we tone down his demands of us. Many of us might maintain that we are living a good life, better than most other people at least. But in fact, we may be like St. Paul was at the time. Apparently he did not take part in the stoning of Stephen but neither did he object. By his silence, he concurred. The same is often true of us. We may condemn the errors of others in private but in public, we are diplomatic. What we need is a "St. Paul" conversion in order to be more zealous and courageous in defense of the faith.

The Jews asked for a sign of proof that Jesus was the Messiah. He complied but they rejected the sign. They were willing to accept his correction that the manna came from God but they could not believe that he himself was like the heavenly manna. Likewise, we are constantly beseeching God for his grace to avoid sin and to obtain favors. When we receive grace, which we always do, there is something we don't like about it—it may demand the rejection of a bad habit or of a sinful pleasure. The way to live is to imitate Jesus who lived the perfect life, who died and rose from the dead. Our faith should present a clear view of the purpose of life and of how to live it.

WEDNESDAY

Acts 8: 1-8; John 6: 35-40

There was a wave of persecution against the Greek-speaking Christians. While Saul was still persecuting, the gospel was spread through the efforts of Philip, one of the seven deacons. Those early followers of Jesus experienced strong spiritual joy that rose over the daily problems of living and dying. Many people in those early days, despite persecution, acted bravely. Some were forced to leave their homes, others were apprehended and thrown into jail, but all continued to preach the gospel. Not only that, but many believed and were baptized because of the signs and wonders that were performed.

Today we have not only the signs and wonders of the early Church, we have the signs and wonders of two thousand years! If the people of the early days could believe the gospel on so little evidence and preached by uneducated people with no test of time; why are we not far more committed to the faith, when we have the blood of countless martyrs, the holiness of many saints, the preaching of brilliant people, and the fact of two thousand years of perseverance upon which to rely?

In many parts of the world, persecution is active and the reaction of Catholic people is generally strong. However, when, from within, the faith is under devastating attack, we lack commitment and courage. The passage of centuries has not changed the problems of society and certainly has not dimmed the cause of our joy. No one who truly believes that Jesus Christ is the Son of God will be rejected. All who submit to him in faith will have everlasting life. So what is needed? We must pray for humility, faith, conversion from this world to God, hope in God's promises, and love for one another.

THURSDAY

Acts 8: 26-40; John 6: 44-51

Today's reading from the Acts of the Apostles tells of the deacon Philip interpreting a passage from Isaiah for an Ethiopian pilgrim. The passage is about the Suffering Servant, and Philip shows its fulfillment in Jesus. The Ethiopian receives baptism and Philip moves on. God works in and through others and not necessarily through ordained priests only. The prospects of Philip converting the Ethiopian were remote at best and his teaching and wisdom alone could not accomplish it. However, it was the gift of faith coming from God that enabled the conversion of the Ethiopian.

As the eunuch said, "How can I understand unless someone explains Scripture to me?" We do need priests and preachers of the gospel. The eunuch could have read Isaiah for years and not understood the meaning of the prophet. The description of Christ that Philip presents from Isaiah is beautiful: "silent, humble, innocent, and therefore, abused by men. He was like a sheep led to slaughter." We are his posterity. He is spoken about on all asides and his greatest, most effective followers are still those, who in silence, humility, and innocence, live fearlessly, faithfully, and obediently in this world as he did. It does not matter whether we are deprived of justice in this world—that will always be the case. If we but follow in his footsteps, we will have a spiritual posterity and everlasting life.

In the gospel Jesus makes clear that no man can save himself, much less the preacher save the non-believer. God's grace draws a person to faith. Each human being must strive to fulfill his mission but the grace of God is all-important. And in this process the words and deeds of Jesus are important because it is only through him that we learn of the Father. If we want faith in the Father, we must go through the Son and, as many have stated, if we want to know the Son, the best way is through his Mother. We can come to know Jesus in many ways, but the one that is most effective is the Eucharist. When we receive the person of Jesus into our very being, he lives in us and acts through us. And if we live this way on earth, we are assured of eternal life.

FRIDAY

Acts 9: 1-20; John 6: 52-59

The demands that God makes of those whom he loves and chooses can be very great. In the story of Saul's conversion, imagine the incredulity of Ananias being asked to visit the very person, who was seeking his arrest and condemnation. If anything, Ananias should have been hiding from Paul in the sight of his companions and the high priests. But the Lord says to Ananias, "I myself shall indicate to [Paul] how much he will have to suffer for my name."

From everyone involved in the event, humility and faith were demanded; denial of self, trust in God, and a practical obedience. God works most often through human instruments, and although there was a vision in this case also, the human situation, the tendency to incredulity, was very much involved. We need to be able to see the hand of God in our lives. The only way to do so, and to accept his will, is to cultivate the virtues of humility, faith, and obedience.

In today's gospel, the promise of the Eucharist was hard for the hearers of Jesus. It demanded the kind of trust in him that results only from humility, faith in the speaker without visible proof, and obedience to his directions. The Jews were lacking in all of these, but especially in humility. They thought they knew what was best for them and believed that they could judge how God was to do things. They were "stiff-necked and hard of heart."

SATURDAY

Acts 9: 31-42; John 6: 60-69

For a time, faith in the risen Jesus was greatly facilitated through God's revelation to Peter and this faith spread to the Gentiles. While the early Church enjoyed a short period of peace, it made great progress especially because of the miracles performed. The faith of Peter and the power of his prayers were tremendous. He feared nothing, promised little, and produced wonders by God's power.

However, not only the crowds, but the disciples, as well, found it hard to believe in the words of Jesus—especially the discourse on the Bread of Life. Ours is a Eucharistic Church and life for us means receiving Holy Communion. "Before Abraham was I Am," Jesus said. If there is ever to be a Messiah, then he must say and do things that are beyond the natural order. The disciples needed humility, faith, and obedience: humility to listen with an open mind; faith in the person worthy of belief; and obedience to his word. We need to be governed, in our thinking and living, by the normative values of the gospels. They breathe a special spirit of joy, simplicity, and holiness that we must make our own—not only in thought but also in action.

Fourth Week of Easter

Monday

Acts 11: 1-18; John 10: 1-10

We do not live in an age of visions and many miracles, although miracles do take place from time to time, and there have been a few authenticated apparitions. Instead of visions and miracles we have been given the Church. And we should react to the Church in the same way that Peter reacted to the vision explained in today's first reading. Is God speaking, revealing himself in some way? This is the only question to be asked. If the answer is affirmative we need to accept God's voice promptly as it is uttered through the Church. As Catholic Christians we believe that God speaks through the Church. What God commands will often enough be contrary to our own ideas and logic because his thoughts and his ways are not our thoughts and our ways. But that should not be any obstacle as long as we are certain in faith that God speaks to us.

The second lesson is obvious: Jesus is the redeemer of all men. "God has granted life-giving repentance even to the Gentiles." It was after incidents such as the conversion of Cornelius that the early Christians remembered this teaching of Jesus in parables such as those of Matthew 13. We need to notice that the opportunity to be baptized is a free gift; man can still refuse. On man's part, repentance or conversion is necessary. Although God wants all men to be saved, only those will be saved who accept his gift and live in accordance with his will.

"The one who enters through the gate is shepherd of the sheep; the keeper opens the gate for him." The sheepfold is the Church, God's People; Jesus is the gate; the shepherds are those appointed by Jesus. Many try to climb over the barriers of the sheepfold to attack the sheep or seduce the sheep into following them; it is the same in the Church. Sometimes these people will be successful but they should be recognized for what they are, "thieves and marauders", rather than true shepherds of the sheep.

The sheep, God's people, must listen for God's voice as he speaks through the Church, and follow no one else, if they wish to be safe. The remarkable thing is that, even in our own day, the sheep are by-and-large faithful to the Master's voice. As Cardinal Wright once stated, "The laity will save us yet." There is every sign that such is the case. A number of shepherds have wandered off; there are those within the sheepfold who attack and try to seduce the sheep, but for the most part—whether through attachment to the shepherd, fear of going outside the fold, ignorance, or whatever—the sheep stay close to one another and to their shepherd.

TUESDAY

Acts 11: 19-26; John 10: 22-30

In today's first reading from the Acts of the Apostles, we learn that at Antioch, a large seaport on the Mediterranean coast, an exemplary church of believers developed. Although immediately after Pentecost, there were large numbers of converts on single occasions, the Acts give the impression that none could compare with Antioch. It was with reason, therefore, that the apostles were concerned about the quality of the converts and that they sent Barnabas to look at the situation. Barnabas is described much like St. Stephen as "a good man filled with the Holy Spirit."

Antioch has often been repeated in mission lands, such as Korea and some African countries in our own day. Simple, good-intentioned people eagerly accept the gospel. One wonders whether or not countries that have lost the faith can regain it. So far there seems to be little evidence that this is possible. But just as surely, there are millions in these countries, as in Europe for example, who live desperate lives without faith. Presently, Christianity in the West is in contrast with Atheism in the East. The next century could very well see Christianity in the East and Atheism in the West.

The Jews continually asked for signs, but they were unwilling to accept their obvious meaning. Our own world is much the same. We certainly have signs in great numbers. The history of the world would be the most obvious one—that immorality breeds violence, crime, fear, social chaos, and war. Saintly people are another sign—their simple lives are happier than the lives of those with great wealth. The birth of every innocent child is still another sign—let us reflect on the fact that we are as children in God's sight. In today's gospel, Jesus portrays himself as the Shepherd of the fold. The sheep are called upon to hear the voice of God, speaking through those whom he has chosen and to follow his word.

WEDNESDAY

Acts 12: 24-13: 5; John 12: 44-50

In today's first reading, we note that in the Antioch community there was a person, who had even been brought up in the household of Herod! In this text, the community seems to be giving the call and ordaining to Holy Orders. On the other hand, it is clear that the apostles had chosen and missioned Barnabas. Also, it was Barnabas who had initially sought out Paul and the passage begins with the remark that Barnabas and Paul had visited Jerusalem, undoubtedly to see the apostles, before being sent to Cyprus. Would that all missionaries were sent on their way with the full support of the laity! Every priest, indeed every baptized person, should paraphrase the words of Christ concerning his relationship to the Father with regard to the mission that we have in the world.

When we accept the teaching of the priest, we are placing our trust in him who sent the priest. For his part, the priest must live in such a way that whoever sees the priest sees God. The priest is neither to judge nor to condemn; he is to devote all his energy to saving sinners.

We will be judged, not so much by an action of God but by an action of our own, namely our acceptance or rejection of God's word. The words of Jesus will condemn a man on the last day, if he has not accepted the gospel. For that word is from God; it is a command from God; and on our acceptance of that word depends eternal life. Well should the priest keep in mind, therefore, that he must speak as God has instructed him.

THURSDAY

Acts 13: 13-25; John 13: 16-20

The early Church still looked upon the Jews as the Chosen People. They have a very special place in God's design. So it is that Paul always went to the synagogue and preached there before going anywhere else. So too he made the connection between the Old Covenant and the New. He did not disparage the Old Covenant but showed how it was fulfilled in the New. It would help us greatly in the present day if we knew more about the meaning of the Old Testament and how it applies to the New Testament. It would greatly enrich our understanding of God's word, especially with regard to fundamental truths that are clearly taught in both Testaments.

By the time that the Last Supper took place many of the faults and failings of the apostles were evident. But Jesus did not renounce his choice of them anymore than the Father rejected the Jews because of their sins and errors. They were the ones who rejected him. Jesus stood by the apostles. The apostles must be "carbon copies" of Jesus, if they are to fulfill their mission of bringing Christ to the people and being accepted by them. This is a tremendous responsibility for the priest, a successor of the apostles. Granted that God can save people in any way that he chooses, the ordinary way that he has chosen depends tremendously on the goodness of the priest. The priest needs to be faithful to the words of Jesus in his preaching and to the deeds of Jesus in the daily example of his life.

Friday

Acts 13: 26-33; John 14: 1-6

The basic message of the apostles to the Jews was that Jesus was the fulfillment of Old Testament prophecy. What was promised to their fathers was fulfilled in this time. Granted that many witnessed his life, only the apostles were witnesses to the Resurrection. As the people had believed in the prophets, so now they were to believe in the apostles. In fact, as the people put to death the prophets, so did they kill the apostles as well.

Why did not Jesus reveal himself broadly after the Resurrection, even as he did before his death? The answer is not available to us, but one possibility is that he wanted to strengthen, confirm, and make abundantly clear the authority of the apostles in the Church. If others had witnessed the resurrected Christ, they would have been in a position to claim his authority to some extent. Even if Jesus revealed himself to thousands, it would not necessarily have converted the thousands. And even if it had, the important thing was that God's truth be handed on faithfully to all generations. Safeguarding that truth, through the authority of the apostles, was much more important than a comparatively small number of instant conversions in the first generation of Christians.

The world has been exposed to the message of Christ over the centuries, first because of the apostles and those who witnessed the Resurrection, and later because of those who came to believe in him and whose numbers have multiplied geometrically. The world has not been converted, however, because there are still not enough witnesses in every age and the witnesses are not as worthy as they are called to be. The witnesses do not follow "the way, the truth and the life" closely enough. We need greater faith in God and in his Son, Jesus Christ.

SATURDAY

Acts 13: 44-52, John 14: 7-14

The preaching of the apostles was characterized by truth in the message, courage in the face of expected opposition, patient endurance in persecution, faithfulness to their mission first to the Jews and then to the Gentiles, and devotion to the Holy Spirit. In all this, they found joy and meaning for their lives.

The world is an amphitheater in which there is contention for the minds and hearts of the people. Opposition to the Church has been, and continues to be, a sign of its remarkable "success" in attracting people. Everyone wants others to agree with him. Where we see that the crowds are flocking to someone else, there is a tendency to be jealous, to attack that person, when the logical thing to do would be to ask why.

Note the influence of women. It is difficult to capture the minds and hearts of a sizable group of people without the women, who are the heart and soul of society. This still remains one of the great strengths of the Church. By and large, Catholic women have retained their faith and love for Christ and his Church, and remained loyal to the priesthood.

Faith in Christ, as the revelation of the Father, is essential to a member of the Church. If we fail to believe in him and in the New Testament time, there is nothing left to our religion. We need to constantly bolster our faith in him and in his teachings because Jesus is the perfect manifestation of God to man. If this faith and love for Jesus are present in us as they should be, then our mission is fulfilled. The Father will live in us, act through us, accomplishing his works. "The man who has faith in Jesus will do the works that Jesus does."

Fifth Week of Easter

Monday

Acts 14: 5-18; John 14: 21-26

In today's first reading, we trace the steady expansion of the post-resurrection faith and church. It was difficult work because of opposition and because of the ignorant superstition of the people. The obligation of the priest, the successor of the apostles, is to offer the gospel to the people. He should do so with perseverance in the most convincing way that he can. However, the gospel cannot be forced upon people; they must accept it freely and with faith or not at all. So it was that, in the face of persecution, whenever it was possible to bow out gracefully, the apostles did so.

Another danger, in addition to trying to force the truth upon people, is the adulation that may be given to a good preacher or one who produces signs and wonders. It is not easy to resist the emotion of the people, nor the emotion within oneself and the temptation to think that much of the acclaim might be due to one's own talents and virtue. Humility is indispensable to the preaching of the gospel; to the degree that it is lacking, God's grace is inhibited. And despite the adulation of the crowd, if their praise is split between the preacher and God, it is not fitting, and the conversion is likely to be temporary rather than permanent, subject to failure when difficulties arise. "Not to us, O Lord, but to your name give the glory."

The preacher, the one who loves God so much that he is impelled to evangelize, is one who keeps God's commandments. "If you love me, keep my commandments." No one will be successful in bringing the gospel to others unless he loves God by keeping his commandments, for it is only to such people that God reveals himself. The same is true of converts. They must have the humility to be ready to do whatever God asks of them because it is only to such people that God reveals himself. Again, we can see that pride, selfishness, egotism are the principal obstacles to love of God. An inflated opinion of one's own importance makes it impossible for God to have much place in that person's mind and heart.

TUESDAY

Acts 14: 19-28; John 14: 27-31

Despite persecution of the most dreadful kind, the early Christians persevered. In today's reading Paul was stoned and left for dead—his injuries must have been severe—but he went right back to his preaching mission, even into the areas from which his attackers had come. He wanted to reassure the people that, although there would be many hardships to endure as Christians, if they put their faith in God, they could overcome all opposition. In the towns that Paul visited he established "parish councils" of elders to govern and guide the Church. "With prayer and fasting, they commended them to the Lord in whom they had put their faith."

In today's gospel narrative, the meaning of peace is established. The "peace" of Jesus is an assurance of spiritual, saving strength that goes far beyond a simple farewell. The peace of the Lord is not given "as the world gives peace." The people still lived in such circumstances that, from a human standpoint, they had every right to be distressed and fearful. But that is the test—to keep one's faith in God in the face of physical and material uncertainty. The test is whether we will turn to human beings and the things of this world for our solace or turn to God. Jesus must return to the Father, both as a symbol of his complete victory over sin, death, and the world and as a sign of our future glory. However, he returns to us through the sacraments to provide us with the spiritual strength to resist and to overcome the world, the flesh, and the devil as he did.

WEDNESDAY

Acts 15: 1-6; John 15: 1-8

The Council of Jerusalem is often used as an argument to prove that Peter did not exercise supreme authority in the Church. That he was not a tyrant or dictator is correct, but that he lacked final authority is false. All the circumstances indicate that Peter and the apostles did have authority. When the problem of whether the Gentiles accepting Christ had to be circumcised before baptism, Paul and Barnabas went to Jerusalem to see the apostles. Along the way they gathered the "sensus fidelium," as it were, but there is no mention that this was used as a club in Jerusalem. Paul and his friends were given a good reception along their route and at Jerusalem also.

The case against Paul was not argued by the apostles but by some converted Pharisees.

Some of the very same people, who urge consultation today by legitimate authorities in the Church, would argue that because Peter and the apostles used that very style, they had no authority. That Peter and the apostles heard arguments on both sides and that they leaned toward the tradition in which they had been raised should be no surprise. These were the reasonable and natural reactions. That they finally decided in favor of Paul, due to the divine revelation that Peter had concerning Cornelius, is a sure sign that the issue was settled on faith, and on what was discerned as God's will.

In the parable of the vine and the branches it is to be noted that not only are the barren branches pruned away but the good branches feel the sharp edge of the knife, as well, in order to increase their fruitfulness. So many people have the idea that no human being is to suffer in this world. Surely we are to be good stewards of the life that has been given to us, but suffering is a part of life, even for morally good people, even for Christ. The Word of God separates the branches from the vine or exposes the branch to new and more vigorous life.

In God's providence, then, we can have our "ups and downs" even in the spiritual life, but we must remain united with Christ. The Word of God can convict us of sin, but as long as we strive to remain united with Christ, repent of the sin, and grow in virtue, we have life and we can regain our fruitfulness. If we try to live apart from Christ, our spiritual life withers and eventually, if this persists, we will be "picked up to be thrown into the fire and burnt."

The key to the spiritual life is the acceptance of God's word. As sap gives life to the branches, so God's word gives life to the soul. God's word made actual and effective through the sacraments does the same. In theology we refer to this life-giving ingredient of the soul as grace. And if we ask anything of God—anything in keeping with his word—"it will be done for us."

Thursday

Acts 15: 7-21, John 15: 9-11

"After much discussion" at the Council of Jerusalem, Peter and James spoke in favor of not requiring anything more of Gentiles than faith in the Lord Jesus Christ as Redeemer. Their reasons were: it was clear that Jesus willed that the Good News be preached to the Gentiles and that they should enter the Church; the prescriptions of the Old Law had been too much for them and their ancestors; faith in the Lord Jesus had been their own means of salvation and all that Jesus asked of them; it seemed to be in correspondence with prophecy; and in the name of Jesus all kinds of wonders had been worked among the Gentiles. All that they should ask is that the Gentiles accept the gospel and put it into practice, and some of the commandments are mentioned explicitly.

The sign that we love God is our keeping of the commandments. That is what Jesus did; that is what we must do—obey the Father. Obedience is the sign of many virtues but it is especially a sign of love, the virtue which encompasses all others. And this obedience and love are the source of all true joy in life. This seems to be a hard lesson to learn, surrounded as we are by so much that gives us pleasure. But we know very well, from our human experience, the truth of Christ's own words. Joy is found in obedience to the one whom we love.

FRIDAY

Acts 15: 22-31; John 15: 12-17

The Council of Jerusalem put in writing its decision that circumcision was not required, but that Gentile converts, after baptism, would be expected to observe the sixth commandment and also refrain from eating meat sacrificed to idols. They were careful to send the letter with two messengers other than Paul and Barnabas, who had advocated such a decision and might have been suspected of fraud, if independent witnesses did not confirm the letter.

From his letter, stating that eating meat sacrificed to idols was not sinful but to be avoided because of possible scandal, it seems that Paul could very well have argued against this restriction at Jerusalem, too, and accepted the ruling only on the grounds of possible scandal. It seems that the apostles felt more strongly about this than he did.

The question needed to be resolved because some people had disturbed the Gentiles because of their private discussions of the matter. The same thing happens today. Even though our people realize that the theologian and others have no official authority in the Church, they can still upset the people greatly and disturb their peace of mind. What is different in our day is that these people persist in their "discussions" even after the Church has officially spoken on the matter. The Gentiles of the early Church had a great spirit of love and reverence for the Vicar of Christ, Peter.

There should be a friendly relationship between hierarchy and people—and there is. The problem exists between the hierarchy, who have received authority from Christ, and those who argue against the legitimacy of any authority but who, in fact, wish to usurp that authority. It is clear in "discussions" that the worst of tyrants are those who wish to push aside established authority. We are friends of Christ, if we do what he commands us, and this major command is that we should get along with one another, love one another as he has loved us.

Saturday

Acts 16: 1-10; John 15: 18-21

We have a glamorized idea of the success of the apostles. Although "the congregations grew stronger in faith and daily increased in numbers," it is also evident in today's reading that their success was hard earned and that the gospel was not well received everywhere. Jesus had told his disciples that this was to be expected. "If you find that the world hates you, know that it has hated me before you." The world loves its own, those who will tell the world what it wants to hear. But we have been chosen and taken out of the world to preach a message of a different world, a different way of life. It must be one or the other. We cannot serve God and mammon. We should not be disturbed when we fail because with our own weak humanity we know how very easy it is to reject God's word and choose the ways of the world. Indeed, we need to be strong in order to keep our own faith, resist the same temptations, and keep working to bring others to the faith.

We note once again that St. Paul, in order to avoid scandal, makes an exception with regard to circumcision in the case of Timothy. Having fought to eliminate that practice when receiving Gentiles into the Church, Paul makes the exception because Timothy's mother is Jewish. This, of course, was not a violation of New Testament law but a matter of doing something over and above what was called for in order to forestall possible dissatisfaction in the community.

Sixth Week of Easter

Monday

Acts 16: 11-15; John 15: 26-16: 4

In today's first reading from the Acts of the Apostles we read about the development of the early Church. Paul and Luke cross over to Macedonia, a country in the Balkan peninsula, and reach the town of Philippi. A very ordinary scene but with extraordinary results is presented to the reader. St. Paul and St. Luke simply take a stroll one day to the river, meet Lydia, a prosperous merchant, and eventually she and her entire household are converted. Later she invites them to her house for a meal, although the context seems to indicate that to accept such an invitation was unusual for the apostles.

This is still the way to make converts. We must go where the people are; they must be able to identify with us so that we can speak to them of God. Granted that most of the work of evangelization is the responsibility of the laity, the priest, too, must get beyond the doors of the rectory to engage the people. We simply cannot bring souls to God without making contact with people.

Jesus sends the Holy Spirit, to enlighten minds and hearts and to draw them to God. However, he tells the apostles, "But you must be my witnesses as well." Personal contact is needed. You must be mission-minded, go out to people, be aggressive at least to that extent. True, you will not always be well received. You may even be persecuted or put to death. But fear not, I am with you to protect you and I keep my promises with regard to eternal life.

Tuesday

Acts 16: 22-34; John 16: 5-11

St. Paul and Silas present us with an example of heroic virtue performed in the name of Christ, and as a result, they are rewarded with the conversion of their jailer and all his household.

St. Paul and Silas had been flogged and then thrown into jail with no treatment for their wounds. They prayed and sang to raise the spirits of the other prisoners. And when an earthquake rocked the prison, broke open the doors, and loosened their chains, St. Paul and Silas did not try to escape. The jailer, seeing how easy it would have been for them to do so and noting their patience under trial, admired them so much that he wanted to have their secret. "What must I do to be saved?" They told him about Jesus and the jailer cleaned their wounds, had everyone baptized, and celebrated with a banquet. It was a great turn of events brought about by faith, hope, and love of God.

Surely it was the power of the Holy Spirit that sustained the apostles and brought so many to conversion. It seems to be most evident in the cheerfulness of the apostles. They were grief-stricken when Jesus first announced his ascension, but he told them that they would be well off with the Holy Spirit who was their advocate or lawyer as they stood trial before the world. And so they were. The Holy Spirit did wonders for St. Paul and Silas on a day that started out disastrously and ended in sublime joy.

WEDNESDAY

Acts 17: 15, 22-18: 1; John 16: 12-15

Paul delivered a brilliant speech at Athens, the center of learning and culture. It was a logical, reasoned speech for philosophically-oriented people and that is how it was received—as an interesting philosophical argument, to be accepted or rejected on the grounds of its reasonableness. It really did not represent a call to faith but ultimately, it became a proof to us that no matter how bright we are, we will never acquire faith in God and Christ purely from reason. We need the Holy Spirit, of whom St. John speaks, who "will guide you to all truth," and faith is a gift, pure and simple. Faith depends more upon good will than knowledge, upon an openness to the transcendent rather than an attitude requiring strict proof.

Still, it is good to note the arguments that Paul uses to prove the existence of a spiritual supreme God because they are attractive. The Athenians worshipped a god who dwelled in human sanctuaries, who needed the service of men, who was the product of human genius or art. But the creator of heaven and earth can hardly be a creation of man's genius or art, nor be contained within a temple, nor need the help of human beings. No, a true God is above and independent of all these. It is foolish to worship that which human beings can in any way control. A true God must be superior to man, not inferior to him and dependent upon him.

THURSDAY

Acts 18: 1-8; John 16: 16-20

In visiting with people and trying to instruct them, we should realize that our principal task is to plant the seed of faith. The increase depends upon God. Therefore, we should not remain with one person or one small group stubbornly trying to convert them. We must give the grace of God a chance to work in them while allowing them time to reflect upon the message. This is the way that Paul approached his mission—in accordance with the instruction of Christ who suggested that he shake the dust from his feet and go on to the next place, if the faith was not given a favorable hearing. Thus after the meager results obtained in Athens, St. Paul left that city and went to Corinth.

It is clear that Paul shunned neither friends nor strangers, nor did he remain in comfortable circumstances long after the faith had been accepted. In Corinth he first stayed with fellow Jews and tentmakers, Aquila and Priscilla, but soon later he lived with Titus Justus, a Gentile. In every new city, even though he knew that almost inevitably he would be rejected, he always began preaching to the Jews then to the Gentiles. Everyone should be given the opportunity to hear the good news, especially the Chosen People who had kept alive the promise of a Messiah for so many centuries.

The personal ministry of Jesus was confined to the Chosen People. True, he could have preached more to the Gentiles instead of meeting with them only by chance. But obviously, according to the ways of divine providence, it was necessary for him to begin with the Jews. We can only speculate as to why he preached only to them, but there seem to be many good reasons: his time was brief; he had three years at most to spread the message; he needed to be rejected as Messiah and not put to death for any other reason; his message and his identity had to be crystal clear and intimately connected with the Old Testament; he could not have covered the then-known world adequately; it was the Father's Providence that human beings participate in the redemptive process and be the Body of Christ to the world.

FRIDAY

Acts 18: 9-18; John 16: 20-23

Corinth was a tough port city with all the vices that one sees in major ports of our own time. It was hardly the kind of place where one might expect to make many converts. That was Paul's thinking, too; he could easily be killed within a short time and to no advantage for the faith. However, with the help of Aquila and Priscilla, Paul preached there because of a prompting and vision from the Lord. He found it spiritually profitable enough that he remained in Corinth for eighteen months. The major problem that he had came from the so-called "religious" community, but the magistrate, who had little regard for any religion, told the Jews to settle their differences by themselves. He did not see that their squabbles were civil affairs and refused to sit in judgment of them.

The apostles learned quickly from personal experience that having the truth on their side, as well as the Creator of heaven and earth, was not going to change the way that the world would perceive them and would not save them from suffering. While the Bridegroom was with them, they were protected; when he was taken away, they learned what it meant to stand in for him. So did Paul learn in Corinth and elsewhere. Loyalty to Christ leads to the Cross.

Just as a woman may conceive her child amid great pleasure and joy, the pregnancy and delivery encompass pain and much discomfort. But once the child is born, all the inconvenience and pain are forgotten and joy reigns once again. So it is with the person who finds God. There may be a joyful first fervor, but the world will change that ardor by its rejection. Only the worldly will seem to enjoy life, while the saintly will suffer. But when comes the day of death, that great day of rejoicing for God's saints, the joy of the saint will never end. Such joy is well worth pursuing.

SATURDAY

Acts 18: 23-28; John 16: 23-28

The reaction of Priscilla and Aquila to the teaching of Apollos is noteworthy. They were two of Paul's closest friends and they could have seen Apollos as a competitor especially since he knew nothing of the sacrament of baptism. Priscilla and Aquila did not fall into the trap of not accepting anyone but Paul. They had room in their lives for anyone who preached the gospel with the energy of Apollos. At the same time, however, when they noted an error in his theology, they did not hesitate to challenge and correct it, while recognizing his good qualities, too. He was an "authority on Scripture"; he was "full of spiritual vigor"; "he spoke and taught accurately about Jesus." So they encouraged Apollos, gave him what they had learned from Paul, and recommended him to others.

The Father is ready to treat us as Priscilla and Aquila treated Apollos. God stands ready to receive our prayers through Christ but even in our own name, if we but ask him in faith to help us. We need to show that we are filled with spiritual vigor, that we know and love Christ and speak of him and the Father's revelation accurately. But if we do so, we shall be well received by the Father; we shall receive his support; the Father will answer our prayers.

Seventh Week of Easter

Monday

Acts 19: 1-8; John 16: 29-33

It is true that Jesus called the people of his time to repent and to believe in the gospel. We should always renew our repentance, be reconverted, as it were, throughout our lives. But St. John the Baptist had nothing further to offer in the baptism he conferred, whereas Jesus had redemption and hope to offer in his own. So it is that St. Paul refers to John's baptism as one of repentance; people were thereby consecrated in that disposition. The baptism of Jesus, on the other hand, offered Spirit and life. St. Paul went on to demonstrate in his discussions at the synagogue what God's grace had brought about in him.

We need to keep in mind that everything we have in this world is a pure gift from God. Conception, life, everything that we have in life, even death at the end of life—all these are God's gifts intended for our good. The apostles, on the other hand, like us, seemed to think that their faith in Christ was something that they had engendered, something that they had developed from their logical thinking. Whatever "faith" in Jesus they had developed on their own was fragile indeed and it was demonstrated that very evening of the Last Supper in the Garden of Gethsemane. What happened to the apostles at Gethsemane? Where were they on Friday?

Christ has overcome the world, but he is the only one who ever will do so. If we wish to overcome the world and truly enter into life, our only sure way is "with him, through him, in him, who is Christ the Lord."

Tuesday

Acts 20: 17-27; John 17: 1-11

In today's reading from the Acts of the Apostles, we hear Paul's speech in Miletus on the way back to Jerusalem. It is a beautiful confession and deserves to be heard. Would that all priests could say what St. Paul told the people. "Never did I shrink from telling you what was for your own good, or from teaching you in public or in private . . . I have never shrunk from announcing to you God's design in its entirety." As a result, there were "sorrows and trials that came my way from the plotting of certain Jews . . . Chains and hardships await me. I put no value on my life, if only I can finish my race and complete the service to which I have been assigned by the Lord Jesus, bearing witness to the Gospel of God's grace."

What a glorious description of the practice of the priesthood, to which we are called! What more could anyone—especially a priest—desire to say than what St. Paul declares. He sets forth the challenge of the priesthood, its mission, including attacks from others, the sorrows, trials, hardships, as well as the rewards the true priest can expect. The life of a good priest demands courage, humility, intelligence, faith, hope, love, and every other virtue. Briefly, it requires prayer, the closest union with God for "without me, you can do nothing." No human being has what it takes to exercise the place of Christ within a community and yet the priest must do so with the help of God.

The purpose of the priesthood is to give glory to God by bringing all men and women to eternal life, which consists in the knowledge of the true God made known in Christ. And so, we must give to others the message of Christ entrusted to us. The glory is to be found in those who have received the message of revelation from the priest and who will see to it that the message is passed on to others. There is nothing else of real significance in this world. God wants everyone to come to the knowledge of the truth. And he is Truth, not only the Truth but the Way and the Life, as well.

WEDNESDAY

Acts 20: 28-38; John 17: 11-19

St. Paul reminds the people of Ephesus that there will always be severe temptations to abandon the faith. It can never be taken for granted. False prophets will always arise because both they and their followers will be deluded by pride into thinking that they know more—have a better way—than Christ; they will be stimulated to continue by the adulation of those who love the new and unusual; many of them, unlike St. Paul, will be seekers of money, power, and prestige. As for us, we must keep in mind that there is only one God, not many; that God is not merely human but divine, infinite, and all-powerful.

In order to keep the faith, unity is a most precious element. We need all the help, all the encouragement, all the support that we can get from others, not purely human support, but especially the support of God's grace mediated by the thoughts, words, and actions of others. That which holds us together in unity is God's truth and that which guarantees the truth is God's divinely appointed teaching authority found in Peter, Paul, the other apostles, and their successors.

God will not take us out of the world that will always be a hostile environment for the believer. But God will give us every grace needed to overcome it. The world is a place of trial, to be sure, but single-minded devotion to God's revelation makes clear that the battle can be simpler if we do not allow ourselves to be tempted by the way of accommodation to the world.

THURSDAY

Acts 22: 30, 23: 6-11; John 17: 20-26

The Resurrection of Christ is still the key to Christianity. If Christ is risen from the dead—because he placed such emphasis upon this sign himself—we can believe in everything else that he said and did. If not, as St. Paul tells us, our faith is in vain.

Christ would not condescend to appear to the Pharisees and the general population. He appeared only to the apostles and a few other followers. It was true beyond a doubt that his body was not in the tomb on the third day. But for this fact we have only the apostles' testimony. Rather than deny the Resurrection, the apostles—these weak, and very human beings—went on to give their lives in martyrdom.

At the Last Supper Jesus prayed not only for his apostles but also for those who would believe in him on the word of the apostles. The world has not known Christ but these men have known him and he missioned them to give that knowledge to others so that all who come to believe in Christ will be one here on earth, and in the company of God in his glory in heaven.

It is evident that Christ depended tremendously upon his apostles. His was a divine revelation but from the beginning it was to be entrusted to human beings—a risky thing to do, but in God's wisdom, the best way to go. Just as Christ was the God-man, so his revelation would be supernatural wisdom and events transmitted by human beings. Apparently that combination was needed. No mere man has ever possessed the wisdom revealed in the words of Jesus; no mere man has ever revealed such sanctity in his deeds. And all with perfect balance!

FRIDAY

Acts 25: 13-21; John 21: 15-19

On the shore of Lake Galilee, in response to the questions of the resurrected Christ, Peter professes emotionally that he loves Christ more than any of "these." Scripture scholars dispute as to whether "these" refers to the other apostles or to the things of the world. "These" could very well refer to both and Peter's answer could also refer to both. He loves Christ more than all other people and things.

It is not easy to come to this total love of Christ without unitive prayer, contemplation. In fact, it would seem impossible. Our lives are so busy that the best we can say usually is that we are trying to serve Christ, to do as he has asked us to do. But this is not likely to occur; we are not likely to serve Christ as we should unless we know him well and love him above all else. The catechism answer is still true. We reach the happiness of heaven by knowing, loving and serving God, and in that order.

We know God by reading about him, listening to others tell of him, and speaking with him in prayer. We come to love God by acts of love, by actually raising our minds and hearts to him, joining our minds and hearts to his. Love is a relationship between people, desire to be one with that person because of that person's goodness. We want to be in that person's physical presence, but love endures and can grow stronger even when that person is not present. This is even truer of Christ. We can encounter him in the Eucharist, penance, and other sacraments only momentarily. So thinking of him, longing for him, conversing with him in prayer is of tremendous importance.

Finally, of course, we grow closer to Christ by acting as he has instructed us to act. But again, this activity is hollow, of little avail, unless it is based in knowledge and love. Human experience reveals the truth of this, whether we reflect on our love of a human being or our love of God. Who knows us, who loves us, who has done more for us than Christ the Lord?

Christ foretells what Peter's love will lead to, and the first reading about St. Paul teaches the same lesson. "Greater love than this no man has than to lay down his life for his friends." Christ's love for us compelled him to suffer and die on the cross. Peter and Paul died as martyrs. Most likely we shall not be required to suffer martyrdom, but we are required to love God above all other people and things, and in that sense to lay down our lives for God and for those whom God loves, namely the people around us.

SATURDAY

Acts 28: 16-20, 30-31; John 21: 20-25

Surely in every positive way we should be solicitous for our neighbor, providing for his needs in both justice and charity. But we should not be concerned about the results. The person may squander what we give him or may use it very well. If he uses it well, he can soon join those who help the poor because he needs less help himself. If he does not use our help well, he still remains among the poor, so we continue to help. We may change the style of our assistance in hopes that we can teach the person to become self-sufficient, but what results from Christian living should not overly trouble us. "How does that concern you? Your business is to follow me."

In the case of Peter and John, it looked as though John was being blessed more than Peter. Peter would be a martyr; John would die a natural death. But which is better? Only God knows. We should leave it to him. John, a more gentle spirit, could have succumbed to fear and abandoned the faith in the face of martyrdom. Dynamic, impulsive Peter, if he had lived to a peaceful old age, could have abandoned the faith out of boredom. God knows what is best for us; we should trust in him.

St. Paul is another example. Imprisoned on complaints from the Jews, he made both the Jews and the Romans do some soul-searching over his case. He forced the Jews to re-examine the question of life after death and whether it was just to persecute Christians, who simply saw themselves as fulfilling the best Jewish tradition. He forced the Romans to act on principle by giving him a fair trial and to look into the life of this remarkable person, Jesus, to examine what he had said and done.

Our responsibility is to follow Jesus, to practice in our lives what he said and did. As for the results in the lives of others, although we surely want everyone to live a good life and to be saved, it is not our business but God's to judge how well that person has responded to grace.

Ordinary Time

Tenth Week of Ordinary Time

MONDAY

2 Corinthians 1: 1-7; Matthew 5: 1-12 **YEAR I**

Today's reading is the beginning of the vigorous second letter of Paul to his Corinthian converts. He greets them by invoking upon them grace and peace from God and the Lord Jesus Christ. Grace and peace, the essential blessings of Christianity are given by God the Father and the Lord Jesus Christ. These blessings are Paul's wish for all his correspondents.

Nothing happens in this world apart from God's holy will. If I have received so many blessings as I have in my life, then I owe glory, praise, adoration, and gratitude without limit to God. It is a privilege to suffer anything in the course of our life, because all suffering is a share in the sufferings of Christ, and suffering is both redemptive for ourselves and others and also an incorporation into the life of God's own Son. We are one with him through creation and baptism, and we live the life that he lived.

Similarly, those who share in the sufferings of Christ will rejoice in the same consolations—the knowledge that we are doing God's will, that we are doing what is right and just, that our actions benefit not only ourselves but others as well, and that an eternal reward awaits us. This is how we share in "grace and peace" from God our Father and the Lord Jesus Christ.

The gospel narrative introduces the delightful start of the Sermon on the Mount—the famous Beatitudes. Jesus teaches that the blessed are those whom worldly standards rank low: the poor, the despised, and the pure. Matthew, the evangelist, emphasizes the quality and the activity of virtue and thus gives us the very same message as Paul gave to the Corinthians. Blessed, happy, and chosen are those who suffer in this world in order to do the will of God. Not only will they be comforted here below, but they will be rewarded with perfect happiness for all eternity in the life to come. At the time of Jesus, the Beatitudes instituted a moral revolution that had not reached its fullness. They were opposed to all the conventional values of the Jewish and Greek-Roman world and pronounced blessings on those who did not share in these values.

1 Kings 17: 1-7; Matthew 5: 1-12 **YEAR II**

In the Beatitudes, the Lord promises that the sorrowing will be consoled, that the lowly will inherit the land, that those who seek justice will have their fill. But these promises make no commitment about life in this world. Even if the lowly will inherit the land and all the other promises are fulfilled, no guarantee at all is given that life will become a proverbial bed of roses for those who serve God. Rather, the promises have to do with spiritual blessings and, although they may be granted in this world, the words themselves, and our experience indicate that the blessings will not be received in their fullness in any one's lifetime.

Still, if we reflect further on the Beatitudes and upon our own experience, we realize that these spiritual blessings are the only ones worth having. As the gospel points out material blessings can disappear overnight. Spiritual blessings bring a joy that cannot be taken away from us by anyone but ourselves; they are long-lasting, more satisfying, and even make the body feel good.

Despite all this, the problem is still clear. Material prosperity is "one in the hand" and spiritual promises are "two in the bush." The key is faith in God. If we have faith in his existence, and therefore, in his love, goodness, mercy, there is no doubt that his way is best. If we lack faith, material blessings will always have the greater attraction. And since faith is a gift of God, we need to pray most earnestly and perseveringly for that grace.

TUESDAY

2 Corinthians 1: 18-22; Matthew 5: 13-16 **YEAR I**

Today, again in his second letter to the Corinthians, Paul writes to defend himself against accusations of insincerity and dishonesty. He insists that he is not insincere and vacillating—just as God is not insincere. "As God keeps his word, I declare that my word to you is not 'yes' one minute and 'no' the next." God is stable, consistent, dependable, and truthful. The message of the cross is foolishness to those who are perishing, but to those who are being saved it is the revelation of God's saving power. This should be a tremendous source of affirmation for us. Christ is our hope. But if we are one with Christ, what is there to fear? If we wish to be secure, peaceful, happy in this life we must simply be as one with Christ. And he has made this possible. He has given us his very spirit in baptism and confirmation, his Body and Blood in the Eucharist. If we are not Christ-like, it is not for lack of resources.

So often we are like salt that has lost its savor, like a light under a bushel basket. We do not radiate and communicate what is in us. We try to hide Christ; we almost seem to be ashamed of Christ, although we are called Christian. Our lives must permeate society and bring society to life in Christ as a small quantity of salt permeates food and water and gives taste to much larger quantities. We must be like a lamp on a stand, which lights up a whole room, lighting up the minds and hearts of people around us with the truth and love, the justice and the goodness of God.

1 Kings 17: 7-16; Matthew 5: 13-16 **YEAR II**

Cardinal Mercier had a practice, we are told, that on days when his schedule promised to be the busiest, he would still insist on taking his normal time for prayer in the morning—and even extending it—in the belief that if he gave God his due, he would have more than enough time to meet the demands of the day's schedule. The day was not necessarily easier; indeed, there were problems but some interviews were perhaps shorter and more pleasant than expected; there was a happy solution to some matter; and if it was impossible to do everything, he discovered, that what seemed so urgent could wait until the next day!

This is the lesson that we learn from Elijah and the widow. Although the widow was definite in her plans to eat a last meal and die, since she saw no way out of her dilemma, she decided that Elijah was of God. So regardless of her plan, she did what God asked of her first. She was not expecting anything to change in her life; she simply accepted God's will. And Elijah, her son, and she were able to eat for a year from the miraculous multiplication of flour.

The gospel does not seem to be directly connected to the epistle but there is a relationship. Elijah was the salt of the earth in the sense that if he had allowed himself to lose faith, the Chosen People would have been bereft of hope. It was bad enough that many were faithless, it would have been disastrous if the prophet also proved to be unfaithful.

Today God calls all of us to be prophets—to hold his truth; to remain faithful regardless of what others do; to be a light on the stand rather than to be hidden under a bushel basket; to allow others to see and understand God's truth and be saved. The world situation is bad enough—it always is—but what will it become if those who have been given the faith and have been called to be the salt and the light of the world should fail? That is our calling, our responsibility in the world. It is not up to us to blame others for their sins. The problem is more likely to be that our proclamation of the gospel in word and in deed is not as appetizing a salt as it should be, and the light that we shed could be much stronger and more illuminating. We are the ones to keep society from spoiling and rotting. We are to present a different, desirable image before an unbelieving world.

WEDNESDAY

2 Corinthians 3: 4-11; Matthew 5: 17-19 **YEAR I**

In today's reading, Paul tells the Corinthians, in self-defense, that he has acted as a true apostle of God's New Covenant. Recalling that on Mount Sinai the face of Moses was resplendent, Paul says that the minister of the New Testament has an even greater glory. He compares the life-giving qualities of the Christian dispensation, the law of love, as opposed to the Mosaic Law, the law of the commandments, which of itself did not bring men to salvation but made sin and the effects of sin manifest and clear. If the Mosaic Law, which can be used to condemn man and which was graven in stone and is passing, could be held in such honor, how much greater regard should we have for the new law of love, which ennobles man, is written on his heart, and endures forever. The law of love affirms that three things remain—faith, hope, and love—and the greatest of these is love. Yet love can easily be pushed aside. In our day, abortion is a good example of love overcome by selfishness. If the law permits something, it overcomes our love for innocent life and allows selfish inclinations to run rampant. Love counsels to self-sacrifice and love of neighbor but, in this case, the law of the land does not. Legalism will one day come to an end; what we love will live on forever.

In Christ's time, the Mosaic Law was thought to be the summary of all wisdom human and divine, the revelation of God himself, a complete and secure guide of conduct. For most Jews the Law was the terminal revelation of God. This value of the Law Jesus did not and could not accept. To be sure, it was not the mission of Jesus to annul the Law and the prophets. His mission was to "fulfill" them—to give the Law that finality which the Pharisees believed it already possessed. Jesus affirmed indirectly that the Law was imperfect and unfinished. His mission was to perfect and finish it. In the gospel narrative, Jesus affirms the enduring reality of the Law found in Old Testament writings; but it is the finished and perfect law that endures, the law of love, not the Law of Moses with its explanatory oral teachings. The Sermon on the Mount is the keynote of the New Testament, the constitution of the kingdom of God, the law of love. "Happy are they who have kept the word with a generous heart, and yield a harvest through perseverance."

1 Kings 18: 20-39; Matthew 5: 17-19 **YEAR II**

In today's reading, there is an account of a very dramatic scene—the duel between Elijah and the prophets of the pagan god Baal. Elijah wanted to prove Baal to be a false god before the Israelites, who were serving it as well as the true God.

Elijah gives us the battle cry of all believers. "If the Lord is God, follow him." Jesus laid down the same challenge several times; one case similar to today's first reading was the accusation against Christ that he drove out demons by the power of Beelzebub. The basic questions remains crucial: Is there a God? If there is, has he made his will known to us? If he has done so, there is only one conclusion: We must obey the Lord our God.

In the gospel Jesus makes clear that he is the same God of creation, who wrote the Law in the heart of every person. He is the God of the prophets, to whom the Law and more was revealed. He has not come to abolish the Law and the prophets but to fulfill them, to confirm them, to make the choice between God and Baal or Beelzebub ever more clear. He came to invite all mankind to consider the basic question once again, to accept God into their lives, and to put God's law and revelation into practice.

Thursday

2 Corinthians 3: 15-4: 1, 3-6; Matthew 5: 20-26 **YEAR I**

Again, in his second letter to the Corinthians, Paul explains the superiority of the New Testament apostle over Moses. The face of Moses shone so that it had to be veiled. But no veil covers the New Testament gospel or the preacher of that gospel. Paul says, "All of us with face uncovered, looking at the glory of the Lord, are transformed into the same image from glory to glory by the spirit of the Lord." In the thought of St. Paul we are to be transfigured by the presence of the Holy Spirit so that the light of Christ may shine in our words and works, be seen by others and convert them. The absence of the Spirit in a person's life is like the veil that Moses' wore so that his followers could look upon him. That veil is removed for those who have the Spirit within them; their knowledge of God can increase and deepen without measure, and the example of these people can help to remove the veil that clouds the mind of the unbeliever. Indeed, today, only those who deliberately immerse themselves in the pleasures of this world have their minds veiled. Made as we are in the image and likeness of God and filled with the Holy Spirit, we have the responsibility to bring these people from darkness into light.

In the gospel narrative, the Lord describes the spirit of the New Testament religion. We are to go beyond just keeping the Ten Commandments. We are to have no enemies, to forgive always. Even worship must be postponed to achieve reconciliation. It is irrelevant to the duty of reconciliation who started the quarrel and it is scarcely possible to overstate the sternness that Jesus voices toward those who refuse to love. The Ten Commandments and all the disciplinary laws of the Church are a bare minimum of virtue. Moreover, these laws are not given to us as ends in themselves, they are the concrete expression of virtues and attitudes that should flood our minds and hearts. The commandments are just more explicit statements of the all-encompassing concepts of justice and charity. Fulfillment of laws is the basic minimum. What the Lord wants us to do is to stretch ourselves to the limit, reach for the ideal, strive in all that we think, do, and say, to be "perfect as the heavenly Father is perfect." Only in this way can we grow in God's love, allow the Spirit of Christ to shine in our lives, and remove the veil which obscures from the minds of unbelievers the way, the truth, and the life of Christ.

1 Kings 18:41-46; Matthew 5:20-26 **YEAR II**

Much is accomplished in the spiritual life only through prayer and fasting. Elijah was a person who, unlike the scribes and Pharisees—and even the apostles at first—understood this reality.

The scribes and Pharisees wanted to justify themselves. In their eyes, salvation had become a mathematical equation. Keep the commandments and fulfill a number of man-made precepts, the civil law, and you will be saved. This may be true, for in heaven there are many mansions, but it is hardly the way of life that God instructs us to live. Elijah realized that, even though God was obviously with him, everything that was accomplished was due to God's power and not his own. His own contribution was to try to discern God's will, accept it, and implement it.

We must not only refrain from murder, anger, abusive language, and the like against our neighbor, we must take "affirmative action," and go out of our way to perform acts of goodness and love on his behalf. What good does it do to worship God and mistreat, or fail to help, those whom God loves? If we are not at peace with one, we are not at peace with the other. We are to have no enemies and we must forgive always. Love of God and love of neighbor are inseparable, even though logically one comes before the other.

Friday

2 Corinthians 4: 7-15; Matthew 5: 27-32 **YEAR I**

In today's reading, Paul, in his deeply personal second letter to the Corinthians, makes a powerful, personal defense after being accused of being an insincere hypocrite. He says that his gospel message comes through him, a weak human being. He tells of his human weakness and human courage for the love of Jesus Christ. If we did not have trials and tribulations in this world, how would we be able to show forth the life of Christ? If we lived in comfortable circumstances, protected from evil and misfortune, would that be an imitation of Christ's life? Christ did not even have a place to rest his head. How could we have so much more? So, we should not be surprised by the troubles we have nor complain about them excessively. They may cause suffering and be hard to endure, but if we do so, we shall be leading others to the compassionate Christ and at the same time saving our souls, "We carry out in our bodies the dying of Jesus so that in our bodies the life of Jesus may be revealed." By living thus, we have nothing earthly to lose and everything heavenly to gain. We are fulfilling God's will and leading others to the reform of their lives and to eternal salvation.

In the gospel narrative, Jesus describes the spirit of the New Testament. He demands that his followers go beyond the commandments, practice purity of mental attitudes, and avoid divorce or remarriage. Sexual morality will always be a subject that draws attention and fire to the Catholic. But the teachings of Jesus are crystal clear. We must not be condemnatory but we must stand up and be counted. By the way we live, we must be a sign of contradiction to the lack of moral values in today's world. How does our faith make our priorities different from those of the culture in which we live?

1 Kings 19: 9, 11-16; Matthew 5: 27-32 **YEAR II**

The power of the Lord can surely be experienced in a strong wind, an earthquake, a devastating fire, but we experience God most intensely when his Spirit touches our minds and hearts. This was the experience of Elijah in today's reading. We could have this experience more often in our lives, if we would welcome it. All the great spiritual writers tell us that the best form of prayer is to be found not by talking to God, but in listening to him. We need to raise our minds and hearts to God in this simple type of prayer, banishing all external distractions, setting our minds and hearts on God alone. And he will make himself known, perhaps not every time or in the way that we want him or expect him to speak to us, but he will make his presence felt and his message known.

Couples contemplating marriage should do something similar. They need not try to psychoanalyze the person whom they hope to marry, but they should try to put aside the externals from time to time and try to see what the other person's soul is like. Externals are not necessarily what they seem to be; externals change. If we fall in love with externals, we are bound to be disenchanted. We must look into the heart, discover attitudes, virtues, philosophy of life. If these are sound, then we can fall in love with the whole person, through whose words and actions goodness is revealed, but we must fall in love with that interior, spiritual goodness, and not with the appearances of things.

Many married people have fallen in love with the superficial, accidental part of a person rather than with the essence. Is it any wonder that divorce is so widespread? This is what the marriage promises mean, namely that one will take the other for better, for worse, for richer, for poorer, in sickness and in health. Better, worse, richer, poorer, sickness and health are externals, accidentals, which come and go. The real person is something else entirely and primarily spiritual, the image and likeness of God within us.

SATURDAY

2 Corinthians 5: 14-21; Matthew 5: 33-37 **YEAR I**

Today's reading is again drawn from the Second Letter of Paul to the Corinthians. Paul tells his readers that, like other Christians, he is a new man. Reconciled to God through Christ, he is also an ambassador for Christ. Paul claims that the love of Christ spurs him on. Christ died and rose for all men and has made us a new creation. Now we do not know, we do not make judgments, according to merely human standards. Paul had once judged Jesus according to purely outward appearances and had persecuted him in his Church. But now Paul does not consider him in this light, but rather according to the revelation he has received. The redemptive activity of Jesus radically changes those who allow themselves to be affected by it. Furthermore, the Crucifixion and Resurrection of Jesus are the dividing line between two periods of the history of all activity in this world. Those who believe Christ died for all men should be living for him and the way he lived. What Christ did was to die for sinners in order to reconcile them to God. He did this despite our unworthiness, and so, since he died for all, we are called upon to die to self in order to reconcile all. We are not to pass judgment upon the worthiness or unworthiness of anyone but in a humble, persevering manner we must strive to bring all to Christ. We do this for love of Christ and for what he has done for us. We should be grateful that he has chosen us to bring about the reconciliation of sinners, no matter who they are. Jesus even allowed sinners to put him to death so that he might show that no one has greater love for man than he. Perhaps someone on a rare occasion will give his life for a just man, but Christ died for us when we were yet sinners.

In the gospel narrative, Jesus tells his followers that their personal integrity and truthfulness should make oaths unnecessary. In ancient Judaism people took oaths on various sacred terms. As God's ambassadors of reconciliation, we are not to swear at all. If a sacred object is mentioned in an oath, it is as if the divine name were being used. The oath is a reflection of the evil condition of man, exhibiting his mendacity and his distrust of his fellow man. In the new ethics that Jesus has come to teach all men, truthfulness is to be secured not by an oath but by inner integrity. The oath can have no place in a society that does not assume evil as a matter of course. We should not use false pretenses, false arguments, to win people to Christ but simply present to them the truth of Christ—his words and deeds.

1 Kings 19: 19-21; Matthew 5: 33-37 **YEAR II**

When we are called by God to a particular state in life, we are to make a full commitment, which is signified in today's reading by Elisha, who burns all his bridges behind him. He not only leaves family and friends, but he sacrifices his animals and burns his farming equipment, leaving himself totally dependent upon God.

Clearly the vowed religious is called to this sacrifice, especially the cloistered. But married people should keep in mind that, even though they do not leave family and friends behind when they marry, they are called upon to give up entirely their past style of life as a single person and are expected to sacrifice other attachments—even family and friends—whenever it is necessary for the good of one's spouse and children. Too often married people and the uncommitted priest, try to have the best of both worlds—their life before marriage or ordination and their new life. We must learn from Elisha to burn our bridges behind us when God calls us to a special state of life.

Exceptions to the above are possible; for example, we may be called upon to give special care to an aged or sickly parent, taking time and energy from our new call in life. However, this is not true with respect to the universal call to holiness, which all of us receive. Baptism for the adult convert, the sacrament of penance, confirmation, marriage, orders for the person baptized in infancy, are moments at which we are called upon to make a total break with our past life. "Turn away from sin and believe in the gospel." Reform and conversion should mean a total change in our way of life or they are without meaning. As Christ counsels us in the gospel, we cannot be wishful thinkers. When we say yes or no, we should mean yes or no; there should be no waffling between the two. When God calls, and he calls incessantly, there can be no middle ground; we must be with him or against him.

Eleventh Week of Ordinary Time

Monday

2 Corinthians 6: 1-10; Matthew 5: 38-42 **YEAR I**

In today's reading taken from Paul's second letter to the Corinthians, we learn much about his sacrifices and sufferings for Christ. He speaks to the Corinthians from his heart and entreats them not to receive the grace of God in vain. For the Christian there is no time to be wasted. That doesn't mean that we should work feverishly to accomplish all kinds of tasks. No, but we should give our total effort at every moment. "Now is the acceptable time; now is the day of salvation." In going about our ministry, we are to be meek and humble of heart, have no enemies, offend no one, give no one cause to reject God because of our conduct. We must be knowledgeable, virtuous, patient, loving, committed to the truth and love of God, persevering, and not afraid of hard work. If we live in this fashion, surely the Lord will be with us and we will accomplish much for the salvation of souls.

Paul's message is reinforced in the gospel narrative where Jesus gives directions on how to react when offended, abused, or oppressed. Jesus tells his disciples not to offer resistance to injury. He gives concrete examples of this kind of conduct. The first area is that of physical violence: "When a person strikes you on the right cheek, turn and offer him the other." The second area is that of legal contention: "If anyone wants to go to law over your shirt, hand him your coat as well." The third area is that of forced labor or service: "Should anyone press you into service for one mile, go with him two miles." The fourth area stressed by Jesus is that of requests for gifts or loans, which are not to be refused: "Give to the one who begs from you." The principle of non-violence and non-resistance cannot be more clearly stated for application to our modern day. In a way, Jesus asks us to be "the punching bags" of society. So although the Christian world as a whole has never been ready and is hardly ready now to live according to this ethic we as individuals should take these words to heart and live accordingly.

1 Kings 21: 1-16; Matthew 5: 38-42 **YEAR II**

When we consider the parable of the wedding feast, we realize that Heaven may be a strange sight to the human eye. When those who were invited refuse, the blind, the lame and all kinds of unfortunate people are welcomed in their poor clothing and with all their handicaps. Those in their finery are rejected. We ought to love the unfortunate and associate with them now if, as it appears, they are to be our companions in heaven.

We as a country, no matter how good we may appear to be to others, treat a great part of the world as Ahab treated Naboth. We are insensitive to the rights and feelings of others. We believe that a financial payoff is all that is needed. We have no deep loyalties to the past nor gratitude to those who have gone before us. Sometimes we have our own way by brute force, when money will not accomplish our ends; sometimes we have others do our "dirty work" or set up a situation, which may have the appearance of an accident but is inevitably ordered to our advantage.

In today's gospel, Jesus tells us how to react when offended, taken advantage of, or forced against our will. Why not align ourselves with the unfortunate who suffer these abuses regularly? We, in the United States, should be more careful about the manner in which we judge progress. Putting the family farm out of business is not necessarily good, and bigger is not automatically better. We need to be more concerned for underdeveloped countries, assist them in their need, and preserve a healthy environment for the benefit of all. We should recognize how power and money not only harm others but have a corrupting influence on our attitudes and our ways of dealing with others.

TUESDAY

2 Corinthians 8: 1-9; Matthew 5: 43-48 **YEAR I**

In today's reading, where Paul is still addressing the Corinthians, he writes to them about a collection. Church collections for the poor are quite biblical. Paul tells his readers that they are rich in Christ and that to give, when one has little, is to give much in God's sight. Paul writes about the beautiful people of Macedonia. Afflicted with great poverty, they are still extremely joyful and most generous in the way in which they have served God and then, for love of God, served Paul himself. Paul credits the Corinthians also as a people who have shown their love and loyalty to him, so he is now offering them an opportunity to show even greater charity by coming to the aid of the Macedonians. The argument is the love of Christ: "What can I render to the Lord, for all he has rendered to me?" The answer is to do whatever we can for others whom God loves as much as he loves us. Christ made himself poor materially that we might become rich spiritually. Generosity costs us very little, while the rewards of spiritual joy are immense.

The gospel goes a step further. The Macedonians are "worthy" of help. Jesus maintains that we should exercise charity even to those who are our enemies. He maintains that we cannot have any enemies, that we must greet, converse with, and love everyone. There must be no limit to our forgiveness or our love for all others. The reasoning is two-fold: 1) They are God's creatures, loved by him as much as we are loved; 2) Even if our charity does no good except to heap coals on the receiver, it will always benefit us spiritually. We shall know that, with a totally selfless love, we have done God's will and done what we can for a fellow human being. The real test of Christ-like love is not to be good only to those who love us, but to be good to those who do not; the latter probably need us more. It is the love of one's enemies that assures the integrity of Christian morality and distinguishes it from merely ethical morality.

1 Kings 21: 17-29; Matthew 5: 43-48 **YEAR II**

We are told that original sin is an absence of the gifts that we should have received from our first parents. We obtain the riches of God's grace only when we are baptized.

The story of Ahab and Jezebel is a reminder of the story of Adam and Eve. Ahab wants more and more possessions for personal prestige and lasting gratitude from his offspring after death. Jezebel perceives how Ahab can be satisfied. She openly admits to the evil of her plan but her husband accepts it for the reasons cited above and also because of his love for her.

Ahab finally discovered that humility provides the right relationship between himself and all others. In humility we should not even try to judge who our friends and enemies might be. Even though others will take advantage of us in so doing, we need to treat everyone with the same degree of charity. If we remember, of course, that some person has abused our kindness in the past, we might deal differently with that person but always in a charitable manner. Not to learn from the past may be an injustice to the person himself or to others. Our goal and everyone's goal is to become "sons of our Father in heaven."

So we should always be kind even to those who have offended us, been unjust to us or even deliberately evil in our regard. The reason is that God loves them and us and continues to do so no matter how we may judge the situation. God is love—that is perfection—and we are called to be perfect as our heavenly Father is perfect. We cannot pick and choose, our love and goodness must be directed to all.

WEDNESDAY

2 Corinthians 9: 6-11; Matthew 6: 1-6, 16-18 **YEAR I**

In today's reading, Paul encourages the Corinthians to contribute generously to the poor in Jerusalem. In classic terms he states why any follower of Christ should be generous to others. In God's plan what we must give first and foremost is ourselves; the more we give of ourselves the more we have. We are called upon, therefore, to give generously and, even though giving is somewhat painful, we should give with a cheerful disposition. "God loves a cheerful giver." We should not fear that our generosity will impoverish us. All that we have is from God. If we should have more than we presently need, surely we should share our abundance with those who have a need for the basics. In keeping with the Scriptures, we should not spend a surplus foolishly, or extravagantly on ourselves, but use it in such a way that we can provide both for our own future needs and for the present needs of those around us to the extent possible.

Another characteristic of our almsgiving is that it should be done in secret or at least without fanfare. We must respect the human dignity of those whom we help and not indulge our pride. God knows all our good works and he is the only one whom we need to "impress."

In today's gospel Jesus supports the statement that our religious duties, such as donating to the poor and fasting must be done single-heartedly to serve God, and not for recognition by others. Fasting, a means of sharing with others, should be done quietly, generously, and cheerfully. The disciple who fasts should wash and anoint himself; washing and anointing were preparations for a banquet, not signs of grief and affliction. "God loves a cheerful giver."

2 Kings 2: 1, 6-14; Matthew 6: 1-6, 16-18 **YEAR II**

The unwavering loyalty of Elisha to Elijah, the man of God, was such that he was given by God a double share of the spirit of Elijah. This reminds us of the promises of Christ that, if we are faithful, we will do even greater things than he did by God's power and we will be rewarded a hundredfold. God will not be outdone in generosity. The only thing that we can really give to God, with the help of his grace, is faith and steadfast loyalty to him. His commandment is that "you love one another as I have loved you" and that includes showing our loyalty to God in our loyalty to one another.

In the whole context of Scripture, Christ did not instruct his hearers to act only in secret. He performed his healings in public; he prayed to his Father in public; he rendered taxes to Caesar in public; thus, others knew of his sacrificial acts.

Obviously, we should not make a great show of everything we do. But even when we are forced to perform in public festive functions we should not act only to be seen. True devotion should be present. If we are to be credible, people must see us practicing what we preach. Such witness can do much good. The Pharisees unfortunately were parading their good works before the people in order to be seen.

THURSDAY

2 Corinthians 11: 1-11; Matthew 6: 7-15 **YEAR I**

In today's reading, Paul defends his motives and actions. He is concerned about the Corinthians because they are so passive, gullible, and willing to accept almost any kind of teaching. This disposition may have been a help to him, when he first preached the gospel to them; he admits that he is a poor speaker but he takes a back seat to no one in the knowledge of God's revelation. The revelation of Christ is definitive; it replaces all other supposedly divine messages; there will never be another to supersede this one. Therefore, the Corinthians must hold fast to Paul's teaching as a bride to one husband.

There is no guarantee that the truth of God is going to prevail in the minds of men. Logically it should. But faith is a gift and men are not always logical in what they do. Carelessness in taking faith for granted can easily result in loss of faith. The Corinthians must be discerning; not every claim is equally true. They must accept the good and reject the bad. In his preaching, Paul emphasizes that he is expecting no material gain. There is nothing in it for him materially speaking whether they believe or disbelieve the gospel message. Rather than ask the Corinthians for support, he depends upon the Macedonians. We know from other citations that he worked also, as a tent-maker. He wonders rhetorically, as we do at times, whether people really appreciate something that is free of charge. In the long run, however, his credibility is gaining because he is not using religion as a source of income.

In today's gospel narrative, Jesus gives instruction on praying, using the "Our Father" as a model. In this familiar prayer, Jesus makes very clear that each of us is to strive to be perfect as the heavenly Father is perfect, but since all of us fall short of that goal, we should at least never judge our neighbor. Instead we should judge ourselves and in so doing find fault enough. With regard to our neighbor we should forgive him seventy times seven times and that means without ceasing. All too often, in prayer, we try to tell God what is good for us. He knows our needs far better than we and the ultimate measure of goodness is God's own will. The prayer of faith consists not only in saying "Lord, Lord," but in disposing our hearts to do the will of the Father. Jesus calls his disciples to bring into their prayer this concern for cooperating with the divine plan.

Sirach 48: 1-14; Matthew 6: 7-15 **YEAR II**

Through the power of God, Elijah did marvelous things in his life. He had fear of no one. Even in death he had great influence upon others. This is the life that is open to all those who fear God, who have faith in him, who love him and have hope in his promises.

The test of a good life is a good death. Whether people are joyful or sorrowful matters not. But if the person dies with equanimity, others have much to learn from that person's life. Peace of soul comes only from the theological virtues.

Although the "Our Father" contains all the forms of prayer—adoration, thanksgiving, reparation, petition—it is clear that adoration is the most important because the Father already knows what we need. We must pray to be accepting of God's will in our life and faithful in carrying it out. This may require much courage at times, but what is required at all times in every life is to fulfill the Lord's commandment to love others as he has loved us. This demands not only justice and charity on our part but forgiveness. Indeed, forgiveness would seem to be the most characteristic attribute of God and one that is most difficult for man. It includes but goes far beyond love.

So our prayer should not require many words; only the constant plea, "Help us to be God-like." Our Father help us to raise our minds and hearts to you, keep us conscious of your presence. Let us love and seek you above all people and things of this world. You, as God, must have your way—that is what it means to be God—so make us submissive to your will which is not only justice on our part but the greatest wisdom, as well. You know far better than we, what is for our good. We do need the necessities if we are to be able to carry out your will with the greatest effectiveness but even this is not nearly so important as loving our neighbor and giving good example. The person who is hungry, homeless and clothed in rags can still be fully accepting of God's will and forgiving towards those who may have caused or continue to cause oppression. Back to the beginning again, help us to be ever conscious of your presence in our lives, our need to give priority to you and your will rather than to the people and things of this world.

Friday

2 Corinthians 11: 18, 21-30; Matthew 6: 19-23 **YEAR I**

In today's reading, Paul compares to his own the efforts for Christ by false apostles. Apparently St. Paul was being "put down" by those who might have been better orators and more attractive to the people in many ways but who, in fact, were betraying the truth of Christ. Do we not have this in our own day, when those who are adept with the media are able to get their message across so effectively. Unfortunately the message is often defective. Paul realizes that the Corinthians are impressed with the work of the false apostles. With frankness and emotion, and to defend himself, Paul tells what he has suffered and done for Christ. In opposing these people, Paul could only cite the truth, namely the sufferings that he had endured both from Jew and Gentile because of his faithful adherence to the revelation of Christ. He was not about to concede anything with regard to that message which does constitute a whole. It is a "seamless garment"; if we concede in one area, it is amazing how quickly this dangling thread can be pulled unraveling the whole quilt of revelation. This is especially true with regard to sexual morality today; HUMANAE VITAE prophesied as much. Surrender on modesty leads to surrender on chastity, the contraceptive mentality, abortion, and divorce. All of these are interconnected. The goal of those weak in morality, who find justification for their immoral approach, even claiming that it is virtuous, is to store up for themselves earthly pleasure. They do not intend to forego heavenly pleasure while satisfying their immoral appetite but they cannot have both. "Where our treasure is, there will our heart be also."

Matthew, in today's gospel, compares the choice between good and evil to a person without sight. Sight brightens up a person's entire life, gives rise to imagination, "three dimensional" thought, and feelings that can have an effect on the body itself. Just as many spiritual and physical faculties of man are impaired when he loses his sight, so when moral sensibility becomes dulled, moral darkness follows and the spiritual senses become insensitive to evil.

2 Kings 11: 1-4, 9-18, 20; Matthew 6: 19-23 YEAR II

There are many similarities in the story of Jehoiada with the stories of Moses and Christ. There is a slaughter of innocents and one is saved; the rescuer is a woman; there is a hidden life and then the revelation of his identity; his enemies are overcome; and he is hailed by the crowds.

In a sense this could be the story of anyone of us with only a few details changed. We are brought into the world by a woman; many "sacrifice" themselves on our behalf. All of us are hidden from the public eye until we hit the newspapers for something—whether good or evil—or until we are at least recognized by our family and friends as a person, independent of others; and who can stand on his own two feet. God willing, others will be pleased by who we are and what we do.

Automatically a covenant is sealed between God and ourselves, when life is given; and between ourselves and others, as they enter into our lives. Our covenant requires that we love God with our whole mind, heart, and soul, and our neighbor as ourselves. If that is what we do, we too shall enjoy the spirit of peace and joy, which prevailed after the death of Athaliah.

Athaliah wished to heap up earthly treasures and lost everything. Jehoiada and his followers were content with a reign of justice, love and peace regardless of what power and money they might possess in the world. We will always have enough; if we live with limited expectations. It is our unsatisfied hopes and desires that cause unhappiness more than anything else. If we have treasure, that is where our heart will be. If we have poverty, our heart—all our love and trust—will be in God. Christ compares the desire of our hearts to good or bad ideas. If the eyes are constantly on the lookout for that which appeals to pleasure rather than for wholesome joy, one's whole being will be pleasure-oriented. Keep control of the senses, if you wish to have a sound and joy-filled life.

Saturday

2 Corinthians 12: 1-10; Matthew 6: 24-34 **YEAR I**

In today's reading, Paul continues to "boast" in an effort to defend his integrity. He could boast of his achievements, as he did to some extent in yesterday's segment, and it would be the truth, but what he "boasts" about is what God has done in him, and through him, and for him. He has come to realize that the statement "In weakness, power reaches perfection" leads to other statements such as "I must decrease so that he may increase" and "I live now, not I, but Christ lives in me." When that happens, the person becomes truly powerful. It is like a new incarnation; through the power of the Holy Spirit, the person becomes like unto God. This happens to very few because we are reluctant to die to self totally. However, if Christ lives in us, the Spirit of God will be active in us and speak through us. And when that happens, whether we are rejected by the vociferous and physically powerful few, our words and example will have tremendous effect on the "silent majority" for years to come, as was the case with the apostles.

Today's gospel develops even further the idea of dying to self, letting go of the world and all that brings worldly success, in order to serve the Lord. It looks like a foolish move and, in a worldly sense, it is. Don't expect the admiration of the world, or freedom from suffering, or consolation—none of these are likely. Faith in God, hope in his promises, love of neighbor for love of God are the theological virtues that hold us on course, support us in our choice, and enable us to accept whatever comes our way. In beautiful words Jesus tells us not to worry about this passing life, but to put God and personal holiness first in our scale of values. Jesus says, "Look at the lilies of the field, the birds of the air; they do not make provision for the future on earth but the Lord takes care of them." Birds and flowers have a comparatively short life on earth, regardless of their beauty. We should learn a lesson from this, too. No matter how attractive we may be as people, no matter what we may accomplish, before we know it, life is all over. And then, what do we have to show for it? It is not wise to play up to others and seek their esteem. We should "play up" to God and seek his esteem.

2 Chronicles 24: 17-25; Matthew 6: 24-34 **YEAR II**

Every person must conscientiously reflect upon life and the various modes of conduct that are presented for living it. We must make the wisest choice we can and follow it with conviction. All too often human beings work themselves into a very unhappy state by failing to stand back every once in a while to make this assessment. Failing to do so, they adopt the values of those around them; they use as a criterion that which gives the most pleasure; they find that the values of pleasure are many times contradictory to one another and, above all, constantly changing. Such false values are bound to cause difficulty. Settling the difficulty on the basis of "the pleasure principle" compounds the problem; this leads to confusion, which finally compels a person to straighten out or give up; live in contradiction or in a life style that one knows is not healthy.

This is what happened to young Joash. After Jehoiada's death, he did not stand on his own two feet. Instead, he weakly allowed himself to follow the values of those around him. These men were not interested in Joash; they were interested in their own pleasure and power. When Zachariah, Jehoiada's son, called Joash to his senses, Joash was at the crisis point. He refused to think things through; Zachariah made him realize the contradiction of his life; but refusing to think and to accept God's revelation, the only way that Joash could find to eliminate the contradiction was to kill Zachariah. The opening verses of the gospel make it clear. "No man can serve two masters . . . you cannot give yourself to God and money." We must make a choice.

In the remainder of the gospel Christ offers a persuasive argument for pursuing things divine rather than things earthly. Notice that God takes care of all that he has created in nature. We are of much more value than plants, birds, and animals. Therefore, we can be assured that God will protect "his own," those who follow his will, even though like everything else in creation we will have our ups and downs, too.

On the other hand, notice what happens to those who do not rely upon God but upon earthly possessions. For example, the man who tears down his barns to build new ones, settles back to eat, drink, and be merry, but dies that night. "Thou fool! Don't put your trust in things, which rust and moths consume; the unbelievers are always running after these things." As for you, place your trust in him, who is Lord of all creation. "Seek first his kingship over you, his way of holiness, and all these things will be given you besides." In beautiful words Jesus tells us not to worry about this passing life, but to put God and personal holiness first in our scale of values.

Twelfth Week of Ordinary Time

Monday

Genesis 12: 1-9; Matthew 7: 1-5 **YEAR I**

Today's reading is from Genesis in which Abram's call is dramatically presented. The initiative is Yahweh's, not Abram's. The first requirement of the call is complete dissociation from the pagan past and the second is migration to a land of God's choice for which the reward is divine blessing affecting Abram himself and his descendants. Abram's response is factual, not verbal. "Abram went as the Lord directed him." Regardless of what one may think of the history of the Jewish people, certainly God has kept the promises that he made to Abraham. They will be a great nation; well known in the world; many nations in many ways have been blessed because of their presence. Even so, the faith of Abraham was extraordinary. He could not know the future. And as he set out for Canaan, he was 75 years old; he didn't even have a child of his own; and although he had some slaves, these and his possessions seem to have been comparatively few. Still, Abraham went faithfully wherever he was directed, built altars in various places, and offered sacrifice to God.

The gospel narrative is a continuation of the fundamental Sermon on the Mount and it is of utmost importance. If we wish to avoid a negative judgment from God, we should not judge other people regardless of what faults they seem to have. We should be like Abraham, simply listening for God's voice and ever ready to follow his judgment. Our harsh judgments will be punished severely, but not unfairly. Acute observance of the faults of others combined with complacency with one's own character is the attitude of hypocrites. If we used only a fraction of the time we spend dissecting the faults of others to search for our own faults, we would be embarrassed to criticize others. The very least we can do is to examine our conscience daily, by reviewing the day to discover what we may have done wrong or imperfectly.

2 Kings 17: 5-8, 13-15, 18; Matthew 7: 1-5 **YEAR II**

Even in non-Christian civilizations, the whole history of mankind indicates that a nation, a religion, a group of any kind remains strong only as long as it adheres to its basic principles and retains the personal and group discipline that this requires. To keep up with the times, legitimate development is needed but this happens gradually. The society runs out of control, when the seven capital sins, or some combination of them, take over. A healthy society is one in which principle, sacrifice, hard work, moderation, self-discipline, authority, unity, prevail. When others use their money, might, and power to flaunt these and an unbridled freedom develops, the society goes headlong into destruction like the swine that rushed over the cliff, after Christ drove them out of those who were possessed.

In today's reading it is clear that the people had rejected the authority of God made known to them by their fathers and the prophets. They were led astray by their own greed, by their moral weakness, by what seemed to be an easier way of life and one which in effect was dictated by their own human cravings. The Scripture author looks upon the exile of the Chosen People as a punishment from God, and indeed it was. Even human wisdom and the personal discipline required to follow it would have shown the people how to save themselves.

It seems obvious that our country is headed in the same direction and only the discipline of self-sacrifice and self-control can save us. Competition for money and power in the world have led us to offer the human sacrifice of the Third World; and we seem to have given up the Judeo-Christian principles of morality for a materialistic-relativistic-hedonistic philosophy that is without principle.

Although it is easy enough to make the above judgments, we are not so quick to recognize that we have been carried along by the tide to a great extent. We are less faithful to principle, less faithful to religious observance, less thoughtful of the poor, less inclined to self-sacrifice and hard work, and resentful of authority.

TUESDAY

Genesis 13: 2, 5-18; Matthew 7: 6, 12-14 **YEAR I**

Today's reading illustrates the absurdity of war. Both Abraham and Lot were doing well but still their families were in competition, disputing with one another, possibly over the use of wells. So instead of engaging in an all out battle, Abraham suggests to his nephew that they separate and Lot acquiesces. Abraham, relying upon the goodness of God, gives Lot the first choice of land. Lot takes that which looks best to him, a fertile plain, but God blesses Abraham as well. Perhaps not all arguments can be settled to such mutual satisfaction, but even if they are not, is it not better to live in peace and contentment among one's fellows rather than to be mutually destructive?

The same point is made in today's gospel narrative. We are to treat others as we would have them treat us. The gate to the road leading to eternal salvation is narrow; the road itself is rough; and it has few travelers; but it is the only way to achieve the goal. If we want to accept God's will, we are sure to encounter difficulties and be tempted to think that the way we have chosen is foolish. We shall also find the way lonely because many friends, even family will leave us to pass through the broad gate, the one leading to perdition where many are entering. We need to have the courage of our convictions. We should try to persuade others to follow the road to life without assuming that we can win them over by forsaking our principles, which would be akin to giving what is holy to dogs or tossing pearls before swine. If we act thus, our would-be friends will look down upon us and cease appreciating our beliefs. When we sacrifice our principles in order to appease the unprincipled, we are no longer of help to them, and furthermore, we can very easily lose our own principles, too.

2 Kings 19: 9-11, 14-21, 31-36; Matthew 7: 6, 12-14 **YEAR II**

It is much easier to speak of faith than it is to put it into practice. With enemies all around, the tendency is to search for compromise rather than to stand in defense of God's truth. This is the meaning of temptation. It can exist in government circles; families seem to have been oppressed in the same way the past many years. Strangely, the last thing that we seem ready to do is turn to the Lord for help. And yet the God of goodness and truth wills that we be holy, that we adhere to his teachings, and he stands ready to help us do so.

That which is missing is prayer. But prayer will not do any good if we expect God to work some kind of miracle. We need to pray for the courage to accept God's truth and to act upon it with conviction. We are God's agents; he will act in and through us, but he will not take our place. We must fight our own battles—with his help, of course, and not presume that he will do everything for us. The cooperation of our own free will is essential.

God gives us what is holy and so often we show about as much appreciation as dogs and swine. That may be an exaggeration but there is much truth in it, as well. We do not usually treat the sacred in a diabolical way, but surely we are careless and lacking in appreciation for what is done for us.

God is faithful; he responds to every prayer. He loves us more than we can possibly love ourselves, and he understands us better than we do, too. So surely he will respond to our needs, keeping in mind that he knows our true needs better than we do. Just as a father will not give something dangerous to a child when the child asks for it, God will not give us what will be detrimental in the long run. Although we may be disappointed initially, we will eventually see his goodness.

And we should treat others in the same manner. Our primary attitude should be one of goodness and love, but our first allegiance is to God. As a result, our first obligation is to do that which God wills, and therefore, that which is for the ultimate good of the person. If we can foresee that granting a request will be ultimately destructive, we should not grant the request. But so often we do grant it—especially in family circles because we can't be bothered to take the longer route of explaining and expressing our love in other ways.

Verse 12 asks us to do unto others as we would have them do unto us. We should preface that with the principle that we should do unto others as God does unto us, the idea being that we would want others to act toward us in the same way, as God acts toward us. All three should be the same!

We need to follow the will of God much more rigidly than we usually do. The options open to a person on a human level are many and can be compared to the wide gate that leads to damnation. However, some of those options are sinful and comparatively few are according to God's will. Indeed, since truth is one, only one of those options is ideal in keeping with God's will. We need to be more careful in our examination of options in life and in the choices we make.

WEDNESDAY

Genesis 15: 1-12, 17-18; Matthew 7: 15-20 **YEAR I**

In today's reading, Abraham complains to God that he still has no offspring. The Lord, having already told Abraham that his descendants would be as numerous as the dust of the earth, points now to the stars to indicate how great his progeny will be. Abraham, rather than arguing the point as we might do, accepts God's promise in faith. And for this the Lord makes a solemn pledge to Abraham that he and his descendants will have the "Promised Land," from Egypt to the Euphrates River. Centuries later it is possible for us to see that Abraham certainly was listening to a true "prophet" and he became one himself. "By their fruits you will know them." God has been faithful to his promises and Abraham has been a true father to his people.

Today's gospel narrative supports Abraham's faith in God's word. Jesus warns his disciples against false teachers of religion. Their deceptive teaching is shown by the results of their doctrine—results very different from those of the Messianic message of Jesus. The true test of prophets or disciples is their life. The words, the actions, the fulfilled promises of God demand a firm act of faith that he exists, that he loves us, that he will do for us what he did for Abraham. They also demand of us a firm commitment to put into practice God's teaching, that is, his commandments and his whole way of life as revealed to us through Abraham and the prophets. We need to believe and to act with the trust that Abraham had.

2 Kings 22: 8-13, 23: 1-3; Matthew 7: 15-20 **YEAR II**

The Lord does not look for vengeance but repentance. It does not matter how long it takes, if eventually the people accept their Lord and vow to live according to his commandments.

It is in keeping with the human condition that from time to time the book of the Law is going to be "lost," as it were. The Holy Father makes clear that he is striving to renew the covenant of the Old and New Law. The question that remains is whether or not we are going to join him as the people of Judah joined the king.

In recent years, the flock of Christ has been decimated, scattered, and confused by false prophets. It is always going to be the case that falsehood and error will be presented to us as something good and true. If that were not the case, we would reject the falsehood immediately. Our minds and hearts are made for truth and goodness; they can accept nothing else.

But we have a means of testing whether or not the prophet is to be accepted. Jesus tells us that by their fruits you will know them. It is as easy to recognize a false prophet as it is to spot a rotten tree. By their fruits you will know them. Christ does not launch into a list of these fruits, but St. Paul does in his epistle to the Galatians and elsewhere. They are charity, joy, peace, patience, et cetera (Gal 5: 22-23).

In the full list of the twelve fruits of the Holy Spirit, it is interesting to note that twenty-five percent of them have to do with purity. It is obvious, therefore, that those advocating sexual permissiveness are false prophets. Although many people who are misleading us today have an approach that seems kind and gracious and appears to promise joy, what they advocate provides pleasure instead of joy. This leads to violence against oneself by the use of drugs and violence against others through various crimes with money as the object.

THURSDAY

Genesis 16: 1-12, 15-16; Matthew 7: 21-29 **YEAR I**

Today's first reading brings us back to the times of polygamy. Surely Sarah did not have Abraham's faith. Invoking the Mesopotamian custom that the maid's offspring would be considered the legal wife's child, Sarah, despairing of ever having children, gives her maid Hagar to Abraham. Because of Hagar's later contempt, Sarah oppresses her. Of the three principals, Hagar was probably the least responsible for her pregnancy. It is a pitfall of human nature to blame our errors on other people! Sarah is jealous and as a result abuses Hagar. It is a reminder of the story that Christ told of a person concerned about the speck in a neighbor's eye, while ignoring a whole beam of wood in his own!

God's goodness to all is made clear. Even though Abraham was his specially chosen, he still came to the aid of innocent Hagar. Like his own Son later, however, God insisted that Hagar submit to temporary abuse so that she might reap a greater reward. This is not always God's way, but it happens in so many cases that it seems to be the "preferred" way. God reveals himself to us in the various human relationships and events in our lives—in friendships and love, as well as, tragedies and joys. All these are vehicles of his personal will for us. Surely we cannot complain. It is an honor and privilege to follow in the footsteps of Christ; we should simply pray for the courage to accept that grace.

Today's gospel narrative is the conclusion of the Sermon on the Mount. Jesus tells us to build our house of faith solidly so as to be prepared for whatever problems life will bring. He makes clear that the key to salvation is obedience to God's will. Christian faith is not an easy answer to life's hard times, but it is a strengthener and a fortifier, a light and motivation with which to face life's problems. Accepting God's will frequently places us in opposition to our fellow men and, regardless of our innocence, others will turn on us as Sarah turned on Hagar. If Christ could face death and make it of redeeming significance, it is possible, through difficulties, for us to realize that no tragedy is without some meaning, even though we may never know what it is.

2 Kings 24: 8-17; Matthew 7: 21-29 **YEAR II**

The book of Kings speaks of the capture of Jerusalem by Nebuchadnezzar and the beginning of the Babylonian Captivity, known as the Exile. It all came about because the king and his forbears had done evil. Only the poor were left in Jerusalem. The sick and the powerful were taken prisoners and brought to Babylon.

In the gospel Jesus indicates that the same thing will happen to individuals and groups unless we put his words into practice. Wishful thinking is not enough; there must be action, as well.

Of course, no one ever does succeed in building a perfectly solid foundation for his "house of faith." It always needs to be strengthened in one way or another and the best way of doing so is through good works. Faith and good works feed one another; they have a spiraling effect. As one's faith increases, good works should increase; as good works increase, faith should increase. Although God may test a person in "the dark night of the soul," this would be the usual process.

And in order to do good works, we must deny ourselves. Good works, as opposed to wishful thinking, require that we give up our time, energy, talent, money or whatever and use them for the benefit of others. Wishful thinkers may even do rather outstanding things, which may even be signs of holiness to some, but the applause that they receive in this world is their reward rather than eternal life.

When all is said and done, the test is perseverance—perseverance in faith and good works, both in difficult times and over the long haul. Can we accept a harsh blow in life and continue to love God? Can we accept betrayal by others and continue to love our neighbor? Even without these negative factors, can we keep building our faith with good works and not grow tired? Perseverance in faith, hope, and love is the ultimate standard, which never allows us to rest on our laurels because it demands that we continue to the very end.

FRIDAY

Genesis 17: 1, 9-10, 15-22; Matthew 8: 1-4 **YEAR I**

Abraham had been faithful to God's promise for many, many years but when he reached 100 and Sarah 90, he was no longer hopeful that he would have a son, so he simply prayed that the Lord would bless Ishmael, the son of Hagar. The Lord did that, but still insisted that Abraham was to have a child by Sarah because the covenant between God and his people was to be passed on by a legitimate rather than an illegitimate heir. The sign of the covenant between God and his people was to be the circumcision of every male child. This covenant imposed the obligation of a religious relationship with God. Circumcision was to be a sign like the rainbow after the flood. This sign was to remind God of his covenant and human beings of their obligations as the Chosen People.

Today's gospel narrative illustrates the faith that Abraham was called to demonstrate in the long years of waiting and searching for the Lord's promises. The faith of the leper is an example of that living faith. "Lord, if you will to do so, you can make me clean." Whatever God wills is as good as done and no circumstance can contravene that will, whether it be the age of Abraham and Sarah or the dreaded disease of the leper. God can do what he wills. So there is never a problem in asking the Lord even for what may be extraordinary as long as we keep in mind that his thoughts are not always the same as our thoughts. And we must always be ready to accept God's way of doing things. This is not easy; this is humility overcoming pride; it is to decrease so that the Lord's control of our lives may increase. Since faith demands the sacrifice of the whole person, mind and heart, it is not an easy act of humility to perform, and many decline the offer to believe.

2 Kings 25: 1-12; Matthew: 1-4 **YEAR II**

Ten years later Nebuchadnazzar besieged Jerusalem again. After a year and a half the Israelites finally gave in and tried to flee the city, but they were apprehended. The king was taken captive to Babylon; his sons were killed before his eyes; the whole city was burned to the ground and the wall of the city torn down. The people, along with King Zedekiah, were led into captivity, but once again the poor were left behind as farmers and vine-dressers.

Jesus shows that he possesses the kind of power that could keep the Israelites from continuing to suffer humiliation at the hands of the Romans. Now the people were not exiled but their country was occupied and being used by a foreign power. Crowds were following Jesus because they had heard of his marvels and they wanted more for themselves and their country. But Jesus was more inclined to give an example of prayer and religious observance. His kingdom was not of this world. If only the people would realize this—if only the people had realized this through the centuries, the Lord would have protected them in accordance with the Covenant; they would have had the best of both worlds, spiritual and material.

SATURDAY

Genesis 18: 1-15; Matthew 8: 5-17 **YEAR I**

In today's reading, the promise is repeated that, even though Sarah seems sterile, she will bear a child. Sarah laughs upon hearing the promise while Abraham offers hospitality to the messengers of the Lord one of whom says to Abraham that he will surely return to him about the same time in a year and that by then Sarah will have a son.

In the gospel narrative, we notice how ready Jesus is to serve those who come to him in faith. As Abraham waited on the Lord's messengers, so Jesus is ready to do whatever he can for the centurion. The centurion also has a great deal of humility, expressed in another way. He recognizes that even as there is a hierarchy in human organizations such as the army, so it is even more logical that there should be a similar arrangement between God and his creatures. If the centurion could tell his men what to do and how to do it, surely God could direct his creatures in a similar fashion. The theme of the story is faith—the kind of faith that sets no conditions. The choice of a Gentile to illustrate this faith gives a strong message. The faith of the Gentiles entitles them to the title of the true Israel that the Jews are forfeiting by their unbelief in the Messiah. The conclusion is the declaration of Jesus that being a member of the Chosen People is not sufficient in itself for salvation. From now on, entrance into God's kingdom will depend upon faith, acceptance of God's authority, willingness to humble oneself before God. Once more, after the centurion departs, Jesus takes up the servant role. He cures Peter's mother-in-law and then, even after a long day, he ministers to the crowds of people who come to the door. God's work is not determined by office hours but by love for others in their time of need. One cannot be faint of heart on the faith journey. One has to be passionate; the lukewarm never make it. There is need of soul and muscle strength to keep getting up and starting again when the plaguing doubts hit.

Lamentations 2: 2, 10-14, 18-19; Matthew 8: 5-17 **YEAR II**

Lamentations summarizes the desolation of all Israel and Jerusalem in particular, after it fell to Nebuchadnezzar. Old men, women, and children are left destitute, mourning their fate.

When they ask what happened, the answer is clear. Israel was the victim of false prophets, who "did not lay bare your guilt." "They beheld for you in vision false and misleading portents." The only thing that could have saved Israel was a recognition of their sinful ways and a plea to the Lord for forgiveness, but it was not forthcoming.

Is not our own country in much the same situation today? We are encompassed on every side by sinful practices but good people don't want to admit it, they turn their eyes from it, and try to lead a virtuous life despite the evil. Their children are engulfed by sin. At the same time even some theologians are temerarious enough to justify the situation and hold that sin is not sin, for example, the practice of homosexuality. They use conscience and the changing times to justify their "false prophecies." As times change, they say, so our moral values should change. If one's conscience permits an action, it matters not what God has revealed through Christ and his Church concerning that action.

The Lord should not need to strike the Israelites nor ourselves with some catastrophe before we convert ourselves. A word from him should be sufficient for us as it was for the centurion's servant. Why? If we believe in God, if we accept who he is and who we are, we should jump when he so much as speaks a word. And he has spoken that word through so many and especially through Christ. Should we not obey as readily as the centurion's soldiers? And if we did, would we not be touched by the healing power of Christ? How is it that some non-Catholics, even pagans like the centurion, respond more readily to God's actual grace than we do?

Try as we will to convert ourselves and our Catholic people, there is something about our baptism that makes us think that we have been saved. In a sense we have been saved, of course, for Christ has died for us, but that is never completely effective until we have persevered for a lifetime in obedience to his will. "The natural heirs of the kingdom" may indeed discover on Judgment Day that the heavenly reward we could have had so easily has been given to others whom, in our eyes but not in God's, we considered to be far less deserving. "There will be weeping and gnashing of teeth."

Thirteenth Week of Ordinary Time

MONDAY

Genesis 18: 16-33; Matthew 8: 18-22 **YEAR I**

In the last reading, one of the three men who visited Abraham was the Lord God, himself. The original goal of the three visitors was to visit Sodom, Lot's city, and Gomorra to ascertain the punishment that those towns deserved although their fate was already sealed. The Lord wondered whether he should tell Abraham what he was about to do, especially in light of the promise to Abraham that he would have a great posterity. The Lord revealed his plan to Abraham and the goodness of Abraham became clear in the way that he asked the Lord to have mercy on a sinful people. Rather than be disturbed by Abraham's audacity, the Lord was undoubtedly pleased that Abraham had a merciful heart. Abraham pleaded for the life of the just within the towns, and the Lord listened patiently and heeded Abraham's prayer. The extremes of divine mercy were emphasized in the Lord's willingness to spare Sodom for the sake of ten just inhabitants.

Still, Sodom was destroyed. What is implied in the conversation is the universality of sin. Some may appear to be more sinful than others, but if we live in a sinful society, all of us are conspirators in some way, at least in our passivity and tolerance of evil. Elsewhere in Scripture the Lord makes clear that not only those who do evil, but those who stand by and tolerate it, are also deserving of punishment. This is collective responsibility that requires collective punishment. Rarely are there innocent people among the guilty. Either the innocent "shake the dust of the place from their sandals" and go off, or they are eliminated by the guilty just as Christ was.

The gospel narrative spells out the cost of discipleship. There are many people of good will who are convinced of the need for justice, but they lack decisiveness in carrying out their convictions. Jesus addresses the question. Those who cannot bring themselves to sacrifice all selfish desires for the Lord cannot be his disciples. The scribe who wants to be with Jesus learns from him that those who follow him must be prepared to have no home, as he has none. The Lord wants our whole mind, heart, and soul. Renunciation of family ties is also one of the conditions of discipleship; one cannot wait until all family connections are satisfied before being able to follow the call. The time is now.

Amos 2: 6-10, 13-16; Matthew 8: 18-22 **YEAR II**

Even though God in his providence has looked most favorably upon the Israelites, he convicts them for mistreating the poor and the handicapped and for involving themselves in heinous sexual acts and in idolatry. To give witness to his eternal truth, the Lord had sent them prophets but the people ignored them. Again, God is not given to vengeance but if the divine plan is flaunted—if we violate the laws of nature, justice, and charity—it stands to reason that nature and those who have suffered will eventually turn against us. This may be attributed to God in the sense that he is the one who has established the laws. Human strength, wisdom, possessions are of no avail, when the forces of nature or the justified anger of the oppressed are released.

Jesus stands in stark contrast to the people of Amos' generation. He identifies with the poor, the handicapped, and the outcasts of society. He makes himself one with them. And if we wish to be his companions, we must do the same with an unconditional commitment. We must make a choice between God and Mammon; we cannot be lukewarm—we must be for or against him. That is the cost of discipleship. Everything and everyone must be held in second place if we mean to follow Christ.

Tuesday

Genesis 19: 15-29; Matthew 8: 23-27 **YEAR I**

Lot is saved from Sodom as a favor to Abraham. Lot does not wish to leave; the occupants of Sodom are his relatives, friends, and neighbors. He knows their sinfulness but even though they are beyond redemption, he hesitates to leave them. The angels literally pull away Lot and his family and they are saved because God "remembered Abraham." Although we should love the sinner, we must also guard against the occasions of sin. Normally, we cannot live in a sinful atmosphere without being infected by sin. Unless we are exceedingly strong, we are more likely to be swallowed up by the culture than to convert it. Proof of this is the general lowering of moral standards everywhere in our world today by virtually everyone, especially in our own country.

In the gospel narrative, the calming of the storm by Christ while in the boat with his apostles could serve as an illustration of the above. He demonstrated his power over nature causing the disciples to wonder about the mystery of his person. Surely the apostles were no competition for the world around them. How quickly they caved in on Good Friday and they continued in fear until Christ had returned to them on several occasions. The culture around us is like the raging sea and the unfriendly sky. It surrounds us, terrifies us, and yet fascinates us with its pyrotechnic violence. The only hope against the storm of life is to stay together and work cooperatively with all our strength coupled with divine intervention. The same is true of the world's immorality. We need a community of opposition to exert extraordinary effort against it, and divine intervention, as well.

Amos 3: 1-8, 4: 11-12; Matthew 8: 23-27 **YEAR II**

The Jews are the Chosen People of God, highly favored by him among all peoples. It is inexcusable that they should reject God's will. Over and over again he has sent them warnings but all have fallen upon deaf ears. He has even permitted them to be afflicted with evils of various kinds and still they have not returned to him.

In such circumstances as these, "Who can but prophecy?" It is clear that the Lord is speaking. It would seem that any person, even without a prophetic charism, could see what was happening. It does not take a great genius. And yet it does take God's grace not to be blinded by the pleasures of the world; to speak out courageously and to be a sign of contradiction.

The prophet is not one who knows the future as such but one who is thoroughly convinced of God's eternal truth. He speaks for God and tells God's message. Amos the farmer strongly condemns the Israelites for their crimes. He predicts dire consequences, which sooner or later are bound to occur as a result of the laws of nature, if nothing else. In the end, when the prophet is proven correct, it appears that he knew the future. In fact, what he knew and adhered to was nothing more nor less than God's eternal truth, his covenant. Sometimes the prophet does not live long enough to be viewed as a hero, but he always suffers opposition, persecution, isolation.

Like the prophets of old, Jesus was a person of faith. The event of the calming of the storm was indeed a miracle. If it had been the Father's will that the world be served by Christ's drowning, he was ready. Similarly we should be prepared to meet the Lord in all circumstances. Our life is a preparation for the time of death.

God does respond to the person of faith. And it does not matter whether his answer is something that seems good to the person of worldly wisdom. In life or in death we belong to the Lord; his will is always for the best, whether we see the wisdom of his judgments or not.

WEDNESDAY

Genesis 21: 5, 8-20, Matthew 8: 28-34 **YEAR I**

Today's reading from Genesis tells of the birth of Isaac, son of the promise. Sarah continued to be very demanding even after the birth of Isaac. She requested that Hagar and her son Ishmael be sent away. Abraham was greatly distressed especially because ancient law ordinarily forbade the expulsion of a slave wife and her child—and he hesitated. The Lord told Abraham to heed Sarah's request and promised him that Ishmael and Hagar would be blessed even though Ishmael was not the child of the promise. Abraham's faith, God's mercy, and the selfishness of human beings stand out in this episode of salvation history.

As both Sarah and Hagar felt sorry for themselves, even though God had blessed them and was protective of them, so did the people of Gaderene after the Lord delivered two men of their demons. It was a dramatic expulsion! The power of God overcame all other power. The men were so savage that no one dared to walk the road where they were. But rather than be grateful, the people of Gaderene were disturbed that they had lost their swine. Jesus had returned two people to their senses and he had rid the village of a serious problem, but they were concerned that it had cost them something! The greed of human beings is well exemplified in this story.

Amos 5: 14-15, 21-24; Matthew 8: 28-34 **YEAR II**

Religious ceremonial means nothing—in fact, it is an affront to God—unless we are living a moral life. This is precisely the problem that many young people have with the practice of religion today. If we wonder why they do not go to church, one of the strong reasons is the hypocrisy which they see in adults. The very same people who worship God on Sunday, are anti-black or anti-Jewish or unkind to their neighbors, whether in word or in deed. The parents may be guilty of other immoral practices, many of them connected with the accumulation of wealth. They may be able to show their affection for their children only in material ways and never with an emotional commitment of themselves. This is often the atmosphere in our "best homes" today. The children usually don't say much about it because the realization grows on them gradually. Eventually they may voice some objection, but it is usually too late and they may be accused of lacking appreciation for what they have. Rebellious conduct of some kind or other becomes for the children the only alternative.

Through Amos, the Lord tries to get across to his people that justice comes first. It is not for charity but justice that we should love God for all that he has done for us. It is not for charity but justice that we should love our neighbors for all that they have done for us. In our language we understand love and charity to be the same thing. Sometimes the words can be used that way. But it is not for "charity" that we should thank and adore God for his goodness. Neither is it "charity," when we fulfill God's command to love others as he has loved us, as a visible sign that we truly love him.

The gospel is a good and realistic illustration as to how human beings deceive themselves; it brings to light our true priorities. Two demoniacs are causing all kinds of problems; their presence must have been a dreadful thing in the neighborhood, frightening everyone, especially the children. The people begged that the Lord would remove the devils from their midst. He did, but when the episode ended up with a herd of swine being lost, they begged him to leave.

Which was more important to them, their material well being or their spiritual well being? They thought at first that they wanted to have spiritual peace, but when it came to a choice, they were convinced that somehow they could tolerate spiritual evil but they could not possibly get along without their material wealth. It is the same today. We lament all the spiritual evils that surround us, but we are not ready to do anything about ridding ourselves of them, if it requires that we get along with less materially. And yet, from the experience of our earlier years, we know very well that we can be happier with less. If we would follow the Lord's advice by giving to others we could bring great joy into our own lives and into the lives of so many destitute people around the globe.

THURSDAY

Genesis 22: 1-19, Matthew 9: 1-8 **YEAR I**

In today's reading, Abraham's faith is put to a severe test. After so many promises and delays, the child of the promise was born and now Abraham is asked by God to sacrifice him! The sacrifice of Isaac by Abraham foreshadows the sacrifice of the Son of God on Calvary. Although some of the accidentals are similar to the Crucifixion in that Isaac carries wood on his back and he is bound by Abraham, the more important similarities are that Isaac was an only son and Abraham freely offered him. It was strictly a case of obedience because there was no other earthly reason for the sacrificial offering. Abraham was willing to give everything. Paradoxically, this is the life of any holy person. The one who freely and fully sacrifices himself to God is rewarded with all kinds of favors. Greater love than this no man has than to lay down the life of an only son, or his own.

In the gospel narrative we continue to see the great power possessed by Jesus, not only over sickness, nature, and demons, but also over sin. Jesus exhibits a climactic power belonging to God alone. This passage of the gospel can be considered a "controversy story" in which the miracle is the resolution of a controversy. The scribes cannot accept that Jesus forgives sin because that is a divine attribution. The appearance of the paralytic and his faith elicit from Jesus not a cure but a forgiveness of sin—certainly not the expected response. Faith in Jesus is an implicit confession of sin and of repentance. Unless sin is cured there is no genuine remedy for human ills. The forgiveness of sin is the fullness of the saving power; a power that goes beyond the working of miracles.

Simply put, Christ does not cure the paralytic at first. He pronounces that, since the man has had his sins forgiven; he is saved. This is what is important: If a person freely accepts to be bound by God's will, whether through illness or in other ways, he thereby purifies his soul and will be saved. It is only in order that he might convince the onlookers of this latter truth that Jesus cures the paralytic. The people are amazed and impressed by the miracle but they still wonder who Christ is.

Amos 7: 10-17; Matthew 9: 1-8 **YEAR II**

In today's reading, we have information about Amos. As a Judean herdsman he is called by God to preach against evil. He does so vigorously although he is opposed by the king and the priest at Bethel. The complaint is made that the people are not able to bear the words of the prophet Amos. Faced with the truth about ourselves, not many of us are able to bear that burden. But we are not expected to do so. We can rid ourselves of the burden in one of two ways, by reforming our lives or doing away with the prophet by blinding ourselves to the truth. The former alternative is difficult but has a happy, consoling ending. The latter course allows us to continue for a time in our foolhardy course but ends in disaster. Too often human beings choose the latter alternative and turn to God in desperation only at the last moment, when they begin to suffer the dire consequences of their choice.

The true prophet is always a reluctant prophet. It was the case with Amos, Samuel, Jeremiah, and the rest. The prophet is not self-appointed; he does something that he believes himself incapable of doing. However, he is absolutely sure that he is impelled by God to speak his message. The prophet is inspired and strengthened by God's grace and his message ordinarily is not something unusual. Calamity is foretold for failure to do God's will, happiness for fulfilling God's will. But the message is God's will, the content of which for any God-fearing person is quite ordinary. The prophet simply proclaims the eternal truth of God; the grace that he needs is fortitude and perseverance. He does not necessarily know the future. What he needs to do is adhere to God's truth which, because it is everlastingly true, will prevail. Meanwhile the prophet needs strength to accept rejection, abuse, and even persecution.

Even Jesus was a reluctant prophet as seen at Cana and in Gethsemane. Although some maintain that he did not wish to reveal his divine identity too early, it could also have had something to do with the mysterious relationship between humanity and divinity. In any event, he was low key among the people; he did not try to overpower them with his divinity; he evidenced much greater interest in the spiritual realm than in the material domain. We need to keep this in mind, too. At a time when many are proposing themselves as healers, we must keep in mind that human beings are finite, subject to imperfection, sickness, and death. The spiritual healing of the soul is far more important.

FRIDAY

Genesis 23: 1-4, 19, 24: 1-8, 62-67; Matthew 9: 9-13 **YEAR I**

In today's reading we learn of Sarah's death. Abraham buys a piece of land for a burial ground and buries Sarah. This small piece of land, legally acquired, becomes the first installment on the promised land. Without the support of Sarah, Abraham continues to be faithful to God. Still in desperate circumstances from a human point of view with regard to the fulfillment of God's promises, Abraham refuses to have Isaac leave the Promised Land and insists that Isaac be espoused to one of his own. By so doing, he is simply remaining faithful to the Lord's promises. He would not relinquish the Promised Land nor allow his son to marry a pagan. Abraham's faith was rewarded; Rebecca came to Isaac from among Abraham's kinfolks. It is interesting to note that Abraham got along well with the Canaanites. He was able to buy from them a plot of land in Hebron to bury Sarah, which was a sign that he had no intention of leaving soon. One can retain his faith and still be civil and cooperative with those of other faiths.

In the gospel narrative, we read about the call of the apostle Matthew who was employed as a tax collector. The nationalist Jews detested those who collected taxes for the Romans and considered them as sinners and referred to them as Publicans. Thus, the association of Jesus with tax collectors was startling in the eyes of the Pharisees who were opposed to the idea of cooperating "with the enemy" in any way. Tax collectors, from a religious standpoint, were about as popular as lepers, but the Lord chose both—tax collectors and lepers—to make clear that no one was to be excluded from his kingdom except those who willfully declined to enter. Matthew accepted the divine mercy rejected by the Pharisees. He humbly recognized his sinfulness while the Pharisees refused to acknowledge theirs and grew in pride. No one can approach Jesus unless he confesses that he is a sinner. The faith that heals demands repentance. This is food for thought for all of us.

Amos 8: 4-6, 9-12; Matthew 9: 9-13 **YEAR II**

When Amos was preaching, the northern kingdom enjoyed great prosperity and luxury—all obtained through social injustice. The Lord speaks of very harsh penalties for those who oppress the poor. He will not stop to punish the arrogant only, but they will suffer the far greater punishment of being deprived of the Word of God. We know what this brings. We can see it in our own times. It is described graphically in the first chapter of St. Paul's Letter to the Romans. Famine and other sorrows are nothing compared to famine for the Word of God, which brings with it all kinds of tribulation. It is a state in which people have no regard for the dignity, the rights, and the needs of others.

Oppression of the poor is still practiced today in much the same way: inflated prices, false weights and measure, poor quality goods, and so on. In these circumstances the poor are willing to hire themselves out for next to nothing, desperate to obtain some means of supporting themselves and their families. Those who practice this injustice lose sight of God's word and are eventually blinded to it.

St. Matthew is an example of such a person, who has reformed his life. It is both for the oppressed and the sinner that Jesus came into the world. In no way did he come to condemn. He came "to give sight to the blind." It matters not whether a person is poor or rich; we are all sinners. And it is for sinners that Jesus has come. "Repent and believe in the gospel" was his message to rich and poor alike. This is still the message that we need to preach, in order that the "deaf" may hear, the "dumb" speak the praises of God, the "blind" see.

SATURDAY

Genesis 27: 1-5, 15-29; Matthew 9: 14-17 **YEAR I**

In today's reading we learn that Jacob aided by Rebecca, his mother, obtains the blessing of Isaac reserved for Esau, the first born. Both Rebecca and Jacob act deceitfully. It is difficult to understand why the Lord permits deceit to be involved in the transmission of leadership among the Chosen People. The most basic answer is that God is dealing with human beings, and although he could interfere and forbid certain things, he is committed to allowing man to use free will. Also, the deceit by which Jacob receives Esau's blessing makes clear that life is not always fair according to human perception. In the sight of God, "fairness" on this earth is not what is important. What is most significant is a clear conscience in this life and the blessing of God himself on entering the next life.

There is a profound meaning in today's gospel narrative. The disciples of John the Baptist found it hard to believe in Christ because his followers seemed to have everything while doing as they pleased. They, on the other hand, had to live a more penitential life. Christ confirms that life is not fair by human standards. He makes clear that eventually, all are tested by God. It is not ours to worry about others and how they appear to be treated by God. We should simply accept what God, in his all-wise providence, sees fit to give us, bend our wills to accept it, and place our hope in his promises.

Everything has a purpose. And if we try to alter the way God has constituted the world we will not succeed. Certainly we are to try to improve our lot; as God told Adam and Eve, we are to increase, multiply, and subdue the earth. But this does not mean that we should strive to overturn the laws of nature or resist God's will. We are to work harmoniously with the Lord, accepting his will.

Amos 9: 11-15; Matthew 9: 14-17 **YEAR II**

The Lord trusts me. He has given me intelligence and free will, with which I can throw back in his face all the gifts that he has given me. He trusts that I shall want to please him. Over and over again, we need to remind ourselves how much we are like children. How upset parents can be—and justifiably so—when their children are trusted, left on their own, simply asked to live in peace with one another while the parents are away! They have everything that they need and more, and how often they end up fighting with one another and disgracing their parents.

The Lord shows us in today's reading how beautiful the simple things of life can be. If we have enough for food, clothing and shelter; if we have loving friends, if we are content in ourselves, at peace with one another, in union with God, what else could we desire? This is what we have been made for; the perfection of such a state for all eternity in heaven.

And so, as the gospel indicates, why should we complain, whether we have little or much, whether we are in relatively good or bad times, as long as we have enough and even when we don't have enough in the material sense. We must be with the Lord or against him, accept his style of life or not. We cannot have the best of both worlds and enjoy the agreeable things of different philosophies of life. Like water and oil, they just won't mix. We need consistency, we need to be satisfied with what we have, we need to find the lifestyle of the Lord. Granted that we will never identify it completely but we can know aspects of it.

Those who are always looking for something that is better for themselves are doomed to disappointment. What we should be looking for—and it is a lifetime task—is the way of the Lord and be content with it. We should pray for the insight to know what true happiness is and for the humility to accept it and persevere in it regardless of the temptation to seek earthly pleasure. This will not only serve us well, but it will inspire countless unknown people who, witnessing such a life, will receive grace from God to do likewise. God's grace is so subtle that others may not take advantage of it immediately, but they will know that they have been touched for a moment by something extraordinary, something transcendental, something that can completely change their lives for the better.

Fourteenth Week of Ordinary Time

Monday

Genesis 28: 10-22; Matthew 9: 18-26 **YEAR I**

In today's reading, young Jacob starts on a long journey from south Palestine to Mesopotamia to find himself a wife. In central Palestine, Jacob stakes himself a pillow out of a stone and in a dream has a vision of personal dealings with heaven and of God's blessings. At the place where God appeared to Jacob, he set up an abode for God. From the exchange between God and Jacob, two considerations become clear: 1) Church buildings are the symbol of God's presence, and 2) Where God is, there we should want to remain.

If the Jews felt compelled to build a temple for the tabernacle of the Law and shrines where God had appeared, how much more compelling is it for Catholics to build churches where the real presence of Christ dwells among us in the Eucharist? For the very same reason, the church or the shrine is embellished. True, we should not exaggerate this at the expense of the poor, but neither should we minimize this need. Is that not the reason why so many churches are built on hills, set apart by lawns, have tall spires—so that the symbol of God's presence becomes visible for great distances? Where God is, there we should wish to remain as Jacob did. How many older people want one thing above all—to live near a church! This is the principal attraction of homes for the elderly and high-rise housing downtown. How many families, when moving to a new community, are interested in being within walking distance of a church! And how anxious should we be to assist at daily Mass and to make visits to the Blessed Sacrament in a nearby church. With the psalmist we can repeat: "In you, my God, I place my trust" because you (God) will be with me in distress.

In the gospel narrative, we read of a miracle within a miracle. A woman is cured while Jesus is on the way to assist the daughter of Jairus. Where Jesus is, there is healing. The people invited him to be with them. Those who were more timid simply wished to be where they could see him or hear him; the more desperate among the timid merely wished to touch his cloak. But the Word of Jesus touched every one in some way. The physical healings were only signs of what was transpiring within his hearers. We need the faith to know that to be near Jesus is to be healed.

Hosea 2: 16-18, 21-22; Matthew 9: 18-26 **YEAR II**

Moses was the first prophet and for some three centuries (eighth to sixth B.C.) there were prophets whose teachings were collated by their disciples. The prophet who came after Moses was Hosea. In today's reading, God speaks through the prophet Hosea in metaphorical terms telling the Israelites that the way back to him is through a desert experience. In order to be converted a person must turn his back on the world; only then can he meditate fruitfully on God and his way of life and become one with him. The important virtues that we must prize are justice, love, mercy, and fidelity. We note that these virtues are characteristic of God's dealing with man and, in order that man may grow in God's image and likeness, man must practice these virtues on behalf of his fellow man. We must act as God acts. And we cannot even begin to do so unless we treat other people justly. Not only are we called to give others what is due to them, we are expected to be merciful. We are to do all this out of love for God and do it perseveringly, with fidelity.

In the gospel there is not much evidence of the practice of justice except that the reading starts off by telling us that Jesus was doing what his Father sent him to do. He was teaching the people what the Father wanted them to know. It is only just that God should not simply create us and then leave us on our own. We must have instruction. Of course, God had satisfied justice by inscribing his law upon our hearts and by commissioning many others to teach us. But when he sent his Son, he was still endeavoring to get across his basic message, which man somehow had yet to understand.

In his dealings then with the young girl and the older woman, the mercy and love of Jesus are most evident. Health is not necessary to salvation, nor are children necessary to parents, but to show his love and concern, Jesus went well beyond justice, restoring the older women's health and bringing the young girl back to life. The whole context of the gospels makes clear that Jesus practiced justice, mercy, and love with persevering fidelity. We are called upon to do the same.

Tuesday

Genesis 32: 23-33; Matthew 9: 32-38 **YEAR I**

Again in today's reading Jacob, who is on his way back to Palestine, has another experience where he wrestles with a strange man. It is a mysterious episode that converts Jacob to spiritual values. The strange person tells Jacob that henceforth he will be known as Israel because he has contended with divine and human beings and has prevailed. Jacob clings to this manifestation of God despite every difficulty. We should do the same.

In the gospel narrative, we read of the opposition of the Pharisees to Christ. He performs a dramatic miracle when he cures a possessed mute boy. For this the Pharisees accuse him of being in league with the devil. He perseveres, however, in curing every sickness and disease and in proclaiming the Good News of the gospel. Jesus compares the multitude to sheep without a shepherd. They become thoroughly confused and exhaust themselves with aimless, nervous running. People are desperately hungry for God. They don't know where to turn; they are under the heavy burden of the Pharisees' rules and regulations. Yet these bring no consolation or hope. As in our own times, the worse things are, the more receptive people are to God's message of mercy, forgiveness, and hope. There is need of more people to spread the Good News, whether priests, religious, or committed laity. God is our only hope.

Hosea 8: 4-7, 11-13; Matthew 9: 32-38 **YEAR II**

In Hosea's day the Israelites appointed their own kings and princes; and they made idols and worshipped them. Although they knew God's ordinances, they looked upon them as applicable not to themselves but to others. All of these actions, of course, led them into trouble, a natural consequence of substituting human wisdom for God's law. The Israelites were, in fact, allowing themselves another "Egypt experience"—but one of their own making which reduced them to the slavery to sin.

When Christ came, the condition of the people was similar. "They were like sheep without a shepherd" and worse. Sheep without a shepherd become confused and exhaust themselves with aimless, nervous running. They did not turn to God, the Good Shepherd, for guidance but they believed in blind prophets, the Pharisees. They had put the law of God far from them. Indeed, they seemed to have put aside the whole spiritual and supernatural element of the Law except for their belief in the preternatural power of Satan. Anyone who appeared superior to them in wisdom had to be the devil rather than God.

Today, the question is raised as to what we must do to proclaim God's revelation to our pagan world. The answer is pretty much, "Try, try again." That is what Jesus did and the ordinary people were able to perceive his authenticity. Eventually they sought out Jesus to heal their sick, give them the meaning of life, respond to their dilemmas. They shunned the Pharisees, who became jealous and decided that Jesus must be eliminated or everyone would be converted from their materialistic teaching to the spiritual truths of the gospel which Jesus was proclaiming.

At the end of the passage, Jesus urges the apostles to join him in preaching and to pray that others through the centuries would also continue to preach his doctrine. "The harvest is good but the laborers are scarce. Beg the harvest master to send out laborers to gather his harvest."

WEDNESDAY

Genesis 41: 55-57, 42: 5-7, 17-24; Matthew 10: 1-7 **YEAR I**

The historical background of today's reading is important for the proper understanding of its message. Jacob had twelve sons, of whom Joseph and Benjamin were by Rachel. Joseph, sold into slavery by his jealous brothers, became the Prime Minister of Egypt. A famine now forces the sons of Jacob to go into Egypt for grain. The immediate lesson in the story comes from the willingness of the Egyptians to share what they had with "the whole world," which was suffering from famine. They had compassion for everyone regardless of race, color or creed. They did not tire; they did not become tight-fisted; they gave to all. In a day when we are much more able than the Egyptians to help the rest of the world, we need to keep this example in mind.

The more profound lesson comes to us as we attempt to understand the workings of divine providence. In this particular case, the providence of God is especially remarkable in that it involves so many people and so many events over such a long period of time. So much was involved from the time that Joseph was sold into slavery by his brothers until they were reconciled many years later in Egypt. Although the events seemed tragic at first, all conspired to bring about happiness for Joseph, his brothers, and their father because they trusted in God. The Lord always gives us the grace of repentance; the question is whether or not we shall take advantage of it, even when our circumstances are desperate. Joseph's brothers did so. We need to imitate them along with Joseph who never lost his love for his family, even after being mistreated: "The eyes of the Lord are upon those who fear him, upon those who hope for his kindness, to deliver them from death and preserve them in spite of famine."

In the gospel narrative, Jesus selects and commissions twelve disciples. They are named individually and because they are "sent out" they are called apostles. Jesus sent them out to the most disadvantaged: those with unclean spirits, the sick, and the diseased. At first, the mission was only to the Chosen People but later it was broadened to the whole world. The apostles had very little in a worldly sense but they had abundant spiritual goods: the revelation and the love of God that they shared with everyone. The gospel should be offered to all regardless of any one's material wealth or lack thereof.

Hosea 10: 1-3, 7-8, 12; Matthew 10: 1-7 **YEAR II**

The picture developed by Hosea is familiar to us. The Israelites have developed a hollow prosperity and the nation is facing a coming doom. Their altars are being torn down; everything seems to be collapsing around them. They trusted in their self-appointed king but what could he do for them in these circumstances? It took them considerable time to analyze and recognize the real situation. When they did, the prophet tells them that their king will disappear, the high places of idolatry will be destroyed. Clearly it will be a time for starting all over, for getting back to the basics of justice and piety, and for seeking God.

Our own age is much the same. Our lack of awareness, our unwillingness to accept and implement obvious answers, our foolish trust in human judgment are almost beyond belief. How blind can we be! And yet we would rather go down with this sinking ship simply because "everyone else" is staying aboard rather than make a leap of faith into the sea of God's grace and providence. Certainly stepping out in faith demands courage but adhering to the ways of the world is leads straight to destruction and perhaps to hell.

In similar circumstances, what did Christ do? He prayed. He chose a small group of apostles. He instructed them carefully and intensively in God's thoughts and God's ways. He fortified them with the grace of faith, hope, and love. He sent them into the world as lambs among wolves. And they were killed, as he was, but their witness and their blood eventually converted a great part of the world.

THURSDAY

Genesis 44: 18-21, 23-29, 45: 1-5; Matthew 10: 7-15 **YEAR I**

In today's story from Genesis we read how Joseph at last reveals his identity to his own brothers. It is a tender account of God's love for all of them. In the ways of divine providence, Joseph had gone to Egypt, not to be lost to his family, but in order to preserve his family. Because of his love for his father and his compassion for his starving family, Joseph forgives his brothers. He sees God's providence in the events of his life. Surely the brothers were unjust to have sold him to the Egyptians but this was obviously a part of God's design. It was God's will that Joseph be sold into slavery in order to save his family at a later date. Forgiveness is the message.

In the gospel narrative we learn that, when sending the apostles to preach, Jesus gave them instructions. They were to go out as poor, sincere, and religious men not looking for gain but dispensing the gifts of God. They were to exercise prudence—not the crafty shrewdness of those who are alert to do harm to others; but the thoughtfulness and perceptiveness of those who are innocent of malice.

Hosea 11: 1-4, 8-9; Matthew 10: 7-15 **YEAR II**

God is a loving parent. No matter how far the child may stray from the parent's principles, God will still seek out the child and express his loving desire that the child reform. The initial response to a child's rejection of parental principles is anger on the part of the parent. He wonders whether he should have expressed himself more clearly. Are worldly influences simply too strong? So God, good parent that he is, suppresses his anger and with compassion constantly reaches out to man.

Certainly this is what we discover in the coming of Christ. Jesus gave up "everything" to come among us as a poor, meek, and humble man. He came with a message of compassion and love—virtues which he preached and practiced through the corporal and spiritual works of mercy. He did not force himself upon anyone but he offered himself to everyone. The only thing that the loving parent cannot do is to make the free act of will to accept the goodness that is offered. And when it is rejected, the love continues but in the form of pity rather than joy.

All this is summarized in the gospel as Jesus sends his apostles "as I have done, so you also should do."

FRIDAY

Genesis 46: 1-7, 28-30; Matthew 10: 16-23 **YEAR I**

Once again God asks a tremendous act of faith from the Israelites. They are to go to Egypt with all their belongings, place themselves in a dependent state under the Pharaoh. However, the Lord will protect them and bring them back to the Promised Land stronger than ever. Israel accepts God's promise, spurred on by the fact that Joseph is already there, and a touching reunion takes place. The family of Israel lives in Goshen, a rich area of the northeast delta region of Egypt. There the twelve tribes of the nation Israel develop from the twelve sons of the patriarch Israel, the former Jacob.

So many times in the Old Testament, events presage the story of Christ. Today's story reminds us of the flight into Egypt, the betrayal by Judas and the infidelity of the apostles, along with the events after the Resurrection. The Lord is betrayed; yet he turns the situation to the advantage of the betrayer and those who have been unfaithful by forgiving them! "What God is there like our God?"

In the gospel Jesus makes clear that the same thing will happen to us—we should be wary of the possibility of betrayal although it is unavoidable. We should be wary, because betrayal can scandalize others and, if we are aware that this can happen, it should be a constant reminder to be careful of what we say and do. We should stay with the deposit of faith and not dilute it with human wisdom. Otherwise, this will give further excuse to the betrayers, undermine our credibility with the weak, and tempt us to act with pride. We might think that we can deal with betrayers on the grounds of rational arguments. Our duty is to adhere to the Word of God as it has been given to us and perseveringly shun rational argument as a means of persuading others.

Hosea 14: 2-10; Matthew 10: 16-23 **YEAR II**

Hosea hopes for the conversion of Israel and utters a fervent plea for this favored nation to forget the political power of Assyria and turn to God. He sends out a message of messianic hope and a final word of wisdom. He tells Israel that Assyria will not save them nor should they any longer say "our God" to the work of their hands. If they heed his word, the help of God will be immediately activated and the nation will come to life once again. However, everything depends upon the free will decision of man to perceive his true relationship to God and humbly invite the Lord of heaven and earth to enter fully into his life. God's way, truth, and life are straight and clear; if man walks along God's path, rather than amidst the brambles on either side of the road, he will be blessed and happy.

Once on that path of God we can be sure that others will still tempt us to leave it. We must be strong in faith and persevering in purpose. Right reason makes God's way the most logical and easiest to follow. However, the irrational temptation to please oneself still has an irresistible appeal for the weak. We can never let down our guard, never cease praying, and never allow ourselves an opening to worldly pleasure. Just a taste of pleasure is likely to whet our appetite and foolishly convince us to leave the diet of God's Eucharistic table. Our resistance to the world will be a source of jealousy and even enmity in others. Against all logic, we may be persecuted for a life of goodness. Certainly, the Lord will not abandon us; he will give us the strength to stand up to any challenge, if we truly will to follow in his way.

SATURDAY

Genesis 49: 29-33, 50: 15-24; Matthew 10: 24-33 **YEAR I**

Despite the fact that Jacob and his family had found a safe refuge in Egypt, his attachment was still to the Promised Land of his fathers, so he asked to be buried among them at Hebron. Joseph, too, believed in the promises made to Abraham, Isaac, and Jacob, so he willingly forgave his brothers. He saw their treachery as a part of God's providence. What was important now was to preserve the fidelity of his family, to God's promises. Despite his good fortune in Egypt, Joseph still saw himself as God's servant, not especially deserving of great favors but grateful for what he received from God.

The gospel makes this point clear. We should not be so greedy or ambitious as to expect in life more than our fathers had; we should expect a somewhat similar fate. It could be different but, by and large, we should expect that life for ourselves is going to be a series of successes and failures. And if we are going to be faithful to God and the principles of revelation we should be prepared for persecution as well. There is nothing in this to fear or to make us unhappy. God sees and knows all, even the secrets of our hearts. Just Judge that he is, he will treat us fairly, rewarding us a hundred-fold for anything that we might be asked to suffer in this world on his behalf. We are worth much more to him than anything else in creation. He will take care of us.

Isaiah 6: 1-8; Matthew 10: 24-33 **YEAR II**

The glory of God is an inspiration to do great things. Isaiah, the greatest of the Old Testament prophets, was called by God while in the Jerusalem temple where he was overwhelmed, cleansed in speech, and sent out as a prophet. He exemplified that "If God is with us, who can be against us!" We must constantly keep before our eyes the glory of God and our own unworthiness in his sight; and realize how foolish our sinfulness and temporizing are in light of this relationship. All the prophets were reluctant messengers, they saw themselves totally unqualified for their task. What they eventually had in common, however, was that they needed no great talent. All they needed was the humility to allow the all powerful God to use them as an instrument of his grace and the courage to take the abuse that goes along with the call to be a sign of contradiction to the world.

Christ had an added argument for his apostles. "The pupil should be happy to become like his teacher." And he added, "If they have harried me, they will harass you." What is important is that God's revelation be proclaimed and that all men have an opportunity for salvation. We should not be intimidated nor should we be concerned about answering our opponents and justifying ourselves to the world. Ultimately everything will be known and "the truth will out" for everyone to see plainly.

God keeps his promises; he will not abandon us. Even as he provides for the natural world, the birds, animals, and plants much more so he cares for us. We need to have faith in him and keep before our eyes that whoever acknowledges him will be acknowledged by him at the end of life on earth. Jesus tells his apostles to have such faith in God that they fear nothing in this world.

Fifteenth Week of Ordinary Time

Monday

Exodus 1: 8-14, 22; Matthew 10: 34-11: 1 **YEAR I**

Today we begin to read the dramatic story of Exodus. The descendants of Jacob after being in Egypt for 400 years were subjected to oppression, persecution, and even genocide. What promoted this turn of events? A new king, who knew nothing of Joseph decided to stop the increase of the Israelites by preventing their multiplication and their possible defection to a future enemy. As happens in most affluent nations, there was a lack of gratitude, spurred on by a loss of a sense of history among the Egyptians. In our own day, they are models of those who always want more, who develop a spirit of selfishness and who seek pleasure rather than goodness.

The message of Jesus in the gospel concerns the cost and meaning of discipleship. One of his missionary instructions is that, "He who seeks only himself brings himself to ruin." Such was the case eventually with the Egyptians and such will always be the case for nations that are depraved in their morals. It is inevitable. The fact that other countries may be as bad or worse than our own is no guarantee to our survival. Indeed, in most nations the evils are due to a small segment of the population; in our country we freely choose immoral options for ourselves. Only adherence to God's truth can save us. And as Jesus states, adherence to truth is like a sword, which has a way of cutting us off from friends and neighbors, even members of our own families. Acceptance or rejection of God's word cuts very deeply. We know it; we try to be protective; we compromise. In the final analysis, we may hold to the faith ourselves, but what about those to whom we give bad example through compromise. "Whoever loves family members more than me is not worthy of me."

Isaiah 1: 10-17; Matthew 10: 34-11: 1 **YEAR II**

When Jesus tells his hearers that he has not come to bring peace but division he appears to be contradicting the whole content of the Bible, especially the gospel. What Jesus is saying is that the result of his preaching will be division because some will accept his word and others will not. We see that what he says is true in some families. Jesus is a sign of contradiction to the ways of the world. Members of the same family choose him; others choose the world.

We need to be aware as Isaiah tells us, that "religiosity" on our part is not enough. There are all kinds of people, who do not engage in blatant immorality, who go to Mass, say their prayers daily, and yet they can be most uncharitable people. If that's the way you're going to be, Isaiah tells us, you might as well forget your incense and sacrifices. They are of no avail; that is hypocrisy. "Learn to do good; cease to do evil; make justice your aim."

We need to do as God does. He sees the evil; he is saddened by it; but he does not turn his back. Like the father of the Prodigal Son, he is always ready to forgive, while we so often are like the older son. Everything God has is ours. We take it and use it but only complain about those who do otherwise. How can we complain about others, how can we fail to love them, how can we turn our back on them, when we have what they need—love of God? God doesn't do so and neither should we.

And we have a test to see whether or not we are hypocritical. If we truly appreciate that we have everything, when we have God's love, we are going to be cheerful, happy, outgoing people ready to share what we have with others. If instead we are sour complainers like the Prodigal Son's older brother—even though everything the Father has is ours—our life is a sham; our pious practices are no better than those of the Pharisees. "He who seeks only himself brings himself to ruin."

When Jesus speaks of the reward that is to be given to the one who practices the corporal works of mercy, he is also speaking of those who practice the spiritual works of mercy. We must welcome not only those who have physical and material needs, but also those who have spiritual and moral needs. Indeed, we should go out looking for them to rescue them. AIDS is a good example. We cannot refuse to help these people on moral grounds any more than we can refuse to help them in their social and medical needs. Jesus assisted the lepers, who were seen in the same light. If we welcome anyone, no matter who he or she may be, we welcome Christ.

TUESDAY

Exodus 2: 1-15; Matthew 11: 20-24 **YEAR I**

In today's reading we read about the infancy of Moses, the people destined to lead the flight of the Israelites from Egypt. Through God's providence Moses received the finest of Egyptian education. The gift of life is of tremendous value. This was recognized not only by the Jewish parents and Pharaoh's daughter, who saved Moses, but by Pharaoh himself, who wanted to stamp out the life of the Jews so that they would not become populous and overcome him.

Moses received his name because he was drawn out of the water, a prefigurement of the sacrament of baptism. The Lord uses water often in Scripture to signify spiritual cleansing. Water is the source of life. It is needed for plants, animals, and humans to sustain life; it was the source of livelihood and food for the apostles; and it was used by John the Baptist and later by Christ and the apostles for baptism.

Today's gospel narrative is a strong antidote to presumption. It appears that we shall be judged according to the gifts and graces that we have received. There will be greater mercy for those who have received less, greater severity for those who have received more. Often we try to comfort ourselves in the fact that we are more holy than other people. As the Pharisees might say: we pray, we fast, we give alms, we work hard for the Church, and so on. Although we do all these things, possibly we could do much more and we sin besides.

As we look upon all the evil in the world, we must admit that many of the perpetrators have lost a sense of morality and don't know any better. Surely they will be held to account, but what about ourselves? Will we not be held to account in a more demanding way for having done little or nothing to stem the tide, when we have been given the grace and the intelligence to counter the evil in the world? Many whom we judge to be malefactors may receive mercy, whereas we will be judged according to a stricter standard. We should not presume anything, but set as our standard the perfection of our Heavenly Father, strive to love him with our whole mind, heart and soul, and love our neighbor as we love ourselves.

Isaiah 7: 1-9; Matthew 11: 20-24 **YEAR II**

"Unless your faith is firm, you shall not be firm." These words of God, delivered by Isaiah to Ahay, should be a watchword for all of us. If we do not have strong, firm convictions about life—how we are to live—we are never going to have the stability and sense of purpose, that are necessary to a happy life.

And although the world may try to convince us otherwise, reason and experience both tell us that if we place our faith in human wisdom, we must be prepared for constant change, contradiction, and a very unsecure life. Human wisdom, even of the great minds, runs in cycles. When all is said and done, unchangeable wisdom—that is, truth—is found only in God, who has revealed this truth principally in Jesus Christ, who in turn has entrusted the Father's revelation to his divinely instituted Church, which lives and acts day by day under the guidance of the Holy Spirit. If we believe this, accept God's truth from the Church, even though it may be unpalatable at times, we have the key to a happy life. If we trust more in the wisdom of the world and act upon it, we condemn ourselves to a life of instability, and constant change, and we end up wondering what life is all about.

Wednesday

Exodus 3: 1-6, 9-12, Matthew 11: 25-27 **YEAR I**

In today's reading we hear of the emotional call of Moses to lead the Israelites out of Egypt. God's first vision to Moses demonstrates God's greatness, power, and love for his people. There probably has never been a hero who has not asked, "Why me?" A hero is not necessarily a fearless person, who is born to greatness. A hero is one who overcomes his fear in favor of a greater cause that motivates him.

The other question in the mind of the one who is challenged is, "How can I do it? I am so weak and the challenge so great." Again, the only incentive that motivates the hero is the righteousness of the cause he is called to espouse and the perception that God is on his side. It is possible that God will permit him to fail in the work to which he is called—but the eternal reward for doing what is right and just, as Christ did, will be similar to the reward which Christ received. Moses seems to be such a hero; not one who thought himself capable of responding to any challenge, but one who was ready to do God's will whatever it might be.

The gospel confirms the same lesson. God chooses the weak to confound the strong. If we try to use our own strengths to overcome the world, the flesh, and the devil, we find that we are no match for the world and that becomes a temptation to join it—to go along with worldly ways, and to succumb to the allurements of the flesh and the devil. What we need to do is deny ourselves and rely on God's strength in dealing with the world, the flesh, and the devil. No human strength and no human wisdom can ever compare with the least assistance that God offers.

Isaiah 10: 5-7, 13-16; Matthew 11: 25-27 **YEAR II**

Isaiah explains that everything which happens in human history is divine providence. The Assyrians overpower the Israelites, slay many, capture great spoils, take the nation into captivity. They may think that they have accomplished all of this through their own power and wisdom, but the fact of the matter is that God has been using the Assyrians to accomplish his own good purposes with the Chosen People. The Assyrians should not pride themselves as being all-powerful; the Lord could cut them down as he did the Egyptians. They are simply like an axe in the hands of a woodsman and just as powerless as the axe without someone to use it. So as God takes retribution on the Israelites, he is in no way favoring the pagan people.

Strangely the mystery of God's providence seems hidden from our eyes. We should be able to discern God's plan to a greater degree than we do. With reference to the Church what is God's purpose in allowing so much power to a materialistic United States? Are the desperately poor countries of the southern hemisphere, where just about everyone has been baptized in South America and there are tremendous numbers of converts in Africa, are these countries colonized centuries ago by plundering Christians, to be compared to the Israelites and ourselves in the northern hemisphere to all Assyrians?

We do not know. What is important for us to know is that no power on earth can compare to God, the Creator and Provider for all. In light of that knowledge of the Father, we are to follow the example of Christ. We are to give praise to him both in our acts of worship and in our daily activity and the model for both is Christ, who went off so often by himself to pray, who praised God before so many important events in his life, who offered himself totally to the Father's will—even to death on the cross—and who loved all others created by God as he loved his very self.

THURSDAY

Exodus 3: 11-20; Matthew 11: 28-30 **YEAR I**

Moses asks for a sign from God in order that he may know himself and be able to convince the Israelites that God has chosen him to lead God's people out of Egypt and back to the Promised Land. In order to believe it is necessary that others know who is speaking and that the speaker is telling the truth. There was no special reason for the people to believe Moses, but if there was a sign that God had chosen Moses as a prophet, then the people would believe him. Moses had his own sign in the burning bush. The sign for the Israelites was to be God's name—I AM—after that it would be necessary to hope in God's promises. Hope of the Promised Land was all that Moses had to offer the Israelites. They were certainly tired and found life burdensome under the Egyptians. They thought they were ready to throw their cares upon the Lord. However, they were not really ready to accept God's yoke, but they certainly needed refreshment. Despite their weak faith, hope in God continually brought them back to him.

The words of Jesus in today's gospel narrative emphasize God's care and concern for his people. Those words are among the most consoling and tender in all the gospels. In ancient Palestine there was a double yoke, under which two animals together pulled the plow. The lesson is that Jesus is beside us through life, helping us to carry all our trials and burdens. We are never alone!

Isaiah 26: 7-9, 12, 16-19; Matthew 11: 28-30 YEAR II

"The way of the just is smooth" and we find perfect justice only in union of mind and heart with God. While we are apart from him, we are bound to be in agony. Peace, the consequence of justice comes only from God; we cannot produce it for ourselves, it is his gift. So it is clear that what we must strive to do constantly is to achieve justice in our lives, give to each his due, whether the other person is near to us or far away.

Surely this is the message of the gospel as well. "Take up my yoke . . . for my yoke is easy and my burden light." That yoke, which holds us in line, is a yoke of justice. If we would only stay in the traces, plod along obediently, doing what we are supposed to be doing what we are made to do—life would seem so much easier, so much more peaceful.

That is not to say that life will be without problems. The oxen must walk over rough grounds, come upon boulders, perhaps stumble, and be bothered by the heat of the day. But all that is due to the imperfect nature of the world and of ourselves. The question that we face is how we make our lives joyful despite the problems. God's answer is to live a life of justice, goodness and love toward others.

Friday

Exodus 11: 10-12: 14; Matthew 12: 1-8 **YEAR I**

In today's reading we realize that nine successive plagues were not enough to compel Pharaoh to allow the exodus of the Israelites from Egypt. Then came the night of the tenth plague. The Israelites ate lamb, prepared for their departure, and sprinkled blood on their doorposts so that their houses would be passed over. Incidentally, this is the origin of the Passover Meal. The Lord had given very clear instructions as to how the Israelites were to escape from the Egyptians. They were to be protected by the blood of the Lamb. The Lord would pass over them in their houses and strike only those who had treated his people so shamefully. All that God required of the Israelites was faith and obedience to his command. Nothing more than faith and obedience are required of us, too. If we have faith in God and obey his precepts, as revealed to us by Christ, we, too, will be protected by the blood of the Lamb and have nothing to fear. In his own way, God will protect us from those who reject or mistreat us.

Today's gospel narrative points out that the pharisaical interpretation of the commandment to honor the Lord's Day was excessive. Jesus revealed himself as the Lord of the Sabbath and he made clear the text that "it is mercy I desire and not sacrifice."

Isaiah 38: 1-6, 21-22, 7-8; Matthew 12: 1-8 **YEAR II**

Although the Lord granted recovery to Hezechiah and gave him fifteen more years to live, the question before us always remains. What have you done with the past 58 years? What did you do yesterday? What are you doing with today? What will you do with tomorrow? Will we be better or worse off with an extra day or an extra year? If better off, great! But the usual result is not especially beneficial and can very well be detrimental to one's salvation. What we really need is a firm purpose of amendment, a spirit of prayer that will keep us constantly united to God in mind and heart. If we spend each day that way, each day is a blessing. But, of course, if we spend each day that way, we have a taste of heaven right here on earth and we would have no worry as to whether God would take us to himself or not.

We need to realize that we shall never save our souls by doing our own thing, even if our own thing involves hard work, penitential practices, and the like. This was the way of the Pharisees, who set up laws for themselves and others and observed them "religiously." In so doing, however, they developed a spirit of pride rather than spiritual union with God. We must be watchful that the same does not happen to us. The demands of daily work are tremendous and, of course, if we accept and fulfill them as God's will, we can make spiritual progress. But it is most important that we retain that motivation, that we see our work as God's will and that we devote ourselves to prayer so that we can discern God's will. Otherwise, we are working our way into a state of colossal pride. The difference between saint and sinner is not that great. The effort to remain one with God is the key.

SATURDAY

Exodus 12: 37-42; Matthew 12: 14-21 **YEAR I**

In today's reading we have the description of the children of Israel leaving Egypt. That they eat unleavened bread is a sign of their hasty departure.

Even though the Israelites had been in Egypt for over 400 years, when the time for their deliverance came, it was very sudden. They had time to prepare unleavened bread only. The lesson is obvious that we, too, who are on a pilgrim journey through life, should be prepared to answer God's call at any time. Death comes as a thief in the night. God has given us directions for our voyage through life and we are to obey them. If we do, God will care for our needs.

The gospel narrative shows that, in the face of adversity, Jesus acted quietly and with compassion. He did not unnecessarily engage in argument with his adversaries, the Pharisees. Rather, he went about his Father's business, healing the physically and spiritually ill. Jesus was always caring.

Micah 2: 1-5; Matthew 12: 14-21 **YEAR II**

Those who scheme to accumulate wealth—taking over the lands and buildings of others in Old Testament times—will sooner or later run into a situation where others will put an end to their wealth. The prophet seems to have in mind a situation like the Exile, when a foreign power will take over everything. But death is also an equalizer. "You can't take it with you." "What does it profit to gain the whole world and suffer the loss of one's immortal soul?"

In the gospel Jesus makes clear that neither he nor his Father is going to use force to compel us to do what is right and just. God constantly invites us to conversion and offers his help, but he is not going to force us. His love, goodness and patience may deceive us into thinking that all is well because he is not going to crush the bruised reed nor quench the smoldering wick. While there is life, there will be hope for us. Perhaps the parable of the grain and the weeds say it best. Both will be allowed to thrive until the harvest, but then the grain will be saved and stored in the barn, while the weeds will be burned.

So it will be with human beings. Jesus will not rant and rave against his tormentors nor cause the wicked of our time any great calamities. He will quietly go about proclaiming the gospel—in person through us until that day when "judgement is made victorious." "A word to the wise is sufficient." Is it sufficient for us, or do we still think that we can do what we please and get away with it?

Sixteenth Week of Ordinary Time

Monday

Exodus 14: 5-18; Matthew 12: 38-42 **YEAR I**

Today's reading reveals a desperate situation for the Israelites. Their dramatic exodus has taken them to the edge of the Red Sea, and Moses announces that they are about to cross. At the same time they see the Egyptians in hot pursuit of them. They are surrounded by desert land, they have no place to hide, and they are pinned against the Red Sea without arms or boats. At this point they would have been happy to return to slavery in Egypt. Despite the lack of faith on the part of the Israelites, however, Moses remains resolute and God is faithful. There can be no more hopeless situation. However, God stands by them and they cross the Red Sea unharmed. This is one of the greatest lessons in history reminding us that God is ever faithful. Why cannot we have faith in him? The worst possible fate is death, but, in a true sense, that means entrance into eternal glory. What is there to fear? And yet we do fear. May our only fear be that we will cease trusting in God. The psalmist reminds us that "my strength and my courage is the Lord, and he has been my Savior."

The gospel narrative confirms the lesson that the Israelites learned when crossing the Red Sea. They realized that God is ever faithful. He has promised to be with us and to love us always. Yet we, like the Jewish people, are forever looking for signs and wonders from God to prove his presence and his love. Jesus reminds the scribes and Pharisees of all the signs already given to them in Old and New Testament history. Moses, Jonah, the people of Nineveh, the Queen of Sheba, and all the prophets are all surpassed in Jesus Christ. We must learn to trust in him, in his goodness, his love, and his compassion for us. Above all, we should not be constantly looking for signs but we should be demanding lively faith of ourselves.

Micah 6: 1-4, 6-8; Matthew 12: 38-42 **YEAR II**

Micah was a rugged prophet who came from the foothills of Judah to preach God's judgment on the nation. He presents to us the Good Friday lamentation of Christ. "My people, what have I done to you? How have I offended you? Answer me!" And of course, there was no answer. The Lord had lavished all kinds of special gifts upon them—giving them life including the necessities of life and what makes life pleasurable. In return, at God's command and at a bare minimum, the people offered God the first fruits of their families, flock, and produce. But that was not what God wanted. That was a token and only a symbol. "You have been told, O man, what is required of you. Only to do the right, to love goodness, and to walk humbly with your God."

What an easy program! What a beautiful, joyful life, doing what is right, loving goodness, walking humbly with God! And yet, like the Israelites, all human beings are prone to be selfish, to love pleasure, and to walk rebelliously along with the crowd. We don't want to be different. We would rather do what everyone else is doing—possibly leisurely going to Hell—rather than doing the simple, beautiful things that God asks of us, but which often make us a sign of contradiction to others.

The Israelites kept asking Jesus for signs. The holiness of his life was a far greater sign than any miracles. The miracles gave validity to what Jesus said and did. What Jesus was expecting from the people was not their admiration—although that was a good first step—but their conversion. Not only did the people of his time have prophets, priests, kings, and judges; they had the words and examples of the Son of God. Still they would not believe and be converted!

"My people, tell me. What have I done to you? What more could I do for you? How have I offended you? Answer me!"

TUESDAY

Exodus 14: 21-15: 1; Matthew 12: 46-50 **YEAR I**

Today we read the epic account of the crossing of the Red Sea. Whether the parting of the Red Sea was as great a miracle as is described in Exodus is unsure. That God's mysterious and wonderful providence was at work, there can be no doubt. The escape of the Israelites could have taken place exactly as described. Or the description could have been much embellished. It could be that a bog had dried that year; the wheels of the chariots could have become entangled in brush or could have sunk in the sand; and then there could have been a torrential downpour that flooded the area. And although it seems that the Egyptians were right on the heels of the Israelites, it could have been that a few days intervened, between the crossing of the Israelites and that of the Egyptians. In any event, what is clear is that God, whether by an extraordinary or a more ordinary providence, protected his Chosen People from the overwhelming power of the Egyptians.

As has always been the case with human beings even to the present day, one's worth is often based upon one's possessions or power or, in this case, on one's relationship to another person. In the gospel the people believe that Jesus' mother and relatives have a special claim upon him because of their relationship to him. That may be true in human relations but, in God's sight, there is only one relationship that matters, namely the relationship that each person has with God himself, and that means one's degree of holiness. The Egyptians had all kinds of worldly power; the Israelites had only their faith in God, but the latter prevailed. This should be our attitude also. "When humanly weak, we are still spiritually powerful through the grace and protection of God."

Micah 7: 14-15, 18-20; Matthew 12: 46-50 **YEAR II**

The Israelites are suffering and they ask the Lord for better material conditions, and unlike ourselves, they are aware of their sinfulness, they realize that their sins are an obstacle to a better life; and they pray for forgiveness. God can very well grant material benefits to those who do not love him, but it is logical that we should beg and receive forgiveness for our sins before expecting him to lavish his goodness upon us. Our God is a compassionate God and he delights in showing clemency. That will be very obvious, if we recognize our guilt, have sorrow for our sins, and appeal to God for mercy.

In the incident where Jesus' mother and relatives seek to see him, the above truth is evident. Jesus certainly had great affection for his mother but, in order to make the point that he was preaching, he stresses that the person without sin, the person in union with God, the person who does the will of God, is closest to him in spirit.

WEDNESDAY

Exodus 16: 1-5, 9-15; Matthew 13: 1-9 **YEAR I**

In today's reading, we find the Israelites in the Sinai peninsula. We note their grumbling over their daily hardships but also God's care of them by miraculously sending them white manna and quails for sustenance. It is strange but true that people who believe in God and, therefore, should know better are continually complaining about his providence. One of their primary beliefs should be that God loves us immensely, more so than we can love ourselves. He knows far better than we what is good for us. And yet we not only complain but we make demands on him and tell him what to do for us. Of course, all this is a sign that our faith is not especially strong. When we begin to complain, it is clear that our faith in God has weakened. Rather than demand things from God, which we think we need, we should redouble our prayers of adoration, faith, hope, and love, asking that we might understand his will better, or at least be able to accept it without complaining and with great trust.

God responded to the prayers of the Israelites, sending them manna in the morning and quail in the evening. This should have restored their faith but, as so often happens, it seems to have "proven them right," and that they knew better than God what they needed. For they continued to be weak in faith, complaining about God's lack of concern. In a sense, the Israelites had far more excuse than we have, however. We have a greater knowledge of salvation history upon which to rely, and our situation is rarely so desperate. All the more, in the face of adversity, should we simply pray for understanding and acceptance of God's will.

The gospel makes clear that the Lord provides grace like manna from heaven for everyone and he provides it in abundance. The difference between men is due not to any discrimination on God's part, but to the manner in which his grace is received or not even accepted. Some are hard of heart, others allow themselves to be consumed by the cares and pleasures of this world; others have varying degrees of openness to God. Most of us are in this latter group. We are only partially committed to the love and service of the Lord. We must constantly strive to increase our love and trust or the temptations of this world will overcome us. We cannot afford to compromise or to dally with evil; we are not that strong; we are bound to lose. So, even though we are weak and will slip into sin, our eyes must be steadily riveted upon the goal, and our efforts steadily devoted to trying to be "perfect as our heavenly Father is perfect."

Jeremiah 1: 1, 4-10; Matthew 13: 1-9 **YEAR II**

The fact that God has given us a free will is mysterious, but the operation of his own will is equally mysterious. Obviously, if God is God, he can do anything he wills, but why he should will to do things this way or that, why he should choose this person or that for a given task, why he should permit evil—these and many other acts of God's will are a mystery to us. Indeed, we would perceive many of them as mistakes.

Jeremiah is a case in point. He is young; apparently he is a poor speaker; certainly he is lacking in confidence; he fears the people to whom he will be sent because of his lack of experience and lack of standing in the community. We would agree with Jeremiah; he probably is not the best candidate in the world to be a prophet. But what Jeremiah and we fail to take into account is that "without me, you (the most capable person in the world) can do nothing." With God as the principal actor, all things are possible.

Surely God does not want a totally passive person as his prophet—although he could work through such a person as well—but certainly he does not want a person who thinks that he knows it all either. Pride in his own capabilities will prevent this latter person from allowing God to work in him and through him. It remains a mystery but, as the Church requires of a candidate for priesthood, it would seem that average abilities are quite satisfactory as long as the person possesses excellent moral character, faith, hope and love for God; in short, a willingness to do God's will.

The gospel also poses a question for us concerning God's will. Why is he so lavish with his graces, even though he must surely know that many people, for one reason or another, will not use them or will not use them well? The answer in this case is a little more understandable from a human point of view although most human beings would hardly be as generous as the Lord. God wills all men to be saved and to come to a knowledge of the truth so, "if without me, you can do nothing" and God truly wishes the salvation of all, his grace must be constantly available even to the hardened sinner. Still, from our own experience, it is hard to understand why an all-knowing God would do so. But that's what makes the difference between God and ourselves. He is also all-good, all-loving, all compassionate—all perfect.

THURSDAY

Exodus 19: 1-2, 9-11, 16-20; Matthew 13: 10-17 **YEAR I**

In today's reading, we find the Israelites finally reaching Mount Sinai. There a theophany takes place. The description of this appearance of God is of a terrifying, unforgettable scene as Moses goes to the summit of Mount Sinai. God can "appear" to us in very dramatic ways, as he did to Moses or he can make himself known in subtle ways, as in the evening breeze. The key to any "apparition" of God to man, however, is that we be prepared for his coming by developing an attitude of prayer so that we may be attentive to his message and that we may not rationalize his message simply because we find it too difficult to accept.

As the gospel states, we must be ready "to see with our eyes, to hear with our ears, to understand with our hearts." When asked why he taught in parables, Jesus answered with a quotation from Isaiah. The knowledge of the kingdom of God is reached only by people who can pass beyond the natural meaning of words and of life. The gospel message is intended for those of good will. When these people hear God's word, whether in parables or in other terms, they easily understand, whereas the simplicity of God's message is repugnant to others. They want the Lord not only to say what they want to hear but also to speak in the manner of their choice.

Jeremiah 2: 1-3, 7-8, 12-13; Matthew 13: 10-17 **YEAR II**

In the early years the Chosen People had a sense of their need for God. Accordingly, they looked to him for help. They worshipped him; they petitioned him; they thanked him for their gifts. They looked to God as their eminent Father, their Creator, their Provider, their Last End.

Then, after the Chosen People were settled in the Promised Land, they began to believe that they could handle things themselves. They turned away from God and sought protection and favors by making treaties with the pagan peoples around them, treaties which were not worth the paper they were written on.

When human beings reach this dangerous state of pride, little can be done for them because they simply are not going to listen to anyone. Anything which contradicts their way of thinking will not only be rejected but destroyed. This was the case, not only in Jeremiah's time, but also in the time of Christ, and is rapidly becoming the same in our country. At the beginning our Founding Fathers came to this country to seek religious freedom; they truly trusted in God. Today the courts are interpreting freedom to mean "do what you please." Freedom cannot exist in a land where there are only rights and no duties. The Ten Commandments, and particular laws based on the commandments are necessary for a balance of rights and duties. But having set human "wisdom" above God's law—and modern "wisdom" above the law of the Land, the Constitution—we have no stable star to guide us on the ocean of life. As St. Paul warned us, we are being tossed to and fro by the winds of false doctrine.

What we are to do in such a situation? Some would advise giving up. What's the use? St. Paul tells us to preach the gospel in season and out of season regardless of the situation. And Christ says the same in a very realistic manner. We are to continue to preach the gospel in a very simple, innocent and clear manner so that the least educated can understand and pray that these people will keep the faith. As for the more "sophisticated" the more one tries to reason with them, the less impression we make. We are only feeding their pride. Something must happen to break down that pride before they will be prepared to listen and to understand.

In these circumstances, when the proud are unwilling to listen, it is not easy for the poor and humble to accept and practice the gospel. Some, like the ancient Israelites, will wish to curry favor with the rich and powerful. But most of them will not; they will retain the humility which is so necessary to faith.

FRIDAY

Exodus 20: 1-17; Matthew 13: 18-23 **YEAR I**

Today's reading gives an account of Moses receiving God's law on Mount Sinai. The Law begins with the Ten Commandments—a remarkably brief but all-inclusive list of the principal temptations facing human beings. God is the author of the list and also the creator of man. He knows whereof he speaks. It has always been a tendency of man, contrary to his better judgment, to grasp at straws when things go wrong for him. So even though he should be well aware of its futility, he violates the first commandment when he trusts in nature or man-made things or people, when God doesn't do what he asks in prayer. Proof of this should be the ease with which human beings can set aside human authority, a violation of the fourth commandment, or remove another person from obstructing the way, violating the fifth commandment, or take from others that which one wants or needs, violating the sixth, seventh, ninth and tenth commandments. God perceives also that man wants more than he has, or is not satisfied or grateful for what he does have, violating the third commandment. In his frustration man tends to be critical of God, violating the second commandment, and envious of his neighbor violating the sixth, seventh, ninth and tenth commandments, and ready to resort to deceit to attain his ends. God knows us so well. Would that we could see the truth about ourselves as clearly and love God and neighbor as we should!

In the gospel narrative, the parable of the sower explains further our reaction to God's commandments. Some of us pay no attention and don't even try to understand God's word because we are so taken up with ourselves. Others are wishful thinkers; we would like to follow God's law but we have no moral courage or perseverance—the slightest temptation leads us astray. Still others are "hooked" by certain pleasures, while even those who keep God's commandments are yet far from perfect. Some people can fall into one of the above categories more or less permanently, but most of us wander from one to another, or we are in one category with respect to some commandments, and in another for others. Total commitment is within our reach, but when temptation comes, we are very weak.

Jeremiah 3: 14-17; Matthew 13: 18-23 **YEAR II**

The prophet Jeremiah condemned evil, but also predicted a future return to God of a small number. The future religious spirit, he announces, will be more spiritual and universal than the superstitious trust in the Ark of the Covenant. Through Jeremiah the Lord speaks of re-uniting his people in a holy bond, free of hard-hearted wickedness, no longer dependent upon the symbol of the Ark but united by other events which are to take place in Jerusalem—the preaching, suffering, death and resurrection of Christ. At that time God's newly Chosen People will be blessed with wise and prudent leaders. Surely the reference would have to do with Peter and the apostles, the Pope and Bishops, as well as to the leaders of the Church through the centuries.

Still there will be unevenness about the manner in which Christ and these leaders—and their word—are accepted. Through God's guidance, the leaders, after the example of Christ, will continue to make God's word available to his people. But free will remains operative at all times. Some will accept that word and live it in varying degrees of perfection. Others will utterly reject it, or accept it superficially for a long time, or accept it with fervor for a short time, and then lose the faith because of the cares and distractions of the world. When God created us as free creatures the terrible possibility arose that we could choose ourselves, our own pleasure and ignore him. To follow Christ is to choose God over ourselves and vindicate his love for us. In order to produce good results, the Word of God has to fall on a receptive soil.

Saturday

Exodus 24: 3-8, Matthew 13: 24-30 **YEAR I**

In today's reading, we learn of the ceremony establishing a covenant between God and his people. Like the Israelites we are quick to express our enthusiastic loyalty and obedience to the Lord; like them too, we easily break our oath. Emotion is helpful in urging us to commitment but something more substantial is necessary—knowledge of what will be needed to keep the promise and a firm determination to persevere. Even with these, we may very well fail, but without them our promise is hardly worthy of the name.

In today's gospel narrative we hear another agricultural parable about the kingdom of God that, in this world, has good and bad elements. That is the reason why it is so difficult to keep our promises to God with regard to a faithful and virtuous life. Temptation will always be present. The weeds sown in the wheat field illustrate the point. The weeds are a danger to the wheat, but, if an effort is made to uproot one, the grain may be destroyed as well. Goodness and evil are allowed to coexist in the world because goodness can be tested only in adversity and success in that test is necessary to attain heaven. In God's good time, in eternity, justice will be had. God is a just judge.

Jeremiah 7: 1-11; Matthew 13: 24-30 **YEAR II**

Today's reading refers to Jeremiah's famous Temple Sermon. In the Jerusalem Temple itself, Jeremiah preached against shallow superstitious trust in Temple sacrifices. He affirmed that true religion is internal and produces works of justice and charity. Some Catholics, like the Israelites of old, think that if they go to Mass on Sunday, they will be saved. Surely that is a good beginning but, as Jeremiah points out, if "Temple worship" is in total contrast to our behavior the rest of the week, we are sadly mistaken. Indeed, we are saying to the world and to our children that there is no such thing as authentic faith and honest behavior—hypocrisy is our road map. Our children stop going to Church because they see through the hypocrisy of our lives. The faith of others around us is shaken. Even the priest becomes tainted with such behavior because he is thought to approve such conduct by urging all to assist at Sunday Mass, by accepting contributions, by urging children to obey their parents, by speaking of God as Father when children can't fully respect their fathers because they see through their hypocrisy.

This is an example of the truth that all in the Church depend upon one another. Immoral or controversial conduct on the part of the priest does severe damage among the faithful. Immoral behavior on the part of the laity also has a bad effect on the priest. Both detract from the credibility of the Church as the Body of Christ, as Christ is the world.

It is a mystery that God can tolerate such a situation, but he does. It has been his plan to give free will to all. As a result we have a Church of sinners and saints—people of varying degrees of sinfulness. Or to use another perspective all members of the Church are sinners who are striving in various degrees to be saints. To live life authentically we must continually go through new cycles of repentance and renewal. The gospel makes clear that the kingdom of God in this world has good and bad elements. However, in God's good time, justice will be had and there will be a day of reckoning as there is each year at harvest time. The grain is stored in barns, and the weeds are burned. Are we grain or are we weeds? This cycle in nature is a warning for us.

Seventeenth Week of Ordinary Time

Monday

Exodus 32: 15-34, 30-34; Matthew 13: 31-35 **YEAR I**

Today's reading continues in Exodus, the Bible's second book. While Moses was on Mount Sinai, the people below made a golden calf. It was an image of the Lord: the strength of a young bull was to represent the Lord's power. However, they were going against God's commandment forbidding them from representing the Lord in any visible form. The Israelites knew very well that Moses was in the presence of God—he had demonstrated as much—but they claimed that they did not know what had happened to him when he went to Mount Sinai for the Ten Commandments. So, they quickly turned to a false god made by their own hands. The revelry shows that what they really did was to rationalize their situation so that they could eat, drink, and be merry, and still be in "good conscience."

The sin of the Israelites is much like that of Adam and Eve, especially the lame excuse that Aaron gives. Aaron agreed with the people instead of standing up to them. He told them to donate their gold; he "threw it into the fire, and this calf came out." How often we agree with popular sentiment rather than adhere to the stricter stance of the Church in order to win over the people. Surely we can bend at times, but we must be careful not to violate God's commandments or have his message lose credibility.

The gospel narrative proposes a few parables from daily life. Each one teaches the gradual development of God's kingdom on earth. A seed must fall into the ground and die for it to grow like the mustard tree. We must die to sin if we expect to spread the kingdom of God. Holiness is like the yeast. It may be unseen and unappreciated, but it can have a tremendous influence on the whole. Similar parables speak of a baptized person as being the light of the world, the salt of the earth. If the salt loses its savor, or the light its brightness, or the yeast its pervasiveness, or the seed fails to die, we have not done a thing for others. We must retain our light, keep our spiritual savor, die to sin, and be as yeast if we are to truly help other people and attract them to the Lord.

Jeremiah 13: 1-11; Matthew 13: 31-35 **YEAR II**

The Lord could not possibly have done more for the Chosen People than he had done. First, for some mysterious reason, he had chosen them and favored them above all other peoples. He had watched over them in his providence ever so closely. He had provided them with divine knowledge and foreknowledge to govern their lives, avoid mistakes, live peacefully and happily. But the Israelites took God's goodness for granted, shoved him aside so that he had no practical influence in their lives. As a result, their faith and their spirit died. They were a prosperous people without a soul and how quickly can such prosperity collapse! When there is no underlying religion and morality, the society breaks apart, falls and crushes the people. This has happened throughout the course of human history. George Washington warned our own country about the possibility in his Farewell Address when he said: "Morality cannot be maintained without faith and religion." The same type of tragedy hangs over our heads in our technological age where so many live without the compassion and wisdom of faith. Nazi Germany proved this assumption, in a gruesome and destructive way. It will happen to us unless we "repent, believe, and practice the gospel."

In the gospel reading, we are informed that the weakness of God is stronger than the power of men; the foolishness of God is greater than human wisdom. That lesson is conveyed by the parables of the mustard seed and the yeast. Both are small and insignificant but they produce results far beyond what one could imagine and they both "die" before they produce anything. We, too, must die to self, be absorbed into Christ and then the power of his grace working in and through us will produce the kind of life we long for—for ourselves and others.

We must trust in God; we must have faith in him. Even if we don't believe in him, at least we ought to believe in his works—the facts of history, which prove him eminently right and correct. What has proven to be of lasting value to humanity, the life of Christ or the life of any other person in history? Through the centuries, nations, governments, and kingdoms have fallen—do we see any of the kingdoms of antiquity still in existence? However, the Church despite its sinful members has lasted through the ages and continues to offer hope to humanity beyond anything that a civil government or human organization can offer! Let us remember that when God goes, all goes. God is the answer to the anxieties of the world. And faith should be our response to him.

Tuesday

Exodus 33: 7-11, 34:5-9, 28; Matthew 13: 35-43 **YEAR I**

In today's reading we learn that during the journey of Exodus, in addition to the tents of the Israelites, there was one special tent or tabernacle of the Lord. There with prayerful words Moses interceded for the sinful, stubborn people. Moses always made time for God. It is clear that God was the leader of his people and Moses his agent. The example of Moses had an effect upon the people. When they saw him in prayer in the presence of the Lord, they did the same, even though as Moses said, "They are a stiff-necked people." Even with them, however, the Lord was kind and merciful. He did not exonerate them of their guilt and at times he punished them. But in final analysis he always had compassion for them. Sometimes when we become discouraged with the response of those we are attempting to evangelize we should remember God's conduct. It should not prevent us from speaking God's truth and adhering to it in practice, but it will give us cause for hope.

The gospel reminds us that, even in the worst of times, there are many good people. Their goodness may be obscured by all the evil surrounding them but still they are there. In the end, the Lord will have no trouble identifying them from among the wicked. We should have no difficulty recognizing them either. Without declaring the guilty guiltless, we should be able to identify many good and holy people who can be an inspiration and a cause for hope to all the faithful.

Jeremiah 14: 17-22; Matthew 13: 35-43 **YEAR II**

Today's reading describes poignantly death and famine in Jerusalem. The Israelites are brought to their knees by utter devastation. Finally, they realize that neither false gods nor unaided nature can help them and the heavens cannot produce rain. They need God's help. They plead desperately for his assistance, asking that he save his reputation among them and among the pagan peoples. They plead for another chance, a time of healing, a period of peace, so that they can "get their act together" again.

The gospel makes us realize that God is not necessarily going to save us from ourselves. The parable of the weeds at harvest time refers to the existence of wicked people where there should be only good people. The Church recognizes that it has unfaithful members represented here by the weeds. God tolerates such members in the Church as he does in the world at large.

However, the last judgment will determine the final destiny of the righteous and of the wicked and thus will purify the kingdom entirely. The lesson is one of patient tolerance. We will be given an almost endless length of rope with which to hang ourselves. At death and at the end of the world, there will be an accounting. The lesson for us is that we need to do more than cry, "Lord, Lord." We need to convert ourselves, amend our lives, accept and practice God's ways.

WEDNESDAY

Exodus 34: 29-35; Matthew 13: 44-46 **YEAR I**

In today's reading we learn of the return of Moses with the Ten Commandments. The radiance of his face is a reflection of the divine glory Moses has confronted on the mountain. That same radiance should shine in our hearts and perhaps even appear in our eyes, if only we prayed with more fervor. The joy that fills our hearts sometimes after prayer or after an especially devout confession is available to us on a daily basis. Granted that only God can bring about this ethereal joy, he is much more inclined to give the favor rather than to deny it, especially because of our need and the good that it can do for others.

When we find God in this way, the gospel narrative tells us that the interior feeling we experience is like that of a person who finds buried treasure or a fine pearl. It is like exploding with joy because we possess something valuable, and realize what it can do for us and our neighbor. The joy of possessing God is so overwhelming that it compels us to share it with others. Indeed, even though we do not have the fullness of God's presence, we should be striving harder to share what we do have with those around us. In God's plan, we never lose but become spiritually stronger by doing so.

Jeremiah 15: 10, 16-21; Matthew 13: 44-46 **YEAR II**

Jeremiah, the prophet, came repeatedly under personal attack during forty catastrophic years. He complained about this situation to God and he even complained to God about God himself! He lamented the condition of God's "Chosen One" meaning himself, Jeremiah! Jeremiah says that here he is, a person who eagerly accepts God's word, lives by it, and preaches it. His is an upright life in accord with God's will. Weeping, Jeremiah asks what has it done for him or for others? He is filled with indignation at what is going on around him but all he receives for his pain are curses. He looks to God for understanding. And slowly, Jeremiah realizes that the understanding is there. It takes time for a saintly person to develop the strength of character to give leadership to the sinful, and it takes time for the sinful to reach that state of utter degradation that renders them willing to turn to God. Certainly this is painful. But the nature of free will is at the heart of the matter. The will of the prophet must be strengthened and the sinful must perceive the state of degradation in which they have fallen and the lack of control they have.

The convert, as well as the holy person, must be a person who gives himself totally to God with no reservations. God is a treasure, but if we are to appreciate him fully, we must be ready to detach ourselves from every other "treasure." As the person who finds a treasure in a field or a most valuable pearl sells everything he has to possess that treasure, so the holy person must be willing to give up all other goods to possess God, and thereby gain the priceless gifts of peace and joy. Renunciation has its rewards.

Thursday

Exodus 40: 16-21, 34-38; Matthew 13: 47-53 **YEAR I**

Moses himself did the work in preparing the dwelling tent for the Ark of the Covenant. It was a portable shrine and place of sacrifice and worship to be used on the journey through the desert. The shrine was an ark or chest to hold the two tablets of the commandments. The cover, formed of two gold angels, was called the resting place of God. Moses, like the priest with regard to the Eucharist, was the custodian of the Law and he took his responsibility personally. Moreover he was careful to obey the command of God in every particular. The priest has the same obligation with regard to the Eucharist. He should be as zealous in its custody, in his personal devotion, and obedient to the commandment of the Church concerning the discipline to be observed. The cloud by day and the fire by night could be compared to today's vigil light. In a sense they were God's presence to which the people looked for guidance on their way. Likewise, we should seek God's presence in the Eucharist where he is always available to us.

Christ repeats in the gospel that both the devout and the sinner will be allowed to live together on the face of the earth, but there will come a day of reckoning. We need to prepare ourselves for that day because it will be definitive. As the Jews should be ready to follow scribes, who really do understand God's kingdom, so we should be ready to follow our Church leaders.

Jeremiah 18: 1-6; Matthew 13: 47-53 **YEAR II**

In today's reading, Jeremiah explains that God is the Creator. The story of the potter's vessel confirms the fact that a creator has the right to cherish, keep, or alter his creation. He also has the privilege to destroy it and start over again. The clay conforms totally to his desires and ability. Likewise, God tries to fashion us according to his designs for us. God the Creator wants us to endure and he does not wish to destroy us! He wants all humankind to be saved and live happily with him forever. The only problem is that human beings are endowed with free will. As such they can refuse to follow the dictates of the Creator and do their own thing. God who is infinitely just cannot ignore this issue and he is forced to disown his creation if it will not conform to his wishes and law. This makes hell credible.

The gospel emphasizes the point that all are called. The dragnet collects all sorts of things—the good are kept but the useless are thrown away. This is a restatement that there are good and wicked people in the Church. God's call is universal in its scope and excludes no one. God gives all people, in the ordinary course of events, many years and many opportunities to convert to him and to follow his way of life. We can understand this easily, when we contemplate others, but somehow we can be blind to the need for conversion in ourselves. "Let him who has ears to hear, hear."

FRIDAY

Leviticus 23: 1, 4-11, 15-16, 27, 34-37; Matthew 13: 54-58 **YEAR I**

Today's reading is taken from Leviticus, the third book of the Bible. Leviticus gives regulations for sacrifices and directions for priests and Levites. It includes a listing of major Old Testament feasts: Passover in the springtime; Pentecost, fifty days later; the Day of Atonement and Feast of Booths, in the fall of each year. The observance of feast days in accordance with the commandment of the Lord consisted: 1) in a gathering of the whole assembly, 2) on a day when no work was to be done, and 3) an oblation made to the Lord. Then, the people were to: 4) mortify themselves and offer oblations to God for seven consecutive days and on the last one the people were to 5) repeat the solemn assembly (#1-3). These took place several times each year.

In the gospel narrative, Nazareth's lack of faith is described. The people of that town were so familiar with their neighbor, Jesus, that they were not ready to accept his teaching. The Nazareth episode forms a climax of the Galilean ministry and the rejection of Jesus. The general conception of the gospels that the miracle is a response to faith is well illustrated here because Jesus did not work any miracles in Nazareth because of the lack of faith of the townspeople.

Jeremiah 26: 1-9; Matthew 13: 54-58 **YEAR II**

For what crime was Jeremiah persecuted? He was simply the bearer of bad news from God. Instead of studying his word to see what the truth might be and how they might reform their lives, the Israelite leaders attacked the messenger. Throughout history, this has always been the case. When we don't want to hear bad news, when we are threatened with the need to reform ourselves, we attack the person who is trying to call us to our senses.

In the gospel it is clear that the leaders reacted against Christ in the same way. They could see his miraculous works. They realized how compelling his wisdom was. Yet, they murmured among themselves and said, "Who is he to be telling us what to do? Isn't he our neighbor? Isn't he just like us? What makes him so special?" In this way they proceeded to "cut him down to size," and failed to deal with the message from God which he was preaching. How similar is our own conduct! As soon as we hear the message, we dislike the messenger for no reason except that he is calling us to conversion. We attack his background, his appearance, whatever keeps us from listening to the message, the Word of God. We reject the speaker because of his message much the way the Nazarenes rejected Jesus. Their response was, "We know him, and therefore, he cannot be anything out of the ordinary." In other words, the message is not worth heeding because it is uttered by one like us.

Saturday

Leviticus 25: 1, 8-17; Matthew 14: 1-12 **YEAR I**

In today's reading we learn that, as the Lord declared that there should be a Sabbath every week, fasting at various times of the year, and other special observances, so he decreed that there should be a Jubilee every fifty years. The Jubilee meant freedom for slaves and a return of property to its original owner. For this reason, the Israelites are reminded that they should never sell property at an unfair price because they or their families must buy it back every fifty years. The word "jubilee" comes from "jubal" meaning trumpet. On the Liberty Bell in Philadelphia are inscribed words from this reading: "Proclaim liberty to all inhabitants of the land."

The Lord demanded a tremendous act of faith from the Israelites in all these celebrations. They were not to work at all; they were not to sow or harvest; they could only live off the land's wild growth and what they had stored. Yet, God always provided. In our culture it would be next to impossible to live that way. Unfortunately, our faith in God's providence is much weaker than our faith in our own abilities to produce and to care for ourselves, even though every natural disaster teaches us the opposite.

In today's gospel narrative, we have, in flashback fashion, a description of the circumstances leading to the beheading of John the Baptist. Here we can appreciate the breadth of the faith of Jesus and John. The faith of Christ in his Father's will was tremendous! Even after John's imprisonment and beheading, Christ went about teaching the same message: "Repent and believe the Good News." John the Baptist had amazing faith, too. In the face of opposition from both civil and religious rulers, death at their hands was the obvious end result of the mission of both John and Jesus. It was inevitable. And yet both Jesus and John continued to preach. In all of our lives there exists a conflict between our desire to please others and our wish to please God. What attempts do we make to resolve this conflict?

Jeremiah 26: 11-16, 24; Matthew 14: 1-12 **YEAR II**

For predicting the doom of Jerusalem, Jeremiah almost loses his life. We are often upset with some one who criticizes us rather than examine our consciences regarding the criticism. The critic has very little choice, if any. He thinks he is telling the truth and trying to help the faulty person. He should try to offer the criticism in such a way that it will be accepted, not rejected. He should not have the manner of a "bull in a china shop."

It is so easy for us to see the defect in the Israelites of Jeremiah's time, and in Herod with respect to John the Baptist. But how blind we can be to our own faults and unwillingness to change.

The Israelites finally accepted Jeremiah's prophecy. It seems that Herod saw some truth in John the Baptist's preaching, too. However, the latter was rejected, not because he was wrong, but because Herod could not bring himself to give up his life of debauchery. The pitiful thing is that Herod had such a good opportunity, he came so close to seeing the truth, but in the end he lost everything. Perhaps the criticisms leveled at us are not life and death issues, but we should give them thoughtful consideration, not just reject them out of hand, and turn against the critic in an uncharitable manner.

Eighteenth Week of Ordinary Time

MONDAY

Numbers 11:4-15; Matthew 14:13-21 **YEAR I**

Today's reading is taken from Numbers, the fourth book of the Bible. The name comes from a census mentioned at the beginning of the book. The reading describes how the Israelites complained and grumbled in the desert. The Lord was miraculously supplying them with manna—cakes made with oil. And yet, family after family complained that they would have been much better off in Egypt where they had a varied diet. Moses could see why the Lord was angry with his people, and yet it was his duty to lead them to the Promised Land. He pointed out to the Lord that the leadership role was beyond his strength—he had not conceived nor given birth to these malcontents. God was responsible so God should do something to bring them into line. Moses was focusing on one moment in time—he was tired and had not yet grown to the stature of the prophet that he was becoming. He persevered and developed the characteristics which would forever mark him as the model prophet: a thick skin, a heart warm enough to forgive and big enough to forget the offenses of others, a willingness to begin anew each day, enough strength of spirit to be unpopular and lonely, a faith that believed the impossible could be realized and that the seemingly insurmountable work before him was only a stepping stone to further challenges. Moses grew with the task! He is a model for all of us to imitate in every aspect of the human experience.

The gospel demonstrates that we can always count on the Lord for compassion. He might not send us manna from heaven or miraculously multiply loaves and fishes, but surely he will care for us as he does for the birds of the air and the flowers in the field. Indeed, in our country, he has supplied us with an abundance of everything, in excess of our basic needs. Shall we recognize that he is the source of our abundance and redistribute it to others in need? Or do we think that this abundance is the result of our own ingenuity and effort. Either way, our surplus belongs to the needy and we have a duty to distribute it to them.

Jeremiah 28: 1-17; Matthew 14: 13-21 **YEAR II**

Today's reading is about the false prophet Hananiah who tells the people that in two years they will be liberated from the king of Babylon, their captor. Jeremiah, a true prophet, contrary to Hananiah, predicts that worse is still to befall the nation of Israel.

No one likes a prophet of doom, but there is nothing worse than a false prophet, one who unrealistically raises the hopes of the people.

In our day, there are false prophets who predict wonderful things for wealthy nations such as our own. Our state of moral degradation due to drugs, sex, alcohol and the resulting violence in the streets, the threat of nuclear annihilation, international terrorism, blatant selfishness—all seem to oppose their prediction. There are still many good people, so society holds together for the present. And certainly we should preach hope because we have great potential for good. But the overwhelming truth to be seen in "the signs of the times" is that we must "reform and believe in the gospel" or we shall suffer some dreadful calamity in the not too distant future.

The times were similar in Christ's day. The calamity did not come until forty years after his death but when it did, there wasn't "a stone left upon a stone" in Jerusalem. Unable to accept what appeared to be bad news from good prophets such as John the Baptist, Christ himself, and the apostles, the Jewish people killed the messengers and continued in their profligate ways. Jesus looked upon the people with pity. They were like sheep without a shepherd on their way to slaughter. And so he prayed for them, he cured their sick, and performed other miracles. Still, they refused to accept his message. He appealed to their sense of goodness and their innate sense of the divine. But they preferred to believe in the people and the things of this world. With no intention of being a prophet of doom, and with every intention of being a prophet of hope and salvation, what can anyone committed to the truth say, except that our present situation in the world is at a similarly critical point? There is only one solution left and that is "reform and believe in the gospel."

TUESDAY

Numbers 12: 1-13; Matthew 14: 22-36 **YEAR I**

In today's reading we learn that Aaron and Miriam saw themselves as much more capable of leading the Israelites than was Moses. They complained to God about Moses. How could God have chosen "by far the meekest man on the face of the earth" to lead his people to the Promised Land, they wondered. The Lord God spoke to them about his extraordinary closeness to Moses and to manifest his opposition to their criticism he transformed Miriam into a snow-white leper.

In this context, meek means humble; someone who will actually allow God to take over his life. The meek person expects no gratitude or praise for efforts made; rather that person accepts to bear the brunt of criticism, sarcasm, scorn, and hostility. The weakness of which we speak is not moral weakness but the humility and the strength of character to accept one's limitations and to look to the Creator for the power with which to deal with the world.

The miracle of Christ walking on the water is a reminder of the same truth. While the apostles were exerting all their strength trying to get across the lake—especially after the storm came up—Jesus was at prayer. Then, calmly, by the power of God, he walked across the waters. So too, Peter was able to walk on water as long as he depended on his faith in Jesus; the moment he thought that he could do it on his own, he began to sink. In both instances, Aaron with Miriam and Peter, in desperation, cried to God to sustain them. And the Lord responded with compassion.

Jeremiah 30: 1-2, 12-15, 18-22; Matthew 14: 22-36 **YEAR II**

Today, again Jeremiah predicts national punishment. However, he goes on to speak of a future restoration of the nation after its punishment in exile. The Israelites should have been able to perceive that all that was predicted was their own fault and they should have returned to God. Alone, without God, they were experiencing hell—with the realization that this utter "aloneness" was their own fault! However, the Lord loves his people. Until their hell becomes a definitive choice, he remains their God. "I will be your God," he has already told them. Where there is life, there is hope.

Even though the apostles were together in the boat and without an overwhelming sense of guilt, they realized what life after death may be for those without God. Although they were all experienced fishermen, the storm was so terrible that it caused them to worry about their safety. Without supernatural assistance, in that dreadful moment, they knew that they could not save themselves. Just then, Christ came toward them, walking upon the water. They called to him for assistance! Peter, displaying the weakness of their collective faith, wondered whether he was the Lord. Jesus remained faithful even at that moment when the apostles were more desperately clutching at straws than believing. When the terrifying storm was over, they finally acknowledged that Jesus was the Son of God.

We are quite like the Jews of the Old Testament and the apostles. When things go well, we want to be left alone by God; we don't want to be restricted by his law or his way of life. It takes a calamity beyond our power to handle to bring us back to our senses. We should realize that we rely upon God for the gift and necessities of life such as air and water not only for us but also for all of creation. As St. Paul told the Romans, if only we would look to God's ordinary providence in nature, we would realize that, even when we perceive ourselves to be self-sufficient, we are not. We need God at all times, every minute of our lives. He alone can sustain us in a worthwhile life that without him becomes ridiculous, purposeless, and absurd. Only the presence of God in our lives makes sense of this world. We need to stop in our round of activities, raise our minds and hearts to him, and then all becomes clear. He is our God and he has power over our lives. If we fail to accept that basic relationship, life becomes aimless and unhappy and we are totally alone to do what we will and that becomes hell on earth.

WEDNESDAY

Numbers 13: 1-2, 25-14: 1, 26-29, 34-35; **YEAR I**
Matthew 15: 21-28

In today's reading, we learn that spies were sent out from the Israelite camp into the Promised Land to collect as much information as possible about the people and the land, its strength and weakness. There is little wonder that the ill-trained and poorly equipped Israelite spies were terrified at the fortified cities of Canaan. These towns often had massive walls fifteen feet or more in thickness and thirty to fifty feet in height. Caleb, leader of the intelligence group, filed a minority report. He suggested that the Israelites attack but the vast majority feared to go ahead. Caleb may have been more in accordance with God's will, but both sides were wrong in that they were thinking only in human terms. Their major difference was that Caleb thought that they could be victorious in arms and the others were fearful that they would lose. Both sides were wrong in not putting their trust in God and making him their major trump. The report led to further dissensions against God and against Moses. As a result God announced punishment for their lack of faith. He condemned them to forty years of wandering in the desert. During that time every one of those presently living would die. Only the second generation would set foot in the Promised Land.

In the gospel a Canaanite woman asked that Jesus cure her daughter. The Canaanites were the original occupants of the Promised Land, which the Israelites eventually took over. There was a deep hatred between the two groups. So when Jesus found a faith that "could move mountains" in the Canaanite woman, it was much more powerful than the prejudice he could be harboring as a genuine Palestinian. Jesus used the episode as an example for the Israelites. They knew how hard it was for him to respond favorably to the woman so if he cured the woman's daughter, it spoke powerfully to the Israelites about faith—she was putting the Israelites to shame. Maybe in their shame, the Israelites would come to believe. Fundamentally, the story asserted that Jesus did not refuse faith wherever he found it.

Jeremiah 31: 1-7; Matthew 15: 21-28 **YEAR II**

Jeremiah looks forward to the future restoration of the nation after its desert captivity. A beneficiary of God's undying love, the nation will return from across the desert to Ephraim in the north, and to Jerusalem. Although in the view of sinners the Lord may seem distant and uncaring, or close and condemnatory, his attitude is always the same—he is loving, ever ready to forgive, desirous of saving sinners rather than losing them to the power of evil. And so, if we show any signs of contrition, he is at our side to aid us with much encouragement. As the father of the Prodigal told the older son, "All I have is yours."

Even though the Son of God came among them in the flesh and lavished miracles upon them, fulfilled the prophecies, preached and lived the very life of God, the Israelites never seemed to be able to understand what was going on. Even non-Jews could see it, as attested by today's story of the Canaanite women. It was not even necessary to have the gift of faith to perceive that Jesus was at least "of God." And if he was even "of God," he could not refuse the Canaanite woman the favor she sought because total goodness is of God's essence.

Physical healings, such as the woman asked for are not necessarily in our best interest. But anything which draws us closer to God is wholly good, and it would be against God's very nature to deny it. This is especially true with regard to sin. Our own free will is always going to be a hindrance, but God's grace is ever present to the person who is sincerely seeking conversion.

THURSDAY

Numbers 20: 1-13; Matthew 16: 13-23 **YEAR I**

Today's reading tells us of the worst episode of rebellion against God during the Exodus. It took place in a barren area southwest of the Dead Sea, later called "Meribah" or "arguing." The Israelites held a meeting against Moses and Aaron. They had already made up their minds that both were "guilty" for having led them out of Egypt to a place where there was not even water to drink. We should recall that on many occasions God had gone to great lengths to manifest to his people his mastery over nature. This crisis in the desert provided another excellent opportunity to manifest that control. God would order Moses to strike the rock and water would gush forth. Once again the people would have proof of God's unfailing providence—in this case by the timeliest of signs. Instead of carrying out this divine plan of mercy, Moses and Aaron used the occasion to upbraid the people. Moses struck the rock and the water flowed out. But by this time the two leaders had changed the whole character of the event as intended by God. Instead of making the occasion a joyful manifestation of God's effortless control over nature, they had turned it into a scene of bitter denunciation. God became angry with Moses and Aaron—they had failed to glorify and hallow God's name before the people and one could say that Moses had failed God. As a punishment he would not be allowed to set foot in the Promised Land. The voices of prophets do not speak only to matters of "sacred" significance. On the contrary, prophets are to bring the reality of the sacred into every sphere of the human experience, thereby penetrating the secular and redeeming it by the very Word of God they have been sent to speak. Moses was partially responsible for the rebelliousness of the people because he had not shown forth sufficiently in his actions the sanctity of God.

In the gospel narrative, the meeting of Christ with his disciples stands in contrast to that of the Israelites with Moses and Aaron. Asking the apostles the question: "Who do you say I am?" could have been chaotic and disastrous. Everyone had his opinion. Under the leadership of Christ, however, it was a very positive experience, and the "authority" of his holiness undoubtedly had much to do with it. The apostles accepted his answer, and then for their loyalty, Jesus began to share with them his mission and authority. What could have been divisive became a source of unity. Because the apostles accepted Christ, they held together among themselves as well. It was not easy. The apostles continued to have their ideas as to how God should operate, but again, that which held them together was the commanding authority of Christ's sanctity. Gentle and humble of heart, Jesus gave them the type of leadership that was needed, even though on this occasion it was necessary to remonstrate forcefully against Peter.

Jeremiah 31: 31-34; Matthew 16: 13-23 **YEAR II**

Today's reading is Jeremiah's finest teaching. It is also his last. Jeremiah prophesies that the Lord will make a new covenant with his people. Often, the Old Covenant had to do with material things especially with the survival or punishment of the Israelites in this world. The New Covenant would be more spiritual. The agreement would not be written on tablets of stone but inscribed in man's heart. The strength of the New Covenant would not be kings, judges, and prophets so much as God himself, working through the power of the Holy Spirit dwelling within the hearts of men.

In the gospel there is an indication of Jeremiah's prophecy. Peter does not declare the divinity of Christ because of any special insight of his own but because the Father, in some mysterious manner, has revealed it to him. Shortly thereafter, Peter reprimands the Lord for talking about his coming death and the Lord rebukes him sharply because he has judged the situation by man's standards rather than by the standards of God.

This is the contest going on within us at all times. All people, having been created by God, have God's teachings written in their hearts. This is especially true of those who have been baptized. It is not difficult to know the will of God, if we make any effort to do so, but human passions and desires often blind us or distract us from considering God's truth. The same type of selfishness makes it difficult for us to choose God's will even when we know it. What good would it do us, if God should help us to get everything we wanted in this world but to the detriment and loss of our soul? Would we not think that he had betrayed us? But God does not betray us; his message is always the same. In failing to learn God's will or in rejecting it, we betray ourselves. We want the best of both worlds.

FRIDAY

Deuteronomy 4: 32-40; Matthew 16: 24-28 **YEAR I**

In today's reading from the Bible's fifth book, Deuteronomy, we picture Moses, just before he died, preaching to the Israelites. Moses reviews for the people some of the wonders that God has performed on their behalf—speaking to them from heaven and from the flaming bush, delivering them from Egypt through many wonders, having them carve out a nation for themselves among people who are much stronger than they. Moses had not simply engineered the escape of a group of displaced people who had been enslaved in Egypt. Acting for God, Moses had made a radical break between Israel's past and its future. Over and against Egyptian dominance, Moses had offered his fellow Semites an alternative reality that included a newly identified people, Israel, with its own land, history, laws, norms of right and wrong, sanctions of accountability, and above all, the freedom to enter into a relationship with the God who had called it into being. Moses, as God's prophet, delivered the message that God was with them. God was for them! Their role was to keep the laws and statutes of the Lord, obeying him in all things. We, in our time, have had far more and far greater manifestations of God's goodness—not only those of the Old Testament but those of Christ, those of the great martyrs and saints, and those of this country when we truly "trusted in God!" Let us counteract the drift away from God and let us rely always upon his goodness, wisdom, and strength.

In today's gospel we read of the profound doctrine of the Cross. The Cross, central to the life of Jesus, must be central to the life of every follower of Jesus. The Christian must deny himself, take up his cross, and follow Christ, if he wishes peace of mind on this earth and eternal happiness in the next. The true and lasting value of the person transcends the condition of the present existence and the whole world is not a sufficient recompense for the surrender of the self. In these circumstances, what does it profit a person to gain the whole world and lose eternal happiness?

Nahum 2: 1, 3, 3: 1-3, 6-7; Matthew 16: 24-28 **YEAR II**

Today, the Lord promises the Israelites that he will give them a new chance. Not only will he help them spiritually, but he will also free them from worldly oppression. Thus, he is granting them a totally new opportunity. However, if anything goes wrong, the Israelites will have no one to blame but themselves.

The gospel makes clear that worldly power is not essential to our happiness. In fact, freedom from all care can tempt us to enjoy this world too much and cause us to set our sights on worldly standards, rather than on God's. Again, what will it profit us if we gain the whole world and lose our souls? No, it is far better to remind ourselves that the world is passing. Even if we are blessed with much in our country, we need to remember through prayer and fasting that "not on bread alone does man live," but on the Word of God. To share our wealth and our abundance with the deprived is a matter of justice and our eternal salvation requires it.

The struggle of life is to seek freedom from dependency on this world and from our own lower nature in order to possess the full freedom found only in the truth, goodness, and beauty of God. God is merciful; God is compassionate; but in the final analysis, God's justice must prevail. If the virtue of justice should be lacking in God, mercy and other virtues would have no meaning. Mercy cannot be the cause of injustice to others. That would constitute a contradiction in God.

SATURDAY

Deuteronomy 6: 4-13; Matthew 17: 14-20 **YEAR I**

Although in the New Testament the "Law of Love" appears as something new, it was as old as Moses and the Israelites were to have burned this into their minds and hearts. They were to have drilled it into their children; they were to have spoken about it everywhere, they were to have the words on signs at their houses and they were even to have worn the words on their wrists and in phylacteries on their foreheads. There can be no doubt that they knew the two Great Commandments, yet like us, they took them for granted. They interpreted them in a human way, often substituting revenge for love of neighbor and man-made prescriptions as the best way to love God. The Israelites had practical proof of God's love, and every reason to love him. For he was giving them a land and houses and wells and fruit trees. in the Promised Land as a free gift, for which they had not worked. He had brought them from slavery in Egypt to a "land flowing with milk and honey." And all he asked in return was their love and loyalty.

Still, when the Messiah appeared, that love and loyalty, based on faith, was weak even among the disciples. Jesus reprimanded them for their lack of faith, when they were unable to drive a demon from a little boy even though he had empowered them to do so. Although they were empowered to be the instruments of God's healing power, miracles came about only through God's intervention. The healer-disciple needs to be convinced of this, acknowledge it at every turn, if God is to act through him. What we need to realize is that this is the case not only for miraculous cures, but for spiritual effectiveness in our ordinary daily ministry, as well. Nothing is going to happen in another person's soul merely through our efforts. Faith, hope, and love for God are the necessary ingredients in us, which somehow are brought alive by God's grace in the other person, the spark having been kindled by our ministry.

Habakkuk 1: 12-2: 4; Matthew 17: 14-20 **YEAR II**

Habakkuk like Jeremiah wrote during Israel's desperate years when Judah, threatened by Babylonia, was collapsing internally. The message of the prophet to Judah is to trust in God and not in politics. He says that one of the greatest deceptions that the ordinary person faces is to believe that he is justified simply because he is somewhat better than the next person. We freely choose to do what everyone else is doing. Thus with the blind leading the blind how can it be avoided that both fall into the pit?

As the Lord points out to his apostles in the gospel, we so-called believers are practically faithless. If we had faith the size of a mustard seed, we would be able to move mountains. And yet we pride ourselves, not on our virtue, but on what God has done for us, giving us the gift of faith, the grace of baptism and the other sacraments. In fact, all this should be to our shame, not to our pride, unless we use God's gifts to become as Christ-like as possible. That presupposes an energetic and resolute determination of dying completely to self and to the world, cost what it may. We should strive to be among the souls that possess this type of courage.

The prophet complains that God has made man like the fish of the sea or like insects that can roam about at will but usually follow "the herd," and therefore, are easy prey to the hunter because they have no wise leader. God has always provided leadership to man—from Abraham to Moses to David with all the other great prophets and kings in between. And in Christ we have the perfect model. What more can we ask of God? We do have a leader. The problem is our weakness of will, our love of the world, our reluctance to sacrifice present pleasure for eternal joy. What can God do with us whom he has endowed with free will? One thing we can do for ourselves is put aside our pride and humbly approach the Lord as the man in today's gospel did and ask that he take pity on us. It may border on despair to admit that we do not have the strength to control our own free will. But such an abject admission will move the Lord. His acceptance of such a plea is ninety-nine percent mercy but there is justice involved, too, because at least we have the minimum amount of humility and faith required to ask for that which we are unable to will for ourselves.

Nineteenth Week of Ordinary Time

Monday

Deuteronomy 10: 12-22; Matthew 17: 22-27 **YEAR I**

The book of Deuteronomy was written centuries after the death of Moses. Today's reading gives us an aggiornamento or updating of the teaching of Moses. Our God is the Lord of lords, Creator of heaven and earth. Of everything and everyone in this vast universe, he has chosen us as the special object of his love. He has done everything for us; he has fulfilled all his promises. And all he asks of us is that we carry out his laws and commandments, which he has given to us out of love, for our own good, so that we might live a happy life in accord with the nature God has given us. In a nutshell, the Law asks only that we love this good and generous God with gratitude for all that he has done for us and that we show this love concretely by the way we treat others. In spite of all these truths we are so often obstinate, insisting upon our own self-destructive ways, which cannot compare to those of the all-wise God, who created us and who knows and loves us far better than we can know and love ourselves.

In today's gospel narrative, Jesus gives a second prediction of his coming death and resurrection. He tells the apostles that he is about to be put to death gratuitously. He who has done everything for his Chosen People is about to be killed for his goodness to man. He was put to death for preaching God's truth, which was contrary to man's ways and man's thoughts, even though God's ways and God's thoughts are far superior to ours and far better for us.

Because the Temple was God's house, Jesus makes the point that he is logically exempt from a tax—but he pays it anyway purely to avoid scandal. In order to please the people, the Lord goes along with human law, even though it does not apply to him.

Ezekiel 1: 2-5, 24-28; Matthew 17: 22-27 **YEAR II**

Today's reading is from Ezekiel, prophet of the exile. His call came when he saw an overwhelming brilliant vision of God. From all that Christ had said and done among his apostles, their image of him resembled Ezekiel's vision of an awe-inspiring, tremendously powerful being. It was normal, therefore, that they were saddened and disbelieving whenever Christ spoke of his approaching death. They could not believe that human beings would be able to overcome the one who had convinced them of his godliness. For that reason, the Resurrection became central. It made clear that no one had overcome Jesus. He had permitted his death for our sake but death could not overcome him. Christ's passion and death were not an exception to his power but the means that Christ used to prove his divinity and his love for us.

So it was with the Temple tax. Just as temporal rulers taxed foreigners more than their own people, why should the Son of God and his apostles pay a tax for the support of what belonged to God? Apparently, this had little significance at the time but later the apostles remembered the incident and it became for them another proof of Christ's divinity. Christ paid the tax so that he would not get into a hassle with the Pharisees over something unimportant to him but significant to them. Jesus preferred to continue his presentation of more important issues. But he wanted to make clear to Peter and the others that the Son of God and his friends had no obligation to pay the Temple tax.

TUESDAY

Deuteronomy 31: 1-8; Matthew 18: 1-5, 10, 12-14 **YEAR I**

In today's reading from Deuteronomy, Moses ends his discourse with the Israelites by encouraging them and his successor Joshua to follow the Lord who walks before them and will lead them into the Promised Land. He repeats the thoughts that he has so often stated to them in the past—have faith in God! But now he hopes that these words will sink in because they are uttered at the close of his life and when they are about to enter the Promised Land without him. Moses had lived for this day. It was his life's mission to bring the Chosen People to the Promised Land and now he would never set foot there. He hoped that the people would heed his advice.

Moses speaks of God as absolute perfection, a person of perfect goodness and justice. All they need to do is reflect on their history; God has kept his promises. In the face of uncertainty he has been like a rock; everything that he has said and done has worked to the benefit of the Israelites. If only they had followed him more closely! But even now, he will be faithful to the Israelites, if only they will be faithful to him. "Be strong, stand firm, have no fear." The Israelites are to remember that regardless of who leads them, it is God who leads them always. And with the Lord, in good times and bad, they need never worry about the ultimate outcome. Faith will make the rough ways smooth.

Today's gospel narrative reminds us that our faith is to be like that of little children, for that is exactly what we are in God's sight. We should not be concerned with our own ability or prestige because it matters not at all with God. Rather than look for power over others, we should simply look to the power of God for our protection. Multitudes of subjects would be of little support to us in comparison to the power, the goodness, and the love of God all working in our behalf. God has concern not only for the multitude but also for each and every one of us individually. He never loses sight of us and he never fails to come to our aid. Call upon the Lord and he will not fail you.

Ezekiel 2: 8-3: 4; Matthew 18: 1-5, 10, 12-14 **YEAR II**

By symbolically eating God's words, Ezekiel is commissioned by God to be a prophet and spokesman to the Jews in exile. He is asked to digest the message of God's revelation and then proclaim it to the Israelites. Ezekiel finds that it tastes sweet but it will be bitter news for the Israelites. Likewise the honor of priesthood is great, but the life of the priest in obedience to the commands of God and his Church is not always easy. His message is true and good and beautiful but often enough it is not well received by the people. Therefore, the tendency of the prophet and of the priest is to change the message so that it will lose its difficult edge. The message eventually becomes sour in the mouth of the speaker and does nothing for the hearer except to allow him to fall even more deeply into a pit of sin. When the priest stands back to look at his life objectively, he should be able to see that only the truth makes one free.

In the gospel the apostles, who apparently discussed the question with great frequency, asked Jesus who was to be the greatest in the kingdom of heaven. His answer was that the person of innocence and simplicity of life, the one who lived like a child was the greatest in the kingdom of God. Jesus went on to illustrate the point. That innocent person often becomes a lost sheep, separated, or even ostracized from the rest of the flock. He does not go along with the crowd. God, like the shepherd, is especially concerned about that "lost sheep," that poor soul who refuses to do what everyone else is doing. He may be lost and abandoned, overlooked and disregarded by his fellow man, but God keeps an eye on him, searches him out, and brings him to a safe haven. The priest, because of his faith, hope, and love for God, is assured that the Lord will never lose track of him and of all those people who are faithful, even though the world may do so.

WEDNESDAY

Deuteronomy 34: 1-12; Matthew 18: 15-20 **YEAR I**

Today we read the final words of Deuteronomy. Moses dies after having a complete view of the Promised Land from Mount Nebo. This Promised Land had been the goal of his entire life. The scriptures, the Word of God, give to Moses the highest praise. "No prophet has arisen in Israel like Moses, whom the Lord knew face to face. He had no equal in all the signs and wonders the Lord sent him to perform in the land of Egypt against Pharaoh and all his servants and against all his land, and for the might and terrifying power that Moses exhibited in the sight of all Israel." Although Moses died without realizing the goal of his whole life and no one has ever found his grave, and although the people often rejected him while he lived, he was mourned for thirty days. The people at last recognized his greatness in their regard and his honor in God's sight, and it seems, as they crossed into Palestine, that they were determined to obey Joshua better than they had followed Moses.

From all this we learn how foolish it is to look for applause in this life. It is not always easy to be sure that we know God's will but that is what we should strive to do, and then follow it regardless of what others may think. God's will is made known not only through prayer but through human instruments as well, so consultation is appropriate. Still, it is not the number of votes that count but the validity of an opinion that should decide the issue, and if we are attentive and prayerful, God will lead us on the path that he wills us to follow. His voice, though insistent, is also soft so it is easy to overwhelm that voice with the clamor of human argument. This is clear from experience and it is what gave Moses so much trouble. Surely through his long life, despite his moments of hesitation and uncertainty, Moses listened attentively and followed God's promptings. He serves as a model to each one of us.

The gospel does not apply directly to the above but it does indicate the manner in which we should carry on debate—openly, forcefully if need be, charitably, and always with God's law and the discipline of the Church as the final arbiter. If we go about our consultation and carry on the business of the Church in this fashion, we have assurance that God will support us.

Ezekiel 9: 1-7, 10: 18-22; Matthew 18: 15-20 **YEAR II**

Today's reading consists of words written by Ezekiel while he was in Babylon and when some Jews were still in Jerusalem. He dramatizes the teaching that sincere religious people will be marked and spared in the coming catastrophe when even God himself will desert Jerusalem. His dramatic approach inspires fear as Ezekiel tells that he hears the angels being commanded to go among the Israelites and designate with an "X" those people who stand with the Lord, those who lament the evil that is taking place in the world. Those who are a sign of contradiction to evil will apparently stand out "like a sore thumb" because they will bear the "X." People think that on the day of Judgment God will have difficulty determining whether a person goes to heaven or hell because everyone's life is a mixture of good and evil. Be that as it may, the judgment will be clear to God. He sees into men's hearts; he knows their attitudes; and it is upon attitude that he makes his judgment. Outsiders might not agree but each one will know in his heart that God is a just judge.

Today's gospel is closely connected with the teaching of the Church. We should correct one another individually. The gospel indicates that in judging and correcting others, we should give each one every benefit of the doubt as Jesus does. First, we should try quietly and privately to win over the person. If that fails, mutual friends together should confront the person. Only when the guilty one makes no change, we should go "public" by seeking Church authority to prevent scandal. At that point, the person, if found guilty, loses the benefit of the doubt and is treated as someone outside the Church. This is to be done kindly, patiently, and with a spirit of readiness to reincorporate the sinner if he repents. However, there should be no compromising of God's truth for the sake of retaining the person as a friend or as a statistic in the Church.

THURSDAY

Joshua 3: 7-10, 11, 13-17; Matthew 18: 21-19: 1 **YEAR I**

Today's reading is taken from Joshua, the Bible's sixth book. Under the leadership of Joshua the people of Israel crossed the Jordan River with dry feet—just as once they crossed the Red Sea. At last they entered the Promised Land. Aware of human nature, God knew that he had to establish Joshua's authority or the fickle Israelites would soon abandon him. So on their very entrance into the Promised Land, he performed a miracle. Even though the Jordan River was at flood stage the Israelites crossed it, as they had crossed the Red Sea, because when the priests waded in with the Ark of the Covenant, the waters ceased to flow, and downstream there was no water as far as the eye could see. All Israel crossed over on dry ground in the bed of the Jordan. Joshua was to face the same kind of doubt and disbelief as Moses did but God was always with them. The story of Israel's infidelity becomes dull and monotonous as we read Scripture. They never learned; we lose patience. If Scripture were a novel, we would put it down quickly because the plot repeats itself continually.

Today's gospel makes clear that the life of each individual person is no different. Peter is inclined to believe that there must be a limit to compassion and love, but the Lord answers in terms which indicate that our forgiveness must be limitless as his is. And God makes the point by telling the parable about the unjust servant, who is forgiven a colossal debt and then, refusing forgiveness, has his fellow servant thrown into jail. If God can forgive heinous offenses, which we throw in his face time and again, should we not be able to forgive the comparatively minor offenses of fellow human beings as often as they occur? We need to keep in mind, "Judge not, lest you be judged." In the measure we give to others, so God will give to us.

Ezekiel 12: 1-12; Matthew 18: 21-19: 1 **YEAR II**

The prophet Ezekiel conveys God's word to the Israelites in dramatic form. He simulates and acts out the final destruction and exile by having exiles leave through the broken walls of a ruined Jerusalem. No one bothers to ask him what all this means! The Lord reminds Ezekiel that he lives in the midst of a rebellious people and he must stand up to them. But isn't that the way that it has been and will always be?

As the gospel points out in parable form, God is overwhelmingly generous and he simply asks us to imitate him. We cannot do all that he does but we can at least follow him in principle. He forgives us over and over again. Why can't we do the same? He often forgives sins deserving of hell. Should we not be ready to forgive our neighbor for the comparatively inconsequential harm done to us? We pray every day—many times per day—that God "forgive us our trespasses as we forgive those who trespass against us." If God were to take us at our word, he would exercise very little mercy in our regard since we are unwilling to forgive others—often for very negligible errors. How we should live our life is exceedingly clear in the depths of our hearts and in the example of Christ. All we need do is treat every one as we would have them treat us or, better still, as God treats us. In word and in deed we are to try to live as God lives. We will still blunder and sin but it will be evident that perfect love is our earnest goal.

Friday

Joshua 24: 1-13; Matthew 19: 3-12 **YEAR I**

After Joshua led the Israelites in the conquest of Canaan he divided the territory among the twelve tribes. Then he gathered the leaders at Shechem in the central highlands and reminded them of God's goodness. He reviewed for the people the whole history of salvation to get across to them that God has always stood by his people, not only in ages past but in the present time as well, when he delivered into the hands of the Israelites the land, the flocks, the vineyards of the pagan people who had dwelt there earlier. None of this was accomplished solely by the sword and bow of the Israelites but by the power of God.

In the gospel the Pharisees again try to trip Jesus in his teaching. They point out that Moses allowed divorce, but Jesus is against divorce no matter what the reason. Once the couple has been joined together by solemn vows in the presence of God, they are to be two in one flesh, never to separate. This is the way God designed marriage and family life from the beginning; man and woman are to complement one another. The apostles conclude that if there is no margin for error in marriage, it would be better not to marry. Jesus does not agree. True, there are some who are incapable of marriage for one reason or another, but the only others who should forsake marriage are those who "freely renounce sex for the sake of God's kingdom." Each one is to accept whatever vocation is given by God. If God calls one to celibacy for the sake of his service or a person is incapable of marriage, for one reason or another, that is understandable.

Ezekiel 16: 1-15, 60, 63; Matthew 19: 3-12 **YEAR II**

The prophet speaks of the magnanimous love of God toward Israel. The allegory used is that of a baby girl thrown on a garbage heap the day she is born and abandoned by all. A benefactor comes along and saves her from this desperate plight. Later he finds her unable to fend for herself and helps her still further. When she is old enough to love, he lavishes all kinds of riches upon her and treats her like a queen. In the end, the orphan who has been given everything by her benefactor, becomes enamored of herself, forgets about her benefactor and seduces every passerby for her pleasure. Unfaithful as she is, tragic as she makes her life, the benefactor remains faithful. God is like the benefactor in his love and fidelity toward Israel, mankind, every individual, the Church, and us. How late have we loved him, if indeed we love God as we should even now! But how faithful and loving he has been!

The gospel concerning the prohibition of divorce brings out clearly that the married person is to regard the other as God regards each one of us. We are to be just and charitable toward everyone, but one's fidelity to a spouse is to reflect that of God—strong, total, and above all, enduring. Hearing this, the disciples decide that, if a married person must be so faithful, it is better not to be married. Perhaps Jesus surprises them when he agrees with them! Only those people should marry who have truly been called by God to that beautiful state in life because only they will have the strength to live out their faithfulness. If one's only motivation for the married state is pleasure, it is better not to attempt marriage. Marriage is not for the self-centered person but for the one who is ready to sacrifice for the other and be prepared to remain faithful, come what may.

SATURDAY

Joshua 24: 14-29; Matthew 19: 13-15 **YEAR I**

Today's reading comes from the final chapter of Joshua. Joshua knew how fickle the Israelites could be. So he spoke to them very clearly and forcefully concerning the false gods that they were worshipping. He told them "to fish or cut bait." Serve the Lord, your God, and abandon the false gods or there can be no covenant with the one true God. Quickly they decided to stay with Joshua and serve the Lord. They agreed too quickly for Joshua's taste, so he reminded them that the Lord is a holy God and they must strive for that same holiness and, if they should falter, they may very well suffer dire consequences. Again, the people swore that they would be faithful to the Lord. So Joshua drew up a code of law, which was a practical application of God's revelation, and he made a covenant with the people. Then, Joshua died.

We need to face the same questions and make the same resolves. Negatively, are we willing to give up the false gods of personal pleasure, to which we are attached? Are we ready to strive for holiness? If we would only start each day with a conscious desire to be as close to God and the Spirit of God as we can and renew that resolve frequently, during the day, we would be a long way on the road to a virtuous, worry-free, happy, peaceful, and joyful life.

The gospel narrative shows the love of Jesus for little children who are symbols of the humble, childlike people—the poor in spirit—who are important to God. We must be like little children, always anxious to be with the members of God's family. If we are among them, how can we help but have a desire for holiness, the support that is needed for such a life, and a constant inspiration? Once we stray, however, we can see how easy it would be for us to fall into a totally different way of life. We need the protection of the whole company of saints. Some would say that this is weakness; if you can't make it on your own with God's grace, what good are you, what merit is there? The answer to this should be very clear. The human situation demands such support; we are social beings by nature. Belonging to "families" of various kinds is a weakness of human nature, if you will, but it is also a fact of life that "families" are absolutely necessary for our well-being.

Ezekiel 18: 1-10, 13, 30-32; Matthew 19: 13-15 **YEAR II**

Granted that parents have a great deal to do with the development of their children since they are their primary educators, they are not entirely responsible for the manner in which their children eventually live. Somehow, God sees to it that everyone has a free and equal chance to know, love, and serve him. Nevertheless, it is important that parents live a virtuous life, for their own sake and for the sake of the children, keeping the commandments, and going beyond that to practice the virtue of charity.

Why should we live in fear? There is every reason to live a joyful life in this world and in the world to come. So we should strive always to live a good life and try to help others to do so as well. And even if we allow ourselves to be negligent and careless about our own salvation, surely we should not live in envy, trying to prevent others from receiving and accepting the grace God offers them. The Lord, therefore, expects three things from us with regard to holiness—to be holy ourselves, assist others to be holy, and, at the very least, not stand in the way of those who are striving to do God's will in justice and charity.

Twentieth Week of Ordinary Time

MONDAY

Judges 2: 11-19; Matthew 19: 16-22 **YEAR I**

In today's reading from the book of Judges, we continue to review the salvation history of the Old Testament—the record of God's relation to Israel. After the death of Joshua, the nation was led by military leaders called Judges. Today's reading describes the chaotic religious conditions. Although God had delivered his people from Egypt, the Israelites soon "put him on the shelf." Like the man who falling from a cliff prays for help and manages to grasp a root growing out of the rocks, and then tells God he will climb back to safety, so once the Israelites were apparently saved, they told God that he could "leave the driving to us." As the root pulled loose from the rocks and the man plunged to his death, so the Israelites broke away from their roots; they began to worship the gods of those around them; they lost their own faith and failed to keep the commandments; one disaster after another afflicted them. In their predicament the Israelites were granted Judges by God to lead them. But no sooner would the people be rescued from one peril, they would fall into another because of their failure to realize that their strength was in their revealed faith.

Catholics in America are repeating the same type of history today. It was faith that made us strong many years ago—a faith that was nourished in the lands of our forbears. But once our Catholic people came to this country, they began to worship the false gods around them. Bit by bit we eased ourselves away from the commandments, revelation, and Church teaching, in order to show that we were good Americans, in order to have money and the materialistic life money, thinking that we too could be as gods. In giving up our Catholic culture, we took up a materialistic culture which dominated the nation. The same thing has happened throughout the "civilized" world until now we realize that the most important mission of the Church in our own day is to evangelize and catechize. That is, we need to convey to our people the very basics of our religion and then to teach the content of revelation as given to us by the Church.

Many unhappy people ask the very same question as the rich young man does in today's gospel reading. How can I attain eternal salvation? They recognize their unhappy state and wish to change the situation. Unfortunately, like the rich young man, however, they may lack the resolution and the need to deny self. The answer remains what it was in the time of Christ—keep the commandments, practice the corporal and spiritual works of mercy, and walk in the footsteps of Christ. Like the rich young man, who believed that he was keeping the commandments, we too "go away sad, for our possessions are many." But that's what life is all about. Do we want temporary pleasure on earth, or eternal happiness in heaven? We must make a choice. We cannot have our cake and eat it, too. "You cannot serve God and mammon." Like little children—and that is what we are in God's sight—we're seemingly puzzled by what is so obvious. We pout; we sulk; we walk around in circles; we experience more and greater unhappiness the longer we resist. Finally, at some point, we give up fighting with ourselves and opt for one alternative or the other—God or mammon, this world or the next, pleasure or sacrifice that alone can bring joy in this life or the next.

Ezekiel 24: 15-24; Matthew 19: 16-22 **YEAR II**

Through the prophet Ezekiel, who often taught through symbolic actions, the Lord tells the Israelites that their children are to "fall by the sword." Whether that is to be taken in a physical or moral sense is not defined. But it is clear that the younger generation will be lost one way or another because of the sins of their elders. The adults will not mourn in the customary way but rather they will "groan" to one another, wondering what has happened.

Something similar seems to be taking place in our own day. More and more, young people succumb to drink, drugs, sexual diseases, violence, and the older generation wonders what is happening. It is difficult and probably not proper to place the blame for this situation on particular people or actions. However, upon reflecting on the affairs of family and friends, is it possible that prosperity has much to do with it? How little we ask of youth by way of work, even around the house, and then they are paid for it! Parents side with children against their teachers, police, and neighbors. Young people have all kinds of leisure time and money to spend. Courts have gone along with indulgent parents and favor complete license to do as one pleases, endangering the rights of the unborn, the elderly, and the ordinary hard-working person.

Is it any wonder that our youth literally "fall by the sword," in auto accidents and violence of various kinds; and morally, by over-indulgence and consequent disease? Is it any wonder that there is no corrective effort, that adults only groan and wring their hands instead of examining society's collective conscience, repenting of its mistakes, and seeking ways of reforming?

It is difficult to say whether the rich young man was the product of such an environment but he could have been. He had marvelous instincts. He wanted to do good and avoid evil but he could not wrench himself free from the prosperous environment in which he lived in order to follow Christ. Sadness was Jesus' reaction. The young man was more a victim of society than of anything else. Nevertheless, he would have a difficult time to save his soul. How many such young people do we have in our society today! And for the most part, all we do is groan like the Israelites. We are afraid to face the real causes of our problems because we would then be challenged to reform our way of life.

TUESDAY

Judges 6: 11-24; Matthew 19: 23-30 **YEAR I**

Twelve Judges are mentioned in the book of Judges, and six are described at length. In today's reading we learn of the miraculous call of Gideon at a time when the Israelites were threatened by the southern Midianites. All the people in the time of Gideon were complaining that although God had done much for the Israelites in the past, he certainly wasn't any help to them now. And why didn't their leaders do something about this? Then, Gideon was given a taste of his own medicine. God chose him to lead his people, Israel. The shoe was now on the other foot. What could he do to lead the people? After all, he was a weak, powerless person. The fact is that every leader realizes this in his inner self; otherwise, he is greatly deluded, or some kind of maniac. The Lord says that he will assist Gideon. But this requires faith, so he quickly perceives how weak his faith is. Therefore, Gideon asks for a sign of God's presence and that is given to him also.

There are many things that are impossible for man. They can only be accomplished through the power of God. It is through the power of God that leaders in the Church are chosen, that they accomplish anything, that they receive a reward. Whether one is a leader or follower, God looks for one thing only from all of us—acceptance of his will. He asks only that we allow him to be at work in and through us. He asks that we allow him to use us as instruments. It is not great strength, great learning, great wisdom that accomplish wonders; it is God's grace. No matter what our station, we are no better nor worse than the next person. The only thing that will ever distinguish us, one from the other, is our correspondence with and acceptance of God's will, evidenced in deeds of justice and charity. This is why Mother Theresa and Pope John Paul, and some hidden lay person whom we may know, are all holy people. The position that they hold in the world has nothing to do with it. In fact, if they were not holy, the position that they hold would be a source of scandal.

Today's gospel reading emphasizes that wealth can easily prove a hindrance to the spiritual life contrary to the belief in Judaism that riches were a sign of God's favor.

Ezekiel 28: 1-10; Matthew 19: 23-30 **YEAR II**

In today's reading, Ezekiel explains a prophecy to the Prince of Tyre. Although a most intelligent person, the Prince has not learned that only one thing is necessary. He has used his intelligence to build a wealthy kingdom and he is so pleased with himself and so filled with pride that he fancies himself to be a god. Ezekiel informs him that uneducated pagan nations will show him how godly he is. Their ignorant armies will overrun the kingdom of Tyre and slay the Prince. Then he will perceive that he is anything but god.

The gospel tells us that in Judaism, riches were falsely considered a sign of God's favor. To deny this belief, Jesus shows that wealth can easily prove a hindrance to the spiritual life. He makes clear that it is easier for a camel to pass through the eye of a needle than it is for a rich man to enter the kingdom of heaven. Riches in themselves are not the problem. What causes the difficulty is the misuse of riches and the attitudes that the rich often develop in using them. Like the Prince of Tyre, the rich man tends to become lord of all he surveys; he usurps the power of God by exercising an unlawful and often an unjust and tyrannical power over other people. Pride predominates. The rich man looks into a mirror and sees a god instead of a human being.

Heaven is gained only by the grace and power of God. Therefore, people like the post-resurrection apostles who seem so powerless and inept in the eyes of the world, will gain the kingdom of Heaven, while others will not. It is necessary to realize that fundamentally we are powerless, dependent creatures, who need the love, protection, and assistance of an all-powerful God. To build such an attitude in ourselves we need humility and faith in God. With those gifts we will know the truth and with hope and love we will be moved to do what is good. Thus, we shall have a righteous life on earth and a happy one in heaven for all eternity.

WEDNESDAY

Judges 9: 6-15; Matthew 20: 1-16 **YEAR I**

In today's reading, we learn that a gangster son of Gideon named Abimelech organized a revolution to become king. His youngest brother, Jotham, proclaimed a fable to show how inadequate Abimelech was. The Jewish people in seeking a king for themselves often enough chose a person who would do them harm rather than serve them well. The parable used by Jotham bears this out. There were many good people in Israel who would have made good kings, but they did not volunteer because they could see how powerless they would be. Who wants to give up the life that he has, in which he can make decisions and determine his own fate, for a position in which he would be just "waving his sceptre" over the kingdom with no effect? If the people truly wanted a king, that is, someone who would reign over them in the name of God, they could find a good one. But since they only wanted a figurehead, who would let them do as they please or who held to the same low standards as themselves, they were sure to get a villain. The same is still true today; we get the political leaders we deserve.

Today's gospel reading illustrates that God is just to all, even if the Gentiles came late to the kingdom of God. Today's parable doesn't have so much to do with the equality of the heavenly reward for those who love God, as it has to do with the fact that acceptance of God's will, a holy life, holding God in one's mind and heart is in itself its own reward. Why should anyone be jealous of another person or angry with God that a later convert should receive the same heavenly reward? After all, the late convert, even if he has prospered to a great degree in the world, has gone through a hell of a life. On the other hand, the virtuous person has lived in union with God all this time. To be sure, the virtuous person may have suffered much, but what is that compared to being one with God, and to the privilege of having worked in God's "vineyard" all his life? It just doesn't make spiritual sense. The late convert has lived his life in spiritual insecurity; the person of faith and virtue has had assurance of salvation. How or why things should happen as they do in a person's life, we don't know, although free will has much to do with it. In any event, we should be just as happy for the late convert as we are for those who have practiced the faith all their lives. And to be truthful, have most of the latter really worked very hard, or worked up to their capacity, in the Lord's vineyard? Certainly the virtuous person of faith has been shown much mercy, too.

Ezekiel 34: 1-11; Matthew 20: 1-16 **YEAR II**

Ezekiel speaks of the Israelites and their leaders in terms of sheep and shepherds. In Ezekiel's time, the leaders took advantage of their powerful position and failed to help the people. They did nothing to assist the weaker, handicapped, and sick members of the community but abandoned them to their fate and treated the rest harshly. This led to violence and depredation, and the weakest members suffered most whereas, in justice, they were the most deserving of protection. The responsibility of a shepherd is to care for the sheep. The leaders are to be concerned for the people, nurture them, and care for the unfortunate. Their duty, so to speak, is to secure the public welfare.

The gospel parable describes a better shepherd. He sent unemployed laborers into his vineyard. He exercised leadership and was not easy with the laborers. He did not give them something for nothing; they had to work, even in the scorching sun. No one could accuse him of being unjust. He gave the men work; he paid all of them the agreed upon wage whether they worked all day or a few hours; and he did not expect to get something for nothing. Every leader of the people can at least do this—he can be just, even though tough; he can be good even though not generous; he can be charitable even though not to all.

The ordinary person should not expect charity but justice. If he gets what is coming to him, works for a fair wage, receives all the protections required by law, then he should be satisfied. He should not be concerned that others get more; he should only be concerned that he and others receive justice. If some receive more, he should still be satisfied and not be envious.

THURSDAY

Judges 11: 29-39; Matthew 22: 1-14 **YEAR I**

The story of Jephthah's vow in today's reading illustrates the primitive ignorance and superstition rampant at the time of the Judges. Jephthah sacrifices his daughter who mourns that she will die childless. This story in Judges is hard to accept, namely that the Lord would allow Jephthah to keep his vow to offer his daughter as a holocaust in thanksgiving for a military victory. We can understand the story of Abraham and Isaac because God, having tested their faith, intervened. For this one, we need to cede to the biblical scholars. What we can gain from the story is the faithfulness of Jephthah to a promise made to God, his deep love for his daughter, and the daughter's difficult decision to accept God's will.

The gospel narrative is a parable warning Israel for not accepting the prophetic message of salvation brought to them by Jesus. Instead of accepting God's will represented by the invitation to the wedding banquet, the people insult God's messengers, even kill some of them and go off to do their own thing. God allows them to do so and this turns out to be hell for them for all eternity. Then God extends the invitation to every person. These latter gladly accept but some, distinguished by the lack of a wedding garment, do not behave as they should and they are cast out to "do their own thing" for all eternity, too.

The power of free will is enormous, it can even reject the will of God. Free will needs immense strength of character to be held in check. Conscience, the commandments, and all salvation history reveal to us that the purpose of life is to test whether or not we are going to keep God's will or, in pride, "do our own thing." The choice truly is obvious, and yet, we choose to sin. Our response to the situation should be to realize that, even though our will seems to be clearly under our control, we surrender to the weakest and most foolish temptations. Why? Because somehow we seem to think that we can enjoy the pleasure of sin and yet not commit our will to it, only to discover that pleasure is as weak as quicksand. The will is easy to control, if we keep a close rein on it, if we don't allow any deviations, any wandering from the straight path. But if we relax our control, we find that it readily runs away from us and leaves us in the quicksand of inertia.

Ezekiel 36: 23-28; Matthew 22: 1-14 **YEAR II**

Ezekiel describes how, after the exile, the nation will be restored—reborn in a fresh new covenant, remade in a completely new relationship between God and man. God promises to prove his holiness through the people. The psalmist describes God's action thus "I will pour clean water on you and wash away all your sins . . . I will give you a new heart and place a new spirit within you . . ." This passage is often used in Masses for baptism and confirmation because it speaks of cleansing from impurity and placing a new spirit in the people.

Possibly the best proof of Jesus' divinity was his holiness. Who could convict him of sin? He performed some marvelous feats but these were quickly forgotten by the people of his own time. Now, we are told that they were psychological phenomena or perhaps figments of the fertile imagination of the evangelists. Disbelievers can fight the miracles and maybe God's providence but there is no doubting the holiness of Jesus. Consequently, holiness should be a characteristic of the members of Christ's Church. At the Last Supper, Jesus repeated several times that the apostles were to exhibit holiness visibly by loving one another in order that others could come to believe in him. Holiness is still the WAY to heaven and the way to faith for others. Ghandi believed that self-sacrifice on the part of one person can accomplish far more than millions of people killing other millions in order, supposedly, to obtain the same end.

Some people, like ourselves, have received a very special invitation to holiness and we have been given the means to respond—not only baptism and confirmation but Eucharist also. There are many who do not have access to these gifts yet live a holy life by turning to unselfish pursuits. God will be known. Others like Ghandi will be given the invitation to love God in other ways. We don't know how God operates outside the Church. But he will be served; he will be loved. All peoples are called to salvation. God's plan will be fulfilled by us or by others despite our collective unworthiness. Why not by us?

FRIDAY

Ruth 1: 1, 3-6, 14-16, 22; Matthew 22: 34-40 **YEAR I**

Today's reading from the book of Ruth tells how a self-sacrificing Moabite woman became the great-grandmother of King David. Moab was southeast of the Dead Sea. The devotion of Ruth to Naomi was exceptional. Ruth had never known the Israelite community and culture; she would be received as an alien. Yet she insisted on staying with her mother-in-law who had no one else upon whom to rely. If Ruth could be so devoted to a human family which had "adopted" her by marriage, how much more should we be devoted to the God, who has adopted us into his family through the sacrament of baptism? Even if others of our human family should die or drift off to some other way of life as Orpah did, how can we conceivably abandon the God, who has taken us unto himself and given us everything? True, he may lead us into "strange lands"—unforeseen circumstances and situations, but what are these, if the Lord is with us? It is not an easy thing to enter the unknown with only

God to lead us and to be with us but this, in a sense, is what one does, when one accepts a religious vocation. To go a step further, or to follow that vocation to its ultimate meaning may be most difficult, but when God is surely with us, what is there to fear in the final analysis? In going with Naomi, Ruth was exhibiting the manner in which a person shows total love of God and neighbor. There seems to be no other motive than these two Great Commandments presented by Matthew in today's gospel narrative. Jesus explains how they summarize the Ten Commandments and simultaneously describe the basic approach to life of any follower of Christ.

Ezekiel 37: 1-14; Matthew 22: 34-40 **YEAR II**

The vision of the dry bones is a symbolic prediction of the nation to be restored and renewed, following its exile in the graveyard of Babylon. It indicates not only God's power but also his great love for man. Above all, it reveals the basic relationship between God and man. God continually offers man the help of his grace. Spiritually, man can remain alive and healthy if he will only keep faith in God, whose love never ceases. But man dries up spiritually, when he turns from God to the things of the world. Even in exile, the Israelites had nothing to fear—God was with them—if they remained strong in faith. Closeness to God is much more important than worldly success, even though it seems to add an extra burden. In our country, material prosperity is a much greater obstacle to the spiritual life and to the love of God than any physical evil we may suffer.

Today's gospel reading provides an important lesson. Jesus emphasizes the two Great Commandments that summarize the Ten Commandments and together describe the basic approach to life of any follower of Christ. The primacy of love for God and love for one's fellow man is revealed in the New Testament as it was in the Old Testament. The greatest and the first commandment is to love God totally; the second is to love one's fellow man as we love ourselves. Beyond that, nothing really matters in God's sight despite worldly influences attempting to convince us otherwise.

SATURDAY

Ruth 2: 1-3, 8-11, 4: 13-17; Matthew 23: 1-12 **YEAR I**

We notice in today's reading how appreciative good people are for even the smallest favors. Since Naomi and Ruth were dirt-poor, Ruth went around the countryside gleaning from the fields. This was a scavenger operation. After the workers had harvested the crop, it was the law of God that the poor could go through the fields and take what little may have been left over. That was a big favor! Apparently women, who gleaned, might often be molested and never would they receive kindness from the workers. Boaz guaranteed Ruth her safety and also gave permission that she might drink from the water supply of the workers. Why was Boaz so "generous?" Ruth's history of fidelity and her humble, innocent manner made her an extremely attractive person. In fact, Ruth and Boaz eventually married and her son Obed, became the grandfather of David.

It is clear that we are called upon to imitate the fidelity, the generosity, and the humility of Ruth, who sacrificed family, country, culture and all that she had and held dear in this world to help her mother-in-law, who was in need. But we need to reflect also upon the goodness, mercy, and love of Boaz, who appreciated and rewarded these virtues of Ruth. He made her feel at home in a foreign land. Sometimes we are hardly willing to do for family and friends what Boaz did for this alien. We pray for the ability to be ever kinder to the poor, especially to poor individuals and not just to the poor en masse.

This would seem to be the lesson of today's gospel, which portrays the Pharisees as being all talk and no action with regard to the practice of religion. The disciples are urged to do what the Pharisees say, but not to imitate their way of life. As the ordination ritual urges us to put into practice what we believe, we should be on guard against the hypocrisy of the Pharisees, which can so readily afflict us. Mother Theresa is an excellent example. Her words were simple and profound repetitions of the same gospel message. It was clear that she acted before she spoke. Many years before anyone ever heard of her she spoke to us much more eloquently in the example of her sacrificial life than by her words. The lesson is clear that virtue—love of God and neighbor, adherence to God's revealed truth in the actions of our lives—is the only thing which counts in the final analysis.

Ezekiel 43: 1-7; Matthew 23: 1-12 **YEAR II**

Ezekiel's vision of God returning to dwell in the holy of holies of the future temple gives our human minds an inkling of the overwhelming glory of the presence of God. There is no need for words, for regulations, nor for ceremony. God's greatness simply flows over to fill every expectation. When God is present with his people, nothing else is needed. Human power, on the other hand, must be cultivated, or "marketed" in today's terms. It must be "earned" in one way or another. It does not come automatically. Usually it is maintained by laws; it is accompanied by ceremony to keep everyone focused on its importance. But when God is present there is no need for trappings, he overwhelms us.

Keeping this in mind, we should be restrained in the admiration that we pay to human leaders. We can, like the Israelites of old, make them into gods; we can sway them to do our will or be swayed to do their will, which may be anti-God, heathen, or atheistic. Instead, we should discriminate and save our greatest admiration for the virtuous person, the one who truly strives to serve the best interest of others. The leaders, the powerful, may not always be included among those most compassionate toward others—the attitude that God wants in rulers. To some extent, compassion makes him present to us while we await the fullness of his coming in glory.

Twenty-first Week Ordinary Time

Monday

1 Thessalonians 1: 2-5, 8-10; Matthew 23: 13-22 **YEAR I**

Of the 27 books of the New Testament, this one to the Thessalonians was probably the first written. Only 20 years after the Ascension, Paul wrote his first letter to the Thessalonians thus beginning the New Testament. This letter written in 51 A.D. was primarily to encourage Paul's converts. He praises the Thessalonians to the skies and the reason for his praise is their vibrant faith, hope, and love. It would be good to know just how they exhibited these virtues—whether quietly, or with great activity, or with great emotion. Regardless of how their faith, hope, and love were expressed, they were attractive to St. Paul and to others because these are the virtues that make us one with God. What more can be asked of a person, what more can one person give to another, than God's presence? Somehow that is what the Thessalonians were projecting, and it inspired all those who were in contact with them.

Nothing in the New Testament is quite comparable to today's gospel narrative. It is a powerful condemnation of the Pharisees who have placed their faith, hope, and love in the things of this world. They are more interested in gold than in the Temple; they place greater value on the sacrifices—which the people bring and which must be made holy—than to the very altar, which symbolizes God and makes the gifts holy. Rather than making it easier for the people to become one with God and enter his kingdom, the Pharisees, by their example, give scandal and drive people away from the practice of faith. They have placed their faith, hope, and love in the things of this world. Jesus condemns with vigor the evasions of truthfulness by the Pharisees and their legalism.

These readings provide good instruction for the priest. Having been gifted with celibacy, the temptation for the priest is material goods. Probably everyone suffers from the latter temptation. But the choice is clear—God or mammon. Theoretically, we make that decision no later than ordination. But how many of us nourish such a relationship with God that our faith, hope, and love for him completely dominate our lives? Rather, are we not often engulfed by more mundane things? And if so, should we not face ourselves more frequently and frankly with the question of who and what rules our lives?

2 Thessalonians 1: 1-5, 11-12; Matthew 23: 13-22 **YEAR II**

St. Paul makes the point that our worship should be directed to God as a spiritual worship. Although we remain in this world and must deal with its realities, it is important that we should be joined in mind and heart to the God who is above. If God dwells in us and we in him, we should be little concerned about bodily suffering. This is not to say that, in an objective worldly sense, life in this world becomes easier but it is endured with less pain when we experience God's peace and thereby increase our faith, hope, and love for God. The spiritual experience of union with God makes other situations less significant.

In the time of Jesus, the Pharisees were quite different. They lived an external and superficial spirituality. The appearance of things meant everything. The devotion of the people was determined by the size of their offering or the ornamentation they put on the Temple. Among their rules were the sacred objects by which an oath could or could not be taken. Jesus condemned their legalism. They appeared to value these objects much more than the God who dwelt in the Temple or the altar which made the gifts holy, or the commandments contained in the holy of holies. Theirs had become a man-made religion.

This type of religious practice is always a danger for us in the Church and Vatican II was intended to correct such abuse. We cannot allow ourselves to become cemented in externals and the danger of this happening is always looming. Peril arises in both change and non-change. The above applies to our personal prayer life as well. We can become bogged down in certain practices of prayer, which eventually can deaden our prayer life.

TUESDAY

1 Thessalonians 2: 1-8; Matthew 23: 23-26 **YEAR I**

St. Paul had great opposition in Thessalonia but he had learned his lesson elsewhere that, come what may, he should speak the Word of God boldly and let the chips fall where they may. He did not resort to trickery, nor did he try to meet the opposition on its own ground. Rather, he preached Jesus Christ crucified. It does seem to be extreme that one would not take the audience into consideration when trying to convert them, so in all likelihood, Paul did so. But what he was trying to make clear to them was that, when the Word of God is concerned, there can be no compromise whether for the preacher's safety or the audience's sensitivity. It is necessary to be gentle and kind with the audience but one should never water down the Word of God in any circumstance.

Today's gospel reading is a devastating condemnation of Pharisaism, a form of religion that makes much of external regulations while missing the genuine internal religious spirit. Pharisaism stands in contrast to St. Paul's approach.

The Pharisees wished to be justified in the sight of men rather than God. Therefore, they were scrupulous in their observance of the externals of the Law—many of which were their own prescriptions—but lax in the fulfillment of the basics which have more to do with internal convictions and attitudes which call for true conversion of heart. They could be very harsh on the people who failed to observe all the externals of the Law but neglected the fact that the Law also called for the exercise of justice, good faith, and mercy.

Without in any way condemning leaders of the recent past, it is clear for anyone to see that the Holy Spirit has recently saved us from a pharisaical situation. It is evident now that prior to Vatican II we were too concerned about the externals of religious schools, hospitals, fish on Friday, rather than internal attitudes and convictions. What Pope John Paul II wants us to guard against is that we not go to the opposite extreme. The pre-Vatican situation was not like that of the time of Christ. Therefore, the changes recommended by Vatican II were not revolutionary. It was not a case of everything being wrong and needing to be thrown out. A few degrees of correction were needed. The danger in the present time is that, in addition to giving less attention to the externals, some would have us eliminate even the Ten Commandments and all moral absolutes. What we need is justice tempered with mercy, hatred of sin with love of the sinner, charity for people and not for monuments, a philosophy based on "the Sabbath is for man, not man for the Sabbath."

2 Thessalonians 2: 1-3, 14-16; Matthew 23: 23-26 **YEAR II**

The Thessalonians thought that the Second Coming would take place shortly. Paul urged them not to give credence to any insinuation that the day of the Lord was near. The end could come at any moment for any of us. But that should make no difference. He encourages them to continue in every good work and word; holding fast to the faith and the teaching of Christ; and practicing justice and mercy. Temptations originating from our own selfishness, our desire to have an easy, untroubled life in this world will arise and many will come from powerful, worldly-wise people, and those who claim to have an "inside track" in interpretation. We must be on guard against them and be faithful to the words and works of the Lord Jesus.

This is as true for the Israelites as for the Gentiles, Christ points out. The religious leaders of the time of Jesus were propounding human wisdom and at the same time sinning against "justice and mercy and good faith." In today's gospel reading, Matthew makes a devastating condemnation of Pharisaism as a form of religion emphasizing external regulations and missing the genuine internal religious spirit. What the Pharisees were asking of the people was not necessarily bad in itself, but these external practices had become the essence of religion instead of signs for the more essential spiritual practices.

WEDNESDAY

1 Thessalonians 2: 9-13; Matthew 23: 27-32 **YEAR I**

In today's reading, St. Paul takes great consolation in the fact that when preaching to the Thessalonians, he did not pull any punches and yet they believed. It would seem that they were won over by a combination of the truth for which the human mind is made and by the fact that St. Paul practiced what he preached. Not only was there an appeal to idealism but there was realism too. The truth appealed to them and the people saw that it worked in Paul's life. Paul had great affection and dedication for the Thessalonians even though he had met with great opposition during his preaching days among them to the extent that he had to flee the city.

The Pharisees once again were just the opposite. Today's gospel gives seven "woes" condemning the hypocritical religious style of professional Pharisees. An honest person could sense that they were not preaching the truth. Although God must reward the good and punish evil, surely the people could sense that the God, in whom they hoped and believed, had to be a loving God, and that did not come through in Pharisaical preaching. That they were deceivers was confirmed by the fact that the Pharisees did not practice what they preached. This was evident in some of their regulations.

A person could tie up his money in "sacred" investments so that he did not need to support aged parents; the poor had to bear impossible burdens at times as shown in some of the laws of the Sabbath. No wonder the faith of the people was weak when Christ came into the world! No wonder people flocked to hear St. John the Baptist and Jesus! They were hungry for the truth and they found John and Jesus credible because they lived their gospel.

2 Thessalonians 3: 6-10, 16-18; Matthew 23: 27-32 **YEAR II**

St. Paul says several times in his epistles, "Imitate me as I imitate Christ." To live the life of Christ is a challenge for everyone of us. St. Paul could have depended upon the people for support, but he did not. He could have eaten the flesh of animals offered to false gods, but he did not. With St. Paul's understanding of the gospel, he probably could have said and done a number of things which although acceptable were outside the tradition, but he did not. His objective was to cause neither confusion, nor scandal, but to mold a unified Body of Christ. He wanted to be seen as one whose outer life was directed by his inner life, his perfect union in the love of Christ. He was a person who practiced what he preached, and "had his act together."

In today's gospel, Matthew condemns the hypocritical, religious style of professional Pharisees. By keeping their man-made laws; by setting their own standards of holiness, the Pharisees appeared in the eyes of man to be holy, but interiorly they were "filled with dead men's bones." They were not what they appeared to be. Jesus points out that some of their man-made laws were opposed to the fundamental laws of justice, goodness, and mercy established by God himself; and some of them could circumvent their man-made laws because of their theological learning but they did not hesitate to place heavy burdens upon the ordinary people incapable of theological subtleties. The Pharisees were like "whitewashed tombs."

Thursday

1 Thessalonians 3: 7-13; Matthew 24: 42-51 **YEAR I**

In today's reading, Paul writes an encouraging letter to the Thessalonians, a young church that he was pleased to have started in Christ. The theme is unity with God and men. He clearly states what every priest knows. It is the faith of the people that encourages him to persevere in his vocation. Surely the priest should be motivated and inspired mostly by God himself, the gospel, his special calling, the grace of Orders, the example of Christ and of the Saints through the centuries. There is no doubt that the faith of our people makes the burden of leadership lighter and fills the priest himself with greater faith, hope, and love.

For such people we are inspired to pray, as St. Paul does, that they will be filled to overflowing with love and that their sanctity may increase and deepen. This is the best gift that a person of faith can receive. The individual person always has a sense of sinfulness, a knowledge as to how easy it is to slip into sin. So the people need to be strengthened by God's grace. The holiness and love, which are evident in the lives of our friends, constitute an encouragement for our own holiness and perseverance in good works.

Our oneness with God, our living of his life, is not something which we should do out of fear. At the same time, everyone likes to put his best foot forward. It is fitting that we should dress and act properly, when we are expecting important guests. Christ speaks of this several times in the gospel, including today's and in the parable of the wedding banquet. Surely, the hypocrite wishes to make a good impression, thinking that he can deceive. The good person also wishes to make a favorable impression, but the major reason is the conviction that there is only one responsible and good way to use his life—the way that the Creator has ordained.

1 Corinthians 1: 1-9; Matthew 24: 42-51 **YEAR II**

Those who have been baptized have been called by God to be a holy person. Moreover, they have been given every grace by God so that true holiness is not an unrealistic ideal but an actual possibility. Indeed, anyone who has been so called and blessed betrays Christ if he does not live up to the ideal. And yet, how often do we say to ourselves that this temptation or that is too strong for us? How often do we get tired of the struggle and allow ourselves to indulge? How often do we put aside thoughts of a distant death to enjoy a present pleasure?

It is a clear conclusion from St. Paul's writings that much of our problem is due to lack of support and example from other people, all of whom depend upon us, for the same assistance. It is clear that weak human beings need all the fraternal support they can get. We depend upon one another and we are indeed "our brother's keeper."

The gospel makes clear that, even in the temporal order, it makes good sense to provide for the future. If we live only for today, we shall have a number of lean tomorrows. It is better to sacrifice a little of what we have in the present so that we will not be lacking anything in the future. And also, so that we can assist others who may not have been so provident. And if this is the case in the temporal order, how much more important is it, when the kingdom of God is at stake!

God has given me every spiritual blessing. This is not true of my body and mind. I have some very positive physical qualities, but my strength is limited; my athletic ability is limited; my endurance is limited. I am subject to sickness, disease, and death. It is the same with my mind. I have been given reasonably good intelligence, but I don't know everything; I am prone to error. My will is also weak. God could have infused great knowledge into my mind. He could have refused to give me free will. Then, I would behave perfectly. But, in his providence, he has not given me every blessing of mind and heart. However, through the merits of Christ, I have received and continue to receive every spiritual blessing. I have the potential to be perfectly holy; God gives me everything needed. And yet I fail in the spiritual life because I allow my imperfect body, mind, and will to prevail. The cravings of physical appetites, my lack of wisdom, and prudence over-rule the promptings of grace. I need to allow God's Holy Spirit to have free reign, to live in me, and to act through me.

FRIDAY

1 Thessalonians 4: 1-8; Matthew 25: 1-13 **YEAR I**

We believe that Scripture, the Word of God, is not only free of error but contains insights that, even from a human point of view, are remarkably penetrating. Paul encourages his converts to greater holiness, chastity, and charity. This reading is food for meditation by any follower of Christ. At this time Paul is speaking to a group of people who have responded well to the gospel message. As Christians go, the Thessalonians are doing very well. But he exhorts them to do better, pointing out that impurity and greed are special temptations, about which we should be concerned. Isn't it true? Human beings, weak and sinful as they are, are especially susceptible to these dangers. All one needs to do is examine one's own conscience; look around among family, relatives, and friends; or check the media. These are the temptations that make the soap opera plots continue endlessly. Somehow the themes of lust and greed are attractive to everyone. Even those who do not sin in this way too often can readily understand their attraction. Since we are no different from other people, by virtue of human nature, we need to be on our guard. Since we are different, by virtue of grace, we should not readily excuse ourselves or rationalize; with God's help, we can remain free of the taint of these sins.

The gospel reminds us that we must always be prepared for the Lord's coming. Our theology tells us that only Christ, Mary, and possibly John the Baptist lived without sin. Rare, exceptional people avoid most sin. The rest of us are always in and out of sin, or at least in danger. To prepare for the Lord's coming we need to develop a spiritual life; we need to flee temptation, not think that we can entertain it or even compromise with it and still avoid sin. We need to have prudence; we need good companionship, and the support of other good people. And above all these, we need faith in God's existence, hope in his promises, and a genuine love for him.

1 Corinthians 1:17-25; Matthew 25: 1-13 **YEAR II**

In religious matters, the Jews were always asking for signs and the Greeks for wisdom, both of which, if given to the degree desired, would eliminate the need for faith. They wanted to be "forced" to believe; they were looking for absolute certainty. They were really seeking from God the one thing that he will never do—take away our free will. And because God would not do that—would not force them to believe—they refused to use their free will to accept him; they used their free will in a negative way only. And with many, this was probably the way that they preferred. That is to say, they wanted to shift the burden of belief totally on God; they were demanding that God justify himself to them. And until he was able to do so, they would continue with their own worldly way of life and with their own man-made religion.

Perhaps the modern scene is not exactly the same but surely there is a danger that charismatic people should become as the Jews and even more likely that those who believe in the "power" of technology should be as the Greeks. There is no question that the charismatic people appear to be deeply religious but there is some question as to whether or not they depend too much on signs and are inclined to develop their own man-made religion (cf. "Enthusiasm" by Ronald Knoc). So far they are attached to the hierarchical church and that is a saving grace but many also have broken away to form their own churches. There seems to be a tendency on their part to see themselves as better than the ordinary Catholic and to want to convert the bishops to their style rather than to accept what the hierarchical Church has to offer.

That "technocrats" are similar to the Greeks, who claimed validity only for what could be quantified in some way, is quite obvious. They pay little or no attention to the spiritual, to that which cannot be measured or mechanized or quantified.

Like the unwise virgins, those who look for signs or physical proof of spiritual realities are not necessarily mean-spirited people, but they have been swallowed up by the culture of this world. They have deliberately shortchanged themselves with regard to faith and tradition and, in their final hour, it will be difficult for them to recover a lost faith, if they ever had it. And, like the unwise virgins, they will find that faith is not something that can be borrowed from others. Faith is something we must "purchase" for ourselves. We need to work at it; most often it comes slowly. Like a flame, the life of faith is delicate, easily damaged, and needs constant attention. It is never too early to develop the faith that we need for salvation.

SATURDAY

1 Thessalonians 4: 9-12; Matthew 25: 14-30 — YEAR I

In today's reading, Paul continues to give spiritual and practical advice to his dear converts in Thessalonica. The Thessalonians have committed themselves to the Christian way of life and Paul congratulates them for it. But one cannot stand still in the spiritual life. To do so is to go backward, to become fearful or self-serving. Instead, St. Paul urges the people to be in even greater earnestness to assist one another and to build peace in the society. Although it is barely possible to make goodness and peace universal, it will never be possible to reach the intensity of the spiritual life, to which we aspire. This will only be realized in heaven. Meanwhile we are to strive, at least, to make ourselves as perfect as possible.

Surely the Lord is not such a heartless person as the master of today's gospel, but the lesson of justice does apply. God does expect something of us. He does not give us life, talent, resources, other people around us for no purpose. We are to help them; they are to help us in accomplishing the mission that God has given us. The lesson of today's parable is to work faithfully while awaiting the Lord's return. God will judge according to talents given.

There is no place in the Christian life for either fear or inactivity. God has given us a mission—to love him with our whole mind, heart, and soul and to love our neighbor as ourselves. We are to use God's grace and other resources, which he has given us, in order to achieve this end. We must be committed to our goal in a stable fashion and we must work at it seriously and perseveringly.

1 Corinthians 1: 26-31; Matthew 25: 14-30 **YEAR II**

Those whom God chose to be apostles were not especially wise, influential, powerful, or well-born. For the most part, it has continued to be the same in the Church among the canonized saints, and the holiest people we know. And if these were wise, or worldly powerful or well born, they sacrificed all of it in order to be God's chosen.

We are not necessarily supposed to give up all these things. For instance, we are not to become fools, nor forsake powerful friends, nor separate ourselves entirely from a "birthright." But we must give up our reliance upon such worldly values, surrender ourselves to God, trust totally in him, and then he will mold us as he wills into a holy people. God's favor is all that counts.

The parable of the talents is an application of the Lord's words that we should learn from the cleverness of the worldly person but not follow his example. And so, just as the worldly wise use their talents, such as money and business sense to accumulate wealth, so in the spiritual realm should we use God's grace.

Just as a person with money invests his wealth in business enterprises or at least puts it in a bank to draw interest, so the person with God's grace should invest his spiritual wealth in good works rather than allow these riches to lie fallow. We must use God's grace and be active in this regard. To stand still "all the day idle" is to lose what we have. Like so many other holdings, such as mechanical assets, if we do not use them, they will grow rusty and crumble when we finally do put them to work. God's grace is similar. We must constantly use God's goodness in works of justice and charity or be in danger of losing everything.

Twenty-second Week of Ordinary Time

MONDAY

1 Thessalonians 4: 13-18; Luke 4: 16-30 **YEAR I**

In today's reading we learn that the Christians at Thessalonica had a special concern. They expected Christ's Second Coming soon and felt sorry for fellow Christians who had died and would not be there to greet the Lord at his coming. Paul explains that the resurrection of the dead will happen before the Second Coming. This periscope leads us to reflect on the value of gaining the whole world while suffering the loss of one's soul. How can that be avoided? Taking at least a few minutes each morning or evening for prayer is vital. It is important to pause for a few moments, set our lives in order, settle our priorities for the day, resolve to carry them out, and work to correct at least one fault. We need meditation of this kind so that we live our lives with a clear purpose in mind. Otherwise, our whole existence can be aimless, monotonous, boring, and unhappy. Rather than live for certain momentary pleasures, if we give purpose to our lives, even work or difficult jobs take on a whole new character. Faith, hope, and love replace drudgery. Life should not be mere existence; it should be truth, goodness, and beauty. These are the things that make life worth living.

In the synagogue at Capernaum, Christ announced the same message as he proclaimed the purpose of his life. He was sent to preach good news to the poor, to heal the afflicted, and to console the downtrodden. His purpose was not to entertain or to improve the material conditions of the people. In the synagogue at Nazareth, Jesus applied to himself the classic Old Testament description of the Messiah and, as a result, the people were filled with indignation. They led him to the top of the hill intending to hurl him over the edge. But he went straight through their midst and walked away. Indeed, he was without honor in his own town.

We must settle on a purpose for our lives. Too many choose mere existence, interspersed with a few pleasures, which satisfy the bodily senses or animal instincts. Far better is it to choose the life of joy, peace, and satisfaction which derives from that which is true, good, and beautiful.

1 Corinthians 2: 1-5; Luke 4: 16-30 **YEAR II**

When St. Paul was in Athens, he tried to win over his audience with a brilliantly reasoned speech. He had no success. So now in Corinth, he speaks only of the "foolishness" of the gospel. It is most uncomfortable for him to do so because he feels weak and fearful. The people have little or no background for the message he brings except their human nature, emotions, and longings. He preaches only about Christ and his death on the cross and lets the grace of God do the rest. And he is eminently successful in this rough and tumble seaport city! We, too, need to stay close to the gospel. Sometimes, it seems foolish to be preaching a homily on the Scriptures when there are so many problems in the world that need to be addressed and that seem to be of vital importance. The objective should be to help the people believe in Christ crucified. He will take care of the rest.

The grace of God can touch whomever he wills. The same message can be preached to thousands of people, yet only a few people—and often the most improbable—heed the message, accept it, and carry it out. As Christ points out, there were many people looking for assistance in the days of the prophets Elijah and Elisha, but only a poor widow and Naaman, the Syrian, were miraculously helped. Human beings set up so many obstacles to grace that only God and not even the most powerful human arguments can overcome them. Therefore, our role is to present God's truth in the best way possible and leave the grace of conversion to him.

TUESDAY

1 Thessalonians 5: 1-6, 9-11; Luke 4: 31-37 **YEAR I**

Most scholars maintain that St. Paul thought that the end of the world was coming soon after Christ's ascension into heaven. His letters are completely compatible, however, with a delayed Parousia. For he is clear on the essential point, namely that the end will come suddenly (cf. Matthew 24) and that we should always be prepared. Readiness for the coming of Christ is motivated by the reciprocal love that we should have for him and by the certainty, suddenness, and finality of death. Since Christians know these things, there is only one sensible mode of conduct. In today's reading, Paul urges the Thessalonians to be prepared always living in anticipation of the judgment that will determine their salvation.

God wants all men to be saved, so there is nothing sinister about death and the end of the world. Indeed, they are not a punishment, but for the Christian they signify entry into a new, more glorious, and eternal life. The demon in the gospel holds to the contrary—he says that Jesus has come to destroy us. By curing the demoniac, Jesus demonstrates that he has come to destroy the power of evil and to heal and save human beings. God cannot work against his own creation.

It is most encouraging in our day to realize that even two thousand years ago it was recognized that Jesus spoke with authority. Whether the hearers were able to accept the teaching or not, they recognized the truth of what he had to say. We should not water down the truth for any reason. We should not be seeking popularity but respect for the truth—God's teaching—whether the people have the fortitude to accept and practice it or not. No matter what a person does with God's word, he has a right to the truth. And we, as God's chosen messengers have an obligation to present that truth to all his people.

1 Corinthians 2: 10-16; Luke 4: 31-37 **YEAR II**

Each person alone knows his or her innermost thoughts. It is true that we may be oblivious to many of our external characteristics or idiosyncrasies and we do not know how we appear to others. However, when it comes to our moral and spiritual character, we alone, apart from God, can penetrate to the depths of our souls.

Followers of Christ not only have this natural ability, but they have been given, in addition, the very Spirit by which God knows himself. As St. Paul says, "We have the mind of Christ." Most of the time, however, we pay very little attention to this Spirit dwelling within us, a Spirit which illuminates our minds and strengthens our wills. We rarely welcome this divine influence; we rarely invite this divine presence to take over our being. Rather, we appeal to the Spirit only in routine fashion, and we allow human passions to prevail even when we are quite aware of the Spirit's promptings.

We are somewhat like the man with the unclean spirit although not as violent as depicted in the gospel. Unfortunately, because of original sin, our spirit has a tendency to avoid God and to want him to leave us alone. That spirit within us can very readily triumph because God will never force us to love him and to do his will. On the other hand, it is clear that our spirit is no match for the Spirit of God and, if we pray earnestly for the favor, he will relieve us of the dominance of our human, disoriented spirit.

WEDNESDAY

Colossians 1: 1-8; Luke 4: 38-44 **YEAR I**

St. Paul gives thanks to God for the Colossians because of their faith in Christ, their hope in God's promises, and their love for those around them. These theological virtues of faith, hope, and love are fundamental to the spiritual life; they are the virtues that relate man to God, unite man with God. No relationship between man and God can exist without them, and, therefore, we can never have enough of them because our union with God must be complete—only fully realized in heaven, of course, but needed here on earth, too, if we are ever to get to heaven.

St. Paul is grateful to God, not only for the good fortune of the Colossians, but also for himself, for those not yet Christian, and for all Christians wherever they are. The Body of Christ is a reality. It is only as strong as its weakest member, and because there are weak members, we must depend on the strong to keep the Body healthy. Paul himself is a strong member but he does not see himself that way; he needs the moral support of others. If he saw himself as not needing this support, it would not only be a lack of truth in him but such pride would make holiness and commitment to his mission impossible. And if Paul needed such support, so do others. It is morally impossible to give oneself completely to the Church without the positive response of acceptance at least on the part of some. It is hard for our people, too, to live the Christian life and teach their children, when all around them there are so many who are weak in their commitment to the Christian way of life.

In light of the above, we need to realize, as Jesus did, that we are constantly to be mindful of others. We must go out to them, bringing the strength of God's grace with us. Not that we can take any pride in it because it is all a matter of God's help. The stronger, more faith-filled members of the Body of Christ must assist the weaker. Love is not love until it is given away and we are not truly religious people—we are not truly in love with God—unless we try to give to others what we are blessed to have.

1 Corinthians 3: 1-9; Luke 4: 38-44 **YEAR II**

Is it not amazing that despite all the gifts that we have received from God our "behavior is still that of ordinary men?" This is an obstacle to God's revelation to us and desire to make us more spiritual. We simply are not ready for God's plans in our regard any more than the Corinthians were. There are still quarrels and jealousy among us as there were among the Corinthians. God would have us know him completely but he cannot because we are too distracted to learn as we should in prayer. We need to concentrate more on spiritual matters such as prayer, spiritual reading, meditation, and contemplation.

We need to be aware that all spiritual development is the result of God's work in us. It is not due solely to our human effort, but it requires turning our mind and heart to God with deep attention. Earthly thoughts and distractions cannot fill our minds to the exclusion of God. Our hearts must yearn for God and shy away from earthly attachments. We must look to God to fashion our minds and hearts, to be our joy, our help, and our shield. This requires time, effort, and attention. And, we are too busy about many things. We must be in search of Christ as were the sick who sought Jesus in today's gospel. Unfortunately their motives were not purely spiritual; they were looking for temporal favors. We need to be anxious for spiritual favors. We must seek the Lord with love, faith, and perseverance.

THURSDAY

Colossians 1: 9-14; Luke 5: 1-11 **YEAR I**

Love of God enables us to grow in knowledge of him, for God is love. Christ did not set forth a series of proofs, when he came into the world, to convince us intellectually that he was the Messiah. Nor was that what was prophesied. He came into the world doing the good deeds prophesied by Isaiah—curing of the blind, the lame, the diseased; freeing prisoners; preaching the good news to the poor. In this way the people came to know Christ. They loved him first and they came to know him, and they learned that God is love. This led them to lead a life of goodness and compassion, and having experienced this divine life, they came to know and love God all the more.

The gospel seems to be chosen as an illustration. Although Christ had preached to the people for a considerable time and they seemed to appreciate his words, the miraculous catch of fish was much more convincing. It made Peter and the apostles see the stark contrast between their own sinfulness and the goodness of God. Despite their inability to understand and appreciate the revelations of Christ in the spoken word, the Lord chose to show his love and concern through the miraculous multiplication of fish. On that day, Peter, James, and John left everything to follow Christ.

1 Corinthians 3: 18-23; Luke 5: 1-11 **YEAR II**

Intelligence is such a great gift that it can become for us a temptation to pride. It can lead us to think of ourselves as gods. St. Paul tells us that such a thought is utter foolishness. The wisdom of man, his intelligence, is nothing compared to the "weakness" of God. However, if we possess Christ, who is God, we have everything and nothing can overcome us—and better still, if we are possessed by God, absolutely nothing can touch us or harm us. God is our safety net and no matter what may befall us on earth, even if the world overcomes us, we simply bounce off the safety net, as it were, to the stars and to the bosom of God!

Today's gospel reading about the miraculous catch of fish illustrates the above. Peter was very proud of his knowledge of the fishing business on the Lake of Galilee. The apparent foolishness of Jesus in directing Peter to do exactly what he had tried unsuccessfully all night proves to be greater than the apostles' human wisdom. After following the suggestion of Jesus, they bring in a huge catch of fish. Their astonishment causes Peter to confess that he had lacked faith in Christ. It is a great moment for him and for James and John, his fishing companions. The three of them bring their boat to land, leave everything, and become the followers of Jesus. They have a profound sense that by leaving everything they gain everything. From proud fishermen they become foolish in the eyes of their friends who do not have their new found wisdom. As Jesus later said to Mary and Martha, "one thing is necessary" and that is Christ, our God. If we are one with him, nothing else in the world is necessary.

FRIDAY

Colossians 1: 15-20; Luke 5: 33-39 **YEAR I**

Due to Christ's appearance on earth as man, his reality as Son of God is often obscure in our minds. Who is this person, who came among us as an infant, preached the gospel, died on the cross and rose again? The Son of God is equal and co-eternal with the Father. This being the case, everything that St. Paul says of Christ is fully true. He is God made manifest! Everything was created according to the Father's idea of it, which already existed in the Word. So all things were truly created in him, through him and for him and their continuance in existence is in virtue of his being. As God-man, he is head of the Church, which can well be called the Body of

Christ. We can be reconciled to the Father only in and through him. The significance, therefore, of the Church and the sacramental system—especially the sacraments of baptism, penance and Eucharist—is enormous! What these sacraments do is to make us one with Christ in a spiritual way, which is even more profound than the physical. And how little we appreciate this grace.

We need to rejoice in the presence of Christ in our lives and act as we would when in the presence of someone whom we love and wish to please. Good husbands and wives have such a love for one another; they can't do enough for one another. Many times we do the same thing just to gain advancement in our employment, or even to be noticed and affirmed. How much more should we be anxious to display our love of Christ—not for the sake of reward, but simply to fulfill the demands of justice!

It is difficult to understand precisely what we should derive from the remarks about patching old clothes and using new wineskins. But surely, it can mean that we ought to give up old ways of thinking entirely and give up old ways of acting and give up our customary stance of compromise (wanting the best of both worlds) in order to dedicate ourselves totally to him, who is all in everything. We need to recognize the importance of God in our lives; the centrality of belief in Christ, if we wish to be reconciled—become one—with God; the need to give up attachment to everything else in this world for love of Christ/God; the need to see and to use all things only in relation to Christ/God. All things, and people, are to bring us closer to God or they are to be abandoned. All people and things are to be judged, not by their earthly value or worldly esteem, but by their value in uniting us more closely to God.

1 Corinthians 4: 1-5; Luke 5: 33-39 **YEAR II**

We are our own worst judges. Even if we should have nothing on our consciences—and no one can truly say this—we can still hardly pass ourselves off as innocent people. I often wonder how God will judge so many instances that I have judged favorably but others have not. As long as I am in good conscience, surely there is forgiveness. But at the same time, with all these unknown or unintended offenses, we can hardly take lightly those of which we are certain. Far less, are we in any position to judge others? "Judge not, lest you be judged," is excellent advice. Make every effort to be faithful to the Lord. Leave judgement to him, simply praying that he will be merciful.

Some people are given to much prayer and fasting but they may be very grumpy or repel other people, seeming to be "too holy." On the other hand, some people are very cheerful and outgoing, seemingly not living a very penitential life, but they attract many people to the faith. Which is correct? Either, both. "The Lord loves a cheerful giver," but some things can "only be done by prayer and fasting." Obviously the happy medium is best, but usually a person is going to have more of one style than the other. Regardless of which approach is used, the one thing necessary is not to envy the other person. There is room for both styles; both styles of life are attractive to certain people or appropriate in certain circumstances. "To each his own" should be our motto in this respect. More power to both people and may God use both for his greater honor and glory.

And it would seem just as well to be content with one's own personality. It is highly doubtful that the penitential person can change his style to an easy-going one, or vice versa. Although we would like to be perfect, it is "better to leave well enough alone." For instance, Christ said that we should "be all things to all men." That is an ideal and we should strive for it. But as so many wise people said when I was appointed, "Be yourself" is the best possible advice. It is our faith that God does the choosing, and he does not proceed at that point to make us perfect. It is his providence that he wants this person in this place at this time with this style for his own good purposes. Don't worry about it. Just be "this" person, plus as holy as possible.

SATURDAY

Colossians 1: 21-23; Luke 6: 1-5 **YEAR I**

St. Paul reminds the Colossians that they were once alienated from God and "nourished hostility" against God in their hearts because of their evil deeds. Isn't this the truth? The more evil deeds we do the more hostile we become toward God. He does nothing to offend us. He simply is truth, goodness, love. And those who are evil cannot help but envy him and eventually hate him for his enjoying a peace and happiness that they know they can never attain as long as they remain attached to their sinful ways.

This is why the Pharisees came to hate Jesus and his disciples. Christ and his followers enjoyed the peace and tranquility of being one with God. They were not concerned for human custom but only for truth, goodness and love. So when Jesus would confound the Pharisees with the truth or heal a cripple on the Sabbath or show love even to lepers and prostitutes, the

Pharisees did not know what to do except to "nourish hostility" in their hearts because of their own evil deeds and their intention to persevere in them. It was because of their own lack of honesty, goodness and love, that they could not abide Jesus and his followers.

St. Paul reminds us that the only way that we can persevere in good deeds, and thereby remain united to God, is to have the greatest faith in him and in his promises. In our own time we understand that this is not easy; the attractions of the world are difficult to resist.

Again, we need to remind ourselves that we become alienated from God, not by anything that he does to us in his providence or by anything that he gives to us in revelation. We alienate ourselves from him by our own evil deeds. We need to have faith in God's existence and in his revealed way of life—Christ—and hope in God's promises that only those who accept his way, his truth, and his life, are worthy of these gifts for all eternity.

1 Corinthians 4: 9-15; Luke 6: 1-5 **YEAR II**

"The present state of affairs" for the dedicated Christian is not an enviable one any more than it was in the days of St. Paul. There is no question that we must be fools for Christ's sake in the sight of the worldly wise. We are comparatively poor, while others are rich; we work hard while others live by their wits; when we are insulted, we must respond with prayers; when persecuted, we must be patient and seek reconciliation. But this is the Christ life. The servant must be as his master. If Christ was treated in this way and responded as he did, so must we.

But one day all this will change. The Bridegroom will return for us, and when we are fully reunited with him, nothing will be able to distract or detract us from the perfect happiness that we shall experience. Meanwhile, it is for us to have faith in God, hope in his promises, and love for him, which is evidenced in the way that we treat those around us.

Twenty-third Week of Ordinary Time

MONDAY

Colossians 1: 24-2: 3; Luke 6: 6-11 **YEAR I**

The Christians of Colossae and the nearby capital city of Laodice did not know Paul personally. From prison, Paul appeals to his sufferings and authority to teach orthodox doctrine concerning the centrality of Christ. Without the slightest bit of boastfulness, he tells the Colossians how hard he is working for them. There is no boastfulness because this is his vocation, to "fill up what is lacking in the sufferings of Christ for the sake of his body."

In God's providence those who believe in Christ are called upon to make up for the lack of penance of other human beings, who will only be converted by example and by that form of prayer. Also, even if they are not converted, those who are virtuous "owe" this to God on behalf of their fellow men. So the sufferings of Paul unite him with Christ; they are an expiatory offering for the sins of mankind; they are an example and a means of gaining the grace of conversion for others. In this letter St. Paul makes clear that his sufferings are a necessary complement to the gospel he preaches. The preaching of the gospel is so urgent that he must accept any and every inconvenience to keep at it and reach as many people as he can in a convincing manner. As he gives himself with this total dedication, suffering and sacrifice are bound to be part of his life, and at the same time they exemplify the life of Christ that he preaches. The reason why he must strive to reach every person with the gospel message is that the wisdom of God, hidden for ages, has been revealed in Christ. Christ is the answer to the mystery of life; the only means by which we can come to know clearly who we are, where we have come from, why we are here, what the future holds—the only means to know all this with assurance is to come to know Christ.

According to Pharisaic teaching, all work was forbidden on the Sabbath. Jesus performs a public miracle on the Sabbath and that angers and confounds the Pharisees. Jesus tells them that they are too narrow and critical in interpreting the Scriptures and that he is Lord over such rules. Jesus knew what he was up against. He knew that his healing act on the Sabbath would be rejected in favor of man-made laws concerning what could, or could not, be done on that day. Instead of wondering what they could do about their laws, the Pharisees "wondered what could be done to Jesus." From the very beginning Christ could see that the proclamation of God's truth was going to demand suffering on his part, but he was ready to face even death for love of the Father and for love of us.

1 Corinthians 5: 1-8; Luke 6: 6-11 **YEAR II**

In today's reading, Paul writes to help a young Christian community in Corinth, a port city, notorious for immorality and wickedness. He advises excommunication for a public sinner so as to keep the community uncorrupted. Paul says that to act as if sin were virtue, or to be indifferent to sin and maintain that one is holy, is the height of arrogance. And such arrogance cannot be tolerated; it will destroy the community. Like yeast in dough or a rotten apple in a barrel of apples, the evil tends to spread. To preserve sincerity and truth either the person must be converted from his ways or expelled from the group. It is false to think that sin is virtuous or even permissible; it is insincere, both on the part of the sinner and of others who tolerate sin in a community supposedly centered in Christ, who sacrificed himself for sin. Boasting of Christ or of your own goodness while being indifferent to sin is hypocrisy.

The gospel states something quite similar with regard to virtue and justice. If a person is suffering and we can be helpful, it is not right to use some lesser commandment to impede the performance of the good action. The whole Law and the prophets are summed up in love of God and neighbor. The prescription against physical activity on the Sabbath was a man-made precept. Perhaps it was established in good faith but it was defeating its own purpose of showing love for God, if its implementation was going to violate both of the Great Commandments. Obviously, the healing was done for love of neighbor and it brought about, as an added effect, the glory of God.

Contrary to what many seem to claim by their conduct, it is never right to perform an evil action even if a good effect is intended. In addition, it is difficult to suppose any case where one would be prohibited from performing a clearly good work which itself would be in violation of a commandment of God.

TUESDAY

Colossians 2: 6-15: Luke 6: 12-19 **YEAR I**

In today's reading, Paul continues telling the Colossians to forget superstitions and live in Christ alone. Jewish observances are in vain. It is as if Jesus picked up our itemized bill of sins, marked it paid, and nailed it to his cross. Paul urges us to continue our faith in Christ and to be eternally grateful for that faith so that we will not be tempted to place our trust in the things of this world or the wisdom of men. Instead we should mold ourselves ever more perfectly in the image and likeness of Christ. The apostle goes on to explain the reasons for this in some detail. The principal reason, of course, is that Christ is God and "of his fullness we have all received" in baptism. Baptism is similar to circumcision but in the former our whole body is spiritually stripped away. We are given the grace to live in the body as if we had no body. We are incorporated in Christ; he is in us and we in him. If we truly believe in this truth and act upon it, nothing can be lacking to us in this world or the next.

Another important reason for believing in Christ and clinging to him is that he has taken away our sins. This favor is owed to no one. It is a totally gratuitous gift, given to us when we were miserably immersed in sin and utterly undeserving. Compare this to a human situation in which you have no obligation to forgive, and every reason not to forgive. It would take a heroic effort to do so. But Christ has done this for us willingly and not easily through his death on the Cross. How close and faithful to Christ we should wish to be.

In the context of these readings we can understand St. Augustine's statement that he rejoiced with the faithful over baptism that he had in common with them; but he trembled at the responsibility that he had for them as priest and bishop. From God's viewpoint he can give us nothing more precious than the forgiveness of sins and his personal presence, both of which we receive in baptism. It is ever so easy for a priest to lose sight of this and so give himself to his responsibilities as a priest that he neglects his responsibilities as a baptized Christian. Prayer, spiritual reading, meditation, devout offering and reception of the sacraments are all elements that keep us united to Christ. It will help, if we not only keep up these spiritual practices but also keep in mind that the object of our ministerial life is to bring the graces of baptism to others. The gospel reading describes Jesus at prayer. The person who puts daily prayer at the top of the day's agenda will make time for prayer. It is a question of priorities.

1 Corinthians 6: 1-11; Luke 6: 12-19 **YEAR II**

Paul, in today's reading, is shocked that Christians in Corinth are suing one another in Roman courts of law. Christians should be charitable and live by the highest moral standards. He further states that it is better to be deprived than to engage in strife to have a wrong redressed. If our gift is to have been made one with Christ, if we are the Body of Christ, why should we be so concerned for the things of this world? If we think it is charitable to call another person to task, is it not far better to bring that person before sacred authority to discuss the matter, thus, helping the person to save his soul, rather than securing retribution for ourselves? Rest assured that God will take care of evildoers in his own time. Be thankful for God's gifts and devote all your energy to leading a good and holy life. In short, if we have been deprived of anything—even unjustly—it may well be for our sanctification. Why bring harm upon another just for our own self-satisfaction?

In the gospel we see that Christ spent the night in prayer before choosing his apostles and beginning a major discourse, the Sermon on the Plain. How and why God chooses those who are to serve him is a mystery. However, it is not done merely by chance. It is essential that we appreciate the gift of our election to baptism and live in accord with God's teachings. We need to remain with him, be healed by him, and be drawn ever closer to him both for our own welfare and to become effective instruments for the building of his kingdom on earth.

If we are called to serve God in a special way, he is doing us a great favor, and he will be more demanding in his judgment of our actions. Let us never think that we are doing God a favor in responding to his call!

WEDNESDAY

Colossians 3: 1-11; Luke 6: 20-26 **YEAR I**

In today's reading, Paul describes how to live in Christ. This new life means death to sin. It means no prejudices, no hatreds. A person who is fully converted to God is one who is totally dead to sin, has no connection or attachment to it whatsoever. He is a new man, completely free to give himself unstintingly to God in every way. True Christian freedom implies no tie at all to sin, and unconditional giving of oneself to the Lord. Not only is this freedom; it is also peace, joy, love, and hope. It is the only means by which we can experience these virtues in any true and helpful sense.

As the Beatitudes imply, freedom from sin and total dedication to God's love and service is not going to free a person from the difficulties inherent to life. It may be quite the contrary. Even so, the woes of this life in the external or material order are not to be compared with the interior joy that one has while united with God, nor can it begin to compare with the joy of heaven for all eternity. Even human reflection, apart from God's revelation, manifests how short this life is, how fleeting too are our great sorrows and great joys on this earth, how insignificant are the events of this life compared to what every human being senses is possible. If we have a capacity for complete happiness, if we long for that state, if we have that potential in our minds and hearts, it would stand to reason that such a life is possible, if not here on earth, then hereafter, in heaven.

1 Corinthians 7: 25-31; Luke 6: 20-26 **YEAR II**

The Corinthians asked Paul for guidance on questions of marriage and the life of celibacy. His response was overshadowed by his belief that the end of the world was not far off and, for that reason, he preached that it was better to be totally detached. Nevertheless his thoughts on the matter are worthy of consideration. The object of life is to save one's soul. That goal should be constantly before our eyes and nothing should distract us from it. Mourning, rejoicing, commerce, marriage are to become conduits for the expression of our love for God and for our neighbor. Paul exaggerates in his statements, but his views are countered to a great extent by the gospel. By offering the joys and sorrows of this life to God, we are drawn closer to him. Since these joys and sorrows are linked to our neighbor, acceptance of them is in keeping with the second great commandment. St. Paul, on the other hand, stresses the first great commandment. But he is not condemning family life or the need to support one's family.

Theoretically, we could assume that we are freer to love God with our whole heart and soul, if we are not deeply immersed in the things of this world. St. Paul's advice is much the same as Christ's words to Mary and Martha: "Mary has chosen the better part"; and this has been the reasoning of the Catholic Church in favor of celibacy for many centuries. However, not all are called to celibacy and those who accept it as a way of life without the grace attached to its calling fall prey to temptations which ruin their lives and the lives of many around them.

It becomes clearer and clearer that the mission of the baptized is to enrich the world by becoming the bearers of God's love to those around them. We are to distinguish clearly between the allurements of the world and all its elements of beauty which are calls to recognize and love the Creator.

The gospel reading accepts the fact that we cannot avoid joy and sorrow, the commercial world, and that marriage and family life are necessary. However, it is more difficult for the wealthy, the well-fed, and the powerful of this world to concentrate on heavenly things. There is little reason for them to look to God for subsistence, guidance, acceptance, and hope. They have no need to be focused on God. The lesson is similar to Christ's statement that it is easier for a camel to pass through the eye of a needle than for a rich man to enter heaven. The apostles were astonished. At the time, they could not understand that the world is not an end in itself, but it is to be used as a means to save our souls and to assist our neighbor in doing the same.

THURSDAY

Colossians 3: 12-17; Luke 6: 27-38 **YEAR I**

In today's reading, although St. Paul is giving an instruction to the Colossians as to how they should live, he is at the same time giving a description of what it is like to live in perfect union with God. In that state our minds and hearts are constantly going out to other people. Our constant question is: "What can we do for them?" The answer is always heartfelt: mercy, kindness, humility, meekness, patience, forbearance, and forgiveness. We are to bind all these virtues together with love, which is the epitome of self-abnegation, service, sacrifice, and concern for others. When all this is ours, we shall be at peace and we should sing hymns of thanksgiving to God for his goodness. It is these virtues, this type of life, the contentment of peace, in union with God, which is God's greatest gift. We should appreciate our material blessings, to be sure, but rich or poor, these virtues are the apex of joy, the prelude to heaven.

In the gospel Jesus spells out in very practical, down-to-earth terms what all of this means. Love your enemies. No matter what another person does to you, react with charity. This is the only way to stay at peace within oneself and it is the only way to convert others. If we love only those who love us, don't sinners do the same? The example of Christ, the martyrs and the great saints through the centuries has been to turn the other cheek and this has been, by all means, the best way of spreading the faith. The gospel teaches that forgiveness and love of one's enemies are major qualities of a Christian. Treat others as you would have them treat you. Do not judge lest you be judged. Do not condemn lest you be condemned. Pardon so that you will be pardoned. Be overly good and generous because the God of infinite goodness will ultimately have a reward of everlasting and perfect happiness in reserve for you. If a person truly needs something and you have the means to provide it, let the person have it. This is especially true where money is concerned. If a person asks for a loan, it is better to give the money with no obligation to return it. If the borrower is sincere, he will either pay back or be more inclined to do whatever he can for others, and thus he will be further converted to the ways of Christ.

1 Corinthians 8: 1-7, 11-13; Luke 6: 27-38 **YEAR II**

The Corinthians asked whether they could buy and eat meat that had been offered to a pagan god. That meat was cheaper. St. Paul said that the question was irrelevant because he knew that pagan gods did not exist. However, at that time, the uneducated masses were scandalized when such food was eaten. St. Paul declared that no Christian should give scandal—thus they should avoid touching meat previously offered to pagan gods.

Objectively, it makes no difference whether the meat we eat has been sacrificed to idols because, in fact, an idol is a piece of stone or wood or other physical entity and not a god at all. But we should realize that the less-learned do believe that eating such meat is sinful. Therefore, if you should be seen doing so, these people would be led to believe that the moral law is not binding in this case, and, if not in this case, why in others? Our "sophistication," our knowledge, could lead others to do what they perceive as sinful. Giving scandal—leading others to sin is sinful. Better that a millstone be tied around my neck and I be drowned than to scandalize an innocent person.

In today's gospel, Jesus teaches that forgiveness and love of one's enemies are major characteristics of a Christian. If that is so, how much more charitable should we be to the weak, the less educated, the easily impressionable? To fail in charity toward such people is the opposite of everything that is considered Christian. Theoretically, the charity of which the gospel speaks seems easy to practice but because self-preservation is involved, it becomes very difficult. The one who brings evil upon me or hates me is attacking my very existence and my right to be as I am. The instinctive reaction is at the very least to protect what I have from this person and to seek revenge. This is a hard lesson but Christ offers three strong and irrefutable arguments for following his advice. First, there is very little virtue in loving those who love us. Secondly, we are to imitate Christ, God himself, who shows mercy to everyone. To make ourselves more and more to his image and likeness, we must follow his example. Thirdly, our reward will be great in heaven.

FRIDAY

1 Timothy 1: 1-2, 12-14; Luke 6: 39-42 **YEAR I**

Paul's three letters, two to Timothy and one to Titus, are known as the Pastoral Epistles. In them Paul gives advice to a bishop on how to administer a church. To young Timothy, Paul tells of his personal weaknesses and strengths, all in an encouraging fashion. We, like St. Paul, are chosen and commanded to be priests by God our Father and Christ Jesus, the Lord. It goes without saying, therefore, that we are under obligation to be good priests. God alone is good, but if he chooses us and commands us to act in his name, it is obvious that he expects us to be the best we can. And if only we cooperate better with his grace, with the Spirit of God who dwells within us, we can be better than we ever thought we could be. God is patient and kind; he treats us mercifully. But this gives us no excuse to take advantage of his goodness. We must not succumb to the temptation of thinking that because, in our judgment, we are doing better than others, we can rest upon our laurels. To whom much has been given, much will be demanded.

In today's gospel narrative, Jesus teaches his followers not to criticize others and to be humble and positive in judging them. It may very well be that the imperfection of the neighbor is equivalent to a speck in the eye and that our own imperfection more the size of a plank. We should concentrate on removing the plank from our own eye and forget about the speck in our neighbor's eye. A blind man cannot guide a blind man; neither can a person of moral evil guide another person to virtue. Somehow the immorality, the insincerity will shine through.

1 Corinthians 9: 16-19, 22-27; Luke 6: 39-42 **YEAR II**

Preaching the gospel, living a good life, is no cause for boasting because one does so either freely or out of a sense of necessity in order to have an everlasting reward. Granted that "the laborer is worthy of his hire," this means nothing compared with the reward which is to come, so why be concerned with present comfort or honor? From a human standpoint this is hard to do, but for one who sees things as God does, there is no other course to follow.

We must do everything within our power to make ourselves acceptable and approachable to other people for the sake of the gospel. It is of the essence, therefore, that we be self-sacrificing, mortified people. This is a necessity for one who preaches the gospel because, no matter what may be the lifestyle of the people to whom we preach, they cannot possibly be receptive to our message unless we practice what we preach. Again, the reward is such that we should consider every sacrifice as nothing. If athletes half "kill" themselves to obtain a perishable prize, how can we do less than they?

It is sad to see some preaching the gospel who think that they "know it all." Such people can, and usually are, blind in practical matters to their own defects. Possibly they don't know as much as they think they do, but even if they do, the application of their knowledge can be faulty. Moreover, it is just such a person who can find fault in others who are much more innocent than himself. Those who take pride in their knowledge often enough are not given to analyzing themselves. But "know thyself" is the beginning of wisdom and the height of wisdom.

SATURDAY

1 Timothy 1: 15-17; Luke 6: 43-49 **YEAR I**

If there is anything we know for certain about Jesus Christ, it is that he came into the world to save sinners. We can only be puzzled by the Incarnation if we are convinced that we are not sinners. If we have no sin, there is no reason for Christ's coming. If there is no reason for Christ's coming, he can hardly be God because God could not do anything foolish. The fact is, however, as St. Paul explains, that each of us, knowing ourselves from the inside, should be able to see ourselves as the worst of sinners. As a result, humility and gratitude should characterize our lives. In today's reading, Paul continues to tell Timothy of Christ's kindness to him. It should encourage young Timothy to look to Christ for strength. A daily examination of conscience is all we need to do to judge whether or not we are sinful people. It will help us realize that evil comes from within, from our mind and heart. In our day we can speak of social sin, in the sense that our very system of living and our culture are tainted. But social or systemic evil derives only from personal sinfulness, and it can continue to exist and thrive only when nourished by personal sin. Systems do not sin; only human beings do. And if we see that the system is evil, we should be able to judge that we are sinful. "By their fruits you will know them."

We must fashion our lives as a good homebuilder constructs a house. That is we must depend upon a strong foundation, which can be none other than the person of Christ, his teaching, and his example. If our "foundation" is merely human wisdom, we are building upon a weak base indeed. It will not stand up under the attacks of people who are worldly-wise, people who live according to the flesh. Our emotions and our weakened human nature are such that when temptations come, we will surely succumb. Jesus Christ is the only foundation upon which to base our hope of leading a good and holy life. Today's gospel reiterates that the followers of Christ, to be genuine, must produce the fruits of holiness.

1 Corinthians 10: 14-22; Luke 6: 43-49 **YEAR II**

In today's reading, Paul tells the Corinthians to avoid pagan idol worship because they have the Eucharist. When we receive the Body and Blood of Christ, we are brought into union with him and through him with one another. The Jews attempt to do the same—enter into union with God—through their sacrifices. Similarly the idol worship of pagans unites them mind and heart with their false gods. So even though these idols in reality have no power, worship of them is to be avoided because it leads a person away from the true God and into false worship.

The parable of the good and bad trees is applicable. One cannot engage in false worship and produce good results any more than a person can engage in true worship and not be pleasing to God. Since these same people, however, may not have given themselves with full heart to their worship, it is possible that the good person may later sin and the person in false worship may produce good works especially if that person is in invincible ignorance. Although deceit and hypocrisy are short-range possibilities, people will usually speak and act in accordance to what is in their minds and hearts. Therefore, we can determine by our actions whether or not we are giving true worship to God. We cannot see within but we can see the fruit of our souls in action. If we tend to buckle under pressure, as the person who built his house on sand, we are less loyal to God and more hypocritical than we thought we were. If we are firm in our basic commitment, if we are true to the two Great Commandments, we may bend and at times sin, but we will hold together, weather the storm, and be stronger in the future.

Twenty-fourth Week of Ordinary Time

Monday

1 Timothy 2: 1-8; Luke 7: 1-10 **YEAR I**

Prayer is a necessity. The more we offer fervent prayer, the more God is pleased. Furthermore, we should not forever be praying for ourselves. We should pray for all people, especially for civil leaders, so that we may have a just society, conducive to peace. For when people are distracted by earthly problems, when they are filled with anger and dissension, it is difficult for priests to reach their people in teaching them how to accept the revelation of God. There are simply too many concerns contending for everyone's attention. To a great extent, today's reading exemplifies this situation. St. Paul, the veteran missionary bishop, offers pastoral advice to the young bishop Timothy. Paul tells Timothy that, among others, civil leaders must be mentioned in the Prayer of the Faithful. Our lives must be filled with peace and justice, and prayer is the way to reach that goal. Salvation and revelation are for all men. Ultimately the major argument in favor of revelation is revelation itself. Revelation is truth and the mind is made for truth. People will accept or reject truth, when they have a chance to perceive it. But in a troubled world, the message of God's truth will not come through in all its fullness and beauty.

Jesus, in the gospel, hears the prayer of a civil servant, the centurion, and he goes to cure the man's servant. At every Mass before Communion we quote the centurion's humble words of unworthiness. The conversion of the centurion could mean the conversion of many others. It could even bring about the internal conversion of many Jews because they pleaded with Jesus to assist the centurion because he had built their synagogue in Capernaum. The centurion was not looking for lengthy argumentation about the divinity of Christ. He had heard about the goodness and power of Christ. He had apparently accepted this as truth. So all he was asking for was a manifestation of the truth in his regard and that would be sufficient. Jesus marveled at the centurion's faith, showed him the truth, cured his servant, and thereby presumably converted the centurion and many others.

1 Corinthians 11: 17-26, 33; Luke 7: 1-10 **YEAR II**

Although we read elsewhere that the people of the early Church shared everything in common, this was not always the case as in Corinth. There, when the Eucharist was celebrated, the people also ate an ordinary meal, and some were overfed while others went hungry. How could the Corinthians do such a thing, when the Eucharist is the sacrament of unity? If the Lord suffered on the Cross for all, how could they fail to have love for one another? In his first letter to the Corinthians, Paul reminds them of the meaning and importance of the Mass.

The Eucharist is re-enacted "in remembrance" of Christ's death for all on the Cross. The Corinthians need to reflect on the meaning of the Cross and the meaning of the Eucharist. If Christ displayed greater love than anyone by his death, the least that the Corinthians can do is to share some of their food with one another.

In the gospel it is evident that the people knew how they should be acting. It is a matter of human decency, not only a divine command, that we should be considerate of one another. Since the centurion had donated generously to the synagogue at Capernaum, the Jewish people told Jesus that he "owed" the centurion a miracle. All the more so, if Jesus won redemption on the Cross for all mankind, we owe every kindness to those whom he loves and redeems.

The remainder of the story about the centurion indicates the humility both of Jesus and of the centurion. In his jurisdiction, the centurion could do anything he wished but he recognized that Jesus was holier, closer to God than he, so his position was one of an inferior. He would not ask Jesus to go out of his way for him. Jesus, on his part, seeing the faith and humility of the centurion, recognized the man's closeness to God. Even though there was no obligation, Jesus cured the centurion's servant. Humility is of the essence for faith, which is the foundation of all other virtues.

Tuesday

1 Timothy 3: 1-13; Luke 7: 11-17 **YEAR I**

St. Paul lists what he considers to be the most necessary qualities in a good bishop. Although there will be different styles of leadership among bishops and different personal traits, the basics given by St. Paul should always remain the same. The bishop should always be a good teacher, morally irreproachable, totally dedicated, given to poverty, gentle but firm, utterly truthful. Although not mentioned by St. Paul, a sense of humor regardless of his serious nature and good physical and mental health are also required. Of course, the bishop should also have the qualities of a good deacon. He should be serious, straightforward, truthful, not addicted to drink, not greedy, faithful to revealed truth, and a good manager.

In the gospel narrative we hear the story of life restored to the son of a desolate widowed mother from Naim. The compassion of Jesus for women is well-illustrated. We do not know how the man died. Had he been executed for rape, murder, or had he died because of an unforgiving illness or disease? What would we have done in the place of Jesus? Every gift from God carries its own responsibility. God's gifts are free but they draw us into the experience of love and the need for response. How did the resurrected man live his life after receiving it back from the hand of Jesus? How would we have responded to such a gift? These are questions that need much thought in our prayer.

1 Corinthians 12: 12-14, 27-31; Luke 7: 11-17 **YEAR II**

In today's reading, Paul expresses his concern about jealousy in the Corinthian Church. He tells the faithful that the various functions in the Church work together for Christ, just as do the members of a human body. By virtue of the Incarnation and baptism, all the faithful are members of Christ's one Body, and jealousies are pointless.

Just as there are many members to a human body, all of which have different functions, so there are many members to Christ's Body, the Church, and all have different responsibilities. Just as one part of the human body should not be envious, but rather grateful to be joined to parts of the body that might have a more noble function, so should we be happy just to be a part of Christ instead of being ambitious for a more prestigious position. This is especially true when holiness is our ultimate criterion and we know that "the first shall be last" and those who take the highest place may be reduced to the lowest.

The gospel is not related closely to the first reading except in a general sense. There is no indication that the widow of Naim and her son had any special place of honor in the community, yet Jesus raised the young man to life on behalf of the widow. Jesus recognizes, loves, and has compassion for all, even the lowliest. And so it will be on the last day.

Wednesday

1 Timothy 3: 14-16; Luke 7: 31-35 **YEAR I**

St. Paul appeals to us to be mindful of our various callings, and of the conduct which should be the consequence of those callings. Christ is the Son of God, equal to the Father and the Holy Spirit, manifested to us in the flesh, believed in throughout the world and now reigning gloriously in heaven, adored by all the angels and saints. We are not to be professional doubters and dissenters, never willing to accept anything as good, any standard as certain. What this amounts to is setting ourselves up as standards. The perennial doubter and dissenter reveals himself as proud with an infallibility complex. If we accept everyone as a law unto himself, this relativism can only lead to chaos in the practical order. No, life is much simpler than that. We need to address and answer the basic questions about life: there is a God; Jesus Christ is the Son of God; he gave us a divinely guided Church to shepherd us; and this being the case, we should follow the way, the truth, and the life marked out for us by the Church.

In the gospel narrative Jesus states that his contemporaries were negative, critical, and interpreting cynically whatever was done. Critical of both John the Baptist and of Christ, they could see good in no one. Is that our usual posture? Do we really believe that everything Jesus teaches is true wisdom, even when it is shocking? Do we believe we should always forgive?

1 Corinthians 12: 31-13: 13; Luke 7: 31-35 **YEAR II**

St. Paul urges us to set our hearts on the gifts that draw us closer to God and not on those that ordinarily gain applause such as prophecy, healing, and others as dramatic. He tells us that the greatest gift is available to all—the virtue of love. In the Church there are many tasks to be accomplished and many talents to be used and Christians are not called to exercise all of them. However, the virtues of faith, hope, and charity are accessible to all humans and the greatest of these is love which all can practice to the benefit of all!

Faith is primarily ordained to belief in the existence of God. If we accept God's existence, we accept his teachings. It is a sign that God is speaking with us when the teaching is accompanied by symbols of God's favor such as miracles, the fulfillment of prophecy, the unquestioned holiness of the speaker, and other indications of his support. Faith in God implies hope in him, too. We expect that one day he will right all the wrongs that we experience on earth. Those who have suffered and sacrificed the pleasures of this world in order to obey God will receive a proportionate reward in time to come. This is the normal expectation of a God, who is good, just, and loving. If we believe in God and we hope that one day we shall be rewarded for our faithfulness, we must in the meantime live according to his commandments. St. John tells us that "God is love," so we must live in love, as well.

In a most sublime passage, Paul says that "love is patient; love is kind. Love is not jealous; it does not put on airs; it is not snobbish. Love is never rude; it is not self-seeking; it is not prone to anger; neither does it brood over injuries. Love does not rejoice in what is wrong but rejoices with the truth. There is no limit to love's forbearance, to its trust, its hope, its power to endure."

No matter what kind of gift we may be given by God, nothing is of any avail unless we have this basic virtue of love. Life styles matter little. We can live like John the Baptist—a very sacrificial life in the desert—or we can live like Christ, who shared the more customary daily life of the people of his time. One is as good as the other as long as it is characterized by the deepest love for God and neighbor. Faith, hope, and love can lead us equally to persecution and death on earth as they will lead to unending joy in heaven. Thus, our major consideration should not be the opinion of men but that of God made known to us by a good and clear conscience.

THURSDAY

1 Timothy 4: 12-16; Luke 7: 36-50 **YEAR I**

In today's reading, Paul gives paternal advice to the young man. Of mixed Jewish-Gentile parentage, Timothy, in his youth, was converted by St. Paul. The advice given is excellent for any priest going into a new parish. He should not worry about what people are going to think of him. His mission is to mirror Christ and be a model of love, faith, and purity. The first thing to do is to be kind to everyone. That will develop trust in him. Trust leads to faith in what one has to say about God. Purity may obviously refer to sexual purity, but in this context it probably has more to do with dedication, purity of intention, and singleness of purpose.

Granted that all the above is necessary to draw the people, then one must be very certain to preach the truth to them. It does no good to attract people to oneself, or even to Christ, unless one is going to give them the full truth of the gospel. This will lead them to have the love, faith, and purity that animates the preacher. Therefore, the preacher must strive always to develop in himself love, faith, and purity. He must study the Scripture and be faithful to it in his preaching. He must present Christ and his revelation exactly as he has received it, and he must practice what he preaches.

In the gospel the basic mistake of Simon, the Pharisee, is that he does not know the Scripture. Instead of studying the Scripture, he has accepted the pharisaical interpretations passed on to him. He does not appear to be a person of love; he doesn't seem to have any real faith in the possibility of the conversion of sinners; and so, he can hardly preach God's revealed truth in its fullness and purity. Indeed, he expects Jesus to have the ingrained prejudices he has, that is, sinners are to be avoided. The lesson that Jesus teaches is that we are all sinners, including the Pharisee. But grace is offered to all. What matters is whether or not we accept God's grace, abandon the life of sin, and are converted. What we often find is that the person who believes that he is a lesser sinner than his neighbor is filled with pride making conversion next to impossible. The great sinner, on the other hand, may have a deep humility. In either case, and in our case, too, this humility is essential. We don't save ourselves; God saves us. We need to persevere in humility all through life and not allow pride to gain the upper hand. The words of the psalmist apply to us: "The fear of the Lord is the beginning of wisdom; prudent are all who live by it. His praise endures forever."

1 Corinthians 15: 1-11; Luke 7: 36-50 **YEAR II**

St. Paul finds out that some members of the Church in Corinth do not believe that Christ rose from the dead. He reminds them that the bodily resurrection of Jesus is at the core of the Christian faith. Without it we cannot be saved and we have believed in vain. In our day, our only claim to honor is that we should hand on to future generations the same message which we have received from Christ through the apostles. It is not to our credit that we should change that message. To change it is to betray a trust; to change it is to place man over God; to change it is to substitute human foolishness for divine wisdom. Yes, we are to apply the gospel message to the new circumstances of the times. But the gospel message is to be the measure of good or evil times. Today too many people assume that the gospel message should be adjusted to accommodate new developments and circumstances. What they are doing is judging the Word of God by the practices of human beings. The whole purpose of God's revelation is to save us from this kind of human error.

The gospel presents us with an illustration. The woman who anointed Christ is looked upon as an ignorant and sinful person, who is doing something foolish—a "no account" person anointing a "no account" preacher according to the ancient Old Testament practices. The Pharisee supposedly knew better. He was above such customs especially if the person in question, such as Jesus, was inferior to him. The Pharisee was more enlightened and the circumstances of "modern times" excused him from the backward practices of the ignorant. Jesus makes clear that virtues are virtues in every age. Perhaps it was not the violation of a commandment to omit the washing of Jesus' feet but certainly it violated the spirit of loving one's neighbor as oneself. Jesus had compassion for the woman but he could have little for the Pharisee because the Pharisee was not disposed to accept it. In his view, he was not only superior to Jesus and the woman but he was also superior to the Word of God.

FRIDAY

1 Timothy 6: 2-12; Luke 8: 1-3 **YEAR I**

In today's reading, Timothy is warned to be faithful and to avoid the weaknesses of false teachers. False teachers are recognizable by their pride, envy, quarreling, and greed for money. Such men value religion only as a means of personal gain. They want to be rich and are letting themselves be captured by foolish and harmful desires, which draw them down to ruin and destruction. The love of money is the root of much evil. We are not to judge others lest we be judged. Regardless of the temptations, St. Paul urges us not to stray from the faith, but to "seek after integrity, piety, faith, love, steadfastness, and a gentle spirit."

As the gospel shows, these same qualities are evidenced in the life of Christ and in the lives of those people most closely associated with him. With St. Paul we are "ambassadors of Christ." Jesus journeyed through towns and villages preaching and proclaiming the good news of the kingdom of God. His was the ministry of reconciliation. Besides being the proclamation of God's forgiveness to individual people, our work is also that of bringing individuals and ethnic groups, different races and nations, into unity of mind and heart with one another. It is the work of peace. We acknowledge our need for forgiveness, we believe God forgives us, and we accept the obligation to forgive others.

1 Corinthians 15: 12-20; Luke 8: 1-3 **YEAR II**

Today's reading takes on great significance. In this passage, Paul helps us to grapple with the meaning of our death and resurrection, a basic problem of faith. Basically, St. Paul asserts that "if our hopes in Christ are limited to this life only, we are the most pitiable of men." However, he adds that because Christ has risen from the dead, we must believe in our own resurrection. If Christ had not risen, our faith would be in vain. But since he has risen, we are to rise as well. Otherwise, his death and resurrection would be useless. What would be the point in his own death and resurrection, if the rest of us had only an earthly life? Indeed, what would be the point of his life? What would be the purpose of grace, and the sacraments, and of our own life? That Christ died and rose again has great significance for us because it was for us and for our salvation that he entered the world.

The Resurrection of Christ is the key to understanding life. If Christ was raised from the dead, it is sure that we will be raised, for he gave his life for us. If Christ had not been raised from the dead, and if we are not raised from the dead, our faith is in vain. Ultimately, everything depends upon the Resurrection and that is exactly the way Christ left it with the Jews and his apostles. The Resurrection would be the sign of his truthfulness, his sanctity, his relation to the Father, and his promises to us.

Jesus went about preaching the Good News of the Gospel—that we are to believe in him, accept his teaching, reform our lives by following his commandments and, as a result, be saved. And all of this was made possible by the death and resurrection of Christ. It was clarified on the night of the Resurrection when Jesus appeared to the apostles. He granted them peace and he gave them the power to forgive sins. Without Christ's death and resurrection, this would not have taken place. But with Christ's death and resurrection, we can be freed from sin and able to follow him.

SATURDAY

1 Timothy 6: 13-16; Luke 8: 4-15 **YEAR I**

Today's reading has Paul's closing challenge to young Timothy. It is a strong, spiritual, lifelong challenge. Along with Timothy, we are urged to remain faithful to God's commandments until his coming. In the final analysis, faithfulness and perseverance in virtue are the essence of the Christian life. All of us keep some of the commandments all the time. All of us keep all of the commandments some of the time. But only some of us, with the help of God's grace, keep all the commandments all of the time. Let us ask God to look down upon us, his people, in all our moments of need, for he alone can assure that we will meet the challenge.

The gospel narrative presents the parable of the sower as a basic teaching of Jesus. The parable is really about the kind of soil—the depth of soul—that receives God's word. God's word is given to all; the Sower sows the seed everywhere. But then, aided by God's grace, it is up to the individual to accept or reject the gift that has been freely offered to him. As the parable indicates, the recognition of God's revelation is very uneven, although the Word and God's grace are given equally to everyone. The deciding factor is man's free will. As the Lord concludes, "The seed on the good ground are those who hear the Word in a spirit of openness, retain it, and bear fruit through perseverance."

1 Corinthians 15: 35-37, 42-49; Luke 8: 4-15 **YEAR II**

In today's reading, St. Paul gives a beautiful explanation of the characteristics of the human person after its resurrection. He cannot say precisely what will be the state of the risen person. In effect, he tells us to use our imagination, basing our thoughts on a few known facts. He says that the seed that is dropped into the ground and dies is nothing like the beautiful plant which grows from it. The first Adam cannot hold a candle to the second Adam, Christ. Similarly, the body of the risen person will be far more glorious than the one we experience now. It is not important that we know the details. Indeed, it is better not to know them because, in this case, our imagination can do a much better job for us than our intellect.

The resurrection should not be a worry for us. God will give us the best. What we should be concerned about is that we "bury ourselves in Christ and die in him" so that, in turn, he can come alive in us and produce beauty in our lives akin to the beauty which comes from the seed of a plant.

Just as many things can prevent the seed from dying in the ground—rocky soil, hard footpaths, and weeds—so too can the cares, the riches, the pleasures of life, certain people, places and things prevent us from dying in Christ and coming to maturity as deeply spiritual people. The Word of God is given to us in various grace-filled ways. We must allow ourselves to be purified and ennobled by that word, and conduct our lives according to God's ways rather than our own. Thus we die to self and live by the Word of Christ. By so doing we begin to live as resurrected people. Living a holy life, informed by divine grace, provides a deep understanding and appreciation of the future experience of the resurrected person.

Twenty-fifth Week of Ordinary Time

Monday

Ezra 1: 1-6; Luke 8: 16-18 **YEAR I**

Today's reading brings us back to a study of Old Testament salvation history after the Babylonian Captivity. The book of Ezra records the developments as the Jews returned to Jerusalem to build the house of the Lord. The Jews in Babylon had already prospered because of their facility in the Aramaic language. Consequently, all of them were not eager to exchange the comfort and security achieved in the land of exile for the fulfillment of a religious urge to rebuild the Temple in Jerusalem. Materialism was a strong impulse to enjoy the goods at their disposal and to put off the return to Jerusalem where they knew they would lack much of their present day advantages.

The gospel narrative about putting a lamp on a stand so that it will give light to all in the room rather than covering it up is an important one for us to consider in our day. So many people ask how we can restore morality to our society, how we can increase church attendance, and how we can save our society from degradation. One clear answer is that each individual person of conviction must uncover his "lamp" and place it on a stand. That is, he must make public proclamation of his faith. In a country like our own, there is nothing to stop us from professing our faith except our own weakness or our embarrassment to do so. There is something about truth and the character of the human person that allows them to find and recognize each other. The answer to the problem of religion and morality is locked up within us. Things will not change overnight; progress will be slow and uneven. But change to a moral society will never begin unless individual people act—and act in a visible manner—in accordance with their moral convictions.

Today we read more and more articles and view more and more programs urging that we return values to our schools and to our young people. It is like Cyrus encouraging the Jews to rebuild the Temple at Jerusalem. Let us seize the opportunity to bring about a cure for society. Some Jews took advantage of the offer made by Cyrus. Let us, in our time, seize the day!

Proverbs 3: 27-34; Luke 8: 16-18 **YEAR II**

Today, the reading is taken from the book of Proverbs—a collection of sayings concerning wisdom. In today's passage, the advice concerns how to relate to other people in life. The root of much evil in the world is our failure to do good and charitable deeds, when the opportunity presents itself. Generally, the people affected are aware of our lack of interest and, even though they may have no strict right to our goodness, our selfishness is resented. They may harm us or others to get what they want or they may develop a mentality of treating others as badly as they have been treated. This attitude can build up over the years and infect other generations producing the kind of strife so obvious today among people of different cultures, especially the "haves" and the "have nots." The roots of some antagonisms are so old and their cause so long-forgotten that it becomes difficult to understand why they exist. Yet, this hostility is very real and is easily rekindled by new real or imaginary insults. When it is within our power, we should do the good that is possible, not postponing and not giving in short measure. Neither should we be the first to find fault with another person or to cause trouble for that person; we should try to turn the other cheek and live in peace. We should not even dispute with others unless there is a clear need. And finally, let us not envy the wicked but let us have faith in God and not be vengeful. God will right all wrongs at the time and in the way which his wisdom determines.

We must become as a lamp giving light to all around us. Our lives must be such that our good example can be seen by all, and so bright that others will admire and wish to practice it. This is possible only when our lives are truly virtuous. The virtuous life is not one that can be turned on and off; neither is it a life that at times needs to be covered up from sight. The virtuous life is a seamless garment characterized by total love for God and for one's neighbor.

TUESDAY

Ezra 6: 7-8, 12, 14-20; Luke 8: 19-21 **YEAR I**

After Cyrus, king of Persia, had decreed that the Jews should be allowed to rebuild the Temple at Jerusalem, his successor, King Darius, determined that expenses should be paid by tax money from the west of the Euphrates. This was remarkable benevolence on his part. Thus the zealous Jews who had returned to Jerusalem were able to celebrate the completion of the Temple;

and then they set up the priestly caste to renew their order of worship as commanded by the Lord.

In the gospel we recall the benevolence of the centurion, who had rebuilt the synagogue at Capernaum and whose servant Jesus cured partly, at least, as an act of thanksgiving. Today's gospel states the attitude of Jesus regarding his family. He tells his disciples: "My mother and my brothers are those who hear the Word of God and act upon it." St. Peter, in baptizing Cornelius, said something to the effect that he now understood that God is not concerned about religion, nationality, color, or race. but only whether a person is righteous and acts in accordance with God's law.

We need to keep in mind the ecumenical inspiration of Vatican Council II. We believe that Christ came to save all men, that one way or another the opportunity for salvation is given to everyone. We need to respect this truth, encourage all people who are striving to live a good, just, and holy life. It would be clearly contrary to God's will to discourage these people or to work against them. We should give them positive assistance; to do otherwise would be pharisaical.

Proverbs 21: 1-6, 10-13; Luke 8: 19-21 **YEAR II**

Regardless of who one is—pauper or king—every person is subject to God. Therefore, it is best that every person, regardless of worldly rank, be meek and humble of heart, realizing that the Lord is his all powerful creator, provider, and judge. This latter role is most important because, in the final analysis, God will right all wrongs and eventually the arrogant will receive their just reward. We are encouraged to be poor in spirit, receptive to God's wisdom, honest, kind, and merciful. In the end, those who practice the opposite vices and are liars, greedy, and pitiless will not only be judged so by God but will be scorned by their neighbors and be without their prayerful support in time of need.

In this world "blood is thicker than water" but fundamentally we are more closely related to God than we are even to our human family. So Jesus can say that the person who is true to God belongs to God's family and should be even closer to the members of God's family than to blood relatives. One day we will be called to account by God and be with him or without him, for all eternity. That relationship to God is the most important and lasting one for us. By virtue of creation and redemption, we have been made brothers and sisters of Christ—children of one heavenly family—so our relationship to "all the saints" is more important and lasting than blood relationships. The lesson to be drawn from this knowledge is that even when tempted to evil by members of our own families or by our very best friends, we are to give our first allegiance to God and to our brothers and sisters in Christ.

WEDNESDAY

Ezra 9: 5-9; Luke 9: 1-6 **YEAR I**

In a time of prosperity, when everything was going miraculously well for the Jews, Ezra gave thanks to God for his goodness and so should we in our times. We cannot very well be grateful, if we are filled with pride, if we think that our good fortune is a result of our intelligence, strength, or other talents. These may play a role, but if we are to be praised, it would be for whatever goodness there is in us. Ultimately, this goodness comes from God who came to save us while we were yet sinners. Along with Ezra we should repent of our sins and thank God for his goodness. It is only this compassion of God that makes it possible for us to live with any degree of comfort, peace, justice, and holiness, and with the hope of everlasting life.

In today's gospel narrative, Christ instructs his apostles to go into the world on their mission of evangelization without the customary "necessities of life." All that really counts in this world or the next is the presence of God in our lives. In God we are to trust, rather than in our talents or in the things of the world like money, prestige, and influence. Our work, at every moment, is to extend the reign of God by our constant concern to reform and renew the structures of society. Are we conscious of having power from God to heal woundedness and to proclaim divine truth?

Proverbs 30: 5-9; Luke 9: 1-6 **YEAR II**

Today, the book of Proverbs teaches us how to live with neither poverty nor riches in this world. The Word of God is a sure protection. Why need a person worry, if he is in possession of God's own truth and acts in accordance with it! Nothing can truly harm us or disturb us, when our lives are governed by truth, for God is truth and he alone is to be feared. The author of Proverbs, therefore, prays to be delivered from material possessions because he might be tempted to deny God's truth or fail to practice it in order to retain the things of this world. How often this is the case! We place our trust in material goods; we lose our fear of God; we put aside his truth and act in accordance with human wisdom.

When Christ sent forth his disciples, they were "armed" only with his truth. He dispatched them as poor, dedicated heralds of the kingdom. They needed nothing else. If the people accepted the truth, they would provide for their sustenance; if not, they should move on to the next town. In any case, the one who proclaims the gospel has nothing to fear as long as he is faithful to his mission and faithful to God.

THURSDAY

Haggai 1: 1-8; Luke 9: 7-9 **YEAR I**

It was through the prophet Haggai that the Lord told the people in Jerusalem that it was about time that they built him a temple. Although they themselves had houses, satiated themselves with food and drink, had fine clothing, they still had not done anything to honor the Lord. History repeats itself. Parishes built in the nineteenth century with money sacrificed by small groups of poor people are now the property of relatively well-to-do families. The spirit of self-sacrifice of those early pioneers must be imitated by present day Catholics who want to preserve their schools, maintain their churches, and assist the less fortunate in our society.

In a way, the situation is something like Herod's perplexity about which we read in today's gospel. Here he is with all his money, power, prestige and the poor Christ is outshining him. He can't figure out why no one loves him. Americans can't figure it out either. Look at all we have done for other countries! Why don't they love us? The answer is that in proportion to what we could do for others, we have done little! Everything in the world belongs to God, it is placed here for the good of all and not just a few. So if we end up in affluence, no matter how hard we may have worked for it, and others end up in dire poverty, we are obliged to share God's goods with those of his people who have a desperate need for them.

Ecclesiastes 1: 2-11; Luke 9: 7-9 **YEAR II**

"All things are vanity!" Truer words were never spoken. The person who sets his heart on material goods, power, or prestige in the world is on a treadmill at best. Having been sated with these things, he always needs more and better in order to have something new and invigorating. It is like rivers flowing into the sea, which can never be filled up. It is like the eye or the ear, which is "infinite" in its capacity to absorb sight and sound. It is the same with admirers; they are always ready to go off with the next person so, if one expects fame to be anything but fleeting, he is living in delusion. It has always been the same, but more so today than ever before, human beings look for instant gratification. But instant gratification usually satisfies a person for little more than an instant.

We need to find our joy and a sense of peace in him who makes the world go round. Rather than desire to possess—and in that sense, to master creation, we would gain much more from contemplating nature, admiring its beauty, its complexity, its order, and thereby coming to know, to respect and to love its Creator, and long to be one with him.

Poor Herod is a perfect example of the material-minded person. Jesus is a perfect example of one who admired the goodness, beauty and truth of creation. Herod could not begin to understand Jesus, he could have no appreciation of Jesus' "world." Jesus, on the other hand, could understand what Herod was about but he was just about powerless to bring him to his senses. All we have is God's grace, as evidenced in nature and in the depths of our soul. After that, it is up to our free will as to whether we will contemplate, appreciate and love the source of grace, give up our attachment to things and serve him.

FRIDAY

Haggai 1: 15-2: 9; Luke 9: 18-22 **YEAR I**

Through the prophet, God tells the Jews to set about rebuilding the Temple, to have faith that he will bring it about. All the people need to do is work. After all, God tells the people that all the silver and gold in the world and all else too belong to him. By his providence, he can bring it about that the Jews will receive all the money needed for the reconstruction. God made a covenant with his people, when he brought them up from the land of Egypt; he will not go back on that pact. He will be their God; all he asks is that they be his people, faithful, hopeful, and loving toward him.

The apostles had been eyewitnesses to a number of miracles, which should have indicated to them that Jesus was indeed the God, who owned all the silver and gold, and everything else in the world. They did their best to acknowledge that he was the equal of John the Baptist. However, they hesitated to go further until Peter, inspired by God's grace, confessed that Jesus was the Messiah, the Son of God. That was a big step in a theocratic society. To be wrong was blasphemy, the worst possible crime. But the apostles eventually took that step, supported by God's grace. They had the faith but to take action was something else. The Jews of Haggai's time had the faith. Every time God calls us to do something for him, he promises to stand by us. We accept this in faith, but then to act on faith is not an easy matter. Jesus prayed before all-important decisions of life. Prayer is the secret to worthy action.

Ecclesiastes 3: 1-11; Luke 9: 18-22 **YEAR II**

These days some people are convinced that the only guiding principle of our lives should be "love, love, love." This is quite true because God is love. On the other hand, it is quite false, when one's understanding of love is superficial and emotional or totally unrealistic as that of a robot. As seen in Christ, love is always present in God but love is identified also with truth and goodness. When truth and goodness are violated, love does not continue to appear as sweetness and light but may change to solicitude, anger, concern, reprimand, and so on. God's love is not for error and evil but for goodness and truth, so God's love is going to have different aspects to it.

The reading from Ecclesiastes brings this out. There is a time for everything—killing and healing, tearing down and building up, weeping and laughing, gathering and scattering and so on. Indeed, God has so made the world and man that these changes should give rise in man to a hope and even a conviction that there is a stable, timeless Being, who does not change. All the change and contradiction in the world reveals an underlying stability and order. The sun rises and sets but it rises again; plants live and they die but they live again; animals live and die but they succeed one another; man laughs and weeps but he laughs once again. As Ecclesiastes says in this way, "God has put the timeless into their hearts."

In the gospel this same thought is developed. "Who do men say that I am?" Jesus asks. The apostles give a "time-conditioned" answer. Jesus is some great prophet returned from the dead, some special messenger from God, who was with us for a time, left, and is back again. That turns out not to be true. Jesus is finally the appearance of the Timeless One on earth; he is God.

SATURDAY

Zechariah 2: 5-9, 14-15; Luke 9: 43-45 **YEAR I**

The greatness of Jerusalem is not to be found in its spaciousness nor in its population, although these have been great enough. Rather, its riches and glory derive from God's special presence there and, since Old Testament days, from the words and deeds of Christ, the Son of God. The Temple was intended to be a rallying point for God's people and it often served that purpose, but often, too, it was a place of division and disaster.

A sample of the latter was the passion and death of Christ on the Cross. It was the culmination of great disunity between Christ and the Pharisees, between revealed and man-made religion. At the same time, coupled with the Resurrection, the same event has been the source of unity among millions of Christians. The apostles did not understand this latter development. But we, who live centuries later, should have the greatest appreciation for the life and death of Christ, and we should live out this mystery in our own lives and in our own cities and towns throughout the world. We should strive as Jesus did and with the help of his grace to establish wherever we are his kingdom of justice, love, and peace.

Ecclesiastes 11: 9-12: 8; Luke 9: 43-45 **YEAR II**

While one is young, he should use his energy for constructive purposes; he should follow his dreams, bubbling with enthusiasm and joy. For, when all is said and done, youth is a short time, so we need to take advantage of this period of our lives while we have the chance. This would have been especially true in Old Testament times and in the time of Christ, when life expectancy was much less than today.

One thing that youth must remember, however, is that life and all he has and all he accomplishes is from God. As is expressed beautifully through the latter part of the reading, youth will need God in old age. If the person does not have God with him in old age, his last days will be sorry indeed, when one begins to lose sight and hearing; when one's world becomes a small room, a bed, a chair; when one experiences irrational fears; when one longs to hear the sounds of nature outside the prison of one's house. Then it is that we learn that all is vanity. Then will we need the presence and the love of God.

In the full bloom of life and power, Jesus warns the apostles that he is facing death. He accepts the advice of Ecclesiastes above. He builds and strengthens his relationship to the Father in good times so that he may be able to bear up, when the time of suffering comes. Like the apostles, we often ignore the warnings. Somehow, we need to strengthen our relationship with God so that at the end, when he is all we really have, we may see him as Father, friend, confidant, total love and goodness, our final resting place. "Our hearts are restless until they rest in Thee."

Twenty-sixth Week of Ordinary Time

Monday

Zechariah 8: 1-8; Luke 9: 46-50 **YEAR I**

In the disappointing days after the exile, the prophet Zechariah encouraged the struggling remnant of those who had returned to Jerusalem. It is interesting to note that when the Lord wishes to describe the peace and serenity of Jerusalem after the return from exile, he speaks of the elderly sitting undisturbed and of children playing in the streets. These are signs that peace and justice exist. We hardly have peace and justice in our time, when abortion and child abuse are common practices, and when euthanasia is becoming a greater threat. All the more should we take these particular issues seriously, when the Lord reveals that the freedom of these innocents is a sign of peace.

Ultimately it is only God who can restore peace to the world. We need to pray to him to accomplish what we human beings seem unwilling to do and we need to be converted to doing this his way—obeying the commandments and living out the Beatitudes. Fidelity to God's way of life is our hope. We need to persevere in good example and in prayer and leave the rest to God's loving providence.

The gospel makes clear that neither physical strength nor political power is the answer to our problems in seeking peace. Rather, holiness of life and being innocent as children are the only ways to obtain a state of perfect peace and justice. Jesus makes it clear that his disciples are to serve others, especially the poor and the helpless. Children are the symbols of the little ones of society. Jesus teaches tolerance towards all, even those imperfectly motivated.

Strangely enough, often in our own time, even as in the time of Christ, people who don't seem to be particularly religious live the gospel message better than we do. People who run soup kitchens, shelters for the homeless, crusade for various causes may not be members of any Church, but they may be doing more than Church-goers. The grace of God, which inspires this goodness, is not to be squelched.

Job 1:6-22; Luke 9:46-50 **YEAR II**

Although Scripture often uses figurative language, there seems to be no question that Satan, or an evil spirit, in some fashion "roams the earth and patrols it." Evil is inferior to God, not superior to him, but it is free in the sense that the Lord tolerates evil for the sake of his people; he allows them to be tested, to prove their desire to do God's will, to be virtuous. The existence of evil and its relationship to God, as described in Job, is the consistent teaching of the Church.

God has no favorites but in human terms, it seems that he does. Why should Job be so favored? Why should we be even more favored with the grace of baptism, the guidance of the Church, and so many other gifts? It is a mystery, but we surely have been favored by God. The question is whether or not we would have Job's strength of will, if the Lord were to test us so severely. In all likelihood, we would not. So we have another motive for thanksgiving and a reason to strengthen our spiritual lives. If we were tested just a bit more severely, we would never survive. So we should thank God for his goodness, never give in to complaints, strive steadily and daily to increase in virtue.

Job's response to God's providence was one of humble submission. What did he have that he did not receive from God? "Naked I came from my mother's womb, and naked shall I go back again. The Lord gave and the Lord has taken away. Blessed be the name of the Lord!" This is the thesis of Pope John Paul II's encyclical Laborem Exercens. There is nothing on the face of the earth that has not come from God in some fashion. That which seems to be new is the product of man's work. Therein is the dignity of work; it is a continuation of God's work of creation. But always we need to recall that work would produce nothing were it not for the goodness of God from the very beginning.

The gospel tells us that those whom the world holds in high esteem are not necessarily God's favorites. God's favorites are the meek and humble of heart, those who become as little children in their style of life. God loves most those who need him most, who recognize their own shortcomings and welcome his help, as children welcome the assistance—sometimes grudgingly but in the end gratefully—of their parents.

True enough, like Job's friends, we are tempted to blame others for our problems. But a child has a certain docility, when he is shown the error of his ways and shown the correct way to do something, which leads to joy in the accomplishment.

Just as we would never ostracize a child from our company, but on the contrary take this child in and offer that child whatever we have, simply because it is a child, so should we welcome anyone who believes in the person and message of Christ. If they are not against us, they are with us, and have the potential of becoming one with us.

TUESDAY

Zechariah 8: 20-23; Luke 9: 51-56 **YEAR I**

In today's reading, Zechariah, through a glorious view of the future, encourages the lonely Jews returned from exile and living in the poor, rebuilt city of Jerusalem. Once that city is established as it should be, they will be God's people. People from all over the world will wish to share the peace of such a kingdom. Unfortunately, although the Jewish people had that potential and Catholics have it now, theirs and our failure to be God's people has often frustrated the fulfillment of that prophecy. God calls us to this task, gives us the grace but we fail to implement his design because we do not wish to follow him who is the way, the truth, and the life.

We can see in the gospel how a human being would judge our conduct. Like the apostles, he would judge that we should be destroyed for our obstinacy. But, Jesus judged more mercifully. As he did with the Samaritans, the Lord permits us to live on so that at least those who are willing to follow him may have the opportunity to do so and be saved.

Job 3: 1-3, 11-17, 20-23; Luke 9: 51-56 **YEAR II**

It is not easy to understand why God allows suffering, especially when we are the ones who are suffering. In today's reading, Job decides it would have been better never to have been born than to suffer as he is suffering.

All God's previous blessings, all Job's prosperity and earlier happiness have been forgotten. For Job the only relevant experience is his current pain and the only light at the end of the tunnel is death. He says that God has "hemmed him in." Job cannot get off the painful path that he is on.

One of the most bitter elements of suffering is the thought that it will never end, that we will never get over it. For Job the prospect of spending the rest of his life on a dung heap is very real and very painful.

Yet experience tells us that suffering ends. Yes, we go through periods of acute emotional or physical pain, but those periods end.

In the gospel, the disciple want to destroy a Samaritan town because its residents would not welcome Jesus because he was going to Jerusalem.

Jesus was well aware that he was going to be put to death. But he refused to let the fact that he was being rejected by the Samaritans and that he would be rejected by the Jews be a cause of destructive anger and suffering to others.

One of the most important lessons we can draw from Jesus' life is that behind all the suffering is love, and that in the end love will triumph over evil and over suffering. In the end every tear will be wiped away, love will reign supreme, and suffering will be no more.

WEDNESDAY

Nehemiah 2: 1-8; Luke 9: 57-62 **YEAR I**

In the difficult post-exilic period, the layman Nehemiah did much to help his people in Jerusalem. Over and over again the Jews had to rebuild either their city or regain an abandoned faith. In today's reading, Nehemiah asks that he might rebuild Jerusalem and he is given the materials with which to do it. God is just as generous to each one of us. He is constantly giving us the gifts we need to rebuild our faith in him and to rebuild a holy and happy life for ourselves. When there is a problem it is not God's but ours. We do not go to him quickly enough or often enough with our needs. When we receive his help, we often squander it or leave it aside to "rust" like abandoned machinery while we go off in pursuit of some pleasure. The most important lesson to remember is that God is ever kind and merciful. He will never turn us down. We must constantly look to him for assistance. This is the only way that even the "strongest" human person can live a holy life.

Jesus makes clear in the gospel that we must be single-minded in following him. His sayings do not mean that we cannot associate with our families, but everything must be done in union with him and God must have first place in our heart and affection. Although the invitation of Jesus will be extended to us often, we cannot be sure when the last time will be. And if we accept the invitation to follow him, we cannot be sure where it will lead. What we do know is that the proper decision, the only safe course of action, is to accept the invitation right now, no matter where it leads, and hold to it steadfastly. We cannot possibly go wrong if we are in union with Christ.

Job 9: 1-12, 14-16; Luke 9: 57-62 **YEAR II**

After questioning God's will himself, Job is reduced to the humble state of submission. Obviously he still has no idea why he and his family are suffering such calamity, but how can one fight God or even dispute God's wisdom?

Job, after much meditation, is overpowered by the strength and the awesomeness of God, and now he is fully convinced of his own weakness, the finite position of a creature in relation to the infinite power of God. He is no longer angry, for he recognizes God and man for what each one is.

Why did God create the sun and the stars, the mountains and the oceans as they are? Why does he, upon occasion, have all these parts of creation act "strangely?" The answer: It is simply beyond our power to know and understand.

Job has learned the meaning of what St. Paul maintains. "Power [of God] is made perfect in weakness [of man]" (2 Cor 12:9). The apostles hardly had the mind of Job. Their idea was to prevail through strength. It is clear where Jesus stands; he rebuked them. The message of Jesus is to leave the apparent disrespect of the Samaritans to the Father to judge. Like the wheat and the cockle, they should be allowed to continue until the Father in due time calls a halt to their lives and makes judgment. Meanwhile, of course, we should present them with the truth, try to persuade them, but not judge, if they fail to accept us.

The challenge is always there before us—to accept God's call or to reject it. Most of the time we don't reject God's will directly but we have something "better, wiser, more humane, more charitable" to do. Job finally came to realize that, even though God's will may at times seem strange to us, human beings simply cannot and should not argue against it.

Thursday

Nehemiah 8: 1-4, 5-6, 7-12; Luke 10: 1-12 **YEAR I**

Today's reading describes a dramatic and important scene: Nehemiah was reading the Word of God to the people, and together with Ezra and the priests, he interpreted it for them. The reaction of the people was to throw themselves upon the ground and lament. But Nehemiah pointed out that the Word of God should be a cause for rejoicing. Granted that they may have ignored God's word or broken his law in the past, now that they had heard it once again and understood its meaning through the prophets' interpretation and were ready to accept it, there should be cause for celebration. The law of God is not something to lament unless we are unwilling to follow it. If we accept it and practice it, the law can turn our lives into great joy and happiness. If we reject God's word, then we shall be sad indeed.

In today's gospel narrative, Jesus, in making his way to Jerusalem, teaches the conditions of discipleship. His followers have a total, lifelong, difficult commitment. The disciples were not instructed to fast and abstain, but to eat what was put before them. They were to look for peaceful people, those truly longing for God's kingdom of justice, truth, and peace. God's peace and joy would be granted to the household that received them well. Accursed and wretched would be those who rejected them. Let us repent for our past way of life, when it was contrary to God's law. What presently in our lives and actions makes it evident that we know and have the truth and that Christ is living in us? Are we happy Christians?

Job 19: 21-27; Luke 10: 1-12 **YEAR II**

Those who claim to know the will of God—or in our own day, to know what Jesus would do, if he were here—make themselves divine. They reject the authority that Jesus has given to the Church and then proceed to set themselves in the very place of the Holy Father—infallible, a law unto themselves. Job asks that his friends not do that but they should have empathy for him in this mysterious hour, in which the Lord has called upon him to suffer for some unknown reason.

In his circumstances, especially with the rejection by his friends, it is not easy for Job to have faith. He must renew his act of faith constantly and he laments how much easier it would be, if he could chisel his act of faith in stone, and go on about life without needing to renew it. But that is the test. Old priests have told me that, in the final analysis, what counts is perseverance in faith. We can overcome sin, lack of support from friends, and so on with God's grace, but God cannot supply perseverance in the act of faith—although he gives us the grace for it. That is not in his plan; we must provide faith of our free will working together with God's grace.

But Job firmly resolves to persevere in faith, sustained by the hope of one day seeing God, who by his presence will put an end to all of Job's anxiety and will give him vindication among his friends. Perseverance in faith is made possible only by hope in God's promises.

The gospel, in effect, urges us to follow the example of Job. In this world we are "like lambs in the midst of wolves"; we are surrounded by enough evil, but even our own friends can tempt us to lose faith. We need the support of others. Accept it, where it is given but do not expect that it is going to be present all the time. You may be an excellent preacher; you may present God's word with impeccable logic; your hearers may even recognize its truth. And still, faith may not be forthcoming. They may be overwhelmed by the cares and pleasures of this world. As for you, you may sympathize with these people, but don't succumb to their ways. Continue on, preach the message of hope—"The reign of God is near"—keep faith yourself and offer it to others. Offering is all we can do; acceptance is made possible to each person by God's grace, but only actualized by the act of free will, which must be provided by the individual person. No one else can do it for him.

FRIDAY

Baruch 1: 15-22; Luke 10: 13-16 **YEAR I**

What Baruch has to say about the Israelites is the life story of each one of us. Very often, the Lord has called upon us in a very personal way to hear his word and obey his commandments, but we have turned a deaf ear. In fact, we have heard him but we have turned quickly to other pursuits as if we had not heard. We have gone off after the plans of our own wicked heart, served other gods, and done evil in the sight of the Lord. We ought to be filled with shame because justice and mercy are so clearly on God's side. We push everything to the back of our minds, bury it as best we can, and continue in our own sinful way forgetting the ideals of perfection which God sets before us.

In today's gospel narrative, Jesus condemns three towns for not accepting his word. He considers them worse than pagan Tyre and Sidon or even wicked Sodom. The people in those towns had not had the opportunity to hear Jesus and his gospel as did Corazin and Bethsaida.

Job 38: 1, 12-21, 40: 3-5; Luke 10: 13-16 **YEAR II**

Job is challenged by the knowledge and power of God. Does he have charge over the dawn and the darkness? Of course. This saying has ever greater meaning in our own time. Do we have charge of the Universe; whose center is the sun? Do we even have charge of the earth, which spins on its axis and circles the sun continuously at such a furious rate of speed? What do you know about life and death? Job is embarrassed. Twice he has challenged the Lord to be more just to him. The response is always the same. What do you know, Job? Do you think yourself wiser or more powerful than God? Accept what is given to you; it is best to do so. Human beings do not know what is good for them in the long run. Job admits his impudence, accepts his finite condition, promises to challenge God no more.

In the gospel Jesus speaks of people who have been treated much better than Job. All kinds of miracles have been performed in their midst and still they do not believe. Who is better off, Job or these other people? Whom does God love more? He loves both equally but it is easy to see that the suffering, which Job endures, is more salutary than the blessings that Jesus bestows in his miracles. These latter people reject the prophets and apostles, even Jesus himself despite the miracles. In so doing they reject the Messiah, God's Son and God the Father, as well. Obviously theirs will be a terrible ending, whereas Job has much to hope for.

SATURDAY

Baruch 4: 5-12, 27-29; Luke 10: 17-24 **YEAR I**

Jerusalem is pictured as the mother of the Israelites, lamenting the fact that her children have been taken from her by God because of their worship of false gods. She reminds the people that the exile is only just and its purpose is not to destroy them, but to bring them back to their senses. She pleads with the people to ask God for his mercy, for that is all he wants. He only wants his people to be reconciled, to be converted to him once again.

In today's reading we can see so many cases of our own day, in which the children have fallen into the worship of money, possessions, illicit sex, and drugs. Possibly some responsibility lies with the parents, but there is no indication that "Jerusalem" is to blame for the sins of the Israelites. Regardless of any fault on the part of the parents, the children have free will; they have been given a knowledge of God, even if imperfect; the children are certainly capable of accepting or rejecting God.

There is no sense in arguing or even reasoning with the children about God. It is best that we simply pray for God's mercy, that the children will see the futility of their ways and return to him. They can reason about their conversion later; now they should return because there is no other direction in which to turn, no other person or thing which ever promises true happiness. Even if they do not understand, they know of God's promise and they have experienced the unhappiness of false gods. Perhaps if we pray enough, they will "come and see" and they will "taste and see how sweet is the Lord."

In the gospel, the disciples return from their missionary journey delighted with what they have accomplished. The forces of physical and moral evil have become subject to them. Jesus tries to calm them down and makes clear that it is through the power of God that they have been successful. If they grow in pride, the situation could be reversed in a twinkling of an eye. They should rejoice, not because they have overcome evil, but because God has chosen them to be his instruments in this demonstration of divine power. The disciples must continue in their innocence like little children, if the Lord is to be with them.

Only Jesus really knows what took place in the souls of those to whom the disciples went. Only Jesus knows how the Father operates among human beings. And so, we return to the thought above. Neither reason nor anger nor enticements of any kind from us will save our children from the worship of false gods. Only God's grace, given to them in mercy, will bring them back. So we need to pray as Jesus did that our young people will simply recognize the Lord God for what he is, accept his grace, be converted to him, and follow in his ways.

Job 42: 1-3, 5-6, 12-16; Luke 10: 17-24 **YEAR II**

Job finally makes a complete confession that God is all-knowing and all-powerful. Man can neither understand all God's ways nor prevent them from being realized. At last Job has the perfect human posture in the presence of God. He is everything; I am nothing; let him do with me what he wills. And of course, what God wills is that we be perfectly happy. In Job's case he returns to him all his material gifts in order to make a point with those who opposed Job. More often than not, God treats his servants otherwise, asking them to accept a life of poverty and humiliation. But happiness is something found within a man anyway and perfect happiness is had only by way of promise in this world.

So it was with the Lord's disciples. Accompanying Jesus, they knew much of humiliation, but from time to time he gave them an experience of happiness in order to sustain their hope and trust in his promises. He can do this because the disciples have become as little children. They recognize God as all powerful and themselves as weak. It is this that the Father has revealed to them. This is the secret that has been hidden for centuries and, strangely enough, still remains hidden from most of us, even though it has been revealed with perfect clarity in the public life, passion, death and resurrection of Christ. It is not as if it could not be seen by people of the present. But we have less excuse because of Christ. Still, even in the things of nature, the lesson is revealed. God is everything; we are nothing; let us accept the fact and do God's will.

Twenty-seventh Week of Ordinary Time

MONDAY

Jonah 1: 1-2: 1, 11; Luke 10: 25-37 **YEAR I**

Jonah is not to be understood as a historical prophet. The book of Jonah is a parable—an interesting imaginary story to teach a profound religious lesson. Jonah, called to preach to godless Nineveh in the east, tries to run away westward. He flees, taking a ship to Tarshish instead. The ship is beset by a dreadful storm and everyone on board prays for deliverance. Jonah confesses that the storm is probably the fault of his God because he is trying to flee the Lord. The sailors are reluctant to throw Jonah overboard in order to appease his God, but eventually they do so and the storm abates.

There are many times in our lives when it is clear that the Lord wants us to do something and we find it too difficult or inopportune. Our rash judgment leads us into greater difficulty than we would have had if we had faced squarely the first problem. Once we run away or once we tell a lie, we inevitably run or lie further. There is no escape unless we convert ourselves, repent of what we have done, and return to a proper course of action. That is always a painful experience but a consoling one as well, because it brings great joy and peace of mind in the knowledge that we are acting in conformity with God's will.

In today's gospel narrative, a lawyer asks Jesus about the Great Commandments in an attempt to run away from the truth. He could have been trying to "trip" Jesus but it is equally possible that he was trying to have Jesus say what he wanted to hear, that love is not totally demanding. Instead, Jesus made clear that the person, who truly loves God and truly loves himself, cannot escape from an act of charity regardless of the circumstances. Jesus tells the lawyer and his hearers the parable of the Good Samaritan. To understand this parable fully, we must remember that, at that time, Jews and Samaritans hated one another totally. Because of historical, racial, geographic, and religious reasons a Jew would not even speak to a Samaritan. In this parable, the victim was a Jew and the travelers were in a hurry to get to their destination, and any demand involving time, effort, and money was not welcome and constituted a risk to any one who would stop to help. Still, one of the travelers, a Samaritan, treated this hated Jew with great compassion unlike the priest and the Levite. Jesus claims that nothing justifies avoiding an act of charity. If we truly love God with our whole mind, heart, and soul we will love our neighbor as we love our very selves totally under any and all circumstances exactly the way the Good Samaritan did.

Galatians 1: 6-12; Luke 10: 25-37 — YEAR II

St. Paul was not one to mince words. In today's first reading, he expresses his distress with the Galatians in very strong terms. Apparently a person or persons had come among them with a watered-down version of the gospel, perhaps, to curry favor with the Galatians. Paul will have none of it. He tells the Galatians that he received the gospel by direct revelation from Jesus Christ. The gospel he proclaims is no mere human invention. Paul protects it and defends it, and in doing so he protects and defends the Galatians.

In Luke's gospel, a man asks Jesus what he must do to inherit everlasting life. Jesus asks him what is written in the Law, and the man answers that he must love God and his neighbor as himself. Jesus tells the man that if he does that he will live. But then Luke tells us that the man, seeking to justify himself, asks, "Who is my neighbor?" Jesus answers with the parable of the Good Samaritan.

Jesus does not soften or water down the message. Neighbors are not defined by geography or blood relationships; they are defined by their humanity and by their need. And in our efforts to live the gospel we must respond to the humanity and needs of those with whom we have contact.

TUESDAY

Jonah 3: 1-10; Luke 10: 38-42 — YEAR I

After incredible misadventures, Jonah, the Jew, reached Ninevah and reluctantly began to preach. Amazingly, the whole city, all the animals, all the men and women, from the king down, immediately did penance in sackcloth and ashes. The spontaneous repentance of the Ninevites stands in striking contrast to Israel who remained obstinate despite all the preaching of God's prophets. The Lord's oracles of doom are conditional and he will forego the punishment he threatens if we repent of our evil ways. If we adhere to God's teaching, conform our wills to his, and carry out his thoughts and his ways in our lives we will be saved. It matters not what judgement human beings make.

The story of Martha and Mary teaches that us that the "better part" is to listen to the Lord. Jesus points out that "wasting time" with him is not wasting time at all. Prayer, union with God, may seem like laziness to some, but it is the means whereby God is implored to help people who may find themselves in difficulty in the world. Generally speaking, God comes to our aid through others—their intercessory prayers and their good example. Trying to be as one with God is the one thing necessary.

Galatians 1: 13-24; Luke 10: 38-42 **YEAR II**

It is important to know the background and the credentials of people who speak to us. It is especially important to know where people are coming from when they talk about the gospel. Today, Paul presents his credentials to the Galatians. He says he began to preach the good news without consulting any of the disciples and, in fact, it was three years before he went to Jerusalem to see Peter. Paul tells these things to the Galatians so that they will understand he is preaching the true gospel and that they should follow his teaching.

In our day, there are many conflicting voices striving to tell us how to live. Some are self-seeking, some are misguided, and some are just plain wrong. There is one voice that speaks with authority, Jesus through the Scriptures, the Church and through his disciples.

In the gospel reading, Luke recounts how Mary sat at the feet of Jesus listening to his words, while her sister Martha who was working in the kitchen became upset that Mary was not helping.

By Jesus' response we learn that being quiet in the presence of the Lord is better than worrying or being anxious or even working hard. It is the better portion. Why do some of us find that so hard to believe?

WEDNESDAY

Jonah 4: 1-11; Luke 11: 1-4 **YEAR I**

After Jonah had preached in Ninevah that the people should do penance or perish, he was bitterly disappointed that God did not destroy the city as he had prophesied. What Jonah had failed to take into account was that the people did penance. God was only keeping his part of the bargain. He doesn't want men to perish, but to be saved. Jonah, on the other hand, even though he had preached repentance, was unwilling to accept the sorrow of the people for their sins and he wanted to continue to condemn them no matter what they did.

In order to bring Jonah to his senses, the Lord grew a large plant in the desert where Jonah was camped. It gave him shade, a great relief from the sun. But then a worm came along and destroyed the plant, upsetting Jonah. The Lord pointed out that Jonah had done nothing to give life to the plant in the first place; through lack of care, the worm destroyed it; if Nineveh did not "deserve" to be restored to God's favor, neither did Jonah have any "right" to a shade tree in the desert. The gratuity of God's grace and his great mercy are the only means of overcoming sin and the other difficulties of this life.

The "Our Father," which we say over and over each day, is a reminder of this truth. All that we have, or hope to have, comes from the hand of God, even the basic necessities of life. And so we pray to God that we will not be sorely tried—at least not beyond our strength—and that God will provide us with the sustenance we need. The implication is that we shall be satisfied and grateful regardless of the amount we receive, because everything depends upon God's mercy.

Galatians 2: 1-2, 7-14; Luke 11: 1-4 **YEAR II**

Again we see the outspokenness of Paul. He saw things with clarity and refused to compromise his beliefs. In today's reading from Galatians, Paul sees that Peter is not being open and above board. In Antioch, Peter had been eating with Gentiles and not observing the Jewish dietary laws. But when Jews arrived, Peter, in order to avoid trouble, drew apart from the Gentiles and ate with the Jews. Paul calls Peter out face to face. It is a good lesson for all of us. We should act according to our beliefs and not alter our conduct because we are afraid of how others will react. That does not mean we adopt a self-righteous, holier-than-thou attitude, it just means that we do what is right without worrying about how others perceive us. There is a tremendous freedom to be found in adopting this attitude.

In the gospel passage, Jesus is asked to teach the apostles how to pray. His response is the Lord's Prayer. It is at once simple and profound. When we say "Our Father," we are affirming our true relationship with God. We are the creatures. He is the provider and protector. Our lives, our well being, our happiness, and our spirituality are in his hands, and that is where they belong.

THURSDAY

Malachi 3: 13-20; Luke 11: 5-13 **YEAR I**

In Malachi's time, people were complaining, as they always do, that God was not fair and just. They claimed that the proud, those who refused to humble themselves and obey the Lord, were the ones who prospered. They were foolish to deny themselves in "this" world, because it does not pay off. Malachi's time was one of much religious indifference and abuse. Malachi predicted that God would come to judge the people and the sun of justice would burn up the wicked but heal the just people. In addition, the Lord promised, through Malachi, to take care of his people. Faith is required. The reward is not immediately apparent; but it is far better that things end well rather than begin well, far better to have perfect and everlasting happiness than imperfect and temporary happiness.

Our principal human weakness is lack of perseverance. It seems that we can believe for a time, hope for a time, love for a time, but the attractions of this world insistently tell us that "one bird in the hand is worth two in the bush" and soon we are tempted to become pragmatic philosophers. In the gospel the Lord reminds us that God is our father and asks us to remember that a loving father never betrays his children. He may not give the child everything at once, but the loving father is compelled by his relationship to the child to do what is in his power for the child. God is our father; he loves us overwhelmingly; everything is possible to him; therefore, he will provide us with everything, and sooner or later we will enjoy complete and everlasting happiness. If he should wish to try us, as he does, so be it. Our major need is perseverance in faith in the basic truths of life, especially in our lasting relationship with God, our Father.

Galatians 3: 1-5; Luke 11: 5-13 **YEAR II**

In dealing with the Galatians, Paul continues to be blunt. In today's reading he asks them if they have gone out of their minds. The issue is the Law versus the Spirit, and Paul is firmly on the side of the Spirit. There is nothing wrong with following the rules. What is wrong is excluding the Spirit in the name of the rules. The Law justifies no one, Paul tells us, and this harkens back to Paul's statement in Romans that those who are led by the Spirit of God are children of God. Relying on the Law rather than the Spirit is a kind of do-it-yourself spirituality. Paul also points out that if the

Law could bestow righteousness, then Jesus Christ died in vain.

The gospel passage picks up the theme of Spirit. Jesus tells his disciples that if they with all their sins know how to give good things to their children, "How much more will the heavenly Father give the Holy Spirit to those who ask him."

The Law was available before Jesus became man. If the Law had worked there would have been no need for Jesus to come. The fact is that we cannot save ourselves. Jesus must do that.

FRIDAY

Joel 1: 13-15, 2: 1-2; Luke 11: 15-26 **YEAR I**

In today's reading, the final minor prophet Joel predicts a coming "day of the Lord"—a frightening day of divine judgment. He announces that the people must pay for their sins. They have given up following God. "The house of the Lord is deprived of offering and libation." The people have given up the worship of the living God. The prophet calls priests, Temple personnel, the elders, and the whole population to penance and formal prayer—the traditional reaction to disaster. In post-exilic times, the efficacy of fasting and other penances was rated highly. Sackcloth was a penitential garment of camel or goat's hair worn about the waist. Ordinarily one would suspend penances at evening, but especially depressing situations prompted sustained self-affliction. We may have a similar situation. We need to rally, reminding ourselves of the power of God, the love of God, but also of the fact that God cannot be deceived.

In the gospel, the crowd accused Infinite Goodness of being totally evil. On several grounds Jesus responded: l) If he is the devil, he is fighting against himself because his preaching is in support of the commandments and all of God's Old Testament message. 2) What is so unusual about casting out devils, when the vast percentage of the population has been able to keep itself free of evil, or at least drive off the evil after succumbing to sin?

Jesus goes on to make the case for the prevention of evil in the first place. It is much better, for instance, for citizens to have a strong defense around their town so that others will not even think of attacking; and if the town should fall once, the people should learn their lesson and build that defense. The same is true in the case of moral evil. It is far better to build a strong defense by means of positive acts of virtue rather than wait for the attack and then try to fight it off. While there is time, a person should be building a defense against evil by performing works of virtue. We still need to resist the attack when it comes, but the previous practice of virtue will help us ignore what would be severe temptations to some, and overcome other temptations.

Galatians 3: 7-14; Luke 11: 15-26 **YEAR II**

During his time on Earth, Jesus performed many miracles. One of the reasons he did so was to manifest God's power, so that people would believe in him. In today's gospel, he casts out a demon. Some who witnessed the event immediately accused him of using the power of Satan to cast out devils. Others demanded that he give them a sign from heaven. Jesus' reply challenges the people to see the truth. In fact, Jesus says, if he casts out devils by the finer of God "then the reign of God is upon you."

That was not what his detractors wanted to hear. They had made up their minds about Jesus and refused to examine the evidence. They were not so different from many people today who have already made up their minds about Jesus even though they have never met him.

In the first reading, Paul tells the Galatians that God justifies by faith. If we shut our eyes and cover our ears, faith becomes impossible and we cannot know the wonder of Jesus in our lives. But if we just look at the evidence and are open to the Spirit, wonders will unfold.

SATURDAY

Joel 4: 12-21; Luke 11: 27-28 **YEAR I**

"The Lord is a refuge to his people." When things look dark and difficult to us in the world, then does the Lord shine forth as our refuge. He is always there, of course, but in good times, "when we don't need him," when everything is brightness and light in the world, we just don't notice his presence.

In the difficult times then, we can see things more clearly—black and white—but that does not mean that we are going to choose the Lord. There is no question that the warmth of his presence, the consolation of his truth, the peace of conscience we have in his goodness, the promise of perfect and eternal happiness he holds out to us—all these are appealing and should be more than enough. But on the other hand, there is the innate desire to be loved here and now in the world, to be admired and popular among the wordly.

That word "love" says it all. The adulation of this world is not love in any sense. It is ephemeral, superficial, self-serving. The person is admired or popular because he has the "courage" to say what the admirers wish to hear, to say what they don't have the courage to say. But the admirers praise this person, not because they have any commitment to him whatsoever, but because they have a commitment to what he says. And what he says is what they love. And what they love is what they think. Thus, their "love" is love of self. When he speaks their ideas, they bask in this "glory." "Here am I," they say, "In that idea. Isn't it wonderful? Am I not wonderful, too?" So obviously their love and admiration of the speaker will be fickle. It will stop, even be turned against the speaker perhaps or turned to someone even more popular, when his attraction is surpassed by the greater appeal of another speaker.

This meditation finishes as it began. "The Lord is a refuge to his people. Blessed are those who hear the Word of God and keep it." Granted that it is possible on our part to make mistakes in this regard, but if we are striving to know God's truth and God's will, he will hardly let us stray. Also, if we remember that "Where Peter is, there is the Church" and try to remain united with the Holy Father, we can't go wrong because he is the divinely appointed Vicar of Christ on earth.

Galatians 3: 22-29; Luke 11: 27-28 **YEAR II**

In Luke's gospel a woman cries out to Jesus, "Blest is the womb that bore you and the breasts that nursed you." Jesus' answer is quick and telling: "Rather blest are they who hear the Word of God and keep it." Although his listeners were unaware of it, there is a double meaning in his reply. Not only is Jesus speaking the Word of God, he is the Word of God.

We are indeed blessed who listen to Jesus and do what he says. But we have to do both. We have to hear his word—that is, we have to receive it and embrace it—and we have to act on it. To the extent that we do not do this, we vitiate the Word of God. To the extent that we do receive the Word of God and act on it we are empowered by the Word of God.

The key to action is faith. As Paul tells us in the reading from Galatians, each of is a child of God because of our faith in Christ Jesus. If we are children of God, we live in the light and the light shines through us to others. We become partners in Christ's work of salvation. Think of it. Is there any greater work than sharing the light of Christ?

Blest, indeed, are we who hear the Word of God and keep it.

Twenty-eighth Week of Ordinary Time

MONDAY

Romans 1: 1-7; Luke 11: 29-32 **YEAR I**

Today's reading is the beginning of a four-week review of Paul's letter to the Romans. The longest of his letters, it appears first in the New Testament among Paul's writings. By his resurrection, Jesus proved himself to be the Christ promised long ago and our Lord God as well. This time the Father has not sent a mere prophet, but his very own Son. Through this Son, we are to learn of the Father and we are sent to offer his message to all men. Everyone has a call to holiness defined as union with God and found by living the message revealed in Christ.

In the gospel, Jesus refers to the Resurrection as the validation of his ministry. He speaks of giving the sign of Jonah to the people in order to prove the truth of his astounding message and to prove that his mission is of divine origin. Indeed, he is divine himself—far greater than Solomon and Jonah, far greater than Abraham, Moses, or St. John the Baptist.

All this should lead us to believe and to accept every word that comes from the mouth of Christ, the God. It is logical that we should believe the teaching of the Church in the same way. It does not make sense to accept Christ and reject the Church. It is essential to Catholic faith that we believe in the Church. That's what is distinctive about us. If we only believe in God, we should be Unitarians. If we only believe in God and the Old Testament, we should be Jews. If we only believe in God and both Testaments then we should be Protestants. But if we also believe in the Church, we should be Catholics. If we deny the authority of the Church, automatically we are "Protesters."

Galatians 4: 22-24, 26-27, 31-5: 1; Luke 11: 29-32 **YEAR II**

With concise reasoning St. Paul, in his letter to the Galatians, compares the Old Testament with the New Testament—slavery compared with freedom. If we have been born into the Church by baptism we are free, while those without baptism are still under the constraints of original sin. In faith, we believe that those who have not received baptism shall have an opportunity to be saved but we, the baptized, have received a special blessing. Our minds and wills still remain human; they are tempted to evil and thus we can and do sin. On the other hand, our consciences are strengthened by the gifts of the Holy Spirit and we more readily know and will the proper thing to do with our life in all circumstances. Others receive less help but our responsibility is greater than theirs, because we have every means at our disposal to live a Christ-like life. So, as St. Paul urges, we are to avoid at all costs falling once again into the slavery of sin.

In the gospel narrative, Jesus teaches his Jewish audience about the sign of Jonah. They were seeking an additional sign in spite of the fact that they had witnessed all kinds of miracles, the fulfillment of prophecy, and heard divine wisdom coming from Christ. It is pathetic that, with all the means of grace at our disposal, we too still complain that God should do more, that he should "force" us not to sin. In the time of Jesus, he promised the Jews his death and resurrection as an incontrovertible sign but still—they did not believe. Do we?

Our difficulty is free will. On the one hand, we find free will to be marvelous, when it brings us pleasure and accords with God's will. But when God's will, made known by our grace-filled conscience, demands that we renounce our pleasure for the sake of doing what is right and just, we scream that God is unfair; he should not make such demands of us. And often enough, we go our own way, shackle ourselves in sin, and call that happiness because we are doing our own will in preference to God's.

TUESDAY

Romans 1: 16-25; Luke 11: 37-41 **YEAR I**

There is always a temptation for believers to be "ashamed" of the gospel because it is rejected by the worldly-wise who are intelligent, even brilliant but pride is their undoing. Just look around at the wonders of the universe, which far surpass the knowledge and power of man. Winds, floods, droughts, lightning, earthquakes are treasures of power which surpass those of modern, technological man. The miracle of life, exhibited in plants, animals, and mankind surpasses and confounds modern day attempts at creation.

Between the brilliant man and these wonders of nature, there is an impenetrable screen of pride, which can be removed only by humility and prayer.

As St. Paul says, it is inexcusable not to recognize and worship the Creator. Those who do not recognize God have knowledge readily available but they prefer to worship gods of their own making which are less powerful and obviously beneath them. They bring approval upon their self-gratification and sensual pleasures by manipulating these false gods whose actions are like theirs. These so-called brilliant people judge the goodness of an action by their man-made standards rather than by its conformity to the higher standards of human intelligence, "written on our hearts," namely, by their conscience which constitutes the image and likeness of God within them and us. To all external appearances, the conduct of these people is quite correct because their conduct matches the man-made standards that they have established. But inside, they are rotten to the core and their conscience reveals this to them. Christ points out that the same was true of the Pharisees and can be true of us. Outwardly, there is a human tendency to go through the motions of being a good person, neat, affable, polite, and clean, fulfilling all the externals of good human conduct, while inwardly living like depraved animals.

Galatians 5: 1-6; Luke 11: 37-41 **YEAR II**

In today's reading, St. Paul scolds the Galatians who had been advised to accept circumcision. Because they are now Christians, Paul says that accepting circumcision would be a denial of Christ; their salvation will come through Christian faith and love. He is very insistent upon spiritual faith rather than the moral concrete precepts of the law. In fact, the Galatians might be tempted to think as Luther did centuries later that "faith alone" without good works is sufficient for salvation. Obviously, faith in God demands good works. The contrast is not between faith and good works but between faith and the law, which in Christ's time, had an accumulation of hundreds of man-made prescriptions, some of which Christ specifically condemned. For instance, there was the practice of failing to support one's parents and instead declaring one's money reserved for the Temple treasury. St. Paul states that the faith of which he speaks is expressed in love.

The law was so rigid that it left no room for love; indeed, to keep the law in some instances amounted to rejection of love as exemplified in the practice of non-support for parents. In the gospel narrative, Jesus severely criticizes the Pharisees for their excessive concern over unimportant rules while neglecting the true interior values of religion. Jesus had neglected the "before dinner ritual" and, when challenged, he tells his host pretty much what St. Paul writes to the Galatians. The Pharisees should not be so concerned about the external appearance of things that they would neglect the internal realities, faith and love—which are essential. The primacy of faith is always clear, whether in the gospels or the epistle readings, but since faith is expressed in love, good works are definitely demanded, too.

Wednesday

Romans 2: 1-11; Luke 11:42-46 **YEAR I**

In today's reading, St. Paul points out how quick we are to judge the actions of others and find them to be evil. He states that in so doing we are condemning ourselves because we are doing the same thing. We are reminded of Jesus' teaching that we should remove the log in our own eye before talking about the sliver in another person's eye. And yet, we consider ourselves blameless, and even if not, we trust that God will be ever so loving and merciful to us. The fact is that he may be merciful to us and to others if they are sorry for their faults. But, it will be difficult for him to have mercy on those who have had no mercy for others. Unless we take an objective look at our lives in light of Christ's teachings, accept his loving invitation to repentance, and strive to live the ideal of Christianity, we are living an unbalanced religion. Our call is to see things as God sees them and to act accordingly as he, Jesus Christ, acted.

Galatians 5: 18-25; Luke 11: 42-46 **YEAR II**

There was dissension among the Galatians because false teachers were insisting upon some Old Testament practices. Paul, in his letter to them, insists on the Christian law of love of neighbor. He describes every sin characteristic of a person living according to the flesh as a selfish action. Self-gratification summarizes all of them in one word. One sin may be more heinous than the next, but all of them are based in a very common human tendency, that is, to look out for oneself first, foremost, and always. The fruits of the Spirit, on the other hand, although all of them are interior virtues of the person concerned, have a relationship to other people. They could not exist in a person without others, with whom or for whom one has acted—peace, joy, goodness, kindness, and generosity. All of them result from sacrificing oneself for the good of other people.

The gospel speaks of the manner in which the law can wean us away from thinking of others to thinking only of ourselves. The law does not lead to the sins mentioned by St. Paul but it can lead us to a rigid allegiance to a man-made standard, which in turn develops pride and a selfish spirit rather than charity in our hearts. The law can become a contest between its tenets and love in my heart and blind me entirely to the spiritual relationship that I should have with God and neighbor. And so, Jesus condemns the scribes, Pharisees, and lawyers—not because they fulfill the law but because they allow pride in its fulfillment to distract them from the obligation to love God and to be just to their neighbor. The Law and the Ten Commandments were intended to do the opposite but human encrustations upon the law deprived it of its life—and love-giving power. Jesus condemns the Pharisees for their unbalanced religion.

THURSDAY

Romans 3: 21-29; Luke 11: 47-54 **YEAR I**

The old idea of justification in Paul's time and the one by which we were brought up prior to Vatican Council II, was that the law justifies. If we keep the Ten Commandments to the best of our ability and try to practice the corporal and spiritual works of mercy, we shall be saved. Not so, says St. Paul. That's an impossible task. No one can live without sin. We simply are not strong enough. Some may do a better job than others, but the best person cannot keep the law well enough to be saved. We all need God's mercy.

In sending Christ, God the Father established a new kind of justice and justification. In effect, he invited all of us to join with Christ. In union with him and by his merits, we sinners can be saved. That is, if we remain one with Christ, even though we sin, we can continue in union with him, or regain union with him, through the grace of the sacraments that he merited for us. This is God's justice that he allows us, encourages us, helps us to be literally one with his Son through baptism and by the power and strength of Christ we can keep the law and live as he did. Therefore, although we must keep the law, the real key to justification and salvation is faith in Christ, which leads to union with Christ in and through the sacraments. No one, then, has any occasion for boasting of his goodness and holiness. All of us are being carried on the shoulders of Christ, as it were. No person is strong enough spiritually to make it on his own. Salvation is found only in and through Christ.

Ephesians 1: 3-10; Luke 11: 47-54 **YEAR II**

In the beginning of his letter to the Ephesians, Paul gives his mature thought on Christ and the Church. He makes a statement on the cosmic importance of Jesus Christ who is the focus of all human history. Every spiritual blessing has been bestowed upon us by God acting in and through Christ. Like him, we were to be holy and blameless in God's sight, we were to become God's adopted children in order that we might give him fitting praise and worship. After our sin, we were redeemed by Christ, and brought back into God's favor. All of this was revealed by Christ, in his words and actions, when he came among us. Everything has been given to us in Christ, by virtue of the Father's love for him, and his incarnation, death, and resurrection. There can be no limit, therefore, to the love and adoration that we should have for our Savior!

The prophets presaged the coming of Christ but one after the other was rejected and killed by generation after generation of the Chosen People. Little by little, the Jews became convinced that they could have salvation on their own terms. They worshipped God materially and according to their own dictates, not in spirit and in truth. Religion was not to be determined by the existence of God, by his providence and revelation, and as an act of thanksgiving. Religion rather was a concession to God, man doing God a favor. The Jewish people had stood religion on its head by the time Christ came. Christ would attempt to rectify that situation, bring God back to a central position—as the beginning and the end of all things and of all people. But the Jews would have none of it.

We seem to be in a similar situation today. Even theologians and so many ordinary people, while paying lip-service to revelation, reject it in practice in favor of their own enlightened insights. They retain their respect for Christ but that sentiment is superficial and deceiving because in practice they reject Christ's Church, and thereby, his teaching.

Friday

Romans 4: 1-8; Luke 12: 1-7 **YEAR I**

If anyone ever deserved to be justified by his deeds, it was Abraham, but Scripture makes clear that he was justified more by his faith in God than anything else. David gives the same testimony. We should not be impressed so much by great deeds as by great faith. Is not this the case with all the saints? Of course, martyrdom is a great deed, but we honor most of the saints for their thoughts, their writings, and their spiritual legacy. We honor them because, like the Little Flower, they did the common, ordinary works of charity well. Among them there were some who showed us the value of chastity and obedience, and especially of poverty.

Most of us are incapable of doing great worldly deeds. Instead, we tend to try to associate ourselves with the powerful of this world in order to bask in their glory or possibly to profit by their influence. In the gospel Jesus points out that this conduct is foolish. It is based on fear. The holy person should have no fear of whatever might happen in this world. God looks after the birds of the air and the beasts of the field; surely we are more important to him than they are. Worldly power will not protect anyone on the last day, when all will be revealed. At that time, we may very well discover that a life, lived even in a pitiful condition in this world, will be far more resplendent than that of kings, princes, and high ecclesiastics deprived the trappings of power and seen in God's unique light.

Ephesians 1: 11-14; Luke 12: 1-7 **YEAR II**

We often think of the priest as God's "chosen one," or at least one who seems to have been especially favored. But St. Paul makes clear that all who have received baptism are a "chosen people." Regardless of what else we may receive from God, baptism will always be the greatest gift. And if God has chosen us, there must be a specific purpose. After all, it is defined faith that God wills the salvation of all people. Obviously, one of our purposes must be to spread the word of salvation to those who do not already possess it. Our missionaries do this in a very direct manner, but all of us have a role to play, whether it be one involving prayer, alms, fasting, or another type of support to those in the missionary trenches. And always we have the obligation of living a holy life, which is probably our most valuable contribution because it helps to Christianize our culture, from which all kinds of good things can arise, such as vocations, support, and aid from our government to those in need.

This holiness of our life is extremely important, both in itself and because it can be so influential upon others. Hypocrisy or lack of virtue can be equally influential and very destructive. Hypocrisy, when detected, and it always is, can be especially harmful because it gives license to other people to do what they know is wrong. If they can say that a supposedly holy person is not really holy, they can quickly generalize that all holy-appearing people are hypocrites, and proudly say to themselves: "at least the evil that I do, I do openly." Many seem to presume that everyone is living an evil life and it is better to do so openly than hypocritically. The way we live our lives should be a challenge to this assumption!

SATURDAY

Romans 4: 13, 16-18; Luke 12: 8-12 **YEAR I**

God made his promise to Abraham because of his faith, not because he had kept certain laws. The promise fulfilled in favor of Abraham's descendants was a free gift of God, a present which he gives to those who believe in him. And if God acted thus with Abraham, so shall he with us. And yet our mentality, particularly in a materialistic culture, does not seem to appreciate this lesson. The American cultural theory is that, if we set our minds to a task, work hard enough, we can do anything. God requires that kind of motivation to be directed to faith in him and not so much toward the task. Human will power and energy are not sufficient for a holy life; only God's grace can make that possible; and God's grace comes to those who believe in him. So it is necessary that we believe in God and love him with our whole mind, heart and soul, and with all our strength. We must use our human powers of observation to view situations as God sees them and then use our human talents to deal with circumstances. Always, we need to realize that we can do nothing good without God's grace, which, although given to everyone, is effective only in those who believe in him and use his grace for his purposes.

We need to acknowledge the power of God and his primacy in our lives. If we disown God in this world—if we make clear that we are going to do things our way rather than his—we will be disowned in Heaven. If we live by his grace and his truth in this life, regardless of what others may think, we shall receive a priceless and eternal reward. We are to have faith that, if we believe in God and trust in his grace, he will, in all circumstances, direct our words and our actions.

Ephesians 1: 15-23; Luke 12: 8-12 **YEAR II**

Again, in his letter to the Ephesians, Paul, filled with the theology of Christ, prays that his readers will be strengthened in their faith. He consistently relates faith in God with love for neighbor; one leads directly into the other according to his theology. It is impossible to have one without the other in any full sense. We can determine, therefore, how great our faith is in God by the way we treat one another, and how great our love is for our neighbor by the degree of our faith in God. If we have faith and love in a genuine sense, what wonders God can and will do in and through us! So we should strive to know all we can about God to strengthen our faith. And once filled with faith, we will be impelled to act with love.

We should make no apologies for our faith and love. Like the apostles, when sent to fetch a donkey on Palm Sunday, we should reply, "The Lord sent me." This is similar to the call of the prophets—the Lord expected them to do only what he had asked them to do; he would care for the rest. Our efforts should be directed to knowledge, love, and service of God and not to determining how to speak to men or defend ourselves against their attacks. If the time comes for defense, the Lord will speak through us and for us. We shall not be disappointed; the Lord will be with us to protect us.

Twenty-ninth Week of Ordinary Time

Monday

Romans 4: 20-25; Luke 2: 13-21 **YEAR I**

Faith is not easy because it calls for trust in a person whom we have not seen. Surely, if God exists as we define him, there should be no difficulty in believing that he can do anything. But the questions remain. Does God exist? Has he "spoken" to man? How can we be sure that he has "spoken."

Answers to those questions are that no human being has ever created life out of nothing. We have no power over water, wind, sun, moon, stars, and distant planets. Yet they operate in a certain pattern and order. We cannot control the largest things nor can we understand the smallest things. When doubts still remain, the ultimate question is, "Well, if there is no God, how did the world come into existence? How is it sustained in existence? What is life all about, if there is no after life, no reward for good and punishment for evil? One of the strongest arguments to me for God's existence is my conscience. Why do I perceive some actions as good and others as bad? Why do I adhere to truth and know it is wrong to deceive? Why do I practice justice and charity, try to live at peace with others? The existence of the One, who made me that way and who rewards and punishes, would seem to be the answer. God "speaks" to us through signs. Creation around us "speaks" of a being who is all knowing, all-powerful, and good. But at times he speaks more directly to human beings through miracles and prophecies. When he does so, we can believe that he has spoken.

As we have mentioned, no matter how long and arduously we examine these questions, there will always be room for some doubt. Our desire to do what we please and our tendency toward evil guarantee it. So faith will always be a problem. But again, the ultimate answer is another question—if there is no God, how do you explain the world and human beings? The existence of God is the only satisfactory answer to life as we know it.

The gospel illustrates the point. The man, who does not know what to do with all his wealth is one who doesn't recognize any life beyond this world. If he did, he would be seeking the favor of a God, who rewards good and punishes evil. Not recognizing this reality, it is logical that the man should keep all that he has for his own purposes. As the gospel says, "This is the way it works with the man who grows rich for himself instead of growing rich in the sight of God."

The gospel calls this man a fool. Is he? If there is a God, he certainly is; if not, he's not a fool, at least not altogether. But everyone dies. Is that the end? Is there nothing further? If there is nothing further, what is the purpose of life? No, there must be something more; there must be a God.

But even if one still remains in doubt about God's existence, what a dreadful risk one takes not to believe. What is there to lose by believing in God and living as he instructs us in Scripture? We know that his way of life is a happy one on earth. On the other hand, disbelieving in God's existence can lead to a loss of everything we have known on earth and to a terrible punishment that will last forever. Who is the fool, the one who believes in God and lives as he instructs us, or the one who disbelieves in God and spends this life eating, drinking, and being merry?

Ephesians 2: 1-10; Luke 12: 13-21 **YEAR II**

Death in a physical sense is the beginning of eternal life—one filled with happiness or sorrow and anger. So when we hear of death, we immediately conjure darkness, absence of life, the end of existence and those thoughts are more rightly connected with sin. Physical death leads to life of some kind; sin leads to lifelessness. The sinner lives, at the level of the flesh, following every whim and fancy without the control which comes from attempting to know the truth and freely choosing the good.

All of us have a strong tendency to live according to the flesh and the standards of the world, and thereby to be lifeless and dead in spirit, and not truly living a human life. Indeed, after original sin, it was impossible to do otherwise because God's grace was absent. But in his mercy and goodness he gave us his only Son to free us from sin. "God brought us to life in Christ!" Of course, the only conclusion an intelligent person can draw from these facts is that we should be grateful to God and, if we wish to retain life which is to live in union with God, we should cling steadfastly to Christ. We should accept his teachings, follow his example so that we may be with him in the bosom of the Father for all eternity.

The teaching of St. Paul is illustrated by Christ's response to his questioner in the gospel. The man wants justice from his brother, his share of the inheritance. Jesus puts aside the question. Surely his brother should treat the man justly. But the possession of material goods cannot begin to compare with the possession of authentic life described above. Physical death comes to everyone, rich and poor, and the quality of life that we have at that time will become definitive and absolute, for all eternity. If we are "living" in sin, if the greedy possession of worldly goods is our goal in life, physical death will be the entrance into "darkness," the total and absolute end of any opportunity for the authentic life in the Spirit of God. We need to concentrate on growing rich in God's favor, rich in virtue. For then, physical death is entrance into life in union with God for all eternity.

We are to use this life to make a choice between life in the Spirit and life according to the flesh. While still on earth, of course, we are in the flesh. But if we long to continue that way for all eternity, that is Hell; if we long to be delivered from the flesh and to live in the Spirit, that favor will be granted to us through the merits of Christ for all eternity and that is heaven.

TUESDAY

Romans 5: 12, 15, 17-19, 20-21; Luke 12: 35-38 **YEAR I**

If sin had never occurred, there would be no death. People would be given a period of trial on earth and, being sinless, they would simply pass from imperfect, temporary life to a perfect, eternal life. That is what God reveals to us through this letter of St. Paul.

But sin and death did enter the world followed by the sins of many, all of whom are taken by death. But just as Adam was the beginning of sin and death, which had consequences for all men, so Jesus is the beginning of grace and supernatural life for all. And what is so marvelous, encouraging, hopeful for us is that grace far surpasses sin. After all, sin is a negative action, which has a negative effect. It is a rejection of God's will, which effectively bars the possibility of God's grace. Virtue on the other hand is a positive action. It is an acceptance of God's will and a welcoming of God's graceful presence in our lives. What we owe to Christ and God's love is beyond measure. Human beings are such that, regardless of their identity, sin and death would have entered the world. What human beings could never do is to bring about salvation, and God's presence into the world. This could only be done by the Son of God. And he has not stopped there; he has given us his divine life in the sacraments, in Scripture, and in the Church!

The lesson to learn from all this is that we can and unfortunately do close the door on Christ. Sin—a negative attitude toward God—is still quite possible. And if that is our attitude, if we are turned in upon our selfish selves instead of looking expectantly to God for his aid, our lives will be a disaster, leading from sin to eternal death. What we need to understand is that halfway measures and compromise are not good enough. We must truly love God, long to have him with us, and dread to have him leave us. Married love is a good example. If the marriage is a healthy one, the partners' truest feelings are those above; they cannot bear the thought of separation. And yet, for foolish reasons, the couple will get into petty arguments and endanger the tremendous happiness they enjoy. How foolish a conduct!

Ephesians 2: 12-22; Luke 12: 35-38 **YEAR II**

For centuries the Jews, as the Chosen People, had been graced to believe in the one true God rather than in a multiplicity of gods. As a result, they had hope, whereas all others who were cut off from Israel, had neither the presence of God in their lives nor hope. They were pagans and atheists. God is the Creator of all, however, so the Son of God is brother to everyone. Therefore, he who is one with all human beings, united them by his birth, his life, and his redemptive death. This is a great opportunity for non-Jews. The authentic God has been made available to them; his teaching brings hope and, together with his grace in the sacraments, the possibility of a more sensible and superstition-free spiritual life. All people once again are on an equal footing and the human family becomes one.

This new opportunity brings with it new responsibilities. There are to be no more excuses. We now know clearly what God expects of us—a life in imitation of Jesus and not an off/on affair nor a hot/cold existence. The way of life we are called to live encompasses our whole way of thinking and acting. Christ has done away with the law, not in the sense that it no longer applies, but in the sense that our knowledge of his way of life and our love for him make the law superfluous. Surely, we shall keep the law but we are not to restrict ourselves to its minimum requirements. Rather, we are to soar to the heights of perfection, to which the example of Christ calls us and which is made possible through his grace.

WEDNESDAY

Romans 6: 12-18; Luke 12: 39-48 **YEAR I**

We have the choice to offer ourselves to the power of evil or to the power of God; we can become slaves of virtue or vice. But we cannot long remain neutral to these great powers. Quite a few of our acts may be indifferent or morally neutral such as eating, sleeping, walking, but we have plenty of opportunities to choose between good and evil so that our lives are colored by one or the other. What most of us seem to do is swing back and forth between virtue and vice. Because we return to virtue all the time or since our sins do not seem to be as bad as those of others, we pride ourselves on being virtuous people. Granted that it is next to impossible to be altogether sinless, but what we don't seem to realize is that every submission to evil makes us weaker and draws us closer to a quagmire of sin. Sin and evil are powerful, insidious forces, much stronger than we are. Grace is always stronger but we cannot presume on the cooperation of our wills to avoid sin. Repeated sinful acts can greatly lessen the strength of the will to resist the next temptation.

The gospel has an application for daily living. The Lord may come at any time for us, perhaps when we least expect him. So we should be ready; we should be living a virtuous life. But even apart from this, we should want to be happy in this life, and live in peace without fear. The only way to achieve this goal is to be obedient, loyal servants of the Lord at all times. This message is for everyone. However, Christ makes clear that it is even more important for the leaders of the Church because they are in a position of trust. "When much has been given a man, much will be required of him. More will be asked of a man to whom more has been entrusted."

Ephesians 3: 2-12; Luke 12: 39-48 **YEAR II**

The message entrusted to St. Paul was a most radical illustration of everything that had been revealed by Christ. The Jews were to show their love for God in the way that they loved one another. Nothing could be a greater test of the acceptance of one's fellow man than to believe that the gospel message and the kingdom of Heaven were open to all men. This was St. Paul's special apostolate. It was not entrusted to one of the original apostles but to one who was learned in the law. The Jews could argue that the other apostles did not know the Old Testament and that they were wild zealots; but the same charges could not be made against St. Paul.

We are the successors of St. Paul. Much has been entrusted to us whether we are priests or baptized Christians. It is our responsibility to preach the gospel to the whole world in one way or another. In our times we seem to have become much less missionary-minded because in our own country matters are unsettled. However, in the first century, the situation was worse in any given community with regard to numbers of preachers, resources, and the security of faith. Our call to preach the gospel requires that we help people persevere in faith; but our most important duty is to see to it that every person has the opportunity to hear the gospel. We should not abandon those to whom the gospel has been preached; however, if the apostles were alive today, they would be shaking the dust from their feet in countries of western civilization where people have the opportunity to hear the gospel and put it into practice and would go to the southern hemisphere in search of people who have never heard the gospel.

THURSDAY

Romans 6: 19-23; Luke 12: 49-53 **YEAR I**

We are not free of justice because on the last day we shall be held accountable and given punishment for our lack of justice. But once immersed in sin, we never think of what we owe to others. Anything goes. We are "free" to do what we please. After all, we say to ourselves, who are we to fear a spiritual invisible God? What can he do to us, here and now? So one feels "free" to do whatever one pleases.

St. Paul points this out in order to explain to the convert that virtue is more than a matter of wishful thinking. We cannot simply withdraw ourselves from sin and leave a vacuum. If we are going to be slaves of God—perfectly virtuous—we must become intensely interested in justice, giving to each person what is his due. If we are not positively determined to move in this direction, the likelihood is that we shall slip back into sin. We shall never be free of sin until we are totally committed to justice, totally committed to giving God what is due to him such as faith, hope, love, prayer and to man what is due to him.

Jesus came into this world to challenge us to choose. He gave us the example of perfect love of God and of man, manifested first in a life devoted to goodness and truth, and culminating in his death on the cross. His life throws down the gauntlet to every person. We must be with him or against him; we must be wholeheartedly dedicated to a life of virtue or given to temporizing with evil; we must love God and man or prefer love of self. We must choose. We cannot equivocate. The choice is between serving God and man or serving oneself. The former is virtue; the latter, on a consistent basis, is sin. Serving oneself may at first seem more a matter of omission but persistently followed, it will end up in a life of clear injustice.

Ephesians 3: 14-21; Luke 12: 49-53 **YEAR II**

St. Paul insists again upon the twin virtues of faith and charity. Christ is operative in us only when we are one with him, when we believe in him as the Son of God, sent by the Father, and filled with the love of the Holy Spirit. When the grace of faith has been fully accepted—when we fully adhere to the truth that Christ is God, and his word and the example of his life are the guiding principles of our life, then he lives in us and gives impulse to all our words and works. This is faith, not in the sense of making a "blind leap," but in that of making a sober, reasonable acceptance of Christ on the basis of what he has said and done.

Since such faith is very personal—acceptance of truth on the authority of another person—it cannot be separated from the consequent love that we have for that person. Love cements the relationship of faith. Thereafter, we need not give so much consideration to the act of faith but concentrate on living the life that Christ prompts us to live. Charity is the root and foundation of life. In this present context St. Paul seems to be saying that love of Christ is the only stimulus which can lead us to practice the Christian way of life as we should.

The Cross was the ultimate sign of faith and love for the Father on the part of Christ. And the Cross thereby becomes the ultimate measure of our faith and love. Can we accept as God a person who is so humiliated as Christ was? This was a stumbling block in St. Paul's time. Likewise, can we accept the Cross in our own lives? Do we have sufficient faith in Christ to accept that if we live as he wants us to live and suffer humiliation in the world, ultimately he will save us? Is our faith so strong and our love for him so steadfast that we will live his life of justice and charity and strive to live a perfectly sinless life regardless of what the world thinks and regardless of the consequences? This is the test which separates even family members. Let us strive to have enough faith and love for Christ that we are able to accept his truth and live it.

Friday

Romans 7: 18-25; Luke 2: 54-59 **YEAR I**

In today's reading, Paul describes graphically the struggle between good and evil going on in the life of every man. Paul adds that only Jesus Christ makes virtue and victory possible. We don't exist without God and his creative power. Goodness is directed toward others but our flesh craves self-gratification. The flesh is not usually satisfied with enough warmth, coolness, food, and the like. It craves for more. And when we respond to this inordinate demand, it could become sinful in two ways. For example, regarding food we could be guilty of gluttony on our part and at of depriving others of food at the same time. However, there is no reason to become scrupulous about these matters. What concerned St. Paul, and what should bother us, is that, when he realized that his flesh was doing something contrary to right reason, he had trouble controlling the flesh with his reason and will. He found that so often he lost the battle. Unaided reason and will are no match for the desires of the flesh. What can we do? Turn to Christ! Thank God for the example of Christ, which shows us the way. Thank God for the death and resurrection of Christ, which provide strength to overcome the flesh by virtue of the grace that we receive in the sacraments.

The gospel reminds us that, if we can be so smart about worldly things, like forecasting the weather from what we observe in nature, why can't we be equally smart about spiritual matters, such as avoiding people, places, and things which can lead us into sin? Of course, we can be that smart. The problem is that we don't want to deny ourselves, our own weakness, and our own pleasure, and turn to Christ. We find ourselves in the situation which St. Paul describes: "I do, not the good I will to do, but the evil I do not intend." The desire to do right is there but not the power. The only answer is to admit our weakness, turn to the Lord for help, and he will supply.

Ephesians 4: 1-6; Luke 2: 54-59 **YEAR II**

This reading contains some of the highest reaches of New Testament thought and describes the life of a true follower of Christ. The life to which we are called is so beautiful. All that is expected of us is that we live in peace with one another by growing in the virtues of humility and patience by quietly putting up with the faults of others. The Holy Spirit gives us the power to do so. We are called to form one community of faith, hope, and love and thus one Body of Christ. There is only one Body, so either we are in it or we are not. The choice is obvious and there is no comparison between the two alternatives. And yet we hesitate.

We want the best of both worlds and the best of this world cannot begin to compare with God and the goodness, truth, beauty, peace, and happiness that he has to offer us. Yet, we hesitate to make a final judgment that we should become one with Christ, when all signs point to the wisdom, the logic, and the benefits of such a decision. All this confirms the power of earthly pleasure and the strong pull that it has upon us. We should appreciate also, our utter need for prayer and the sacraments. Unless we depend upon Christ, unless we strive to be more closely united with him, we are in a losing situation. Only he can save us from ourselves. Left to ourselves, we are foolish, and only the grace of God, humbly sought and appreciated, can save us from that foolishness.

SATURDAY

Romans 8: 1-11; Luke 13: 1-9 **YEAR I**

St. Paul shows us the difference that being a believer makes. Those who are one with Christ, who have received his Spirit in baptism are able to live as Christ did. The Spirit gives us that extra strength that we need to overcome the tendency of the flesh toward evil. We need to keep in mind, however, that there is nothing automatic about this. Just as the sinful person must agree to go along with the flesh, so the virtuous person must make an act of will to go along with the Spirit. As St. Paul says elsewhere, there is a battle going on within every person between the flesh and the Spirit. But let it be clear that those who are blessed with the Spirit of Christ have little excuse. Moreover, we have the responsibility to be giving the same Spirit to others, persuading them by word and example to accept Christ and his Law of Love. Failure to live according to the Spirit ends up in depriving others of the opportunity to follow good example.

There is no doubt about the reality of personal sin; each one of us must stand before the judgment throne of God and be accountable for our personal lives. We cannot blame anyone else for what we, of our own free will, have done. On the other hand, Jesus makes clear in the gospel that there are social and cultural dimensions to sin. We are our brother's keeper. Things that I do or don't do have an effect upon others, just as their thoughts, words, and actions have their effect upon me. Depending upon the environment, in which we live, it is easier or more difficult to serve God as we should. Those who are guilty of very visible, external, highly publicized sins, therefore, may be less responsible than others whose sins are not known. Can any of our lives stand up under the spotlight of thorough investigation and the insinuations that can be implied against us?

We are all in need of God's mercy, always in need of another chance like the fig tree that for three years failed to bear fruit despite all the farmer did to help. Like the tree, we have been given grace upon grace for much more than three years. How much fruit have we produced? God has been exceedingly patient. Some day, God will call us to account and time for repentance may be running out. It may not be too early to repent!

Ephesians 4: 7-16; Luke 13: 1-9 **YEAR II**

The Body of Christ is built initially by faith in God and knowledge of his Son. Then, the members of the Body are bound together through love.

Our young people need this understanding of the Body of Christ. There is no possibility of building it up without knowledge. The initial step is the acceptance of the gift of faith that there is a God and Christ is the Son of God. Then, we grow Christ-like in proportion to what we learn about him, Who is the revelation of the Father, and in proportion to what we put into practice. The only thing that provides motivation for banding together and sacrificing to serve others is the knowledge of the person, the life, and the teachings of Christ. Otherwise, everything we do is in danger of fragmentation.

It is true that some with the knowledge of God and of Christ may have fallen away from the Church. However, one who has the knowledge of Christ and later falls away will always have a memory of the good things which he has lost and may very well have the incentive, when things get bad, to regain what he has abandoned. Today, our young people need a personal experience of God and the normal way to receive this is by learning about him rather than expecting a vision. They need something substantial, they need faith supported by knowledge.

Our children are being exposed to various excesses and vices and we tend to look upon them in condemnation. As Jesus told the Jews, those who suffer from the world's ills are not necessarily to blame for those ills. We may be much more responsible. The tragedies of life may be salvation for our young people and for us. What is clear is that all of us need to see ourselves as creatures in relation to our Creator and accept what he, in his mysterious providence, sees fit to give us as our role in this life.

Thirtieth Week of Ordinary Time

MONDAY

Romans 8: 12-17; Luke 13: 10-17 **YEAR I**

In today's reading, St. Paul continues his major theological treatise. The baptized Christian, dead to flesh, lives a new life. Indeed, it is much more than a new life. It is a new relationship to God: being God's adopted child and heir. We are certainly indebted to God, because of the Spirit he has given us. Not only are we made like God, but we are given his very Spirit, a share in his own life, by which we are united to him and made one with him.

This truth is one of the most remarkable of our faith. The Spirit of God is actually given to us in the sacrament of baptism through the merits of Christ's death on the Cross. The Spirit once given cannot be taken away because through it we become members of God's own family. Adopted though we are, we are truly God's children with a right to everything that our Father has, namely, heaven with perfect, everlasting happiness. This gift of the Spirit, this right to heaven, can be lost through sin by the one who receives it. Truly, as St. Paul says, "We are debtors," but if grateful debtors, we should hold at all cost to what we have received.

In the gospel, Jesus shows the goodness and mercy of God by curing the woman who had been afflicted with back problems for 18 years. He gave her this gift freely, without a request from her. Despite the objections of the Pharisees, he did not take back what he had done. Jesus points out that the Pharisees have lost perspective; they treat animals with far greater kindness than they treat human beings. In this instance, he has only done for the woman what the Pharisees do for animals. The first reading reminds us that God is ready to do much more. "If God has so loved us, should we not also love one another?"

Ephesians 4: 32-58; Luke 13: 10-17 **YEAR II**

Today, Paul describes the way of a good moral life. We are to be kind and compassionate to one another. Just as Christ loved us so much, that he gave his very life for us, so should we be ready to give our lives for the sake of our neighbor, at least by way of service.

One type of unkindness in which human beings often enough engage is impurity in thought, word, and deed. Our actions can degrade others and ourselves, but thought and word also contribute to lowering standards of morality. There is nothing so powerful as impurity to make us like animals. We lose our human dignity bit by bit. St. Paul advises that we should not speak in an impure manner. With sins of this kind the conduct of the impure person tarnishes the image and likeness of God in him. God is pure love.

In the gospel Jesus shows the kindness and compassion with which we should treat other people and how man should be considerate of women. Jesus points out to the Pharisees that in many ways the people treated their animals better than they treated women.

Today's readings are most important for the present world. Because the pace of life prevents us from becoming acquainted with those around us, we lack kindness and consideration for them. We simply do not care for or about them. In fact, our animalistic attitudes especially with regard to sexual relations flow from our non-caring attitudes and so does all the violence in our society. We need greater respect for the human person in general and for our own in particular. That we are made to the image and likeness of God is an idea that should enhance our every thought and action and be the motivating power animating our kindness and consideration for ourselves and others.

TUESDAY

Romans 8: 18-25, Luke 13: 18-21 **YEAR I**

In today's reading, St. Paul, after describing the difficulties in living a spiritual life, describes the glorious destiny ahead—for ourselves and all of creation. So, we should live with great hope. "Creation was made subject to futility." There will always be disappointments in this world. Earth is not heaven and never can be. The things of this world are inevitably going to fail us. People are going to fail us or at least not live up to expectations. We are going to fail too, whether physically, mentally, or morally and eventually wear down. What is left to us?—Hope! But it is a well-founded hope. Our hope is in God's goodness and in God's promises. And if we are to retain this hope, it is necessary that we have patience and perseverance for "the sufferings of the present are as nothing compared with the glory, to be revealed in us!"

The realization of God's kingdom, our hoped-for promise, is like the mustard seed or the yeast in a loaf of bread. It is frail to begin with, it is slow to germinate; in fact, it undergoes death and resurrection before it begins to flower. When it begins to make its presence felt, it becomes sturdy; it flowers; it attracts the attention and admiration of others; and eventually its promise is fulfilled. The mustard seed becomes a great tree; the lump of dough becomes a nourishing loaf of bread; the person is made holy by the power of God's grace and reaches sanctity; that is, complete union with God, with perfect and unending happiness.

Ephesians 5: 21-33; Luke 13: 18-21 **YEAR II**

In today's important reading, Paul exhorts married Christians to demonstrate strong mutual love. In Paul's view, Christian marriage should mirror the love between Christ and the Church. If taken out of context, this passage from Ephesians can be very offensive to women. However, it should not be. Someone must be head of the family and St. Paul assigns that role to the husband. Likewise, Christ, and in his place the hierarchy, is the head of the Church. The hierarchy must ultimately make the decisions and the rest of the Church must submit to them. If no one is in charge, society is paralyzed or chaotic.

The major problem in misunderstanding this letter is that two sentences are taken out of context and the duties of husbands, as described by St. Paul, ignored. Husbands are to serve their wives as Christ has served the Church. Surely no one can say that Christ lorded over his people. He was their champion. He constantly suffered indignities for their sake, in their defense, even to death on the cross. If husbands are to do the same, and base their decision on such love, surely wives and children will benefit greatly because at all times they will be the husband's principal concern.

The gospel reading is connected to the epistle only in the general sense that the family, like the kingdom of God, will flourish only if holiness is at the heart of the enterprise.

It seems altogether impossible that a large tree can grow from a tiny seed or that yeast can have such an expansive effect on bread. But they have that God-given power. So it is with the spiritual life. Apparently weak, invisible, easily put down by that which is material, holiness not only can survive but can transform all that seems so powerful in the world. So too, can the family. The good family is a "domestic church," in which clearly Christ is the unmistakable head of the household.

WEDNESDAY

Romans 8: 26-30; Luke 13: 22-30 **YEAR I**

Once again St. Paul insists that without God we can do nothing. We cannot even pray or pray in a manner appealing to God, except when the Spirit of God is praying within us. True, God knows from all eternity, before we are created, whether we are going to heaven or hell, but that certain foreknowledge does not deprive us of free will. God knows not only our final status; he knows all our actions along the way, so the path to heaven or hell is clearly set before him. But we can see it too, if we only look at life more objectively, or ask ourselves more bluntly, how well are we serving God? We are free to change the direction of our lives, if we will to do it. Not only will God know it beforehand. He always prompts us by his grace to do so, whether we fully cooperate or not.

Jesus knew that his mission from the Father was to set his gaze firmly on Jerusalem, upon death on the Cross at the hands of the scribes and Pharisees. He could have refused this mission but he continued to exercise his free will in unison with that of the Father. Indeed, he tells his questioners that we cannot be lackadaisical about working for salvation. We are not to choose the least common denominator; we are to accept and act upon the ideal. The gate is narrow. "Many will try to enter and be unable." So take no chances. Yes, you are my specially Chosen People, the Lord admits, but the Creator must love everyone and give to everyone according to his own merciful providence an opportunity to know, to love and to serve God. Even though Jews and Christians—again, in God's mysterious providence—may receive greater gifts than others, greater demands will be made of them, one being the duty of evangelization. Depending upon how we respond, so shall we be rewarded.

Ephesians 6: 1-9; Luke 13: 22-30 **YEAR II**

St. Paul urges good relationships between children and parents. The obligation is primarily on the children. Just as we creatures are to love and obey God in everything because he is our Creator, so children should love and obey their parents. Generation establishes the relationship. St. Paul also points out that this is one commandment which has a reward attached to it. Obedient, loving children are promised happiness and long life.

Since children grow and mature and must eventually take responsibility for their lives as adults, it is both a matter of wisdom and proper education that parents should teach their children responsibility and not stunt their growth. Children, like little birds, must learn to fly. If they are to do so, they should neither be pampered nor left on their own too much. The parent should give clear instruction, good example, and stand aside to allow trial and error. They should be ready to help and then encourage the child to be on his own.

In St. Paul's time, there were sixty million slaves in the Roman Empire. Nowadays, the general connotation of "slave" is sometimes linked to a person for whom there is no felicitous set of circumstances in his favor. The "victim" should not be overwhelmed by the situation, miserable though it might be. Victory over this condition does not consist in worldly success but in mastering oneself to such an extent that the person becomes like Christ in thought, word, and deed. Once again, the person involved must not necessarily be subservient in every thing, especially if this should involve moral evil, but he should have reverence and work willingly. And certainly the master, realizing that control in this world is no guarantee of God's favor, should exercise justice and charity toward those in his charge.

The gospel makes clear that "the last will be first and the first will be last." This is the standard that we should use to govern our conduct. Humility, obedience, service, justice and charity, make one "last" in this world but "first" in the kingdom of Heaven. Worldly influence and power will be to no avail in the next life. It will not be a case of whom we know but who we are. We must become saints; we must make ourselves holy. Holiness is union with God, brought about by the theological virtues of faith, hope, and charity. And we cannot possess these virtues without a basic humility—a recognition of God's perfection and our own imperfection and a realization that every person has a relationship to God. This requires that I love God with my whole mind, heart, and soul and all my strength, and that I love my neighbor as I love myself.

THURSDAY

Romans 8:31-39; Luke 13:31-35 **YEAR I**

In today's reading, having explained how in Christ we receive salvation, hope, and a family relationship to God, Paul says we should have no fears. He explains that nothing in this world or the next can ever separate us from God's love. In light of the fact that the Father gave us his only begotten Son for our salvation, and that the Son accepted to die on the Cross for us, what else will he not do to help and protect us? If God has already made the supreme sacrifice on our behalf, surely he will do lesser things to aid us in our life-long effort to become one with him. And if we should sin, he will not condemn us but assist us to rise again.

Eventually, therefore, if we should fail to unite ourselves with God, it will be altogether our fault, not his. This is not to say that our lives will be free of trials and difficulties. Based on what God has done for us, our faith, hope, and love for him should be so strong that nothing should be able to deter us from pursuing steadfastly the goal of perfect union with the Trinity.

The gospel illustrates this latter point, namely that God has done everything for us, to the point that any appreciative person should be saved. However, it is still possible for us to reject God's gift despite his continuous offering of it to us. Christ says as much. But even though some will reject him, he is not about to shrink from crucifixion for the sake of the elect. Herod may do what he wills but he cannot overcome the power of God; the Resurrection will make that clear.

Ephesians 6: 10-20; Luke 13: 31-35 **YEAR II**

"Our battle is ultimately not against human forces" but against evil in all its forms. No matter what anyone on earth may do to us, that person has no power over our eternal reward or punishment, so we should not worry too much about him. What we should be concerned about is the judgment of God. And because God sees such virtues as important, we must be steadfast in truth, in justice, and in charity and try to make the whole world such a place by proclaiming steadfastly the revelation of God which has been given to us in and by Jesus Christ. For all this, especially the latter, we need constantly to pray for the gift of faith.

Certain Pharisees could see that Herod and others of their number were "out to get" Jesus, so they warned him to flee. He resisted. After all, those who were opposed to him could easily catch him and flight would be an admission of guilt. Far better was it to stand one's ground depending on the weapons of truth, justice, and charity to prevail in the minds and hearts of all people with a conscience. Far better was it to trust in faith that no matter what would happen to him on earth, Christ could depend in faith upon the goodness and justice of the Father.

St. Paul speaks of the above virtues in terms of military weapons, but "the Word of God as the sword of the Spirit" is more than a metaphor. Words are concrete and ideas are spiritual, so the expression cannot be totally literal. On the other hand, the Word of God does the work of a sword even separating members of a family from one another, depending on whether they accept the Word or not. The Word can also cut to the very heart of an individual, making clear that he must choose between God and self. If we accept the Word, the wound heals and we are stronger than ever. If we reject the Word, the wound will fester continually—our conscience will nag no matter how hard we try to seal off the poison.

Unfortunately, the Pharisees and so many in our own time depend upon real weapons of war to defend themselves and to enforce their ideas. But this cannot be the way of Christ and his followers.

Friday

Romans 9: 1-5; Luke 14: 1-6 **YEAR I**

When Paul wrote to the Roman Church, the Jewish people were generally not accepting of Jesus as Savior. This realization astonished and puzzled Christians. In today's reading we hear Paul speaking in strong terms of his own people who do not believe in Jesus. He was overcome with grief for the Jewish people, who were given everything but did not appreciate what they had and lost it all. He exaggerates in saying that he would separate himself from Christ, if it would do any good for the Jews, but that would solve nothing. Paul cannot give them more than God has already given them, that is, grace upon grace. Unfortunately, if we do not respond to God's spiritual promptings, nothing human can save us.

Is this not the case of every person, every sinner. We must admit that we have been given all kinds of favors by God: good parents, excellent education, call to priesthood, good friends, the inspiration of so many people of great faith, the sacrament of penance, so many other experiences, along with those little whisperings of God's grace which make clear the path of virtue. The only thing that God will not do for us is to deprive us of free will. We must make the choice between virtue and vice, joy and pleasure, God's will or my will, future promise or present gratification. Which shall it be? All the weight of both reason and faith favors God's way and yet we weaken so easily in the face of temptation.

In today's gospel narrative, we hear that the Pharisees were keeping Jesus under close surveillance. In all his ways and without hesitation, Jesus always chose God's Law over man's law. When Jesus pointed out to the Jews the alternatives of God's or man's law, they had nothing to say. Good as man's law might be, it should yield in every instance to God's command. Instead of looking to God for guidance and making our laws correspond to his Law, we make our law first and try to bend his to justify what we have done or plan to do as with abortion, nuclear armaments, embryonic research, and other matters. There are all kinds of arguments in favor of the human law, but when we get to the "bottom line" and see clearly that our human wisdom is contrary to God's Law, we should summon the humility to admit our mistake and change the law.

Philippians 1: 1-11; Luke 14: 1-6 **YEAR II**

Today, we read from Paul's letter to the Philippians in northern Greece. He had converted them on one of his missionary journeys and they remained generous and grateful to him. He thanks them for their steadfast support of him in spreading the gospel. Paul implies that they did much "good work" in promoting the gospel. When he was in prison or when he was being challenged to defend the faith they stood by him and did not deny him. St. Paul did not demand that the people defend the faith as articulately as he did. They were not prepared for this. But he expected, at the very least, that they would not oppose him or desert him. And he was grateful that they went beyond this minimum to provide more positive support. In our own day the Holy Father and the missionaries who proclaim the truth of the gospel are worthy of similar support.

Christ should have been able to expect such support from the scribes and Pharisees of his time. First, they should have given more serious consideration to his credentials as a prophet. Second, if in doubt about those credentials, they should not have opposed him until they were certain of their position. But they did oppose Christ because they could not overcome their prejudice, which was based on a fear that they would lose their power with the people. By pride in their own ideas, they were blinded from giving a fair hearing to the teaching of Christ.

Theologians should be free to study the teaching of the Church and even to disagree with it privately. But they should not allow their pride to establish their own ideas as the criterion for truth and they should not undermine the Holy Father and the Magisterium. They should be giving support to the teaching authority of the Church until final judgment has been passed.

Saturday

Romans 11: 1-2, 11-12, 25-29; Luke 14: 1, 7-11 **YEAR I**

In today's reading, Paul tells of the mystery of Israel—prepared for the Messiah but not accepting him. Paul says that the Chosen People, Israel, is not permanently rejected. Israel will accept Christ after the Gentiles do. God's call to the Jews is irrevocable. Forgiveness is always extended, always possible for anyone. As happened often in the Old Testament, God has not rejected his people but they have forsaken him. The rejection of Christ by the Jews opened to the Gentiles the possibility of belonging to God's kingdom upon earth. There is room for all. A welcome to the Gentiles does not mean exclusion of the Jews. What it does mean is that the Jews have had ample opportunity as God's Chosen People and, although salvation is open to them through their conversion and God's forgiveness, others who have not had such a grace-filled history will now become a Chosen People, if they convert themselves to total love of God and love of neighbor for love of God.

Somehow the leaders of the Jewish people had become convinced that they held the keys to the kingdom of Heaven. By their works and their rules and their efforts, they could gain and lead others to gain salvation. However, they worshipped God in name only. They did what Adam and Eve wanted to do. They became as gods, at least in their own sight and in the sight of their people. This is an ever present danger for us too. We do well, especially the leaders of the Christian community, to have a wholesome, realistic humility. We are not chosen to be priests and bishops because we are necessarily holier than others but because God has a job for us to do. From among sinners, God chooses some to be priests! Amazing, when one thinks of it! And if one remembers that key concept, it is possible to become a good Christian leader. For a good Christian leader is one who allows Christ to live in him and through him. A good Christian leader is one who concentrates on loving God with his whole mind, heart and soul, and serves his neighbor out of love for God.

Philippians 1: 18-26; Luke 14: 1, 7-11 **YEAR II**

It must have been especially difficult in St. Paul's time to live in hope. After all, the memory that everyone had of Christ was that, although he was a good and wise man, he had been put to death. And for all those who missed the fact of the Resurrection his death was the end of an era. This may have been the reason why St. Paul expected a quick return of Christ. But he did not return. To be sure, there were some miraculous signs, but these came and went and were disbelieved by many. How hard it must have been, day after day, to retain one's faith that Christ is God and will fulfill his promises of eternal life and perfect happiness! We have 2,000 years of history. Although it may be difficult for us at times—certainly, believing was more of a problem in the early centuries.

If we really believe in Christ, our attitude should reflect St. Paul's that it is far better to die and to be one with him than to continue in this life. If we do not think as St. Paul did, there can be only two reasons, both of which are probably present. First, we may not be living a sufficiently holy life to be welcomed directly to heaven. Second, maybe our faith and hope are such that we do not go about fulfilling our baptismal calling with the total dedication which should animate us. Does life mean Christ to me, here and hereafter? Do I have a personal and meaningful attachment to him? It would be well to develop and strengthen that personal relationship to Christ. We should imitate the Pharisees in at least one respect; we should "observe Christ closely." We need to reflect on his words and example, see clearly the person he was, and follow him in everything as closely as we can.

Humility does not mean that we must sit in an isolated corner, lose all significance, have no influence on others, and live very passively. What we are called upon to do is to think little of ourselves so that God may take over in our lives and speak and act through us. If we think much of ourselves, we shall be forever trying to accomplish much by ourselves. And when human beings try to do this, ninety-nine percent fail miserably. There is a small percentage of people who do seem to "succeed"—after all, someone must hold power, wealth, land, prestige—but even these people will look foolish when the question is asked, "What does it profit . . . ?" Far better is it to make room in one's life for Christ in order that we may live and move and have our being in him.

Thirty-first Week of Ordinary Time

Monday

Romans 11: 29-36; Luke 14: 12-14 **YEAR I**

In today's reading, Paul says that both Jew and Gentile, in spite of their faithlessness, have received the gift of faith in Christ. God's grand design of salvation is open to all men and women. St. Paul speaks of God allowing all to be disobedient so that he could manifest his mercy. Paul marvels at the wisdom of God, which is so unlike human wisdom.

In the gospel narrative, Jesus demonstrates his special concern for the poor, lepers, Samaritans, publicans, soldiers, shepherds, and public sinners. God will treat us the way we treat these unfortunate people. In exaggerated fashion, Jesus instructs us not to invite family, relatives, and friends to celebrations, but our emphasis should be upon the poor. That is, before we spend huge amounts of money to feed our own, who are already well fed and clothed, we should think of those in society who lack the very necessities of life and go to their aid first. In a true sense this is one of the sacrifices that the priest and religious make—they are unable to entertain family and friends on a frequent or extravagant basis.

Philippians 2: 1-4; Luke 14: 12-14 **YEAR II**

In today's reading, St. Paul presents us with marvelous advice for our times marked with so much controversy. Everyone clamors to be heard; few wish to listen; and often those who argue a point are talking from little knowledge, not knowing what they speak of, or mouthing the words of someone else, often as ignorant as they are. We live in a media-dominated age. Everyone is supposed to have an instant opinion on every subject and be able to articulate it in thirty seconds or less. This is extremely dangerous, if we have any regard for the truth. And it is most perilous for a person representing the Church because, in our agnostic times, the listeners rarely understand the religious message without a considerable background briefing. Humility that prompts a simple admission of little knowledge and a recognition that other people might be more aware than the one speaking is important and necessary.

In Catholic circles another need is for unity of spirit and ideals. Most theologians, bishops, and others in the Church want to be heard. We of the Catholic faith should strive to make it possible for Christ to be heard. The only guarantee we have of this is that we maintain unity with one another by adhering to conciliar statements and to the guidance of the Holy Father and the bishops who speak in union with him. It matters not what I think about a subject but what Christ thinks. I should not be clamoring for attention but trying to gain attention for the Word of God.

In the gospel, Christ demonstrates a special concern for the poor, lepers, Samaritans, publicans, soldiers, shepherds, and public sinners. He emphasizes the need to have the gospel preached to the poor. This is always a concern of the Holy Father who is constantly trying to touch the hearts of the poorest as he travels around the world. This is also the clear responsibility of bishops, priests, and informed Catholics. So many are bullied into silence or, out of a desire to be loved or accepted, desert the teaching authority for worldly respect!

TUESDAY

Romans 12: 5-16; Luke 14: 15-24 **YEAR I**

The thoughts of the passage from Romans are so numerous, rich, and important that one could reflect upon them for days. The passage centers upon the image of the Church as the Body of Christ.

The human body has many different members and individual cells but works well only when each one is fulfilling its particular function. No part of the body does everything. Each has a limited role; the body functions best when each part fulfills that given role perfectly. And so it is in the Church. Some have charismatic gifts; they should use them to inspire. Some have great physical strength; they should use it for service. Some are bright; they should use their intelligence for teaching. Some are wealthy; they should give generously. Some have positions of authority; it should be exercised in a positive way for the good of all.

There are certain virtues that everyone should exercise such as the total love for God and love of neighbor for love of God, detestation of what is evil, zeal in serving God and one another, hope in God's promise, patience in difficulty, perseverance in prayer, and even love for one's enemies. If we use

God's special gifts to the fullest even if we have only one of these gifts we are fulfilling our responsibility and role as members of the Body of Christ.

The spiritual masters remind us that every person has one predominant fault, which he must battle all through life, but if he does so, he is not likely to be beset by others. The battle strengthens his will power. So too the converse seems to be true. Most of us have one predominant virtue and if we cultivate that virtue to the fullest, the degree to which we develop other virtues is amazing. In a very real sense, all virtues are one and illustrate different aspects of virtue. So too, all vices are one, but different aspects of sin. At the heart of the life of holiness is free will and the choice between God and self. We need to make a determined choice to love and serve God rather than self.

The parable of the wedding feast bears this out. Those who were invited preferred to use their considerable gifts for their own selfish purposes instead of showing gratitude to the king. The king then invited those with lesser gifts to join him, because he would rather celebrate with those of less talent but more good will. Indeed free will is the only gift that we have to give to God; everything else is his and not under our complete control. Free will is his too, but it is a unique gift in that, once given it is no longer under God's control by its very definition. Unfortunately those who use their freedom for selfish pursuits find themselves enslaved by the pleasure of things, whereas those who use their freedom to serve God and neighbor all become free spirits experiencing the joy of unlimited love.

Philippians 2: 5-11; Luke 14: 15-24 **YEAR II**

To teach humility to the Philippians Paul quotes a hymn describing how God emptied himself to become our suffering Savior who is now exalted. "Your attitude must be that of Christ!" Would that we could always keep this admonition before our eyes. Humility characterized Christ's attitude. Because of this disposition, Christ accepted any assignment, any indignity, any suffering out of love for his Father and a desire to save souls. As God, Christ could exercise rank and power and he could have dominated the world. However, he sublimated all this because it was his Father's will.

If this was the attitude of Christ—an attitude that we must imitate—surely we must look with indifference upon whatever rank and power we may have. We must always give first place to God's will, love him, look to him in prayer as our strength, and love our neighbor by constantly fostering the desire to do what we can, by word and example, to save souls. Thus the corporal and spiritual works of mercy should fill our lives. And our minds, hearts, and voices should resonate the teachings of Christ.

The attempt that so many of us make, consciously or unconsciously, to save ourselves and others by our own "lights" does not conform with the demands of humility. Rather than follow the gospel, as explained by the Church, we interpret the gospel for ourselves and live accordingly. For a Catholic, to whom the full truth as proposed by the Church is available, this is nonsense. And the basic, anti-humility decision that one makes to follow his own inspirations, vitiates just about everything he does.

The dependence upon one's self and the love of personal pleasure are illustrated in the gospel. The master has far more to offer than the guests can provide for themselves; indeed, they are dependent upon him. But the guests become enamored of their own possessions; they can do without the master; they go their own way; and they find that others take their place. How easily we are diverted from the simple purpose of life to an inordinate esteem of ourselves and of our possessions. The eventual result of the desire "to do it myself" is hell where for all eternity we will be allowed to do it "my way."

WEDNESDAY

Romans 13: 8-10; Luke 14: 25-33 **YEAR I**

The only thing that we owe to our neighbor is to love that person. First, it obliges us to justice, to give everything that is due without holding anything for ourselves. Then, it obliges us to treat the other person as we would treat ourselves, forcing us to put the interests of the other person first, sacrifice ourselves so that the other person can receive what we would wish to receive. Granted that such charity is often heroic, we can hardly say that we fulfill the gospel unless we practice that kind of love. This is what it means to be perfect as the heavenly Father is perfect. In all probability, we shall fall short of the perfection of the great saints, but we must strive for that ideal.

Today's gospel narrative speaks of everyone who has accepted Jesus as Lord. This means a lifetime of prayer, holiness, and imitation of the master. God's commandment of love is such that it may even set us at odds with our family. Granted that family is first in line as our "neighbors" and we owe them much by way of justice and charity, we cannot simply lavish our love on those who love us, for even the pagans do that. When God gives a calling to the total consecration of priesthood or religious life we must be ready to respond to the will of God to forsake family, who are well able to take care of themselves in most instances. Since there is such a lack of love in the world, some people must give their whole lives to this work in imitation of Christ, in order to keep the love of God alive, and in order that there may be a visible example of the Christ-life for all to follow. This is not an easy task for the one who is called; one should give serious consideration as to whether one can make a total commitment to such a life; but it is a beautiful life, if lived to the full.

Philippians 2: 12-18; Luke 14: 25-33 **YEAR II**

The Philippians were living "in the midst of a twisted and depraved generation." Sometimes we think that our own are the worst of times but the truth is that sin abounds everywhere. So compared to the perfectly happy state in which this world could be, it is rather always twisted and depraved, sometimes to a lesser and sometimes to a greater degree. This should not be a matter for discouragement. It is a challenge to make God present in the world, always striving to live in such a way as to turn others to God and thereby save our souls and theirs as well. Regardless of sufferings, sacrifice, deprivation and even death which St. Paul could foresee, ours is a glorious mission because God is with us and he gives us strength. He waits for us "on the other side" to welcome us into the everlasting happiness of his kingdom.

We must be single-minded with regard to doing God's will and achieving our salvation. Surely we are to live and work for God's kingdom as a community, but if others—even family—do not wish to be included, we are to leave them behind in order to pursue the one thing necessary, the God-given goal of loving and serving him. This we accomplish by loving and serving those around us as the examples of the gospel make clear. Like a contractor, or a military commander, or even a sports coach, if we are to attain our goal, total concentration is demanded of us. We cannot afford distractions nor interests which divert our attention from the goal—the kingdom of Heaven. For this, a lifetime of prayer, especially contemplative prayer, holiness, and imitation of the master are necessary.

THURSDAY

Romans 14: 7-12; Luke 15: 1-10 **YEAR I**

In today's reading, Paul says not to judge others. We are all subject to Christ and we all face God's judgment. "None of us lives as his own master and none of us dies as his own master." We have received life from God; we depend upon his providence to continue living; and our life on earth will come to an end, when he decides to call us. Everything is in his hands. Therefore, who are we to judge others? The fact of the matter is that we are being judged right now. There is no good in comparing ourselves to others and claiming to be better. Only God and the individual know the blessings and favors that he has given that person. Although we may complain about others, we have no complaint against God. We must simply answer to him at the hour of our death.

The gospel is a practical application of the epistle. The scribes and Pharisees stand in judgment over the people. But Jesus turns the tables upon them, making clear that their own laws could be applied against them. They were more interested in the laws of men rather than the law of God, more interested in things than in people, more interested in worldly success than in union with God. If they practiced the spiritual life as they lived their material life, they would save their souls. Every human person is precious in God's sight because each one has been made in his likeness. He has love and mercy for each one; he wills everyone to be saved. "And if God has so loved us, we ought to love one another."

Philippians 3: 3-8; Luke 15: 1-10 **YEAR II**

St. Paul had excellent credentials as a Jew. Perhaps some could equal his claims but few could surpass them. He was not only circumcised, he had been a zealous defender of the faith. But once he came to know Jesus and the gospel, he did not temporize. He put aside Judaism totally and embraced Christianity completely. He was not about to compromise. Granted he was a person of his culture, so many cultural traditions stayed with him. But he had the mind of Christ; his was much more a religion of the Spirit than of the law. The law was not abandoned by any means but the Spirit of Christ calls for us to go so far beyond the law that the law, in that sense, should have very little hold upon us.

Christ wanted all of us to be missionaries—to go after lost souls and to bring them back to the fold. He gives two examples in the gospel—the lost sheep and the lost coin. We need to go in search of souls with the same intensity, the same "desperation," that people generally devote to finding something of material value. Is that the way we proclaim the faith? And when we bring one soul to the truth, we are to rejoice more over that person than over all the others who are already in the fold. Of course, in the practical order we will lose souls, if we neglect those already in the fold. The only way to keep them from envy is to convert them fully to the missionary mind of Christ. Then, the whole community, unmindful of itself and one with Christ, will be able to rejoice as one over the conversion of another person. Our love of Christ, and our following in his way, must be total.

FRIDAY

Romans 15: 14-21; Luke 16: 1-8 **YEAR I**

In closing his letter to the Romans, Paul states that he has spoken very strongly, even though he knows how knowledgeable they are about the faith and how good they are. This is what he has been called to do. Today our people, although much less knowledgeable in the faith and engulfed in a sinful world, to which so many family and friends have fallen victim, are insulted or hurt or feel "put upon," when we preach God's moral law. Somehow because we must work so hard to earn a living or because we have done so well to provide a living for others—a work of justice and charity—our people are offended, when we remind them that what we have we must share with others. Yes, we must share even with strangers, those on welfare, and those in the southern hemisphere. Instead of being grateful to God that we are able to work, that we have prospered materially, and that we are able to show our gratitude by our goodness to others, we tend to complain at least subconsciously, that God could have made it easier for us. He could still give us more so that we would have no material worries whatsoever. He should free us of physical illness because we have been so good to him and worked so hard. He could somehow help these poor people who disturb our conscience without any need for us to be his instruments in coming to their aid.

We don't seem to understand that God gives good things to some, not because those "some" are so good but in order that the "some" can share with the many. We don't seem to understand that we are to be Christ to the world, living the same life, exercising the same virtues. We don't seem to understand that, in God's providence, we could just as easily be the people in need and not the people he asks to provide for the needy.

Through today's gospel narrative, we should learn from the unjust steward. He at least knew how to prepare for the future. Should we not be just as practical about gaining heaven? Learning from the steward we should imitate his business efficiency rather than his, unethical practices. Every kind act of ours is earning credit toward heaven! We not only gain by our good deeds, we gain from the prayers of those to whom we have been kind. And even in this world, we gain peace of mind—a limited experience of heaven itself. Compassion, of course, is a better motive for justice and charity, but even selfish motives can influence us to the practice of these virtues.

Philippians 3: 17-4: 1; Luke 16: 1-8 **YEAR II**

We now live in times when our prayer must be, as it was St. Paul's for the Philippians, that we "stand firm in the Lord." The great saints, Thomas More, Vincent de Paul, the apostles stood courageously against those who opposed the faith, those who insulted them, accused them in court, and did everything to plague them. In their time, they stood tall and firm in the Lord! In our day, all of this is still true, but there can be a difficult battle within the heart and mind of a person. One can doubt one's sanity, when all seems to be against one's convictions. One can fear the presence of pride when people brighter and seemingly holier are in opposition. One can always ask the question, with so many adversaries, "Could I possibly be wrong?" The answer to that, of course, is "yes." Our strongest support is Peter, the Vicar of Christ, the Rock upon which the Church is built, he who is to confirm the faith of all. On the negative side, there is assurance, too, in the fact that those who oppose the Magisterium are clearly associated with the world and its pleasures. This is very evident with those who engage in various kinds of over-indulgence. It is also apparent in so-called "sophisticated Catholics" who try to persuade us that we must make accommodations to the world because times change; what was wrong a few years ago such as abortion, sexual practices, occasions of sin is not wrong now. It is one thing to be concerned for the poor; it is quite another thing to abandon God in order to "help" them. It is one thing to apply gospel principles to new circumstances; it is quite another to change the principles because, when applied, the answers are contrary to what we want them to be.

The gospel reading about the unjust steward illustrates the point beautifully. Those who are well off in this world are usually those who bend and then break the Law of God. They cater to this world; they seek glory and comfort, power and prestige, in the here and now. We on the other hand, although stewards only, must nonetheless be dedicated, active in upholding God's way, and living it. We are not to be passive. We are to be alive and at work always, proclaiming the gospel and living it in such a way that God's presence and God's call will be heard in the world. Indeed, if we were more dynamic and imaginative like the unjust steward, we would perhaps draw many more people to the Lord!

SATURDAY

Romans 16: 3-9, 16, 22-27; Luke 16: 9-15 **YEAR I**

In today's reading, Paul ends his letter to the Romans with a remarkable listing of friends and fellow workers in Christ. They have proven faithful and trustworthy. He has confidence that they are good spiritual leaders and the Christians in Rome can depend upon them. This list helps us to picture the early Church in real life. If we can depend upon a person in smaller matters, there is a good chance that we can depend upon him in greater matters, too. But if he cannot be responsible in easier situations, how can we trust him in the more difficult? If we cannot be depended upon in earthly situations—even in minor matters and those that concern others—how can the Lord look upon us as trustworthy people in spiritual matters, which affect eternal life and death?

In the gospel narrative, Jesus warns his followers against the spiritual dangers lurking in money and worldly possessions. Avarice is always one of the great temptations. If we cannot manage money with justice and charity, it may be a sign that we are not serving God as we should. We cannot serve God and money. God is justice and charity in love. We need to work constantly to be less dependent upon the world, more dependent on God. The Pharisees believed that God was on the side of money. They thought that he allowed sinful people to prosper. The lesson of poverty, although clearly taught in the Old Testament, was not understood and lived by the Jewish people. Christ's message came as a totally new revelation so different, not from the Old Testament, but from the Jewish tradition that it was difficult for them to accept it. How many of our choices are influenced by the desire to make money? How many are influenced by the desire to help people? Do, we experience any conflict between these two desires in our work? One key to understanding Jesus in this passage as well as throughout the gospels is to realize that he teaches through examples while allowing us to figure out the general principle behind them. Jesus worked hard to keep his religion from being turned into a set of laws. Instead of presenting rules, he gave concrete examples of how we should act allowing us to draw our own conclusions concerning the principles animating those examples.

Philippians 4: 10-19; Luke 16: 9-15 **YEAR II**

We must learn to cope with every circumstance. The generation that experienced the depression especially in the thirties has seen both good and bad and the people who lived through those years should adjust fairly well. However, the generations that have known nothing but plenty since the forties have a more difficult time. We are called upon to give them good example by showing how the theological virtues of faith, hope, and love for God can sustain us in every circumstance. We do not have the harsh experience of St. Paul in being "brought low" but we should be able to show some self-sufficiency—or rather God-dependency—as he did. Only faith, hope, and love can sustain us. If, instead of complaining, we look to the essentials, we shall discover the God-given dignity, nobility, and strength which set man apart from the rest of creation.

In hardship we discover the more profound realities. "What man thinks important, God holds in contempt." We need to have this same mind, which is the mind of Christ. Only when we have little, will we realize how badly or foolishly we have squandered our abundance. And in so doing we have shown our lack of gratitude to God. The old saying of Christ is so very true: "You cannot serve God and money." We either need to live without, or to live as if we had nothing, or at least to live with a conscious awareness that we are nothing without God. Jesus often warned his followers against the spiritual dangers lurking in money and worldly possessions. Our worth comes only from the "unbelievable" fact that God loves us. He loves us enough to have created us, to have given us countless blessings in this life, to have died for our sins, and to be offering us the everlasting happiness of heaven. All that we need to do in return is to show a little gratitude by loving others through the corporal and spiritual works of mercy.

Thirty-second Week of Ordinary Time

Monday

Wisdom 1: 1-7; Luke 17: 1-6 **YEAR I**

Today, we read from the book of Wisdom. Written in Greek at Alexandria of Egypt around 100 B.C., this book contains highly developed doctrine that prepared for the New Testament. It begins with a general recommendation of wisdom in life.

The Spirit of God is kindly but it is so repelled by evil that it cannot exist in a soul which is given to injustice, disbelief, and sinfulness. God surely wishes to give himself to everyone but his Spirit and wisdom are such that he can only be with the person who strives after goodness and justice all his days.

In today's gospel narrative, Jesus speaks about not giving scandal, forgiving other people, and having strong faith. The just person is to correct evil in others and, if there is repentance, he is to forgive that person any number of times. This is not to say that evil is a light matter at all; scandal is a horrible thing. However, we must understand that the flesh is weak. Thus we are to hate the sin and love the sinner.

Titus 1: 1-9; Luke 17: 1-6 **YEAR II**

Today's reading is from the beginning of the letter of Paul to Titus who was organizing a diocese on the island of Crete. St. Paul sees his task and that of Titus to promote the knowledge of the truth as Christianity embodies it. God has manifested this word in Christ, in the preaching of Paul, which has been handed on to Titus, and which Titus is to provide for the people by appointing in every town presbyters, who "hold fast to the authentic message and who will be able to encourage men to follow sound doctrine and to refute those who contradict it."

Like Christ himself, Paul says nothing about writing treatises. He speaks of oral tradition, passing on the message of faith from one person to another. This may be a risky way of doing things, in human judgment, but it is God's way.

This particular section does not mention God's grace, but grace is obviously necessary in the preacher, the one who hands on the message. He should be "blameless, not self-willed or arrogant, not a drunkard, violent, or greedy man. 0n the contrary, he should be hospitable, a lover of goodness, steady, just, holy, and self-controlled" and, of course, faithful in teaching. It is most interesting to note that Paul also excludes from the ministry of preaching those who have been married more than once and those whose children are non-believers, wild, or insubordinate. One's family, therefore, does have a bearing on whether or not one is to be accepted for the preaching office. When giving the call to deacons, we should keep these factors in mind, as well as other impediments which may not at all be the fault of the candidate.

In today's gospel, Jesus speaks about not giving scandal, forgiving other people and having strong faith. Granted that we should be most forgiving, when a person repents and expresses sorrow, still we must guard against scandals. This is especially true with respect to deacons and priests. We may forgive previous mistakes but we may not forget them. "Woe to him through whom scandals come" refers not only to the person who commits the scandal but to those—bishops, who knowingly and willingly permit the scandal.

Faith is like a mustard seed, like yeast in dough. A little bit goes a long way and can accomplish wonders. Likewise are defective attitudes and faults of character. These spiritual qualities seem small, weak, impossible to quantify, but the influence they can have on one's own life, the lives of others, and on the culture is incalculable. "Great oaks from little acorns grow." Great scandals from little flaws of character also grow.

TUESDAY

Wisdom 2: 23-3: 9; Luke 17: 7-10 **YEAR I**

Today, the book of Wisdom speaks of original sin and life after death. The words about immortality are frequently read at Masses of Christian burial. They are among the finest in the bible. The "time of visitation" is the last judgment and "sparks" are images of triumph. God made man in his own image and one of the characteristics which he gave us was that we should be imperishable. Immortality was intended to be shared with God, living with him for all eternity. But man, in the guise of our first parents, fancied that he himself could be God, and with that act of pride and presumption, sin and death entered the world. When sin entered the world all people were to perish and die. However, they could still be imperishable, if they carried out God's will during the course of their lives. Keeping God's will is not easy. Indeed, many people consider it utter foolishness because they see death as the end of everything. So, why suffer any pain or inconvenience in this world? But, death is not the end of everything. The just end up in the hands of God and with him realize their fullest potential, which is immortality. Everyone undergoes trials in this world; the innocent may suffer more than the wicked. It may even seem that God punishes arbitrarily. Whoever suffers willingly is being purified—made more holy—like metal in a fire, being fashioned into a more beautiful form, and taking on a greater resemblance to Christ. So despite sin and death, we have the possibility of immortality, if only we have the patience to suffer a little now. But even that suffering is quite bearable because God is with us. We must be wise and consider looking at everything in the light of our last end. The wise or sensible person is the one who evaluates everything—every option, every decision, and every choice—in light of what life is about, its ultimate purpose.

The gospel parable reminds church leaders to be unceasing in hard work. We must be totally dedicated. None of us is qualified to criticize or judge God. We are simply to obey and carry out his commandments and programs. If we wish to become God's friends, we must show that we are trustworthy and faithful like the good servant. We have received all we have from our divine master; we owe him everything. Our relationship to God requires that we serve him faithfully, love our neighbor, and hope in his promise of eternal life. Do we ever do anything that goes beyond religious obligation?

Titus 2: 1-8, 11-14; Luke 17: 7-10 **YEAR II**

Today, in his letter to Titus, a gentile Christian, Paul counsels and gives spiritual lessons to the organizing Bishop of Crete. It is difficult to summarize or even to present in more expressive language what St. Paul has to say to Titus. "Let your speech be consistent with sound doctrine." It is so easy for the priest to be intimidated by the culture and by what everyone else is doing. As the saying goes it is hard to swim against the tide of public opinion. For instance, older men and women should be taught that they should not retire from giving good example. As they get on in years, they must be stronger in faith, sensible, sober in all ways, use time constructively, not be a burden, and contribute their wisdom and good judgment to society. It is easy to be negative, to gossip, to become useless, and to convince oneself that one is not wanted or needed. The priest must preach and emphasize the positive aspects of getting older, both for the dignity of the person and the good of society.

The above may seem acceptable even in our day but what of St. Paul's advice to wives? They must love their husbands and children; they must be chaste, busy at home and not neglect their growing children; kindly, and submissive to their husbands! That is quite an agenda for our times. Yet, any unprejudiced person can see the need for these. We complain about the evils of separation and divorce, infidelity, promiscuity, "latch-key" children, the drug culture, and so much else. We plead for peace in the world, while there can be no world peace without kindness, love, and tranquility in the home. As long as there is egoism and selfishness, there can be no peace. Being submissive to a husband is strong language when taken out of the context of the gospel but, when understood in terms of the husband's obligation to have a total sacrificial love for wife and family, it simply means that eventually one person must take responsibility for decisions. This is exemplified in different contexts by the Pope, the President, the heads of organizations.

The main teaching for man, young and old, is self-control and here St. Paul refers in a special way to sexual control. Today, the general attitude is that sex, particularly for the male, is uncontrollable. Surely women need to be more modest, but there should be overwhelming rejection of rape and the belief that there cannot be a good relationship between male and female without sexual activity. In the face of all this, often the priest is reticent and passive. As St. Paul says, eventually, "Hostility will yield to shame," if not in this world at least in the next. The priest's teaching must be "serious, sound, rejecting godless ways, rejecting worldly desires, defending what is just." Then, if some reject the teaching and scorn us as people, in the depths of conscience, the truth will be clear, even in this world. We must be tireless in our commitment to serve God, the truth, and the gospel. Even when we have exhausted ourselves doing whatever is in our power to serve, in the end, as creatures of God, totally dependent upon him, we must confess, "We are useless servants. We have done no more than our duty."

WEDNESDAY

Wisdom 6: 2-11; Luke 17: 11-19 **YEAR I**

Today's reading from the book of Wisdom is addressed to kings and rulers of nations. That includes the "princes" of the Church as well. They are reminded that God is the source of authority and that they will be judged by

God. So they need wisdom! I, as bishop, have often reflected on the thoughts in today's reading. In our culture we are engulfed by evil and there is a tendency to condemn the people who are involved in it. And yet I often wonder if I will not be held more to blame than they. After all, without the slightest bit of pride, but simply because of family and Church background, I know better. In regard to others, I think I have been guilty, as I am sure other priests have been, of understating the demands of the kingdom of God. None of us wants to put a guilt trip on anyone or make religion into a burden. Therefore, we make suggestions such as, "Would it not be nice to read Scripture every day?" or "It would be really helpful to go to Mass daily if you can." We have to be more passionate about the kingdom of God! Christ is not casual about wanting to share his mind and heart with us through his word, and wanting to give us his body and blood daily in the Eucharist. There was nothing casual about his offering of himself on the cross. I may be held responsible for the wrong doings that others commit because of my failure to teach them properly and effectively. However, the Lord will treat kindly those who come from broken homes, who were never taught religion, who have known nothing in their neighborhoods but poverty, drunkenness, sloth, theft, sexual misconduct, and drugs. These people never had a chance. We should heed the warning of wisdom. Those who have positions of power and prestige will be judged by the Lord according to a strict standard. It behooves us, therefore, to be just, kind, loyal to God, and obedient to his commandments. Power on earth is no guarantee of an exalted place in heaven. Quite the contrary. "The lowly may be pardoned out of mercy, but the mighty shall be put mightily to the test."

All good gifts are from God. It is not a matter of charity but of justice, then, that we should use his gifts for his intended purposes and not for evil. We owe God praise, glory, and thanksgiving for all that he has done for us. But all humanity is like the ten lepers, only one of whom returned to give thanks to Jesus for his cure. You too have received great gifts from God, perhaps others have received greater and some less—but it is clear that whatever one receives from God is more than his due. Give thanks to him, then, and bless his name! Wisdom says "keep from sin."

Titus 3: 1-7; Luke 17: 11-19 **YEAR II**

Today, in the first reading, Paul advises Titus about the Church on the island of Crete. The people should have a different way of life because of Christ. That there are so many good people in this world is marvelous especially when there seems to be so little faith. How can one forgo the things of this world unless one believes in God? Probably, there is more faith than we think. In any event, we can tell that there are many good people because even in ourselves we sense the desire to give vent to our passions, to enjoy illicit pleasures, to be envious of others, malicious, and end up hating others as well as ourselves. St. Paul says that he was that kind of a person. However, when he came to believe in Christ and began to practice Christianity, he realized that striving for self-satisfaction was of no great benefit in this world and most detrimental to one's prospects for eternal salvation. He refers to his former conduct as foolish, disobedient, and far from the faith.

What St. Paul offers as a substitute is not passivity or indifference in the sense of not caring but a holy indifference to the things of this world. He came to the realization that anger, envy, hatred, and self-seeking accomplish nothing for anyone. Although the life of virtue is not acquired easily, and needs the support of many, it provides serenity for oneself and those around as well as the assurance of a reward from God. So it makes sense to obey the civil law, to take any honest employment, to think, speak, and act with charity toward others. This is the message of the Church with regard to peace. The true peace-makers, the Church would maintain, are those who are at peace with themselves, who are sincerely interested in the welfare of others over their own, who perseveringly strive for liberty and justice by the practice of great charity in their own lives.

The story of the Ten Lepers in the gospel illustrates perfectly the above principles. In the time of Jesus, the attitude toward lepers was one of dread, anger, self-defense rather than compassion. Jesus treated them in just the opposite manner. He spoke to them; he listened understandingly; he loved them; he acted in their favor and cured them. He treated them with justice and charity, restoring their freedom to be human beings once again. We learn from this episode not only to do the same, but also not to expect any praise or gratitude for a good life. The world sees self-sacrificing love as foolishness. Only one of the ten lepers returned to give thanks. Only God is truly appreciative of such a life.

THURSDAY

Wisdom 7: 22-8: 1; Luke 17: 20-25 **YEAR I**

In today's reading, wisdom is beautifully described, leaving no doubt that this is the aspect of the human person, which is the image and likeness of

God. Every word of the description is appropriate. However, I shall concentrate only on a few ideas. Wisdom is a spirit. Although one, it is multifaceted; it can penetrate all things and learn the truth about them. It can apply itself to every aspect of life, gain certainty about what is to be done, always directing the person to that which is right, good, and holy. In this way wisdom brings the calm and tranquility of peace to the person, who is otherwise restless and uncertain. Wisdom is "the aura of the might of God, a pure effusion of the glory of God, the spotless mirror of the power of God, the image of God's goodness." Wisdom, dwelling within us, is what makes us like God and makes us lovable.

At the time of Jesus on earth, the people were concerned about the coming of God, whether as the Messiah or as marking the end of the world, both of which could be simultaneous but not necessarily so. Jesus addresses a somewhat ambiguous question to the people leaving them and the Pharisees guessing. But he makes one point that makes the question meaningless. He says that "The reign of God is already in your midst." If the Jewish people had realized that they already possessed God by means of revelation, actual grace, in nature, and by virtue of God's promises, in which they could place firm hope, there would have been no need of the question. They would have realized that in an inchoate state they already possessed God. In light of the first reading, we can say that they had rejected God-given wisdom, or at least they were ignoring it in favor of human, worldly wisdom. By so doing, they were led away from truth, goodness, and beauty; they were afflicted with doubt and insecurity; they were not of one mind and heart with God as they could have been, if they had accepted God's gifts, appreciated their value, and put them to good use in their lives.

Philemon 7-20; Luke 17: 20-25 **YEAR II**

Today, we read from Paul's personal letter to Philemon. Philemon's slave, Onesimus, had stolen something and then fled and sought sanctuary with Paul. He must have been filled with fear when he arrived at the latter's doorstep. A slave in those days had no rights, whether at home, in slavery, or abroad as a fugitive. Slave or free, St. Paul was only interested in bringing a person to the love of God. He converted the runaway to Christ and sent him back to Philemon calling him "a beloved brother, especially dear to me; and how much more than a brother to you, since now you will know him both as a man and in the Lord." Onesimus means useful. St. Paul could have used the help of Onesimus in prison but he thought it better for all and for the faith that Onesimus go back to Philomen who owed everything to Paul because Paul had brought him to Christ. Paul asked for no favors for himself; rather he asked Philomen to love and accept Onesimus as Paul had loved and accepted him, as God loves and accepts all of us. It was not to be a repayment of a debt but a recognition of God's image and God's grace even in a slave.

The gospel makes clear that religion is not a matter of living for oneself now and expecting a heavenly reward for having minded one's own business. The kingdom of God is present now on earth, not in a finished form but is "under construction." We are called to build that kingdom of justice and truth, peace and goodness right here on earth. It will not be perfect but our mission is to strive for the perfection of the Father. On earth we must "be about our Father's business," which involves the practice of justice and charity toward one another in the name of God.

FRIDAY

Wisdom 13: 1-9; Luke 17: 26-37 **YEAR I**

If anyone is serious about seeking an explanation for the universe and our place in it, it should be relatively easy to identify a Supreme Being as the ultimate cause. But so many people become distracted by the things of this world and end up worshipping them instead of God, their source. For example, people see something of startling beauty and they worship the beauty instead of the Creator of it. They witness the power and energy of fire, wind, water and they become enamored of these—worship them—instead of continuing on to search for the One who made them. The book of Wisdom does not excuse these people, but the author does give them credit for at least searching for God, while others remain indifferent.

Among the Chosen People, or among those who have received God's revelation and come to believe in him, the situation unfortunately is not much better. Although they have been introduced to God, they become fascinated with the things of this world and devote their time and attention to them. When the Lord calls, whether at the end of life or at any time, without hesitation we should go to him; we should do his will. We cannot become so caught up in the things of this world that we fail to hear his voice or remain indifferent or unresponsive when we do hear his call. Dire consequences await those who choose this world over the world to come, which is simply the presence of God for all eternity.

2 John 4-9; Luke 17: 26-37 **YEAR II**

"Anyone who is so progressive that he does not remain rooted in the teaching of Christ does not possess God." And of course, the guarantee of being rooted in the teachings of Christ can only be given by his Church. Progress, or development in doctrine is not synonymous with newness of doctrine. Christ is the full revelation of the Father. We can learn more about Christ and his teaching and how to apply it to our times, but we cannot know more than Christ did about the Father. The way to make real progress in the faith—the only progress worth making—is to live in love, love of God and love of neighbor, giving up self for the good of others.

In today's gospel, Jesus speaks of the second coming at the end of the world. The day will come without warning! Thus, as followers of Christ we should be ready for the catastrophe. Worldly progress is not the be-all and end-all of life; but it is growth in the eyes of God that is the one thing necessary. People in the time of Noah and Lot thought that "they had it made." They were enjoying their "success" when they were all destroyed in the twinkling of an eye. The same could happen to us. Keeping the commandments, practicing the virtues, making progress in God's judgment, constitute the only true success to be gained from this world.

SATURDAY

Wisdom 18: 14-16, 19: 6-9; Luke 18: 1-8 **YEAR I**

The beautiful, poetic qualities of the book of Wisdom are noted in today's reading. Wisdom speaks of God bringing deliverance for man. The figures remind us principally of the Exodus but also of the Incarnation. The Lord is seen as coming suddenly with majesty and power. He remains in heaven but has his effect upon earth, destroying evil and restoring right order in all of nature, renewing all things as they were intended to be. And those whom the Lord saves rejoice in him, give him praise and adoration. Our role in life is to keep faith with God. We are to persevere in our hope that he will set all things right at his coming, in his own time, just as he has promised. On our part, we are to live in love, love of God above all things and love of neighbor as ourselves. Surely, if on earth a person eventually grants a request if only to be rid of the annoying pleader, how much more fully will the God, who loves us, come to the aid of human beings who trust in him and call upon him?

God has the power and the will to save us. Also he has promised to save us and he keeps his promises. God has already saved us in Christ, his Son. The means of salvation are available to us in the sacraments. That is, God is in the world already; he offers us his hand, as it were, in the sacraments. It is up to us to accept salvation and to persevere in that determination, not allowing ourselves to be distracted by the allurements of this world. God is always present to us with the offer of salvation; we must persevere in our will to accept his outstretched hand and to walk with him, through this life, along the path to salvation.

3 John 5-8; Luke 18: 1-8 **YEAR II**

Today's first reading is from The Third Letter of John. Once people have accepted the faith, we should not abandon them but give them the help they need to sustain their faith. St. John speaks particularly of those who are in material need. It is difficult to sustain faith in a good and loving God, when one is destitute. It is doubly difficult to do so when faith requires those who are able to share with those in need and they fail to do so. How can the two live under the same gospel? Although this passage speaks primarily of material need, it justifies the existence of parishes. These groupings under the leadership of a priest are not so much a means of "saving the saved" as they are a means of sustaining the faith of those already baptized. They are a sign of the Body of Christ to others, and a source of assistance for the missionary work of the Church.

Frequently it can seem to us that God does not hear our prayers or, if he does, he is not quick to answer them. This life is a time of trial. God permits those trials to exist; so we need to persevere in faith. This is made easier with the support of a community such as a parish. If we have that support and we are steadfast in prayer, God will surely hear and answer our supplications. Perseverance in prayer may be the most important virtue and we all need the help and encouragement of others to sustain our faith, hope, and love for God.

Thirty-third Week of Ordinary Time

Monday

1 Maccabees 1: 10-15, 41-43, 54-57, 62-63; Luke 18: 35-43 **YEAR I**

The Books of Maccabees are late Old Testament writings. Originally written in Hebrew around 100 B.C., First Maccabees tells of developments from 175 to 134 B.C. and of the successful Jewish Revolution. We read first of the Syrian King Antiochus Epiphanes and of his campaign to secularize the Jews. Thus, not long before the coming of Christ, some Israelites were persuaded to give up the faith in favor of the pagan Gentile practices and they won the support of King Antiochus. "Whoever observed the law was condemned to death by royal decree." A gymnasium was built in Jerusalem to glorify the body; the Sabbath was profaned; sacrifice was offered to idols as pagan altars were built everywhere; scrolls of Scripture were confiscated and burned. In the face of all this, however, many held fast to the faith and even suffered death rather than go along with the fad of abandoning the faith in favor of "do as you please" paganism.

The choice was clear as it is in our day and alarmingly similar. Many people abandon faith in God and worship of him. But "nature abhors a vacuum." Something or someone must—and does—take the place of God. Certainly we tend to glorify the body today through fitness exercises, health improvement, and advertisement of beautiful women and virile men. If Sunday is put aside, exercise time or TV time or time for some other activity becomes sacred. Praise and glory are heaped upon athletes, actors, and other "idols" rather than God, although they are torn down and replaced at will, a sign that they should not have been "worshipped" in the first place. For the most part, copies of Scripture are not confiscated and burned, but surely the twentieth century pagans have been in complete control of the media.

In these circumstances it is not easy to keep the faith and yet, like the blind man of the gospel, we subconsciously know that the culture is leading us where we do not wish to go. How do we fight our way out of the darkness and confusion and break the chains in which society binds us? The only answer, as the blind man realizes is to go to Christ. "Lord that I may see." "You alone have the words of everlasting life."

Unfortunately there are many people surrounding us—at times members of our own families—who tell us, as they told the blind man, to keep quiet, to go along with the crowd, to prefer darkness to light, the pleasure of sin to the joy of virtue. We need to keep in mind that Christ, the Lord, can overcome all these. "If God is with us, who can be against us?" We need to learn that we cannot break the chains of a sinful society by ourselves, but we can do so by the grace and love, power and goodness of our Savior, Jesus Christ.

Revelation 1: 1-4, 2: 1-5; Luke 18: 35-43 **YEAR II**

The mysterious, consoling book of Revelation, the last book in the bible, is from God's angel to John—either the apostle or a disciple—about something to happen soon. It is also known as the Apocalypse. Exegetes have taken divergent positions regarding its author. According to tradition the apostle John was the great authority in Asia until about the end of the first century; he would have inspired all the Johannine writings but the redaction would have been carried out by different disciples, more or less familiar with his thought. In today's reading, the Church at Ephesus is characterized by patient endurance. It had turned aside one false prophet after another. But now it is growing weary, having been through so much. In Revelation, the members are exhorted to return to their first fervor.

The gospel offers an example to the Ephesians in the story of the blind man. He too has been forced to endure patiently with his blindness. But even now, although he may have gone repeatedly to the Pool of Bethsaida or to various charlatans, he has not lost his original desire to see. If anything, it has grown stronger. And finally, his faith and perseverance have been rewarded. Like the blind man, the Ephesians who typify us are exhorted to be strong in faith, never to lose hope, always alert to the temptation of false doctrine. We, as the Church in America, have been tempted and our metal tested from time to time. It will continue to be in varying ways and, at times, with great severity. We need to be strong in faith, and never to lose hope.

TUESDAY

2 Maccabees 6: 18-31: Luke 19: 1-10 **YEAR I**

Second Maccabees is less historical, more religious than First Maccabees and covers the period of 180 to 161 B.C. Today we read the edifying story of Eleazar's martyrdom during the persecution. Under King Antiochus, when loyal Israelites were being put to death for their faith, Eleazar was a sterling example of steadfastness and belief in God. Even his friends tried to persuade him to save his life by substituting kosher meat for the pork that the pagans were demanding that he eat. But Eleazar would not dissemble. His refusal of the deception suggests a conscience alert to the possibility of scandal. It would also bring shame and dishonor upon him; and in any case, he could never escape the judgment of God, even if he escaped the hands of men. And so, he went to his death joyfully. Would that in time of temptation, we would consider the four arguments of Eleazar. Sin is a shameful and dishonorable thing to do; our conscience will never let us forget it; we have an obligation to society, to lead others to appreciate what is truly good, true and beautiful, and we have a responsibility to elevate culture and not pollute it. Finally, regardless of all else, God knows what is in the heart of man; we cannot deceive him; we need to examine all of our actions, conscious of the fact that he is our judge and not our fellow man. Righteous conduct is to be preferred to popularity.

Eleazar seems to have been a virtuous person all along but Zacchaeus, as a tax collector, had been unethical in some of his business practices. Still, he came to understand what Eleazar perceived. Why should he live on in the minds of men as a thieving tax collector? Why not gain an honorable reputation? Others have rights too, especially the right to live in an unpolluted culture, in which they can have an opportunity to discern clearly what is true, good and beautiful, and to pursue these ends. Zacchaeus also began to see that life is short, better to suffer loss now than later. And in this connection, he came to realize that God was his judge; better to please him than to seek riches and pleasure for himself. As death approaches, we learn, if we do not already know it, that we are not in control of our origin nor of our final destiny. Our life is in God's hands so why not strive to please him.

Revelation 3: 1-6, 14-22; Luke 19: 1-10 **YEAR II**

Again in Revelation we read about Sardis, one of the seven churches through which John wanted to reach all the churches in Asia. The Church of Sardis had the reputation of being alive but the prophet sees that its spirit is dead because it has wandered from the original revelation. It would be similar to a modern diocese which has every material advantage, has the name "Catholic" emblazoned everywhere, but has lost touch with revealed truth. Sardis apparently was a hollow shell rather than a vibrant community fully committed to the Lord. The Church of Laodicea was even better off materially but clearly indifferent to the faith. It did not even keep up a facade of virtue. The Laodiceans seemed to have reverted to practical atheism while pretending to be Christian. However, actions speak louder than words.

On the contrary, in today's gospel, Zachaeus appeared to be an immoral, irreligious person; all because he was a tax collector. However, he had an inner conversion and was far more zealous than the Pharisees and scribes who were considered religious. Externally, Zachaeus might not have appeared to be the most religious person of his entourage. Yet actions speak louder than words. This rich man climbed a tree to see Jesus; he gave half of his possessions to the poor; he repaid fourfold those whom he might have cheated. Yet, many looked askance at this "sinner." It is difficult to generalize about the spiritual condition of other people, and we should not judge. Today, there are Catholics who exhibit a great deal of materialism, practical atheism, religious superficiality, and hypocrisy. It is not our privilege to judge them or any one else. On the other hand, it is very important to judge ourselves. We need to see the world around us for what it is and to ask very honestly whether we have converted to its ways or are striving to overcome it as Christ did. Self-deception is very easy to achieve!

WEDNESDAY

2 Maccabees 7: 1, 20-31; Luke 19: 11-28 **YEAR I**

We are presented today with another example of tremendous heroism on the part of a mother and her seven sons. In the course of responding to King Antiochus and encouraging her sons to accept death rather than deny the faith, she gives eloquent testimony to the existence of a Creator and to the fact that God is the author of all life from the moment of conception. The lessons to be learned are on the surface. If there is a God, as the mother firmly believes, it is a good and glorious act to surrender one's life rather than to deny him. There is really no choice. It is only they of little, weak, or no faith who could do otherwise. This should raise a serious question in our own minds. How strong is our faith? Until we face that question, we imagine that our faith is very strong. But would we be willing to die rather than deny him? Very few of us would be. If that is the case, how fervently and frequently should we pray, "Lord, I believe, but please help my unbelief?"

The story of the talents is somewhat similar. The noble man who became king was rejected by many of the people who did not want him to rule over them. They were put to death but others who did not reject him were given money by the king. Two wise ones invested it, while the third merely saved the money and did not use it. Those who multiplied the king's money were given a number of villages to rule; the third was left with nothing. We need to make a firm determination as to our faith in God and live in such a way that our every action is a manifestation of our faith. In addition, have we thought of the gifts that God has given us to use in his service? It is never too late to discover those talents and put them to good use in doing God's work. Should we be asked to give our life for our faith, that is the time when God would give us the grace to respond by a heroic act. Our belief should be that God gives the grace for the work at hand if we pray for it and especially he gives us the grace to persevere to the end if we are strong in our faith and use the gifts that are ours.

Revelation 4: 1-11; Luke 19: 11-28 **YEAR II**

In the gospel Jesus speaks of the manner in which an earthly king deals with his subjects. He rules by power and woe to the person who does not respect it. At the same time it is clear that no one paralyzed by fear can serve the king well. Fear may enter in as an incentive but the major motivation must be a desire to gain the king's recognition and perhaps affection. Another helpful motive is to gain a certain reward. In the parable the people who oppose the king outright are put to death. But the one paralyzed by fear does not fare much better. Since he has done nothing positive to offer the king, he is deprived of all he has. Only those who work for the king's benefit are rewarded.

The book of Revelation describes, in human and mystical terms, the heavenly court. Obviously it is not like that of a worldly kingdom, but there are similarities. There is no one present who is opposed to God, and all are active. "Day and night without pause they sing . . . whenever these creatures give honor and glory and praise . . . the 24 elders fall down before the One seated on the throne, and worship him who lives forever and ever." Heaven is peopled only by those "who have kept the word with a generous heart and have yielded a harvest through perseverance" for the honor and glory of the king. Thereby, they have attained an eternal reward and have gained the king's love and affection. They now enjoy the fruits of their service.

THURSDAY

1 Maccabees 2: 15-29; Luke 9: 41-44 **YEAR I**

Mattathias was another example of utter fidelity to the faith. When he and his sons were approached by the king's men to apostatize, Mattathias killed one man who was about to sacrifice, killed the king's messenger, tore down the altar, invited others to join him, and then fled with his sons into the desert leaving behind all their possessions. Many others who wanted to live righteous lives according to their religious customs also went in the desert and settled there.

The gospel speaks of Jesus lamenting for those in the city of Jerusalem, "If only you had known the path to peace . . . but you have completely lost it from view!" We think of the other saying of Jesus that those who lose their lives for his sake will live, while those who try to protect their lives and possessions in this world will lose everything they have. Peace will come to Jerusalem but only through the most tragic sorrow and sternest detachment.

What we are really asked is to give up the love that we have and receive from family, relatives, and friends for the love of God in times of crisis when the two loves are antagonistic. Love on this earth may and is often illusory. How often love "until death do us part" ends in divorce? Although human love is beautiful, it is fragile. On the other hand, the life of love that God promises is far superior to human love because it is perfect and everlasting. As he did at Jerusalem, the Lord looks at us with concern and perhaps sadness. "If only we knew the path to peace" which is love of God through a sinless life and love of neighbor through the practice of justice and charity!

Revelation 5: 1-10; Luke 9: 41-44 **YEAR II**

Both readings speak of the fact that the revelation of God is hidden from the eyes of God's people, even the Chosen People. God willed to make himself known to the Israelites and he did so, but through the centuries they often rejected the prophets and put them to death. In these our times, the Son of God, portrayed in Revelation as the Lamb who was slain, has brought his knowledge of the Father to earth and has revealed him to us. Strangely enough, however, we remain no more open to God's word than the Jews of ancient times. As St. Paul told Timothy, we have itching ears, ready to believe the kinds of fables we want to hear, but taking an attitude of "show me," when it comes to truths we do not wish to hear. Through the centuries, figuratively or literally, such people have always suffered the same fate—their church and their nation have fallen apart. In our times, will we listen, be converted, and be saved, or will we turn a deaf ear, remain self-centered, and be lost?

We must prepare ourselves for the inspirations of the Holy Spirit. Do we wonder that we are not better? The saints are always thanking God that they are not worse. The more we ask the Holy Spirit to pour his illuminating light on our souls, the more we notice our faults. The choice has never been clearer. It is within our power to turn to God with the help of his grace, but human beings just will not take the step. We must throw up our hands and give ourselves entirely into God's keeping. Only God can save us from our willfulness.

FRIDAY

1 Maccabees 4: 36-37, 52-59; Luke 19: 45-48 **YEAR I**

Today we read that the revolution and guerilla warfare of the Maccabee brothers succeeded. They defeated the Gentile army, took Jerusalem and reconsecrated the Temple. It was December 14, 164 B.C. and this marked the origin of the Jewish feast of Hanukkah or Dedication. All places of worship are solemnly, publicly dedicated to this very purpose of worshipping God. Even when memory of the dedication ceremony passes away, custom makes it clear that "my house is a house of prayer." In the Old Testament, any time that a building was erected in God's honor, or even when the Ark was being carried around the countryside and kept in a tent, it was clear that those who entered that area should be intent on worshipping God, talking to him. We would never walk into another person's home, ignore the host, and set up a business. If we did, it would not be surprising if we should be thrown out. And it would be our fault, not that of the owner. So, and more so, should it be when we enter the house of God.

Today's gospel reading tells of the cleansing of the Temple by Jesus. He entered the Temple area and proceeded to drive out those who were selling things, saying, "It is written, 'My house shall be a house of prayer' but you have made it a den of robbers.' " Our bodies themselves are the temples of the Holy Spirit. What attitude of mine reveals to those around me that I consider my body a house of prayer?

Revelation 10: 8-11; Luke 19: 45-48 **YEAR II**

It seems that the highly symbolic book of Revelation was written to encourage Christians suffering savage persecution from the Roman Emperor at the end of the first century. Using code language such as visions, symbols, and numbers it predicts that Rome will fall, the risen Christ will triumph, and victory will come soon. While Christ is with us, when we are listening to him or adoring him in prayer, all seems to be sweetness and light. His message makes sense to us as we digest its meaning, but it can become tasteless and indigestible when it comes to putting the message into practice. We must have courage and realize that the seemingly distasteful aspects of the Christian life last but a moment compared to the blessings of eternity.

The experience of Christ in the Temple illustrates the lesson from the book of Revelation. Most of the people were with Christ because of his miracles; they found his teaching to be true, good, and beautiful; they savored every word. The Pharisees, on the other hand, had developed their own man-made religion, with which they were very content because it served them well. The traders too, because the Pharisaic law protected them, were no more disposed than the Pharisees to listen to the Messiah. They rejected him because they did not hear what they wanted to hear. Later on the people rejected Christ too because they feared the Pharisees and desired their own material prosperity more than they loved and honored Christ.

SATURDAY

1 Maccabees 6: 1-13, Luke 20: 27-40 **YEAR I**

At this time King Antiochus was tempted to make a foray into Persia to pillage a city, Elymais, which held a great deal of the treasure which had been accumulated by Alexander the Great. He failed in his mission, when the Persians learned of his coming and rose up in defense of their city. Meanwhile the Maccabees had gained strength and had taken Jerusalem. Antiochus was caught between the Persians and the Maccabees. There was nowhere to turn. He knew that he was about to die and he repented of his cruelty to the Jews. Otherwise he had ruled well. And so he feared greatly.

The gospel makes clear that those who believe in the true God have nothing to fear from death. In fact, death releases believers from the problems that are often so painful on earth. Death, for the just person, removes all fear, all worry, all doubt, all problems, and difficulties. We shall be free as the air in death; we shall live as the angels.

The Sadducees did not accept the later Old Testament doctrine of life after death and tried to make the belief ridiculous. In the gospel reading, Jesus answered them effectively. Only life after death, to be determined by an all-loving, all-powerful, all-just God, can impose restraints upon people. Only those who believe in God, trust that he has told us how to live, and believe in an after-life. They moderate their conduct according to God's will. The testimony of Christ, who has given ample proof to those of open minds that he is God, proclaims that there is an after-life. When both faith and reason come to the same conclusion, how can we believe anything else? And yet, at times, we do. It is good to pray always, "Lord, I believe; please help my unbelief."

Revelation 11:4-12; Luke 20:27-40 **YEAR II**

In the present as it was through the centuries, truth, beauty, justice, and goodness are overwhelmed by those who refuse to allow principle to play a part in their lives. We have been created in such a way that we crave truth, goodness, beauty, and justice and they will always have their God-given champions like Moses and Elijah. Evil eventually bores us. But selfish greed of one kind or another will almost always prevail upon earth; the good will be overcome; evil will seem to triumph. Still, God reigns over the world he has created and he will eventually have the last word. He will raise up the good to everlasting glory and he will leave the wicked to their own selfish designs, which they find to be Hell—the realization that their way of life is wrong and they burn bitterly with remorse for their foolishness.

The Sadduccees, who did not believe in the Resurrection posed a problem for Jesus, which made the after-life seem ridiculous—if a woman is widowed six times and marries seven husbands, whose wife will she be after death?—Jesus points out that this type of reasoning is the cause of their leading a life that God does not condone. The Sadduccees weigh everything in material, earthly terms; they have no concept of a truly spiritual life. As the soul is entirely different and superior to the body in every way, so God is to man and heaven is to earth.

The real life is heaven, our after-earth existence. We should not take earth as the norm of truth, beauty, goodness, and happiness. God himself is that norm. The things of earth can give us only a very pale image of the after-life, as if looking at something through a veil. The purpose of life on earth is not to provide a foretaste of heaven, although a very holy life can do so, but rather to test our attitudes, to discover whether we are with God or against him. Depending on the answer we give to that question, we can have God, who is everything, for all eternity, or we can have ourselves apart from God for all eternity and that is Hell.

Thirty-fourth Week of Ordinary Time

Monday

Daniel 1, 1-6, 8-20; Luke 21: 1-4 **YEAR I**

Today's reading is from the fascinating book of Daniel. It was written during the persecution of Antiochus to encourage Jews persecuted by the system. The first story tells of wise Daniel and his three friends and greatly encouraged Jews not to compromise on forbidden foods. When King Nebuchadnezzar of Babylon conquered Judah, he decided wisely to educate a number of the most promising young Jews at his court so that they could assist in the administration of his kingdom. Among these were Daniel, Hananiah, Mishael and Azariah. They won the favor of the chief chamberlain, who agreed to feed them vegetables and water rather than non-kosher meat and wine for ten days. When their health proved to be better than that of all the rest, the chamberlain continued the practice. Not only were they the healthiest people at court, but they also proved to be the wisest and most prudent. In addition, Daniel proved to have a gift for understanding visions and dreams. The lesson of this story must have been clear to the Jews when they were forced to eat pork by their conquerors. Their God who did not allow the young men of the Babylonian Exile to suffer harm when they refused to partake of the food and drink of the pagans would also come to the aid of those who refused to violate the Mosaic Law.

So it is that Christ praises the widow's mite. There were receptacles in the Temple for the Jews to place their offerings. The poor widow had little in the way of material things and could not match others in their physical gifts. But she had a great heart; with faith she contributed the last penny that she had, trusting that God would provide as he had for Daniel and his companions who with little food became healthier than their pagan counterparts. We should not fall into the sin of presuming that God will provide everything for our lives without any effort on our part, but that is not the danger of our times. What we need to guard against is the presumption that somehow we can save ourselves by our own resources and that we do not need God's grace. This is the heresy of our times. Either we do not hope in God because we do not believe in an after-life or because we think that we can save ourselves by our own power and abilities. In either case, we don't need God. "Lord, I believe; please help my unbelief."

Revelation 14: 1-3, 4-5; Luke 21:1-4 — YEAR II

In this final week of the liturgical year, the reading concerns those in heaven who did not surrender to the immorality of emperor worship. The number is huge! In metaphorical terms, John describes the glory of the blessed. They have been "ransomed" by the Lamb, so it is not due to their own merit that they have been saved. On the other hand, they have given their most precious asset—their free will acceptance of God's invitation to follow in the footsteps of Christ. Their lives on earth were innocent, uncorrupted by deceit of any kind. They were pure and holy and in that sense they did "merit" eternal glory.

In today's gospel, the widow, who gave a mite out of her want, is representative of those who are saved; the rich, who, out of their surplus, gave a much larger sum to the treasury, are representative of those who are not saved. The free will gift of self is all that is necessary. Free will seems easy to give; it is a small gift in a way; but human beings hate to part with it, even though paradoxically one has a much greater sense of freedom after surrendering it. We cannot buy or even work our way into heaven. Money and great works are accidental. Whether we are rich or poor, the only thing that counts in our relationship with God is the acceptance of his will and the demonstration of that acceptance in the performance of the corporal and spiritual works of mercy.

TUESDAY

Daniel 2: 31-45; Luke 21: 5-11 — YEAR I

Today's reading again taken from the book of Daniel was written during the bitter persecution by Antiochus and contains lessons to encourage the Jews. When Daniel, who could interpret dreams and visions, interpreted to the king the meaning of his vision he gave the following explanation. Although the kingdom would last for a few more generations, it would eventually come to ruin, when God would establish his spiritual kingdom on earth. This could possibly be understood as the coming of Christianity or the Second Coming of Christ. In any event, there is a time limit to earthly kingdoms but there is no such restriction on the kingdom of God.

Likewise, in today's gospel reading, Jesus foretells the destruction of the Temple. In the time of Jesus, the newly-rebuilt Jerusalem Temple was a glorious, elaborate structure. Jesus speaks first of the future destruction of the Temple and then of the end of the world. In the gospel Christ repeats Daniel's prediction. He tells the Jews that Jerusalem and their Temple will be leveled. Their political power will cease. Nations will quarrel bitterly among themselves. The one thing necessary in such times is to remain true to God. No matter what happens, only he has power to save us. If we will to be saved, therefore, we must remain one with him. There is absolutely nothing that can sever us from the love of God. The love of God holds us through every turn in our lives.

Revelation 14: 14-19; Luke 21: 5-11 **YEAR II**

Today's reading is of a dramatic scene from the book of Revelation. John, the author, describes the coming judgment on the ungodly as a great harvest of the earth. In his parables, Christ often likened the kingdom of God to a field, in which healthy plants and weeds grow together. Both are harvested or destroyed when the crop has fully grown. The book of Revelation speaks of a "grim reaper" of grapes and the King of Heaven as the reaper of the good fruit of the harvest. Little is said in detail. What is clear is that our opportunity to show whether our love is for God or for ourselves will come to an end at a given time and there will be a final judgment with appropriate reward or punishment.

In today's gospel, Jesus speaks, eschatologically, of the end of the world. As the gospel indicates, all who believe in an afterlife—in a final judgment—are anxious to know when it will occur so that they will be ready. But no one knows the time; only God does, and he is not telling because that would be tantamount to "forcing" us to do his will. The only strategy to follow is that of the Boy Scouts: "Always be prepared." The signs that will precede the end of the world are not so much the immediate prelude but rather warnings that the end could come at any time, in an instant, through some "act of God." And even if the end is long delayed for the world as a whole, for the individual, the end is sure to come and possibly quite suddenly. It makes no sense to do anything but live a life of virtue.

WEDNESDAY

Daniel 5: 1-6, 13-14, 16-17, 23-28; Luke 21: 12-19 **YEAR I**

Again, today's reading is from the book of Daniel. The adventures of Daniel were written and circulated as little pamphlets to encourage the Jews during the savage persecution of Antiochus. The dramatic episode of the writing on the wall taught the Jews that the kingdom of Antiochus would collapse soon!

The account read as follows: King Belshazza gave a banquet and, for the occasion, he used the precious gold and silver chalices, which had been taken from the Temple in Jerusalem. While the guests were eating and drinking, they suddenly saw a hand writing on the wall in a language which they could not understand. So the king called for Daniel to read and interpret the message. Daniel told them that it was a warning that the kingdom was about to collapse because the king had been found wanting. He and his followers had worshipped silver and gold gods, fashioned by man, but failed to recognize and worship the God who gives life to all things.

Today's gospel contains a prediction that is deeply prophetic. Within the framework of the end of the world, Jesus speaks of the coming trials of his followers and encourages them to patient endurance. Jesus states that those who worship false gods will persecute and punish those who worship the true God. Such foolish actions should not cause us to worry about our defense. When that time comes, God will enable us to make a profession of faith. Not a hair on our heads will perish. People committed to such foolishness are not about to listen, they have closed their minds and hearts to the logic of common sense so we should not worry. We should concentrate only on God's word, be stouthearted, pray for even stronger faith, and our resolve will be rewarded with eternal life.

Revelation 15: 1-4; Luke 21: 12-19 **YEAR II**

Today's reading is from the book of Revelation written to encourage Christians under persecution during times of emperor worship. Nero stood for the persecuting emperors. The reading is an encouraging vision of victory. The song of Moses indicates liberation after oppression.

There will be all kinds of calamities before the end of the world and there are all sorts of troubles which come into the life of an individual before his death. So the readings from the book of Revelation and also from the gospel apply to both. It is not a pleasant prospect to face persecution, physical punishment, and even death. If one is not concerned at all by such a future, that person is probably much more confident in human strength than should be the case. As St. Paul has indicated our only hope of triumph is weakness. If we depend upon ourselves, we are sure to cave in. What we must do is come to the full realization of our weakness and then depend utterly upon the strength of God's grace to fortify us. This is the message of Christ in today's gospel. Within the framework of the end of the world, Jesus speaks of the coming trials of his followers and encourages them to patient endurance. For our part, we contribute "patient endurance" inspired by the scenes of future glory in the book of Revelation. We rely on the Lord for the rest.

THURSDAY

Daniel 6: 12-28; Luke 21: 20-28 **YEAR I**

The interesting episode of Daniel in the lions' den was an encouraging message for those suffering persecution for their Jewish religion. It showed the complete triumph of Israel's God over the pagans. This is the story. King Darius wrote a proclamation that no one in the kingdom was to address a prayer to God or man; they were only to pray to the king for thirty days. Daniel was discovered praying to God and, despite the efforts of the king to save Daniel, he had to throw him into the lions' den. Miraculously the lions did not eat Daniel, so the following day, when he was found alive, King Darius released him and had Daniel's opponents thrown into the lions' den where they were promptly overpowered. Then, the king made another proclamation that Daniel's God was to be reverenced throughout his kingdom.

Two things stand out in the story: 1) Our allegiance to God comes first; above every earthly priority, we should worship the Lord, our God, and have faith in him. Even if Daniel had been eaten by the lions, his faith would have been justified. It would have been a horrible death to be sure, but the early Christians suffered the same fate and did so cheerfully because of their faith in the existence of God and his power to triumph even over death. 2) Although King Darius allowed himself to be persuaded to throw Daniel to the lions against his better judgment, it is clear that he recognized goodness in Daniel and truth in his faith. We need to appreciate how important it is for us to develop that kind of goodness, which will appeal to the minds and hearts of others and lead them to the Truth. Rational argument is not nearly so important an example, as fearless adherence to principle.

Today's gospel reading tells of the end of the world. It will be a fearsome spectacle, putting dread into the minds and hearts of all. The implication is that everyone somehow at sometime will be faced with something similar that will force them to choose between acceptance of the worst that the world can offer or faithful allegiance to God. In a very real sense, trying to escape death, no matter how horrible, will get us nowhere. God is the only viable choice. And yet, if our faith is weak, we shall try to flee from him even then. We need to recognize the goodness and love of God, so that we shall never forsake our faith in the truth of his existence. Let us remind ourselves, every time we read of crimes and catastrophes, that Jesus is Lord and he has triumphed over all evil.

Revelation 18: 1-2, 21-23, 19: 1-3, 9; Luke 21: 20-28 **YEAR II**

In the book of Revelation special code names are used so that the book cannot be held as evidence against Christians. Babylon is the code name for Rome. The book of Revelation describes how the mightiest nations on earth will be brought down at the end of the world. No more shall there be any simple pleasures—hence no music, no honest labor, no light, no sound, no marriage or birth or family joy. But the last sentence seems most appropriate for the industrial nations such as ours. "Because your merchants were the world's nobility, you led all nations astray by your sorcery." Our sorcery is that "money counts" when, in the final analysis, this is not at all true.

Just as material prosperity gives the appearance of great power, the feeling of being indestructible, and the impression of great happiness, so the devastation which follows when all that has vanished seems more desperate and total—all because there are no spiritual values left in such a society. At the end of the world there will be natural disasters, violence, war, terrible bloodletting on every side. The only hope will be faith in the coming of the Lord. This expectation will be the only thing that will sustain a person in those terrible times. But Christ, the Son of Man, will come to fulfill that hope and raise the faithful to eternal glory!

FRIDAY

Daniel 7: 2-14; Luke 21: 29-33 **YEAR I**

Daniel has an elaborate vision of four horrible looking animals, which represent the kingdoms of the world. Then, the Lord comes among them on a throne of glory and destroys them all. Finally, the Son of Man appears and God gives him dominion over all the earth. First, as in the vision of Daniel, we should realize that earthly empires come and go, usually because they have the seeds of destruction within. Great as our country has been, we should be able to see the seeds of destruction all around us. If we don't react and stamp them out of existence, our downfall is clear. Somehow we seem to think that God is on our side, and that we are more virtuous than others. Many times a supposedly "better" country may fall to a more evil one. This happened in the early centuries when the pagan hordes overran Europe. But how do we compare in virtue with the poverty-stricken countries of the southern hemisphere? By gospel standards, on which side would God be, theirs or ours?

In today's gospel, the parable of the fig tree explains the need to wait for God's kingdom to come. No Palestinian tree seems so dead in the winter as the fig tree, and so suddenly alive in the spring. We should read the signs of the times regarding our personal lives and try to judge the state of our souls in light of the gospel. Do we come off poorly in that comparison especially if we make an objective examination? Are we moved to change? Today the Lord asks us to make adequate changes in the way we live.

Revelation 20: 1-4, 11-21: 2; Luke 21: 29-33 **YEAR II**

In today's reading again from the book of Revelation, the Last Judgment is described. The dead rise from their graves. All are present before the judgment throne of God. The book of life is opened. Those whose names are inscribed therein are welcomed to "the new Jerusalem, to the new heaven and the new earth." The martyrs are specially honored. All others are condemned to the eternal flames where the devil and his angels have been confined.

There is no sign of revenge or anger or anything of the kind in the account of the Last Judgment. There is only justice. There is little judgment; the good and wicked have already judged themselves, as it were, by their conduct on earth. The Last Judgment seems to be more of a formality than anything else.

The Lord begs us to read the signs of life concerning death and judgment. We understand many other signs in nature, which signify good weather or a storm, which distinguish good from bad trees, which tell us of the change of seasons, and we act upon them. But we don't seem to be that attentive to the signs of our own mortality, or if we do, we fail to take the proper action. Every person, even the young, should quickly learn through sickness and injury that they are quite mortal; every person begins to realize in their fifties that old age and death are inexorably approaching; every person in the present day should realize the dangers of imminent death through a nuclear war or explosion. Still, we try to shut these thoughts out of our minds or we fail to act upon them.

It is not healthy, of course, to be living constantly in fear of death. It is healthy, however, to recognize our own mortality—the prospect of death at any age—and to take the very positive step to live a life of total virtue so that we won't need to worry about anything. The realization of this inevitability should not lead to inaction or to a continuance of an indifferent life, which will always be joined to fear. It should lead to the decision to be active, to lead a life of virtue, which banishes all fear—a life which is based on faith and leads to the greatest hope, joy, and peace about the next world and to a life of justice and charity in the present.

SATURDAY

Daniel 7: 15-27; Luke 21: 34-36 **YEAR I**

Daniel is upset by the vision he was given because the monsters were so terrible. He requests an explanation. It is that the kingdoms of this world will lord over the good and the innocent; they will fight among themselves; however, in the end, goodness will prevail and the kingdom of goodness will be everlasting. There is always the temptation for us to go along with the kingdoms of this world, that is, to become a part of the system and to think that we have no responsibility to avoid evil and do good. We accept the syndrome that "This is the way things are done. Everyone's doing it. You can't buck the system. Why not go along?" We develop this mentality even though we know quite clearly that it is contrary to God's thoughts and God's ways, even though we know that many people must be getting hurt because of the way we act. Still, we choose not to look at God's truth, not to look at the suffering around us. And as long as the truth remains clouded, as long as we are not forced to face it squarely, we go on as we have before in blissful, but deliberate, ignorance.

Today's gospel reminds us that this situation cannot last forever. There will be a day of reckoning! A day when we must respond to God! And perhaps those who will be the worst off in God's sight will not be those who have chosen to do what is evil, but those who have deliberately chosen to remain ignorant of the truth. We are reminded of the Lord's words to be either hot or cold; the lukewarm he vomits out of his mouth. God's final message to the Church and to us is to be watchful and to pray constantly. We should try seriously to find out what distracts us from the reality of God, from life's real purpose, and from preparing to meet Jesus Christ at death.

Revelation 22: 1-7; Luke 21: 34-36 **YEAR II**

Today, a glorious vision of heaven climaxes the book of Revelation. The message is that, in spite of false prophets, faithless Christians, and relentless persecution from the world, the Church is guaranteed victory because of the Risen Christ. The perfection of heaven is described in terms contrary to daily inconveniences or handicaps under which the people of the first century suffered. Heaven is depicted as a place where clear water is available in abundance, there is good fruit all year round, there is medicine to cure sickness and disease, there is no darkness, only light. And the most wonderful characteristic of heaven is the faithfulness of the people; all are perfectly united with God, and with one another as well.

This description is hardly one that we would use for heaven because good water is so readily available to us, though threatened by pollutants; good food is accessible all year round; medicine is close at hand; and there is no lack of light. No, we have succeeded so well in turning nature to our own use that we might describe heaven as a place where we have enough money to obtain an infinite amount of what we already have or to supply the means of obtaining those things that we could potentially have. Many earthlings today would see heaven as a place where we could handle everything by ourselves—have a perfectly happy life—if we had enough money to buy it. In the time of Christ, some people were no different. They looked upon heaven as the perfection of what they had on earth. However, the author of the book of Revelation makes clear that the true happiness of heaven is unity with God: the fulfillment of faith, hope, and love for him.

The gospel contains the final message of Christ to the Church: be watchful, pray constantly, and be wary of earthly-mindedness. We are not to give in to indulgence, drunkenness and worldly cares. This is not what heaven is all about and it should not be the focus of our present life. We cannot afford to postpone virtue, while we first enjoy the pleasures of this life to the full. Rather we should do everything, and use the goods of this world while always having in mind the things of heaven—faithfulness, hope, love of God, justice and charity toward our neighbor.